D1364842

ESSAYS AND STUDIES IN HONOR OF CARLETON BROWN

Carleton Brown

ESSAYS AND STUDIES

IN HONOR OF

CARLETON BROWN

Essay Index Reprint Series

BOOKS FOR LIBRARIES PRESS
FREEPORT, NEW YORK

First Published 1940
Reprinted 1969

STANDARD BOOK NUMBER:
8369-1408-2

LIBRARY OF CONGRESS CATALOG CARD NUMBER:
79-99693

PRINTED IN THE UNITED STATES OF AMERICA

CARLETON BROWN

For nat oonly thy laude precious
Parfourned is by men of dignytee . . . .

OUR birth is but a sleep and a forgetting. Carleton Brown's star rose on our academic scene late in September, 1900, under the appropriate sign Libra, when he was translated to the mundane study of philology at Harvard University. Not ours to trace the clouds of glory he came trailing from the Minnesota college which presciently bore the given name of its most distinguished graduate; from the Andover Theological Seminary, which made so appropriate his development of religious elements in our older literature; and from the pastoral care, which was transmuted into fatherly guidance of his graduate students. The Carleton Brown to whom his colleagues, associates, and former pupils dedicate this volume is the English scholar whose career typifies our ideals of industrious and fruitful research.

Our list of his published writings reveals clearly his range throughout Old and Middle English, both linguistic and literary, but eminently Chaucerian, as befits one baptized in the Child-Kittredge school. Apart from deferential bows to the Shakespearians he has remained austerely mediæval, and his newly completed *A Manuscript Index of Middle English Verse* gives a *finis coronat opus* to one of his most assiduous labors—an exhaustive exploration of the mediæval literary manuscripts extant in England. Ever faithful in teaching and annually consecutive in publication, he steadfastly pursued this major work, broadening from the religious and didactic to include the secular, till it comprises well over four thousand titles.

What the list of publications fails to reveal is his collaboration as a silent partner—editorially in *PMLA* since Volume XXXV and tutorially in a host of papers published in three decades elsewhere. The gift of a documentary lead, the entering wedge of an idea, critical guidance in interpretation of evidence, suggestion of points unperceived, emendations of phraseology, a timely word to an editor—But by the mouth of children thy bountee / Parfourned is. . . . It is not unusual for teachers to be the onlie begetter, planting their seed in fertile soil. With Carleton Brown it was almost usual, and many An Holy Medytacion passed into a Wreched Engendring without paternal acknowledgement.

And the Children are culling
On every side,
In a thousand valleys far and wide,
Fresh flowers . . . ,

Of Carleton Brown the 'slender thread' suspending the Modern Language Association in 1922, Volume L of *PMLA* has adequately spoken in recounting his achievements for the Association. These involved a measure of toil not widely realized, and comparable to the early struggle of A. Marshall Elliott. Despite one doubting Thomas after another, with painstaking personal care he reëstablished order and numbers and prestige. Farsightedly he set long-term enterprises afoot. Patiently, by reiterated correspondence, he nursed nesteggs into considerable funds. With frugality and tactful suggestion, unfailingly exercised with courtesy, he improved the Publications and initiated series of books. This is our tribute to the Scholar Militant.

Behind the scenes—in departmental meetings, and committees, and the chance converse of colleagues—there is a Carleton Brown whose conscience and kindness are tempered by a quizzical humor. It delights in spreading pitfalls for the unwary, and proceeds on the blind assumption that his *vis-à-vis* is catholicly informed. Even in publications let him beware who hears his praises sung in the opening lines. Neddie Sheldon used to argue: 'You say it is black? Do you not detect a tinge of brown—rather pale brown—even grayish—or, one might say, perhaps white?' But *re* provenance, one may rather suspect this Socratic procedure to be a relic of Andover dialecticism. In any case a more searching query ensues, followed up by a proffered fact, a suggestion of its significance, and other facts till the *vis-à-vis* has

Blank misgivings of a Creature
Moving about in worlds unrealized . . . .

Teste those who have recently conversed on the *Poculum mortis*.

The highly specialized scholar of today comes to be less and less a fair target for wide ranges of queries, and, more seriously, less and less susceptible to wide ranges of interest in languages and literatures. The scope of this volume is in itself a tribute to the breadth of interest of Carleton Brown. When a committee at New York University—consisting of Professors Homer A. Watt, Albert S. Borgman, Margaret Schlauch, Oscar Cargill, Karl J. Holzknecht and the writer, with LeRoy Elwood Kimball and Dean John Musser—first considered the present volume, it was decided that his range of reading interest must have become perforce at least coextensive with that of the Modern Language Association. There should doubtless have been also an article like Madan's on Bradshaw, but we too thought best to do a small thing and get it done.

To picture Carleton Brown alone is not to see the whole man. One should be a shipmate, seeking refreshment in his cabin—or a fellow diner, at high table or low, in ferne halwes—to perceive the analogue to a marchal in an halle. Nearly every writer in this volume can visualize him in his home—the tender husband and father, the genial and unsparing host who almost, in old English fashion, kept open house for colleagues, and associates, and pupils. By the hearth, or presiding at the board, he lacked only some Milward or Boswell to garner a store of learning and wit. Here the shrewd observer of public affairs, the searching critic of educational trends, the example of plain living and honest thinking round out his phase as the scholar *en rapport* with life.

Carleton Brown emerged as Ph.D. with Walter Morris Hart, J. S. P. Tatlock, and William Witherle Lawrence, a quartet who touch't the tender stops of various Quills. With Lowes he exchanged Chaucerian notes as intellectual refreshment from English A themes. At Bryn Mawr (from 1905–1917) he grew to international prestige: with Kittredge he represents for America the Early English Text Society. Then—*c'est la guerre*—he went to Minnesota and drew the Modern Language Association to its furthest point west.[1] It rebounded and Bryn Mawr reclaimed him

---

[1] To quote from a letter dated Oxford, Jan. 29 [1920]: "I can't think that Grandgent, with his enthusiasm for simplified spelling, has forgotten my own unconquerable aversion to *ar*, *shal*, and *wuz* . . . but if the M.L.A. in convention assembled should be determined to try the experiment of a raw Westerner for this responsible post, I dare say I should regard it as a mandate which could not be refused, not merely because it would be personally flattering, but because it would be a notable recognition of the Western universities."

till in 1927 he led it back to its birthplace in the City of New York. There for twelve years New York University reaped the fruition of his maturity, and made him Doctor of Letters. Time has broken many of his closest ties: J. W. Bright, Hermann Collitz, J. D. Bruce, Eduard Prokosch—to name a few. And of his English friends, who in happier days should have been represented here, a host from Henry Bradley and Napier on to Pollard and Herbert found Carleton Brown an ambassador extraordinary of American scholarship.

The year 1940 finds him in the *vita nuova*—as Edward C. Armstrong puts it—of the professor emeritus; freed, when one no longer craves freedom, from stimulating personal influence on youth; bound, as one would not be bound, by the growing urgency of dreams still to be realized.

> Hence in a moment of calm weather
>   Though inland far we be,
> Our souls have sight of that immortal sea
>   Which brought us hither . . . ,

From 1900 to 1940—they say the forties. But what Astrolabe could have determined the course of the erstwhile editor and proprietor of the *Solida Mail* (Tuesdays and Fridays), of Chaffee County, Colorado? Hence, our Bibliography alone ventures on a prophetic strain; on solid accomplishment we base the intimations in this legend of the worth of Carleton Brown.

P. W. L.

CONTENTS

HAGBARD AND INGELD

KEMP MALONE

The Johns Hopkins University

IN the seventh book of his *Gesta Danorum*,[1] Saxo Grammaticus tells one of the great love stories of the world, the story of Hagbard and Signe (Hagbarðr and Signý).[2] The following may serve as an outline of the tale:

King Ungwinus (Yngvinn) of the Danes fell in battle against one Regnaldus (Ragnaldr), leaving a son Sywaldus (Sigvaldr) and a daughter Sygrutha (Sigþrúðr). Sywald had a daughter Syritha (Sigríðr), who married a certain Otharus. In due time Sywald sought to wreak vengeance for the death of his father. The battle between Sywald and Regnald took place on the Danish island of Sjælland. It was decided in Sywald's favor by the valor of Otharus, who broke through the Swedish ranks and cut Regnald down in the midst of his men. No less than forty of Regnald's Swedish champions, including their leader Starcatherus (Starkaðr), disgraced themselves by fleeing from the battlefield. After the death of Regnald they took service with Haco (Haki), son of Hamundus (Hámundr); Saxo calls Haco *maximus piratarum* 'the greatest of vikings.' Upon the death of Sywald, his son Sygarus (Sigarr) became king of the Danes. Sygar had three sons, Sywaldus, Alf, and Algerus, and a daughter, Signe. One spring, Alf and Alger, in the course of a viking expedition, came upon three other sons of Hamund, the brothers Helwin, Hagbarthus, and Hamundus. The two Danish princes and their men fought against the three sons of Hamund all day, but were unable to overcome them. The two sides made a truce for the night, and made friends the next day, compelled by mutual exhaustion. Thereafter, Hagbard (and his brothers as well?) accompanied Alf and Alger to the Danish court, where Hagbard saw and fell in love with the princess Signe. She already had a suitor, a German of noble birth and good looks named Hildigisleus, but she thought little of him because he had performed no feats of valor and she held him to be a coward. Her love was turned rather to Haco, because she had heard of his great deeds. Hagbard paid court to her by stealth, and she agreed to become his secret mistress. Her brothers knew nothing of this, but Hildigisle suspected what was going on, and bribed Bolwisus (Bölvíss) the blind, an evil counselor of King Sygar's, to sow

---

[1] The latest and best edition of the *Gesta* is that of Olrik and Ræder, Copenhagen, 1931. Our story begins in VII, iii, 2; *ed. cit.*, p. 187.

[2] In the present paper, Saxo's Latin forms of proper names, and their Danish equivalents, e.g., Hagbarthus and Hagbard, Starcatherus and Starkad, are given without special indication, while the corresponding Icelandic forms are given in round brackets.

dissension between the sons of Sygar and the sons of Hamund. The slanders of Bolwisus led Alf and Alger to slay Helwin and Hamund while Hagbard was away, but Hagbard took swift vengeance for his brothers' death, killing Alf and Alger in battle. Hildigisle was pierced through the buttocks with a spear, and slunk away in disgrace. Hagbard now returned to the Danish court, alone and disguised as a *pugnax Haconis famula* (vii, 6) or *bellatrix Haconis vernula* (vii, 8). He claimed that Haco had sent him on a mission to Sygar. By virtue of his disguise he gained admission to Signe, who received him and backed him in all he said. They spent a night of love together. But he was betrayed by maidservants, and Sygar sent armed men to take him. He fought hard and long against them, and killed many at the door, but had to yield in the end. At his trial he was defended by the good counselor Bilwisus (Bilvíss), but the arguments of the evil counselor Bolwisus prevailed, and he was condemned to death on the gallows. Shortly afterwards the queen, handing him a cup, told him to slake his thirst before he died. He took the cup, but, since she had given it to him in mockery, he paid her back in the same coin, boasting that he had killed her two sons, and dashing the drink into her face. Meanwhile Signe made ready to die the same death that was about to befall her lover. She had a watch set, and, when the watcher told her that Hagbard was being hanged, she and her faithful maidservants set fire to the palace and hanged themselves. But Hagbard had asked that his mantle be hanged first, and it was this mantle, not Hagbard himself, that the watcher saw. By this ruse Hagbard learned, before his own death, that Signe had died for him; when he saw the palace burst into flames he went happy to his death. His brother Haco, as soon as he learned what had happened, left his Irish kingdom and set sail for Denmark, where he overthrew and slew King Sygar in battle. Sygar's only remaining son, Sywald, now took up arms, but was killed in battle with Haco Hamundson's comrade Haco Fastuosus, a battle in which Haco Fastuosus also fell. Haco Hamundson went away to the land of the Scots, and died there two years later.

Of the characters named in the tale, Sygar (Sigarr) answers to the Sigehere of *Widsith* 28 and is generally reckoned a historical figure.[3] The element *Sig-* appears not only in Sygar's name but also in the names of other members of the family: Sywald (Sigvaldr), Sigrutha (Sigþrúðr), Syritha (Sigríðr), and Signe (Signý). These names have a genuine look, and may well have belonged to historical persons, members of Sygar's family. It was contrary to old custom, however, to use the same name twice in a given family. Of the two Sywalds, then, only one can have been historical—whether Sygar's father or his son we have no way of saying with

[3] He lived in the fifth century, according to P. Herrmann, *Erläuterungen zu . . . Saxo Grammaticus*, II (1922), 490.

Saxo's second book has been derived from the Hadbardish name, and the king himself explained as an eponym,[10] and the name of Haki's brother Hagbard can be given a like etymology.[11] One explanation of the name Starkad makes it mean 'the strong Hadbard.' Moreover, the Hadbards had an alternative name. In *Widsith* 47 they are called Wicingas (vikings), and this, in all likelihood, not because they were given to piracy but because they lived in Bardowiek.[12] In other words, the viking name, as applied to them, was tribal or geographical in sense, and this is the earliest sense of the word on record. Now we have seen that Haki was known to Saxo as the greatest of vikings, the viking *par excellence.* If he was actually a Hadbard, the viking name would obviously be particularly appropriate for him, and we should have an explanation of the fact that he rather than some other pirate of history or story came to be thought of as the viking *par excellence,* and as the leader in whose service Starkad learned how to live the life of a hero. The association of Haki with Starkad is the more indicative because Starkad in heroic story represents the Hadbard of Northern tradition. As Herrmann puts it,[13]

> Dass der alte Speerkämpfer des Beow. bereits den Namen Starkad gehabt habe, ist natürlich nicht zu beweisen. Aber ein Greis ist er sicher schon gewesen, und ebenso hat er eine bevorzugte Stelle am Hofe innegehabt; darum darf man weiter annehmen, dass er auch durch Stärke, Unbesiegbarkeit und rauhes, rücksichtloses Auftreten berühmt war. . . . Die dän. Heldendichtung hat in ihm die Eigenschaften verkörpert, die die Dänen ihren Erbfeinden, den Hadbarden, beilegten: Stärke, Streitlust, grimmigen Trotz. . . .

It is not impossible, indeed, that the viking name came to lose its geographical or tribal sense, and to win its heroic implications, be-

---

[10] S. Bugge, *Home of the Eddic Poems* (1899), p. 160. It will be noted that Haki, like Hothbrodus, is localized in Sweden.

[11] There are two possibilities here. Hagbard can be derived, by dissimilation, from earlier *Hadbard. Alternatively, if, as seems likely, the Hadbards spoke an Anglo-Frisian dialect, their name for themselves may have been *Haoðubardan (compare OE Heaðobeardan from earlier *Hæoþubæordan), and in Scandinavian mouths the ð of this name form would become *g; see* A. Noreen, *Altisl. Gram.*, 4th ed. (1923), p. 188. Subsequent leveling between Hað- and Haogu- might have given rise to the extant Hag-. In any case, the change from ð to spirant *g* is phonetically easy, especially before -*u*-.

[12] *See* the discussion in my edition of *Widsith*, pp. 155 f.

[13] *Op. cit.*, pp. 419 f.

cause the original bearers of the name, the men of Bardowiek, and in particular the two Hadbardish tribesmen Haki and Starkad, became symbols of heroic piracy. Here, too, we may have an explanation of the fact that the Hadbard tribe came to be forgotten: if in the North *Wicingas* drove out *Heaðobeardan* as the tribal name, the tribe would be left with a name which in time ceased to be distinctive of the tribe and finally lost all tribal application.

A peculiar—indeed, an enigmatic—feature of our story is the relationship between Signe and the brothers Haki and Hagbard. Saxo writes (VII, vii, 2–5; ed. cit., pp. 192 ff.):

2. Per idem tempus Hildigisleus, claro Theutonum loco ortus, formæ et nobilitatis fiducia Sygnem Sigari filiam postulabat. Apud quam maximum ei contemptum obscuritas peperit, quod fortitudine vacuus aliena probitate fortunam instruere videretur. Præcipue eandem in amorem Hakonis magnalium eius spectata deflexit opinio. . . .

3. Hagbarthus vero cum Sigari filiis Daniam petens iisdemque ignaris sororis eorum alloquio potitus, tandem eam ad clandestini concubitus promissionem fide sibi obligandam adduxit. Quæ postmodum, forte pedissequis insignes procerum titulos conferentibus, Hildigisleo Hakonem prætulit, in illo nihil præter speciem laudabile reperiri, in isto oris lituram animi flore pensari testata. . . .

5. Quæ vox ita ad astantium aures delapsa est, ut Hagbarthus Hakonis laudari vocabulo putaretur. . . .

[At that time Hildigisle, a German of illustrious descent, sought the hand of Signe, daughter of Sygar, counting on his good looks and noble birth. But his want of fame gave her the greatest contempt for him, because, without courage himself, he thought to build up his fortune on the worth of others. What moved her to love Haco was particularly the proved fame of his wonderful deeds. . . . Now Hagbard went to Denmark with the sons of Sygar and without their knowledge managed to pay his addresses to their sister, and finally he brought her to give him her word that she would become his mistress in secret. Afterwards, when her women fell to comparing the princes' titles to distinction, she gave Haco the preference over Hildigisle, saying that in the latter there was nothing worthy of praise except his looks, but in the former high-mindedness fully made up for a scarred face. . . . These words led the bystanders to think that she was praising Hagbard under the name of Haco.]

The natural interpretation here is the one which Saxo seems to make; namely, that Haco and Hagbard are two names for the same person. But, later on, our historian represents Haco as the brother and avenger of Hagbard. I conceive that Saxo (or his source) knew and combined two versions of the tale. In one version, the earlier, the hero's death was left unavenged[14] and the hero's name was Haki Hagbard (originally Haki the Hadbard). In the other version, the hero's death was duly avenged; the hero went by his surname, Hagbard, while his true name, Haki, was given to the avenger, who, appropriately enough, was made the hero's brother. Alternatively we may say that in the later version the hero as lover figured under his surname Hagbard, while the hero as viking was made into a separate figure, the avenger, under his true name Haki. Such a differentiation need not give us pause. In real life the same man may well be both a great viking and a great lover, but in popular story the complexities of reality tend to be simplified, and characters tend to represent one aspect or 'humor' only, becoming typical or even ideal in the process. The Starkad of history presumably had love affairs, but love won no place in his literary life. And in the course of time love came to be felt equally unsuitable for Starkad's master, Haki, the greatest of vikings. His love affair with Signe was therefore attributed to an *alter ego*, the Hagbard of our story, for whom, as it happened, a name was available, since Haki had a surname as well as a true name. But the differentiation was late, and remained incomplete. Hagbard in particular, though primarily the lover, kept much of the viking, and this the more since the ideal lover was expected to be a fighter too (compare Chaucer's squire).

The secrecy of the lovers and their failure even to consider the possibility of marriage suggest yet another explanation of the fact that the hero in Saxo's version is called both Haco and Hagbard.[15] From the Icelandic version (to be considered below) we may infer that the hero came to the Danish court to seduce Signe, by way of taking vengeance on Sygar for his rape of the hero's sister. If Haco

[14] Saxo's verse source stops with the death of Hagbard, and Herrmann, *op. cit.*, p. 497, inclines to the belief that the original story went no further.

[15] The oldness of the tale keeps us from explaining this secrecy and avoidance of marriage in terms of courtly love convention. Herrmann (*op. cit.*, II, 493) compares the tale to *Romeo and Juliet*, where the secrecy is a natural consequence of the hostility of the houses to which hero and heroine belong. But our tale differs from Shakespeare's play in that the hostile parties have made friends, for the time being at least. Saxo makes no attempt to motivate either the secrecy or the avoidance of marriage.

had this in mind, he would make friends with the Siklings, and win an invitation to visit the Danish court, under an assumed name, without revealing the fact that he belonged to a hostile house. And Hagbard (an arbitrarily modified form of his surname Hadbard) may have been the name which he assumed for the occasion, and Signe's recognition of him as Haco may have been added as a dramatic touch. But, whatever the hero's intentions when he came, he fell in love with her and she with him, and both felt it needful that their love be kept secret. The love story may be said to begin when Hagbard first came to court, but we are told (VII, vii, 2) that even before she saw him Signe was inclined to love him (under the name Haco) because of his achievements—an inclination which does credit to her head, certainly. Her conduct after he came was none too discreet, the rival suitor suspected the worst, and his jealousy led to a renewal of the old feud between the Siklings and the sons of Hamund, with tragedy behind.

The tale of Hagbard and Signe has many points of likeness to the tale of Ingeld. The background of both tales is the old blood feud between Danes and Hadbards, and the course of events in the two tales runs in the same direction. In the following, I have undertaken to analyze the stories and to compare them trait by trait. Analysis and comparison may be expected to throw light on various features and to make more precise any relationships which may be found. I begin with the traits themselves, presented in outline form:

Hagbard and Signe (Saxo)	Ingeld (*Beowulf* and *Widsith*)
1. Danes defeat Swedes in battle. Regnald killed, and forty Swedish champions (including Starkad) flee.	1. Danes defeat Hadbards in battle. Wiðergyld killed, and other Hadbards (including Starkad) retreat or flee.
2. Starkad and other Swedes take service with Haco (Hagbard).	2. Starkad and other Hadbards take service with Ingeld the Hadbard.
3. Danish princes after drawn battle make friends with Hagbard and brothers.	3. Danish king (occasion not recorded) makes friends with Hadbards.
4. Danish princess looks with favor on Haco (Hagbard).	4. Danish princess offered to Ingeld the Hadbard.
5. Hagbard (presumably with brothers and followers) comes to Danish court for visit.	5. Ingeld with followers comes to Danish court for visit (with betrothal or marriage in view).

6. Danish princess agrees to become Hagbard's mistress.	6. Danish princess betrothed to Ingeld.
7. Feud breaks out anew.	7. Feud breaks out anew.
a. A bribe from the rival suitor moves an old counselor (Bolwis) to make trouble.	a. The insolence of the fæmnanþegn moves an old spearman (Starkad) to make trouble.
b. He incites the sons of Sygar against the sons of Hamund.	b. He incites the son of Wiðergyld against the fæmnanþegn, the son of the slayer of Wiðergyld.
c. The sons of Sygar slay Hagbard's two brothers.	c.
d. Hagbard slays the sons of Sygar.	d.
e. The rival suitor gets a spear through his buttocks.	e. The fæmnanþegn is slain by the son of Wiðergyld.
f.	f. The son of Wiðergyld is pursued by the Danish avengers, but gets away safely because he knows the country well.
g.	g. Ingeld's love cools and his thoughts turn to the old feud.
8. Hagbard returns to Danish court, alone and in disguise, bent on love.	8. Ingeld returns to Danish court at the head of an army, bent on war.
9. Hagbard is caught by the Danes and put to death.	9. Ingeld is defeated in battle with the Danes and presumably falls.
10. In connexion with Hagbard's death the Danish hall burns to the ground.	10. In connexion with Ingeld's defeat and death the Danish hall burns to the ground.

I add the following comments on the various traits:

Trait 1. We learn of this defeat of the Hadbards from the speech of the old spearman (Starkad) in *Beowulf* 2047–2052. The information given is general in character, except for one detail, the fall of Wiðergyld. We are told that the Danes *weoldon wælstowe* (2051); in other words, the Hadbards were defeated and had to retreat or flee. Starkad speaks as *se ðe eall genam* (2042). His knowledge of the battle was evidently that of a participant, and, since he survived to tell the tale, he must have been among those Hadbards who saved themselves by retreat or flight. It is customary to presume that Froda as well as Wiðergyld fell in this battle, but the English text, taken for itself, does not admit of this presumption; in later Scandinavian story, Froda is killed and Wiðergyld is not mentioned, but this may (and probably does) mean that, as history became story, Froda was *substituted* for Wiðergyld. The Regnald of Saxo's seventh book answers in part to Wiðergyld, in part to the Froda who took Wiðergyld's place in Scandinavian tradition. He is like Wiðergyld in two respects: (1) he was killed in battle with the Danes, and (2) his fall brought with it a retreat or rout of the opponents of the Danes, Starkad included.[16] He is like Froda in two respects: (1) he is represented as a king, and (2) he was slain as an act of vengeance. Wiðergyld was only a retainer, of course, and the English poet does not say or imply that the Danes attacked the Hadbards in retaliation for a previous attack of the Hadbards on the Danes. According to later Scandinavian story, however, Froda had killed Halfdan, and, therefore, deserved death at the hands of Halfdan's heirs; in like manner, Regnald had killed Ungwin, and, therefore, deserved death at the hands of Ungwin's heirs. The vengeance motif seems inconsistent with the localization of the battle on the Danish island of Sjælland; if Sywald was trying to wreak vengeance for his father's death, one would expect him to take the offensive and invade Sweden. In the original story of the battle, however, the Danes in all likelihood were merely repelling a Hadbard raid and Sjælland was actually the scene of the conflict. Saxo's localization, therefore, is best taken as a survival from the original form of the story. That the Hadbards reappear as Swedes is not without parallels (*see* above), and is in any case a mere detail; the important thing about them was not so much their nationality as their enmity to the Danes, and this enmity would be better marked by making them Swedes, once the Hadbard tribe had been forgotten. The change of nationality took place by the viking route, of course: the opponents of the Danes began as Hadbards or Vikings; later they were known simply as

---

[16] Only in connexion with the fall of Regnald and that of Wiðergyld do we find Starkad taking part in such a retreat or rout. For a different view, *see* A. Olrik, *Danmarks Heltedigtning*, II (1910), 80 and 124. Oddly enough, Olrik overlooks the *Beowulf* passage. The parallels to the fall of Regnald which he does cite are beside the mark. In them, Starkad fights (or refuses to fight) in single combat with a formidable opponent (who is the center of interest and by winning gains more glory than would otherwise be possible), and a wound, usually a very serious one, is given Starkad by that opponent. Here both these fundamental features are wanting. Starkad does not have a single combat with any particular hero, and receives no wound. Nor is his flight an individual matter; he flees with the rest. Our interest lies not in Starkad or his opponent but in Regnald and his bane. The Saxonian and Beowulfian passages agree in all these points.

vikings (with a small v); finally they became Swedish vikings or Swedes. Saxo tells the story from a Danish, the *Beowulf* poet from a Hadbardish, point of view. This difference brought it about that the central event, the fall of Wiðergyld or Regnald, is presented differently. In *Beowulf* no particular bane is mentioned by name; indeed, we are given to understand that it took many Danes (certainly several) to fell him. In Saxo's account the matter is reversed: Sywald's son-in-law Otharus singlehanded overcomes Regnald and the bravest of the Swedes together. The heroic stature which Saxo gives to Otharus thus originally belonged to Wiðergyld, I take it; the transfer presumably took place in Danish tradition.

Trait 2. In Saxo the Swedish retainers are represented as followers of Regnald who upon his death entered the service of Haco. In *Beowulf*, however, the Hadbards who retreated from the battlefield were retainers not of Wiðergyld but of Froda, and their service with Froda's son Ingeld began with the death of Froda. Since we do not know when Froda died we cannot say just when Starkad and his fellows entered Ingeld's service. We can say only that this new service began after the events of trait 1 and before the events of trait 3.

Trait 3. The drawn battle, leading to a truce and compulsory friendship for a season, is a motif that plays an important part in the Finnsburg tale, where, however, it is combined with another motif; namely, the defense of the hall. In Saxo the drawn battle motif serves as a device whereby the Danish princes make friends with their enemies, the sons of Hamund (i.e., the Hadbards). In *Beowulf* no such formal device is employed, but the underlying principles at work are the same. In the one case a hard-fought battle, in the other a *wælfæhða dæl*, ends in war weariness and longing for peace, and the two sides make friends. A difference remains, nevertheless: in *Beowulf* it is the Danish king himself who makes friends with the Hadbard leader, while in Saxo it is only the king's sons who make friends with Hagbard and his brothers. In the English tale, the attempt at reconciliation is a political matter, a stroke of statecraft, while in the Danish tale it is a personal matter only, without effect on the political situation (so far as one can judge). This difference answers to a general distinction between English and Scandinavian heroic story: the national or tribal element remains in English tradition, but tends to become confused or lost in Scandinavian versions of some of the old stories, and this tendency is particularly marked in the traditions about the warfare between Danes and Hadbards, presumably because the Hadbard tribe early came to be forgotten. The brothers Alf and Alger, as we have already seen, were hardly at home among the original Siklings, and there is good evidence that Sygar (Sigarr) himself once figured more largely in the tale than he now does.[17] I suspect that Alf and Alger, when they made friends with Hagbard, were playing a part which earlier belonged to their father. In any case, the drawn battle motif can readily be explained as a dramatic sharpening of a deal of deadly feuds and quarrels.

Trait 4. Ingeld's love of his wife (or betrothed) is mentioned in *Beowulf* 2065 f., where we are told that it became cooler. The poet says nothing about the lady's love of Ingeld, and, in general, the love motif is played down in our episode, and the betrothal presented as an affair of state, in which it was the lady's function (like her mother's before her) to do what she was told and become a *friðusibb folca.* Since the English poet's interest lay not in the personal but in the political aspect of the betrothal, he makes the Danish king play the active part which, no doubt, he played in real life, while the Danish princess gets a passive part equally realistic. In Saxo's tale, however, the interest lies in the personal not in the political aspect of the affair. Here, then, we find the active and passive parts interchanged: the Danish princess is active throughout, while her father does nothing until all is lost.[18] The princess even betrothes herself, in effect, when she feels inclined to Haco (Hagbard) before seeing him, and rejects his rival. This choice between rivals her father presumably made for her in real life (like Hroðgar in *Beowulf*), but in Saxo's tale she herself made the decision, without the advice or even the knowledge of her father. Her reason for choosing as she did has its interest in this connexion. She preferred the man who had already made his mark in the world, unattractive though he was in physical appearance. Such reasoning and such a decision would gladden a father's heart in any age, but strikes one as a bit cold and calculating, and not

[17] Note the allusion in cap. 25 of the *Völsungasaga* (ed. W. Ranisch, Berlin, 1891), p. 43.

[18] We have already seen that not he but his sons make friends with Hagbard.

wholly in harmony with the passionate, reckless Signe that we learn to know as the story proceeds. It seems not impossible that the father originally made the choice, and made it for the very reason which Saxo puts in Signe's mouth. Certainly none but a man whose fame was secure could forgo vengeance and marry his foe's daughter.

Trait 5. Hagbard's visit to the Danish court took place by invitation of his new friends and former foes, the sons of Sygar. In the story this new friendship had the function of bringing Hagbard to court and so to the lady. In like manner, the friendship between Ingeld and the Danish king had for its specific purpose the bringing together (in betrothal or marriage) of Ingeld and the Danish princess, and this purpose was accomplished when Ingeld came to court.[19] But the sons of Sygar, unlike Hroðgar, did not invite Hagbard to the Danish court for betrothal or marriage, or indeed for any particular purpose other than a demonstration of friendship.

Trait 6. Hagbard here figures as secret lover, whereas Ingeld plays the part of betrothed or bridegroom. The great difference between the tales lies, of course, in the fact that one is a love story while the other is a political event (or series of events) in which the lovers (if we may so call them) are mere pawns. The political marriage motif does not appear in the tale of Hagbard and Signe. The lovers, therefore, since they belong to hostile houses, must keep their love secret, while Ingeld and Freawaru, though their houses too are traditionally hostile, are duly betrothed—betrothed, indeed, for that very reason.

Trait 7. A satisfactory interpretation of the fæmnanþegn in the Ingeld episode of *Beowulf* has never been found. His immediate function, it is true, offers no difficulties to the interpreter. He is there to give the old spearman an opening whereby the feud may again be set going. But why is he called a fæmnanþegn, and what is his motive for behaving as he does? Clearly he, no less than the old spearman, wishes to make trouble. The latter's motives are evident: his side had lost in the last fight, and the blood of the Hadbards then slain was still crying out for vengeance. No such motives can be imputed to the fæmnanþegn, who belonged to the

[19] That the Ingeld episode of *Beowulf* deals with the betrothal or wedding of Ingeld at the Danish court seems reasonably clear; *see* my paper in *JEGP*, XXXIX (1940), 76–92.

winning side and had no slain kinsmen to avenge. By all the rules the fæmnanþegn ought to have supported his lord, King Hroðgar, in the move for peace and reconciliation. The key to his disloyal and deliberately provocative conduct may be found, I think, in the epithet *fæmnanþegn* which the poet applies to him. This epithet in the editions is regularly printed as two words, but, since it is preceded by the nom. sg. masc. *se* of the definite article, it must be taken as one word.[20] The meaning of this word is not immediately obvious. In an earlier study, I put it into modern English as 'maiden-thane' and, comparing such modern expressions as 'maiden voyage' and 'maiden effort,' suggested that a maiden-thane was a young man who had had no experience in battle.[21] Now the Hildigisle of Saxo's tale seems to be such a man; certainly he lacks the scars of battle. But he qualifies as a fæmnanþegn in another sense besides: he dances attendance on Signe, pays court to her—is, in short, a suitor for her hand. Moreover, his trouble-making is well motivated. Naturally enough he hates to see his rival preferred and himself rejected. I conceive that the fæmnanþegn of the *Beowulf* episode was in like case, and revenged himself by conduct designed to stir up the feud anew and thus hinder or spoil the marriage. The old spearman struck at the root of the trouble when he pointed to the fæmnanþegn, although the latter may well have found confederates, as lines 2036 f. would indicate. Saxo represents Hildigisle as a German, and gives him a name to fit. No indication of the rival's name and nationality, however, appears in Saxo's verse source (preserved to us by Saxo in a versified Latin rendering), and it seems not unlikely that Saxo himself was responsible for Germanizing the rival, a change which enabled him to vent yet once again his well-known hatred of the Germans. Since the hero was an enemy of the Danes, the proprieties would call for a Danish rival, and we have reason to think that the rival was originally a Dane, answering in this respect to the fæmnanþegn of *Beowulf*.

That Saxo made the rival a German on the model of Haldan's rival Siwar (whose story Saxo tells in the same book) is a conjec-

---

[20] A. J. Barnouw, *Textkritische Untersuchungen* (1902), p. 23.

[21] *MP*, XXVII (1930), 259.

ture of A. Olrik's,[22] which seems reasonable enough. If, however, Olrik meant to say that not only the Germanism of the rival but the very existence of a rival in the Hagbard tale was due to the influence of the story of Haldan, I cannot agree. Hildigisle is specifically mentioned (though not by name) in the verses, which show not the slightest indication of any influence of the Haldan story. The following lines speak for themselves (VII, vii, 4; *ed. cit.*, p. 193):

> Huic [i.e., the hero] pretium non forma facit, sed fortior ausus armisque parta claritas.
>
> Ast illum [i.e., the rival] capitis decor approbat et nitor oris vertexque crine fulgidus.

Moreover, even in Saxo's prose Hildigisle has little in common with Siwar; on the contrary, the careers of the two are markedly different. The story of Haldan's love affair with Guritha may be summarized as follows (VII, ix, 9–20):

> The Danish princess Guritha, granddaughter of Sygar and only survivor of the Sikling family, vowed to remain chaste rather than marry one beneath her in station. Haldan (son of Borgar, a chieftain of Skåne), however, urged his suit. She denied him, because of his rank and misshapen mouth (a mutilation which he had come by honorably in battle). He did not lose hope, however, but told her he would come back after winning glory enough, in war, to make up for his rank and mouth; he urged her not to take a man to her bed until she knew he (Haldan) had come back or was dead. Haldan now went abroad to win fame in warfare. He was away for some time, and a rumor reached Denmark that a certain Hildiger had overthrown him in single combat (he had actually killed Hildiger in this duel). Then Siwar, a Saxon of high birth, became a suitor for the hand of Guritha. She finally accepted him (though at heart she preferred Haldan), being constrained or overpersuaded by her guardians, whom Siwar had bribed, and the two were formally betrothed. Haldan learned of this and hurried home. He reached the Danish court just before the wedding festivities began. After talking to the bride, and learning the true state of her heart, he killed the bridegroom and (with some help from his followers) cut down all the Saxon guests. The wedding then proceeded, but with Haldan as bridegroom.

In this story the rival does not pay court to the heroine until the hero has left the scene, while in the Hagbard tale the rival pays court to the heroine before the hero appears on the scene. Moreover, Signe rejects the rival and accepts the hero, while Guritha

[22] *Kilderne*, II (1894), 246.

rejects the hero (for his scars, the very reason that moves Signe to accept Hagbard!) and accepts the rival. The return of the hero to the Danish court is the culminating event of both love stories, but here the rival does not figure at all in the Hagbard tale, while he figures largely in the Haldan tale. The rival does bribing in both tales, but for quite different purposes. The contrasted pictures of hero and rival are given great prominence in the Hagbard tale, but in the Haldan tale hero and rival are not contrasted at all. Hildigisle and Siwar are not alike even in name. When we say that both are represented as Germans of high birth, we have exhausted their likeness. The Germanism of the rival is wholly appropriate in the Haldan tale, where the hero is a Dane, but inappropriate in the Hagbard tale, where the hero is an enemy of the Danes. Here one may agree with Olrik that the Haldan tale was the lender. Otherwise the two rivals must be reckoned independent literary figures.

The fate of Hildigisle gives us a further clue to his proper connexions. He is disposed of by a spearcast through the buttocks. Here we have the handiwork of Starkad, as Olrik noted (*loc. cit.*), though he did not draw the logical conclusion; namely, that Starkad, the faithful retainer of Haco (Hagbard), was the man who gave Hildigisle that *klámhögg*. Saxo does not tell us who cast the spear through Hildigisle's buttocks,[23] but the old spearman was just the man for the job and we have good reason to think that in an earlier form of the tale he threw the weapon. Saxo, it is true, says nothing of Starkad's presence at the Danish court with Hagbard. Here he was presumably following the later version of the tale (see above), a version in which the lover (Hagbard) was distinguished from the viking avenger (Haco). In this version Starkad of course served the viking, not the lover, and consequently had to be relieved of the spear-throw, which therefore is told of without mention of the thrower. The manner in which the rival was put to shame, however, reveals Starkad at work, even though he has been removed from the scene. In *Beowulf* too the old spearman downs the rival (that is, the fæmnanþegn), but he does it by

[23] The common presumption that Hagbard was the spearman is not borne out by Saxo's text.

word, not by deed. He incites the son of Wiðergyld to attack the fæmnanþegn. The difference between the English and Scandinavian accounts here is characteristic. In the English poem, Starkad is a man of words; in the Scandinavian monuments, he is everywhere a man of deeds (in spite of his age), though he has words enough besides.[24] It follows naturally enough that in the Hagbard tale no character appears who answers to the son of Wiðergyld. Such a character, a son of Regnald, in all likelihood figured in an early form of the story, and slew Hildigisle at Starkad's prompting. But when Starkad took the deed for himself, the son of Regnald became superfluous, and was accordingly dropped from the tale. A mark of his former presence, and of Starkad's original function of whetter, remains in the tale, however. The whetting speech characteristic of Starkad was not discarded when the man that Starkad whetted was dropped. The speech was kept and given to another old man, the evil counselor Bolwisus. This character does not belong to the Ingeld tale, but he probably had a place in the Hagbard tale from an early date, though not in the very earliest form of the story. His original function will be considered below in connexion with trait 9. Here it is enough to say that his existence as one of the characters of the Hagbard tale made him available for the part of whetter when the whetting motif was shifted from the Hadbardish to the Danish side (that is to say, when the son of Regnald dropped out of the tale, leaving Starkad with nobody to whet).[25] The correspondence of Hildigisle to the fæmnanþegn of *Beowulf* now becomes clearer. Hildigisle was originally a Dane, and his father in all likelihood was one of the banes of Regnald.

[24] A. Olrik noted this difference (*Danmarks Heltedigtning*, II, 81 f.), but wrongly represented the *Lay of Ingeld* to be an exception to the rule; *see* my paper in *MP*, XXVII (1930), 267 n.

[25] In the version of the Hagbard tale alluded to in the *Völsungasaga* (*see* note 17 above), the whetting was kept on the Hadbardish side, although here too the son of Regnald seems to have been dropped. The development in this version was parallel to that in the Ingeld tale as told in Saxo's sixth book: the duty of taking vengeance was shifted from the son of Regnald (compare the son of Wiðergyld) to the brothers Haki and Hagbarðr (compare Ingeld), whose father Hámundr (compare Froda) presumably had replaced Regnald (compare Wiðergyld) as victim of the Danes. The whetter is not mentioned by name in the *Völsungasaga* passage, but we may safely presume that Starkaðr was the whetter.

When Otharus, the son-in-law of Sywald, was brought into the story (a late change), and took the place of Regnald's banes, Hildigisle's father lost all connexion with the tale and Hildigisle himself in consequence lost his function as victim of an avenger and served henceforth only as rival of the hero. For this reason his death became needless and the fatal *billes bite* of *Beowulf* 2060 answers to the humiliating but not fatal spearcast of the Hagbard tale.

We have already seen that Alf and Alger were late poetical creations (or importations), not original members of the Sikling family. I conceive that their father Sygar once did the deeds which, in Saxo's version of the story, are given to them.[26] This conception helps greatly in reconciling Saxo's version with the Icelandic version alluded to in the *Völsungasaga* but unluckily not otherwise preserved. The Icelanders knew Sigarr and his daughter Signý; they likewise knew Hámundr and his two sons, the famous vikings Haki and Hagbarðr. They knew nothing of any sons of Sigarr, or of any other sons of Hámundr. The *Völsungasaga* passage, however, makes reference to certain unspecified members of the family of Haki and Hagbarðr. The reference reads as follows (*loc. cit.*):

> Miklir váru þeir [i.e., Haki and Hagbarðr] ok ágætir, en þó nam Sigarr systur þeira, en hefir aðra inni brenda, ok eru þeir seinir at hefna.

The *aðra* 'others' of this passage I take to be the brothers Helwin and Hamund named in Saxo as victims of Alf and Alger. In spite of Saxo, however, the Hamund in question was not Hagbard's brother but his father, as it would be contrary to old custom in name giving for Hagbard to have both a father and a brother of the same name. The other victim, Helwin, if brother of Hamund, would be Hagbard's uncle.[27] Sigarr burnt his victims in, while Alf and Alger defeated and killed their victims in a naval battle. Presumably, Sigarr took Hagbard's sister in order that Hagbard's seduction of Sigar's daughter might be motivated as an act of

---

[26] *See* the discussion of trait 3 above, where I suggest that in the original tale it was Sygar rather than his sons who made friends with Hagbard.

[27] The rarity of the name *Helwin* (on which *see* H. Naumann, *Altnordische Namenstudien*, p. 90) may be reckoned an argument for Helwin's antiquity in the tale, although the Icelanders say nothing of such a character. His name duly alliterates with his kinsmen's.

vengeance, on the principle of an eye for an eye and a tooth for a tooth. In other words, this deed of Sigar's had no place in the original story, but was added later by some sagaman concerned to make vengeance rather than love the driving force behind Hagbard's seduction of Signe. The other deed attributed to Sigarr in the *Völsungasaga* passage had a more complex history. According to Saxo, as we have seen, the Danes under Sywald defeat the Swedes and kill the Swedish leader Regnald. Some forty Swedish champions, including Starkad, survive the battle and take service with Haco (who according to Snorri was King of Sweden). It seems clear that Haco and his men are duty bound to avenge the defeat of the Swedes and the death of Regnald, and Haco finally takes vengeance on the Danes, but this vengeance is long delayed. Haco's brother Hagbard actually makes friends with the Danes and visits the Danish court. This visit, however, leads to a second attack by the Danes in which Helwin and Hamund, the brothers of Haco and Hagbard, are defeated and killed. Hagbard avenges his brothers by killing the Danish princes Alf and Alger, but is himself captured and put to death by King Sygar of the Danes. Haco then bestirs himself and avenges his brother's death by killing Sygar. This long and complicated business makes a striking contrast with the brevity and clean-cut lines of the Icelandic version, where Sigarr answers to three generations of Danes (Sywald, Sygar, and the brothers Alf and Alger) in Saxo's account, and the burning-in answers to two Saxonian battles. The simplicity of the Icelandic version reflects, I think, an older stage of the tradition, an earlier form of the tale, than that recorded in Saxo. Sigarr, the Sigehere of *Widsith*, was the one and only antagonist of the brothers originally; his father and his sons hardly played a part in the tale when it first took shape, and never won entry to the story among the Icelanders. The sons, indeed, properly belong to another story, that of Alf and Alvilda, and were brought into the Hagbard tale by means of an arbitrary genealogical construction, in the course of an attempt to build up a group of stories dealing with the theme of love.[28] And Saxo's two Danish victories (the fall of Regnald and the fall of the brothers Helwin and Hamund) are

[28] Compare A. Heusler, in J. Hoops's *Reallexikon*, IV, 178.

merely variant accounts of one and the same battle.[29] But the version of Saxo has its points for the historian. In it old and new appear side by side, with no attempt to iron out the inconsistencies; thus much old material has been kept, relatively unchanged. The Icelandic version, on the contrary, is beautifully balanced, and neatly rounded, with an eye to a unified, symmetrical, artistic effect. This effect has been triumphantly achieved, but at great cost to the historian. We have already seen that Sigar's rape of Hagbard's sister was added to the tale, to balance Hagbard's seduction of Signe. In the same way, Sigarr burns his victims in, to balance the burning of Sigar's hall at the end of the tale. There is good reason to think that the sagaman modified the love story for the sake of perfection in the taking of vengeance. For the same reason the fall of Regnald was discarded, or, rather, replaced by the fall of Hámundr (the father of Haki and Hagbarðr), and the whetting was obviously directed not at the son of Regnald but at the sons of Hámundr, who (we are told) were *seinir at hefna* 'slow to take vengeance.' The pressure upon the brothers to act was made as strong as possible: their sister had been ravished, and the others, the rest of the family (apart from themselves), had been burnt in. The allusion takes us no further, and, though by conjecture we can supply the rest, it will be wiser, no doubt, to forbear. We may be certain that Hagbarðr seduced Signý but was caught and hanged by Sigarr.[30] But did Hagbarðr go twice or only once to Sigar's court? In other words, did the Icelanders keep or give up the trait according to which the Siklings made friends with the sons of Hámundr? My guess is that they kept this trait; hence the *seinir at hefna* of the allusion. If so, did Haki and Starkaðr go with Hagbarðr on his first visit, and did the old spearman do the whetting in its proper dramatic place; namely, the court of his foes, as he did in *Beowulf?* One wonders also whether a fæmnanþegn or rival suitor figured in the Icelandic version, and just how the sons of Hámundr and their men got away with whole skins. Hagbarðr presumably returned to Sigar's court in disguise, but hardly in the

---

[29] It is characteristic of Saxo's literary art that he neither chooses between these variants nor tries to combine them, but records them both as separate and distinct episodes. Cf. note 25.

[30] Snorri in *Skáldskaparmál*, 64, tells us that Sigarr hanged Hagbarðr.

guise of a woman.[31] I fancy he was betrayed much as he is in Saxo's version. It seems evident that Haki avenged his brother, but one cannot say whether Sigar's hall was burnt as part of Haki's vengeance or in connexion with Signý's death; indeed, one cannot be sure that Signý died with her lover in the Icelandic version; she may have died with her father.

Let us now leave the Icelanders and return to Saxo. After the feud had broken out again, Hagbard was no longer safe, of course, on Danish soil. We are not told how or when he left the Danish court, nor is anything said of the parting of the lovers, but obviously they were parted by events, even though bound to each other by vows. We find a like situation in *Beowulf*, where Ingeld and Freawaru are parted by events, though bound to each other by vows. But there is a great difference here: Ingeld's love cooled and vengeance got the upper hand, while the reverse was true of Hagbard. This brings us to the next trait.

Trait 8. Here the tragic conflict between love and honor ends. In this trait we see Hagbard giving himself wholly to love, and Ingeld giving himself just as wholly to vengeance. The other differences between the two stories follow logically enough.

Trait 9. The *Widsith* poet gives us no details of Ingeld's last expedition. We are not even told that Ingeld was killed. We know only that the Danes defeated him decisively at Heorot, and the presumption is that he fell in the battle. Saxo, on the contrary, tells in detail the story of Hagbard's night of love and death. Here we will confine ourselves to two features of this story: the disguise and the betrayal. The Eddic hero Helgi once disguised himself in women's clothes, as we learn from *Helgakviða Hundingsbana, II;* a certain Blindr inn bölvísi saw through the disguise (in spite of his name). The bearded Hagbard of Icelandic tradition could not have disguised himself in this manner, and it seems likely that Hagbard's disguise, as we have it in Saxo, did not belong to the original tale, but was borrowed from the Eddic story, along with the blind Bolwisus, who obviously answers to Blindr inn bölvísi.

---

[31] As Herrmann points out (*op. cit.*, II, 492), *Kormákssaga* gives a beard to Hagbarðr. The hero's return meant, possibly enough, that his vengeance had miscarried: he fell in love with the woman whom he had set out to seduce. If so, Saxo and the Icelanders are not so far apart after all, except in the beginnings of the love affair.

Disguise in women's clothes goes with betrayal by the blind Bolwisus, but Saxo (or his source) took from this character his original and proper function (presumably because he thought a blind man unsuitable for this function) and gave him other work to do. The betrayal by maidservants belonged, in all likelihood, to another version of Hagbard's death, a version in which he did not disguise himself as a woman. If so, Saxo has taken the disguise from one version, the betrayal from another version of the tale.

In the Hagbard tale, the hero dies for love. In the Ingeld tale, he dies for honor. The two deaths are correspondingly different. But in each case the tragic end is, in some sort, a triumph. Ingeld sacrifices love and life itself in order to wreak vengeance; he does his duty, and does not count the cost. Hagbard puts himself in the hands of his foes in order to be with his love once again; he too does not count the cost. Hagbard and Ingeld are heroes of equal stature, though of different ideals.

Trait 10. From *Beowulf* 82 ff. we learn that the fall of Ingeld brought with it the burning of Heorot, the Danish royal palace. The Danes overcame their foe, but their hall was burned. This trait is unusual. Ordinarily, in story at any rate, it is the hall of the vanquished, not that of the victors, that burns. The appearance of this same trait in the Hagbard tale is, therefore, worthy of remark. So far as I know, these are the only two stories in which the trait occurs, and the agreement of the Hagbard and Ingeld tales here can hardly be dismissed as a coincidence.

We have finished our analysis and comparison of the two tales. What conclusions are we entitled to draw? It would probably be unduly simplifying the matter to say that the stories of Hagbard and Ingeld are different treatments of the same historical material: King Sigehere may in fact have hanged his daughter's lover. But it seems clear that our stories have too much in common to be fully separable in origin or development. Both have their roots in the same feud between Danes and Hadbards, though this feud may have involved two Danish dynasties, the Siklings as well as the Scyldings. And both make use of the same sequence pattern of events, however much they diverge in their treatment of the items that make up the pattern.

THE 'DREAM OF THE ROOD' AS PROSOPOPOEIA

MARGARET SCHLAUCH

New York University

As succeeding generations of scholars have studied the body of Old English lyric poetry and given tribute to its enduring literary qualities, an almost incredulous amazement has been expressed repeatedly concerning the originality of form and the extraordinary emotional intensity manifested in it. These qualities are particularly striking in the anonymous verse monologues which make up a considerable part of the whole lyrical offering. It is generally admitted that these poems show exceptional skill and mastery of technique; they are not the fumbling efforts of untaught beginners. For poems such as *Wanderer*, *Seafarer*, and *Banished Wife's Lament*, classical models have been suggested more than once. These lyrics represent persons as speakers. As partial explanation of their genesis, it has been pointed out that any cultivated Englishman of the time would have known and admired such declamatory passages as the speech of Æneas (most famous of exiles) to Dido and Dido's own lament at the involuntary perfidy of her guest in Vergil,[1] and the more lachrymose epistolary monologues in Ovid's *Heroides*. Hilda Reuschel has recently suggested that Ovid's personal expressions of an exile's woe in the *Tristia* and *Epistolae ex Ponto* may have contributed to the very wording of Old English lyrics.[2] The originality of treatment by Anglo-Saxon writers is generally conceded,[3] but it is undisputed that Latin models were near at hand and well loved.

As a literary type, *The Dream of the Rood* stands somewhat apart

---

[1] Rudolf Imelmann, *Forschungen zur altenglischen Elegie* (Berlin, 1920), especially pp. 188 ff. and 225 ff.

[2] "Ovid und die ags. Elegien," *Beiträge zur Geschichte der deutschen Sprache und Literatur*, LXII (1938), 132 ff.

[3] Ernst Sieper, in *Die altenglische Elegie* (Strassburg, 1915), stresses the Germanic tone and content of the poems, and argues for kinship with Celtic (Welsh) poetry (pp. 55 ff.).

from the other elegiac monologues in Old English. Here for the major part of the poem the speaker is an inanimate object, not a person. The discourse of the Rood is enclosed in another one, that of the dreamer who heard it speak; but the inner monologue is the essence of the poem. To endow the Cross with power of locution was to use a device of unexampled effectiveness in making vivid an event about which, for all devout Christians, the entire history of the world revolved. The object most intimately associated with that breath-taking moment when 'the veil of the temple was rent in twain from the top to the bottom; and the earth did quake, and the rocks were rent' might well be given speech with profound literary effectiveness. Yet this was not commonly done at the time. The Old English poet was not following a literary tradition concerning the Rood; he was making an innovation with the originality of genius.

Concerning the independence of models manifested by this author, A. S. Cook remarks in his introduction to the poem:

> The second part, the address of the cross, is unique in its composition. The notion of representing an inanimate object as speaking to him who stands in its presence, and communicating information or counsel, is as old as the Greek epigram. This was originally an inscription on a monument, a statue, or a votive offering preserved in a temple, and not seldom represented the work of art, or the dead who reposed beneath the monument, as addressing the passer-by.[4]

As literary analogues Professor Cook cites some of the Greek epigrams from the *Anthology* and several in Latin in which a dead person, or the statue of a dead person, speaks briefly from the tomb. He also refers to an epigram which Ovid puts into the mouth of a parrot (*Amores*, II, 6) and another, perhaps spurious, at the beginning of *Heroides*, IX. Such simple statements in the first person singular were inscribed on bells, swords, and house fronts. Beyond these, however, he offers no literary parallels before the Old English period. If this were all, the originality shown by the author of the *Dream of the Rood* would indeed be all but unbelievable.

Now I have no desire to diminish the glory of the Old English

---

[4] *The Dream of the Rood* (Oxford, 1905), p. xliii. Citations from the poem follow the edition by Bruce Dickins and Alan S. C. Ross (London, 1934).

poet, whose literary gifts remain beyond dispute no matter how many models he may have had. But I do wish to point out that Professor Cook has neglected to consider a number of poems in Latin which bridge the period from the Greek *Anthology* to eighth-century England and perceptibly diminish the appropriateness of the term 'unique' as applied to the speech of an inanimate object—even if it is to be the Rood—in the literature still extant in the eighth century. Moreover, I should like to point out that even without any models in Latin, a gifted writer might have found the suggestion for such a poem as the *Dream of the Rood* in Latin rhetorical texts of the time which discussed prosopopoeia, or discourse by inanimate objects. The poems suggested so far as direct sources or models for the *Dream* differ from it most conspicuously in being third person narratives instead of monologues. Thus Ebert[5] proposed a fourth-century poem *De Cruce* by Cyprian, also called *De Pascha*,[6] as a direct inspiration for the Old English poem; but this is allegorical exposition with but a slight modicum of narrative *in the third person*. Such texts are pertinent in a general way, since they exemplify interest in the Cross as a theme, but they leave out of account the interesting aesthetic problem of the innovation in Rood literature: the use of elegiac monologue.

In the golden age of Latin literature there was already a marked development of imaginary discourses by inanimate objects. This was a device particularly favored by the elegiac poets. Among the better known examples of this and later ages are: the discourse of the Tress of Berenice by Catullus; the apologia or *exculpatio* of a courtesan's doorpost in a dialogue also written by Catullus;[7] a similar theme, *Verba Januae conquerentis* by Propertius;[8] the discourse attributed to his book of *Tristia* by Ovid;[9] a panegyric on the emperor composed by Ausonius and put into the mouth of the

[5] Adolf Ebert, *Allgemeine Geschichte der Literatur des Mittelalters im Abendlande* (Leipzig, 1887), III, 70–72; also in Sächsische Gesellschaft der Wissenschaften, *Berichte*, Phil.-hist. Classe, XXXVI (1884), 81–93.

[6] S. Thasci Caecili Cypriani *Opera Omnia*, ed. G. Hartel, Part 3, in *Corpus Scriptorum eccl. Lat.*, III (Vienna, 1868–1871), 305 f.

[7] *Carmina*, 46 and 67.

[8] *Elegiae*, I, 16.

[9] *Tristia*, III, 1.

Danube River;[10] a discourse delivered by a statue of Dido and another by the petrified Niobe, also by Ausonius.[11] An anonymous writer of the days of decline and fall represents the City of Rome itself speaking in its desolation:

> Vix scio quae fueram, vix Romae Roma recordor,
> Quae populo, regnis, moenibus alta fui.
> Cesserunt arces, cecidere palatia Divum,
> Jam servit populus, degeneravit eques.
> Quae fueram totum quondam celebrata per orbem,
> Vix sinor occasus vel miminisse mei.[12]

Elizabeth Hazelton Haight has pointed out the popularity of this literary device among the Roman elegiac poets. Speaking of *The Lock of Berenice* by Catullus, she says:

> The fact that the speaker in this elegy is a Talking Tress associates it with all those poems in which inanimate objects (tombstones, statues, doors) are given voice. The common device of the Speaking Door Catullus uses in another poem, which is not a monologue, but a dialogue, between House Door and Poet Catullus. . . . The House Door poem [of Propertius, she continues later] (I, 16) may have been suggested by Catullus LXVII. It is not specifically stated to be the door of Cynthia's house, but may be the door of any courtesan. . . . House Door speaks a monologue about its disgrace in having sunk from the portal of a consul whither triumphal cars drove, to the barred door of a Light o' Love where all night excluded lovers chant their lamentation.[13]

Of such themes the speaking tree, or the wooden statue which recalls that it was once a tree, presents the closest classical parallel to the monologue passage in the *Dream of the Rood.* A poem long attributed to Ovid, *De Nuce*, represents a nut tree as complaining about the hurts and indignities to which it is exposed because passers-by shake it and throw stones at it in order to obtain the ripened nuts.[14] The tree protests its innocence, and laments the failure of the gods to act as husbandmen and protect the trees which were formerly in their charge.

---

[10] *Epigrammata*, 3.

[11] *Ibid.*, 118 and 27.

[12] N. E. Lemaire, *Poetae Latini Minores* ex recensione Wernsdorfiana, IV (Paris, 1825), 536.

[13] *Romance in the Latin Elegiac Poets* (New York, 1932), pp. 22 and 102.

[14] P. Ovidii Nasonis *Carmina*, ed. A. Riese (Leipzig, 1871), I, 220–224 (Poetae Ovidiani: *Nux*).

1 Nux ego iuncta viae, cum sim sine crimine vitae,
a populo saxis praetereunte petor.
obruere ista solet manifesta poena nocentes,
publica cum lentam non capit ira moram.
nil ego peccavi: nisi si peccare vocetur
annua cultori poma referre suo.

Fertility is a curse, not a blessing; if it were sterile it would be unmolested: 'Certe ego, si numquam peperissem tutior essem.' It has suffered mutilation not because of hatred but because of desire for the booty:

37 at mihi saeva nocent mutilatis vulnera ramis,
nudaque deiecto cortice ligna patent.
non odium facit hoc, sed spes inducta rapinae.
sustineant aliae poma: querentur idem.

The tree also laments because it is suffering from thirst, because it is not permitted to bring its fruit to maturity, because winter, hated by most creatures, is necessarily welcome to it on account of the peace it brings, and because it cannot escape from threatened wounds ('nec vitare licet mihi moto vulnera trunco'). These manifold ills cause it to desire death:

159 o! ego, cum longae venerunt taedia vitae,
optavi quotiens arida facta mori!
optavi quotiens aut caeco turbine verti
aut valido missi fulminis igni peti!
atque utinam subitae raperent mea poma procellae,
vel possem fructus excutere ipsa meos!

The poem ends with a direct exhortation to the traveler by the wayside: if I have deserved this punishment or been harmful in any way, burn me or cut me down at once; if not, leave me in peace and pass on!

The resemblances of this poem to the *Dream of the Rood* are largely generic, because both are laments and both are spoken by trees. The chief difference lies in the important circumstance that Nux complains of its own misfortunes, whereas the Rood solicits pity for the crucified Christ whom it bore. Certain verbal parallelisms result from the similarity of theme: 'ac ic sceolde fæste standan' and 'hyldan me ne dorste' (ll. 43b and 45b) recall 'nec vitare licet mihi moto vulnera trunco, / quem sub humo radix vinclaque firma tenent?' (ll. 169 f.). The general statements 'Feala ic on þam beorȝe ȝebiden hæbbe / wraða wyrda' (ll. 50 f.) and 'Sare ic wæs mid sorȝum ȝedrefed' (l. 59a) seem to echo the equally general sentiments of Nux such as 'sic ego sola petor, soli quia causa pe-tendi est: / frondibus intactis cetera turba viret' (ll. 45 f.). There are specific references in both poems to the wounds suffered by the tree. Rood says: 'eall ic wæs mid strælum forwundod (l. 62b), and Nux refers to its "mutilatis vulnera ramis' (l. 37). Nux protests its innocence: 'nil ego peccavi: nisi si peccare vocetur / annua cultori poma referre suo' (ll. 5 f.). There is at least an implied protestation of innocence in the Rood's repeated emphasis on its inability to do otherwise than carry out the Lord's will (ll. 35 and 42) even though its part in the crucifixion made it seem for a time most loathsome to men ('leodum laðost,' l. 88a).

In the *Dream of the Rood* a few lines are devoted to a description of the tree's life in the forest, and an account of the day when men came and bore it away on their shoulders (ll. 28–33). In Latin literature too the wooden statue of a god sometimes refers to the time when it was transformed from a block of wood into an image. The most conspicuous examples are to be found in the group of poems giving speech to the god Priapus, of which Horace's satire (I, 8) *Canidia* is probably most famous:

> Olim truncus eram ficulnus, inutile lignum;
> Cum faber, incertus scamnum faceretne Priapum,
> Maluit esse deum. Deus inde ego, furum aviumque
> Maxima formido. . . .

Not all of the Latin *Priapea* are composed in the first person, but many which are contain a few lines on the transformation from tree to image,[15] and many stress its tutelary function.

---

[15] See *Priapea* in Catulli Tibvlli Propertii *Carmina*, ed. L. Moeller (Leipzig, 1901), pp. 95–119. There are 85 poems in this collection. Only those representing the image as speaking are in any way pertinent. Number 10 is typical: "Insulsissima quid puella rides? / Non me Praxitiles Scopasve fecit, / Nec sum Phidiaca manu politus. / Sed lignum rude vilicus dolavit / Et dixit mihi: tu Priapus esto! . . . " In number 63 the image recounts the history of its origin, his sufferings, and the final insult put upon him: "Parumst, quod hic cum fixerint mihi sedem,/ Agente terra per caniculam rimas / Siticulosam sustinemus aestatem? / Parum, quod imos perfluunt sinus imbres, / Et in capillos grandines cadunt nostros / Riget-

Familiarity with the Ovidian *De Nuce* on the part of the author of the *Dream of the Rood* is by no means improbable. The poem was commonly included among the authentic works of Ovid. The earliest English manuscripts known to contain it postdate the Norman Conquest,[16] but this does not preclude knowledge of it in England at an earlier date, since collections of the Ovidian poems are extant in continental manuscripts from the eleventh and twelfth centuries.[17] The collection of *Priapea* was not lost in the Middle Ages; it was preserved partly, no doubt, because the poems were attributed to Vergil. A ninth-century manuscript of Murbach, Germany, contains these poems together with other short ones traditionally ascribed to Vergil.[18] The text of Horace's *Canidia* was also known in Europe before the time of the Conquest, though there is no record of an 'Oratius totus' in England before 1170.[19]

Besides these Latin discourses by trees or wooden images, there are, as Professor Cook has pointed out, a few riddles which bear a remote resemblance to the *Dream of the Rood*. Number 17 by Eusebius (eighth century) represents the Cross as speaking briefly in the first person, but the discourse is a form of enigmatic definition, entirely lacking in the narrative element so conspicuous in the *Dream:*

---

que duro barba vineta crystallo; / Parum, quod acta sub laboribus luce / Parem diebus pervigil traho noctem. / Huc adde, quod me vilem et a rude fuste / Manus sine arte rusticae dolaverunt, / Interque cunctos ultimum deos numen / Cucurbitarum ligneus vocor custos . . . . " In number 85, written by Catullus, the speaker stresses his role of guardian: "Quercus arida, rustica fabricata securi, / Nutrivi ut magis et magis sit beata quotannis / Huius nam domini colunt me deumque salutant . . . . " Cf. also number 84, likewise by Catullus. In an elegy by Tibullus (I, 4), Priapus makes a reply to a speech addressed to him.

[16] Canterbury, Christ Church (dated 1170); Durham (twelfth century). *See* Max Manitius, *Handschriften antiker Autoren in mittelalterlichen Bibliothekskatalogen* (Leipzig, 1935) (=*Zentralblatt für Bibliothekswesen*, Beiheft 67), pp. 62 ff. *De Nuce* is specifically mentioned as part of both of these MSS.

[17] *Ibid.*, p. 67.

[18] *Ibid.*, p. 47. *See* Moeller's edition of the *Priapea*, p. xlvi, for reference to a fragmentary codex of the eighth or ninth century containing a few of the poems.

[19] *Ibid.*, pp. 55 ff. The earliest surviving mediaeval MSS of Horace were done in France and Germany in the ninth and tenth centuries.

Per me mors adquiritur, et bona vita tenetur;
Me multi fugiunt, multique frequenter adorant;
Sumque timenda malis, non sum tamen horrida justis;
Damnavique virum, sic multos carcere solvi.[20]

It is because of their continuity with this distinctly classical tradition that some of the Old English riddles composed in the first person singular show similarity of phraseology with the *Dream of the Rood;* for instance, number 72, which concerns a spear, begins 'I grew in the mead, and dwelt where earth and sky fed me, until those who were fierce against me overthrew me when advanced in years.' (Compare this with 'me vilem et e rude fuste / Manus sine arte rusticae dolaverunt' in number 63 of the *Priapea.*) The riddles are not, however, the sole or nearest source of inspiration available. Discourse by an inanimate object, making use of narrative, was a form known and practised according to the precepts of mediaeval rhetoric.

That form was known as prosopopoeia, and was usually discussed in conjunction with ethopoeia, or imaginary monologue attributed to a human but fictitious character. The two cannot be very well separated, since prosopopoeia assumes that an object feels and speaks like a person.

Priscian, following his source Hermogenes, gives the following brief description of the two germane forms under the heading of *adlocutio*, which is the ninth of his topics:

Adlocutio est imitatio sermonis ad mores et suppositas personas accommodata, ut quibus verbis uti potuisset Andromache Hectore mortuo: conformatio vero, quam Graeci προσωποποιίαν nominant, est, quando rei alicui contra naturam datur persona loquendi, ut Cicero patriae reique publicae in invectivis dat verba.[21]

The example from Homer—the discourse of Andromache—had been used by Hermogenes; the Ciceronian instance of prosopopoeia—the discourse by the City of Rome to Cicero—was Priscian's substitute for a similar but less familiar instance from Greek oratory in which the sea is made to speak.[22] After a brief definition

[20] Quoted by Cook, *op. cit.*, pp. xlix.

[21] Prisciani *Praeexercitamina* ex Hermogene versa, ed. Carolus. Halm in *Rhetores Latini Minores* (Leipzig, 1863), pp. 557 f.

[22] The text of Hermogenes is to be found in his Προγυμνάσματα, ed. Hugo Rabe (Leipzig,

of *simulacri factio* (εἰδωλοποιία), or the attribution of speech to the dead, Priscian makes some general remarks on the appropriateness of certain types of speeches to certain circumstances and individuals. He classifies all monologues into three groups according to their style or emotional tone: *orationes morales*, *passionales*, and *mixtae*.

Passionales sunt, in quibus passio, id est commiseratio perpetua inducitur, ut quibus verbis uti potuisset Andromache mortuo Hectore; morales vero, in quibus obtinent mores, ut quibus verbis uti potuisset rusticus, cum primum aspexerit navem; mixtae, quae utrumque habent, ut quibus verbis uti potuisset Achilles interfecto Patroclo; habet enim et passionem funeris amici et morem de bello cogitantis. Sed operatio procedit per tria tempora, et incipit a praesentibus, recurrit ad praeterita et transit ad futura: habeat autem stilum suppositis aptum personis.

As prosopopoeia the *Dream of the Rood* appears to be an *oratio passionalis* (a specific Cross speaks, not one of a class; moreover, the aim is certainly to evoke 'commiseratio perpetua'). Emporius used the term pathopoeia for such impassioned fictitious orations.[23] The *Dream* observes the suggested time sequence of present-past-future by means of the introduction in which a dreamer recounts his vision of the Cross as an event in the present time, by the Rood's narrative account of the Crucifixion in the past, and by the closing references to a future life. The Rood says:

119 Ac ðurh ða rode sceal rice ȝesecan
of eorðweȝe æȝhwylc sawl,
seo þe mid Wealdende wunian þenceð.

The dreamer adds:

135 7 ic wene me
daȝa ȝehwylce hwænne me Dryhtnes ród,
þe ic her on eorðan ær sceawode,
on þyssum lænan life ȝefetiȝe,
7 me þonne ȝebrinȝe þær is blis mycel.
dream on heofonum. . . .

In discussing imaginary monologues, some writers like Em-

1913), p. 20: Ἠθοποιία ἐστὶ μίμησις ἤθους ὑποκειμένου προσώπου, οἷον τινας ἂν εἴποι λόγους Ἀνδρομάχη ἐπὶ Ἕκτορι. Προσωποποιία δὲ, ὅταν πράγματι περιτιθῶμεν πρόσωπον, ὥσπερ ὁ Ἔλεγχος παρὰ Μενάνδρῳ, καὶ ὥσπερ παρὰ τῷ Ἀριστείδῃ ἡ θάλασσα ποιεῖται τοὺς λόγους πρὸς τοὺς Ἀθηναίους . . . .

[23] Ed. Halm, *Rhet. Lat. Min.*, pp. 561 ff.

porius limited themselves to ethopoeia, stressing the general advice that discourse must be made to harmonize with the characteristics (*mores;* the ἦθος of Hermogenes) of the type of person being presented. Isidore of Seville echoes Priscian in his definition of prosopopoeia; he quotes the same example from Cicero's speeches: 'Etenim si mecum patria mea . . . loqueretur. . . .'[24]

Another type of Latin discourse may be found represented in the *Dream of the Rood*, subordinate to the narrative embodied in prosopopoeia. Although not intended as an exculpation or speech of defense from an implied charge, the Rood's narrative contains certain phrases suggesting a desire to dissociate itself from the cruel tragedy to which it served as instrument. For a time it suffered reproach for this:

87 Iu ic wæs ʒeworden wita heardost,
leodum laðost, ærþan ic him lifes weʒ
rihtne ʒerymde, reord berendum.

But throughout the narrative the Rood's helplessness has been emphasized. Just as the voluntary character of Christ's sacrifice is underscored in certain locutions,[25] so the involuntary function of the Cross appears in such phrases as: 'þær ic þa ne dorste ofer Dryhtnes word / buʒan oððe berstan' (ll. 35 f.); 'Bifode ic þa me se Beorn ymbclypte; ne dorste ic hwæðre buʒan to eorðan' (l. 42); 'Ac ic sceolde fæste standan' (l. 43b); ' . . . hyldan me ne dorste' (l. 45) and 'Ic þæt eall beheold. / Sare ic wæs mid sorʒum bedrefed' (ll. 58 f.).

Literary defense from a charge, whether overt or implied, was known as *purgatio*. All of the longer mediaeval rhetorics discussed it. Cassiodorus, for instance, shows it graphically charted as a subdivision of a technique of defense known as *concessio* ('I admit that I did this, but . . . '), which in its turn is a subdivision of *qualitas assumptiva* in the class known as *iuridicalis*. His definition is:

---

[24] *Origines*, "Capita quae sunt de Rhetorica," in Halm, *Rhet. Lat. Min.*, pp. 507–522, § xiii.

[25] *See* William O. Stevens, *The Cross in the Life and Literature of the Anglo-Saxons* (Yale Studies in English, XXIII) (New York, 1904), p. 74.

Purgatio est, cum factum quidem conceditur, sed culpa removetur. Haec partes habet tres: inprudentiam, casum, necessitatem.[26]

This definition of *purgatio* is to be found with but slight verbal changes in Martianus Capella[27] and Isidore of Seville.[28] Alcuin elaborates it by presenting hypothetical cases:

Purgatio est, per quam eius qui accusatur non factum ipsum, sed voluntas defenditur: ea habet partes tres, inprudentiam, casum, necessitudinem. Inprudentia est, cum scisse aliquid is, qui arguitur, negatur, ut . . . [an example follows taken from a typical *controversia*]. Casus autem infertur in concessionem, cum demonstratur aliqua fortunae vis voluntati obstitisse, ut . . . [example follows]. Necessitudo autem infertur, cum vi quadam reus id quod fecerit fecisse defenditur, hoc modo . . . [an example of shipwrecked persons who involuntarily violated the law of Rhodes about its harbor: 'vi et necessitate sumus in portum coacti'].[29]

The Cross indicates repeatedly that it performed its dolorous function 'vi et necessitate'; it is for this reason that parts of its speech sound like a *purgatio* using the technical plea of *necessitudo*. The approximation to this particular form of *concessio* or defensive pleading also explains the resemblance to Middle English and other poems in which the Cross tells of its unwanted function as part of its defense in a disputation with Mary. Professor H. R. Patch has already called attention to the slightly argumentative tone which anticipates the disputes between Mary and the Cross.[30] Mary is mentioned in the Old English poem, but the defense, if such it may be called, is directed not to her but to the dreamer. The epithet *reus* is probably more appropriately applied to the Cross in the later disputation than in the *Dream of the Rood*, but a knowledge of rhetoric may have caused the author to bring out the element of *concessio* in its speech.

The Latin poems and rhetorical theory here presented are

---

[26] "De Rhetorica" in the *Humanae Institutiones*, ed. Halm, *Rhet. Lat. Min.*, pp. 495 and 497.

[27] "De Rhetorica" in his *De Nuptiis Philologiae et Mercurii*, V, ed. A. Dick (Leipzig, 1925), p. 227.

[28] *Op. cit.*, p. 509.

[29] *Disputatio de Rhetorica*, ch. 15, in Halm, *Rhet. Lat. Min.*, p. 532.

[30] "Liturgical Influence in the *Dream of the Rood*," *PMLA*, XXIV (1919), 233.

intended to illuminate the literary genesis of the *Dream of the Rood* rather than to supply specific sources for lines and phrases. Its relationship to the general body of literature of devotion to the Cross, as demonstrated by Ebert, Stevens, Patch, and Williams, is not to be doubted. But if Cyprian's allegorical exposition *De Cruce*, the hymns of Fortunatus and acrostic poems glorifying the Cross give important evidence for the prevalent appeal of the theme, its poignant effectiveness of form can be better accounted for by pagan theory and practice of prosopopoeia. The Ovidian *De Nuce* is not in any sense a source for the *Dream of the Rood*, but its existence helps us to understand the element of tradition which shapes the work of even a great innovator like the Old English author. After all, his greatest innovation was in the style and intensity which made of his poem an *oratio passionalis* (pathopoeia) in every sense of the word. Emporius had said that there were three levels of discourse possible in the composing of this (as any other) type of speech; 'vasta, humilis, temperata.' These three, as he was well aware, were but three variant terms for the ancient Greek schools of oratory: Asiatic, Attic, and Rhodian.[31] The English poet chose and successfully handled an *oratio vasta*, the only appropriate one for a monologue by the Rood. That he did this is truly his chief literary glory. No amount of defining of rhetorical tradition, and no number of literary analogues on any level, can lessen that great distinction.[32]

---

[31] Halm, *Rhet. Lat. Min.*, p. 561.

[32] It is significant that a later rhetorician, Geoffrey Vinsauf, proceeds from a brief definition of prosopopoeia to a discourse by the Cross as his most ambitious example of the type: "Vocis in hac forma sanctae Crucis ecce querela. / *Crux ego rapta queror, vi rapta manuque canina / Et tactu polluta canum. . . .* " The speech is interspersed with frequent addresses to man (*homo*). *See* Geoffrey's "Poetria Nova" in Edmond Faral, *Les Arts poétiques du xiie et du xiiie Siècle* (Paris, 1924), p. 211.

MEDIAEVAL WINDOWS IN ROMANTIC LIGHT

ERIKA VON ERHARDT-SIEBOLD

Vassar College

Gedichte sind gemalte Fensterscheiben
—GOETHE

THE great formative international influences which the civilization of antiquity exercised on later ages have received full recognition. We still need, however, to evaluate the continuity of mediaeval traditions and achievements, the legacy of our own past, and those interests and aesthetic values which the Revival of the Middle Ages have brought to modern life and art. Now that attention is being focused on the mediaeval period and one more chapter is beginning to take shape in the monumental history of ideas which modern scholarship is writing, a new perspective can already be envisaged, the transition from the Middle Ages to modern times becomes clear, and the whole range of thought from antiquity to the modern age may be surveyed.

This essay attempts to link two intellectual worlds, the mediaeval and modern, and at the same time to carry the imagination back to the world of later antiquity, the Hellenistic Age. It shows how one creation of the mediaeval artist comes to life again and represents a favorite motif in romantic literature. Mediaeval windows as seen in romantic light recapture the glamor and glory of the Middle Ages, evoke metaphysical speculations of later antiquity, stimulate in many ways the poets' imagination. These windows painted in colored light appear now as a closing horizon shutting out the world, now as an expanding horizon opening out into the realm of reverie; they yield color visions that transform interiors, suggest warmth, depth, seclusion—and color vistas that invite a flight of the imagination, offer an escape.

It seems strange that the mediaeval window had to wait many centuries until at last it found its poets. Much as the dramatic composition, in particular of thirteenth-century glass, must have tempted poets to transpose such stories written in glass, yet the *ecphrasis*, practised so widely by the writers of the Middle Ages and the Renaissance in connection with tapestries, wall paintings, and *objets d'art*, real or fictitious, would seem to have neglected the subject matter vividly presented by the painted windows. Though we find references to painted windows in mediaeval and Renaissance literature, Milton is apparently the first poet who in his *Il Penseroso* sensed the singular appeal of the mediaeval church window. So all inclusive is this short poetic description and so firmly placed in the framework of a couplet that we are reminded of the mediaeval *tituli*, but Milton gives no indication of the legend in the picture, gives only atmosphere tinged with emotion:

> Storied windows richly dight
> Casting a dim religious light.

There lies a power of suggestion in Milton's age-old words.

With the rediscovery of Milton in the eighteenth century, poets suddenly discover the mediaeval church windows, see them in the light of Milton. They respond to their solemnity and admire their 'religious gloom,' their twilight effect, sunbeams fading, moonlight dimmed—holy light.

In 1782 Thomas Warton published a 'dichromatic' poem in celebration of the window designed by the painter Reynolds, which in monochrome and clear glass—a concession to the neoclassical taste of the period—replaced the beautiful fourteenth-century stained-glass window in the Gothic chapel of New College, Oxford. The poet duly emphasizes the 'chaste design,' 'genuine line,' 'Attic art from lucid surface,' 'universal pattern'; he sets 'the purer radiance' against 'the doubtful radiance of contending dyes' and praises 'the tints that steal no glories from the day, nor ask the sun to lend his streaming ray'—nevertheless, the jewel colors of the former mediaeval window still glow so vividly in his heart and in his poem that verses like

> . . . hues romantic tinged the gorgeous pane
> To fill with holy light the wondrous fane

continued to live in the imagination of the romantic poets and were to outshine 'the new lustre' that had been 'added to religious light.'

The Gothic Revival originated in England in the latter half of the eighteenth century and was soon hailed also on the Continent; it represented one of the most creative impulses of that great international Romantic Movement. The painted windows figured as colored mirrors in which the imagination of the Romantics saw the Middle Ages. Mediaeval windows became a romantic property, a treasured possession. Poets, like Walpole and Beckford, collected eagerly every fragment of mediaeval glass so as to bring the atmosphere of the Middle Ages to their fantastic Gothic castles. Even Goethe shared the general interest, and his estate contained a valuable collection of Gothic and Romanesque glass.

The stained-glass windows appear henceforth so frequently in English literature that it is possible to trace a definite tradition in the use of this motif. Gleaning our illustrations from poems, novels, plays, prose treatises, journals, and letters of the romantic period we become aware of one common factor in all the many forms of description. The poets are not interested in the pictorial values; to them painted windows merely represent impressions of colored light. They are a grander version of their beloved 'Claude Glass' which tinged and transformed reality, a magnified replica of the kaleidoscope whose everchanging play of gleaming colored patterns thrilled the romantic age. The mediaeval window, once designed to present a story in the language of religious symbolism or armorial emblems, now turns into a medium of impressionism.

In the course of this study it will not be possible to quote more than a few pertinent examples to show the general trend in the use of this poetic motif. We are able to discern a scale of gradation in the values of light, from Milton's half-light, half-shade to such dominant color notes as yellow and red, and, finally, to a blaze of light in polychrome effects. However, an ordered, chronological development is not apparent. Of two quotations belonging to the later period of Romanticism, both using the metaphor of the stained-glass window for the same conception, the first may well be considered as still adhering to the Miltonic tradition, whereas the second shows altogether independent treatment.

The enchantment of the church service is described by Scott in

Old Mortality (1816), where, in chapter XVIII, he attributes to the sermon:

a rich and solemn effect, like that which is produced by the beams of the sun streaming through the storied representation of saints and martyrs on the Gothic window of some ancient cathedral.

That same enchantment finds expression in Thomas Hood's little known poem, *The Two Peacocks of Bedford* (1822):

Now in church, time-sober'd minds resign
To solemn prayer, and the loud chaunted hymn—,
With glowing picturings of joys divine
Painting the mist-light where the roof is dim;
But youth looks upward to the window shine,
Warming with rose and purple and the swim
Of gold, as if thought-tinted by the stains
Of gorgeous light through many-coloured panes.

In following the course of the motif of the stained-glass window in romantic literature one more tendency can be shown. The poets gradually substitute reflected light for direct light, and they introduce moonlight as painting colored patterns on white surfaces; but again these transitions are not clear-cut. Further examples will illustrate the variety of emotional responses.

The dim religious light of Milton acquires a definite tint of color. Poets, such as Beckford and Shelley, discover on their journeys to Italy windows gleaming in saffron light, that product of a fourteenth-century invention when a thin veneer of yellow color applied on glass left it delicately stained and highly translucent. Filtering light appears pale and visionary, imparting a hue of sanctity. Beckford thus experiences a church in Florence as 'breathing Divinity.' For Shelley this yellow light in the Cathedral of Milan is an inspiration to read Dante. He writes in 1818 to his friend Peacock:

There is one solitary spot among these aisles, behind the altar, where the light of day is dim and yellow under the storied window, which I have chosen to visit, and read Dante there.

The yellow color note is handled very effectively by the romantic critic A. W. Schlegel, who uses it to describe the hallowed atmosphere of a Gothic cathedral, the first impression when entering the strange world of the Gothic novel, *The Monk* (1795). But

'Monk' Lewis himself strikes the real keynote of the highly charged atmosphere of fantastic colors of his novel when in one of the opening passages he makes the moon, which in Gothic novels shines dim and pale, here all at once paint magic colors:

The moonbeams darting into the church through painted windows tinged the fretted roofs and massy pillars with a thousand various shades of light and colours.

'*The lovely moon des Anglais*' of which the Marquis de Girardin spoke when in 1775 he tried to introduce and explain 'the English word' *romantic* to his French compatriots, this romantic moon as a painter of magical colors is no mere invention of the English Romanticists; actually moonlight falling through colored glass produces, because of the absence of strong diffused light, on white surfaces very distinct colored patterns.

Moonlight and colored or ornamented panes conspire to create the atmosphere for interiors which poets now begin to introduce as settings in literature. The moon reflects diamond patterns on the floor of a room, all Gothic gloom and Oriental splendor, 'a gorgeous room but somewhat sad,' which Keats in the poetical fragment, *The Castlebuilder* (1818), furnishes for himself:

It should be rich and sombre, and the moon,
Just in its mid-life in the midst of June,
Should look thro' four large windows and display
Clear, but for gold-fish vases in the way,
Their glassy diamonding on Turkish floor.

Poe who was especially responsive to the mood of a milieu makes full use in his works of colored glass; the light as seen from without or within acquires fantastic effects. His ideal room described in the *Philosophy of Furniture* (1840) shows two long deeply recessed windows with crimson-tinted glass.

Brilliantly stained windows flooded with moonlight call forth an interplay of colors. In the luster which falls on the white pavement one color stands out, the color much admired in mediaeval stained glass, 'flashed' ruby light. This clear red becomes heightened until it seems to clash with the moonlight, quiet and pale and silvery. As a spotlight the color red assumes uncanny powers. Scott introduces this motif into romantic literature. He did not discover it himself. Among the manuscripts of Scott which have recently been examined in the library of Abbotsford, one of his translations from the German came to light entitled *Wolfred of Stromberg, A Drama of Chivalry from the German Meier* (1797). The original play, Jacob Maier's *Fust von Stromberg* (1782), belongs to the large class of Gothic tragedies written in imitation of Goethe's *Goetz von Berlichingen* (1773), a play which Scott translated in 1779. There is a midnight scene in an abbey. The moon shines through a painted window, shines through images of saints, and throws a blood-red circle on the floor, on a stone, under which something mysterious is hidden.

This sensational picture has been closely copied in the scene laid in Melrose Abbey of Scott's *Lay of the Last Minstrel* (1805). Moonlight enters through a painted window, casts the blood-red cross of the stained-glass saint on the floor, marks a stone, which finally is raised and the book of magic discovered:

> The silver light so pale and faint,
> Showed many a prophet and many a saint,
> Whose image on the glass was dyed;
> Full in the midst, the cross of red
> Triumphant Michael brandished,
> The moonbeam kissed the holy pane
> And threw on the pavement a bloody stain.

And once more in poetry the color red is mirrored, never to be forgotten again. Literary critics have sought in vain for the source of Keats's fantastic vision of colors in *The Eve of St. Agnes* (1819/20). Moonbeams and softly tinged heraldic light play a subtle decrescendo of colors. The winter moon illuminates in red, rose, purple, and gold the figure of lovely Madeline in prayer:

> A casement high and triple-arch'd there was,
> All garlanded with carven imag'ries
> Of fruits, and flowers, and bunches of knot-grass,
> And diamonded with panes of quaint device,
> Innumerable of stains and splendid dyes,
> As are the tiger-moth's deep-damask'd wings;
> And in the midst, 'mong thousand heraldries,
> And twilight saints, and dim emblazonings,
> A shielded scutcheon blush'd with blood of queens and kings,
>
> Full on this casement shone the wintry moon,
> And threw warm gules on Madeline's fair breast,
> As down she knelt for heaven's grace and boon;

Rose-bloom fell on her hands, together prest,
And on her silver cross soft amethyst,
And on her hair a glory, like a saint. . . .

Milton's religious light, here tinged with 'the rainbow's varying hues' of the Romantics, the reflected color red from 'Gothic' literature dominant! Manuscript versions show how Keats had toiled to keep this color of red from intruding too much, how by the very sound of its name, borrowed from the language of heraldry, he had attuned it to romance, divorced it from reality. Keats introduced this color note not as a medium of mystery but for the vision of warmth and love which it brought into a cold, lonely, moonlit interior.

The still-life figure of the girl kneeling in prayer is in itself a stained-glass picture of Gothic art, or a statue come to life when romantic art made it a practice to cast colored light on sculptured figures, thus lending a spark of life to the cold white marble.

The living-picture motif of Romanticism!—a human figure transposed into a portrait or statue—a portrait or statue coming to life! In the enchanted atmosphere of moonlight shining through fantastic windows the worlds of reality and imagination blend. In such an atmosphere sculptured saints in prayer seem to stir with life as in Byron's poem, *Lara* (1814):

and as the moonbeam shone
Through the dim lattice o'er the floor of stone,
And the high fretted roof, and saints, that there
O'er Gothic windows knelt in pictured prayer,
Reflected in fantastic figures grew,
Like life, but not like mortal life to view.

Romantic moonlight, colored moonlight, no colors on earth can match this visionary light! Such is also Shelley's experience when in his *Queen Mab* (1812/13) he writes:

Those lines of rainbow light
Are like the moonbeams when they fall
Through some cathedral window, but the teints
Are such as may not find
Comparison on earth.

In 1862 a romantic artist, the pre-Raphaelite painter Millais, thought he could give reality to Keats's dream of colors and paint the scene in *The Eve of St. Agnes*. He carefully built up the vision following the details given by Keats. A winter night, midnight, and full moonlight streaming through a painted window, no fire burning on the hearth to mar the effect of the moonbeams. Starting his painting at Knole Park, Millais then tried to finish it in London. As his son and biographer states, it was there that the painter became aware that light even from a full moon was not strong enough to throw through a stained-glass window such definite colored lights on objects that these tints could be put on canvas. The artist was forced to finish his picture in the unromantic light thrown from the bull's eye glass of a lantern and to reduce the colored reflections to the single color of red.

Experiments have convinced me that through colored filters perceptible reflections can indeed be thrown by strong moonlight on white surfaces. Our romantic poets were too faithful observers of nature and too eager experimenters with light and color to invent facts not true to nature. However, the sensitivity to faint light effects varies considerably with individuals, and especially the painter, trying to render permanent such evanescent shades, may have to contend with difficulties unknown to the impressionistic poet.

But all these various emotional responses aroused by painted windows do not yet comprise the whole gamut of reactions. Strange to say, colored light calls forth in the minds of some of these poets philosophical speculations; a train of reasoning is awakened which may be said to conflict with the artistic and sensuous pleasure experienced by the poets. This reaction is strong in those Romantics who are metaphysically minded and who, as is usual at that time, incline toward Neo-Platonism. These poets see in colored light a depotentiation of the pure or white light, the symbol of the highest Deity. True to Neo-Platonic metaphysics of light, they regard colored light as white light deteriorated or stained; colored light is comparable to the lower grades of Being in the Neo-Platonic ontological scale, it represents diversity instead of Oneness and thus becomes a symbol of the corporeal world.

Coleridge in *Anima Poetae* under the date 1804 writes: '*White is the very emblem of One in being the confusion of all.*' We find here

Coleridge's favorite '*Multëity in Unity,*' which in his *Principles of Genial Criticism* he explains as rooted in Neo-Platonic philosophy. '*What is Life*'? asks our poet in a poetical fragment, dated 1805:

> . . . all colours of all shade
> By encroach of darkness made?,

darkness being related here to the Neo-Platonic conception of Matter (ὕλη).

When Coleridge to please his audience introduces in the tragedy *Remorse* (1813) a scene which pictures the interior of a chapel with painted windows, this setting at once calls forth in his mind metaphysical associations: white light, of which we partake only to a certain extent, is contrasted to colored light as absolute truth to relative truth:

> These rays that slant in through those gorgeous windows
> From yon bright orb—though coloured as they pass,
> Are they not light?—Even so that voice, . . .
> Which whispers to my soul, though haply varied
> By many a fancy, many a wishful hope,
> Speaks yet the truth. . . .

It is not likely that even the careful reader of Coleridge's play would have detected the Neo-Platonic background of archetype and image, of *Nous* and Soul, in the metaphor.

A similar metaphor occurs in Shelley's *Adonais* (1821) where among much Neo-Platonic imagery the following revealing lines are found:

> The One remains, the many change and pass;
> Heaven's light forever shines, Earth's shadows fly;
> Life, like a dome of many-coloured glass,
> Stains the white radiance of Eternity.

White light against colored light symbolic of Eternity against Time!

These conceptions of white light and colors among the romantic poets are especially significant, if we remember that at the beginning of the nineteenth century a vehement controversy about the nature of light was agitating the intellectual world. It is well known that Goethe in his *Beiträge zur Optik* (1791–1792), in his *Farbenlehre* (1805–1810), and other works took a decided stand against Newton's doctrine of color, against white light being a mixture of the primary colors instead of these being a product or deterioration of the original unitary white light. Goethe attempted to invalidate Newton's theories by experiments which he carried on over a period of eighteen years and some of which have proved of lasting value in physiology and psychology. But it seems to me that we have good reason to assume that Goethe's attitude was considerably influenced also by metaphysical considerations. Goethe regards color as *Trübung* of white light, a conception not unrelated to what Coleridge calls *encroach of darkness*. Goethe speaks of his *Farbenlehre* as *Platonic* and it is known that the word *sonnenhaft*, which he coined to describe the eye in the poem prefixed to his *Farbenlehre*, is a rendering of Plotinus's ἡλιοειδής. In the same introduction a phrase such as *Die Farben sind Taten des Lichts, Taten und Leiden*, to my mind, can hardly be divorced from Neo-Platonic thought: ἐνεργήματα καὶ παθήματα. Likewise, in a chapter of his *Farbenlehre* entitled *Intentionelle Farben*, the poet speaks favorably of Roger Bacon's comparison of white light and colors with archetype and image. Goethe expresses his aversion to the atmosphere of Faust's 'Gothic' study, so remote from Reality, by introducing colored window-panes through which clear sunlight shines *trübe*. Many references may be found in Goethe's works on color which connect white light and colors with ethical values, thus reminding us of the Neo-Platonic scale of white light = Spirit, *Nous;* colored light = Life, *Logos;* darkness = *Hyle* or Matter, something negative.

This opposition to Newton is no isolated occurrence, but is also evident in the attitude taken by the romantic poets, Blake, Shelley, Keats, and especially Coleridge, who all resented Newton's mechanical explanation of light and color, whereas the pre-Romantics such as Akenside and James Thomson, including here also Wordsworth, had known nothing but praise for Newton. Most enlightening is a letter by Coleridge which has only recently been published. This letter of July 4, 1817, is addressed to Ludwig Tieck, the German Romanticist, shortly after the latter's visit to Coleridge. The poet inveighs against the Newtonian conception of light as a *physical synodical Individuum* comprising *seven specific individua*, capable of mechanic dissection by a prism, in short, against its being not a principle but the result of a plurality of prime colors. He confesses that to him Newton's *assumptions . . . years before I ever heard of Goethe, appeared monstrous Fictions*. Coleridge shows himself in this letter a faithful adherent of certain ancient doctrines of the nature of light, a point of view emphasized by him also in some marginal annotations to *Naturphilosoph* Lorenz Oken's *Erste Ideen zur Theorie des Lichts* (1808), annotations published by Alice Snyder in her article on Coleridge's *Cosmology;* with reference to Goethe, Schelling, and Steffens he there speaks of *this ancient doctrine of Light and Shadow on the grand principle of Polarity* as opposed to Newton's optics. Like the Neo-Platonists and the *Naturphilosophen*, Coleridge thinks of 'Nature' as the unfolding in various forms of a unitary principle, the One, the Neo-Platonic Ἕν; to him the different phenomena are, therefore, only different aspects of one and the same law. Thus in his letter he professes to have always upheld the idea that *Sound was = Light under the praepotence of Gravitation, and Colour = Gravitation under the praepotence of Light*. Plotinus in his *Ennead*, IV, 5 had similarly thought of sound and light as being intrinsically cognate phenomena, as revealing the Oneness of all manifestations of the unfolding Deity, or, as Goethe expresses it, *alle Manifestationen der Wesenheiten sind verwandt*. This intrinsic sameness of all phenomena is a conception very different from the purely mathematical structural identity or analogy which we nowadays sometimes see in the laws governing, for instance, the behavior of sound and radiating energy.

In conclusion we may state that the Romanticist in reviving the enthusiasm for the mediaeval window imparts to these windows new values, values not immediately associated with the windows themselves but with the light effects produced by them. In the field of aesthetics the romantic poet thus enriches the feelings which the stained-glass window may evoke. However, with those romantic poets in whom the light effects stimulate metaphysical thoughts, the mind is fettered by ancient theories, the poet shows no understanding of the progress of his own age in the field of natural science, the subdivision of knowledge into several well-defined disciplines, each with principles of its own.

TWELFTH-CENTURY SCHOLARSHIP AND SATIRE

FREDERICK TUPPER

University of Vermont

THERE are clerks of two kinds in Chaucer. Over against the good clerk of the Prologue, him of Oxford, who 'unto logic hadde longe ygo,' and an even better man, the good Parson, a learned man, a clerk 'That Christes gospel trewely wolde preche,' we must set far less savory persons, another clerk of Oxford, 'hende Nicholas' of the Miller's Tale—

> Of derne love he coude and of solas
> As clerkes be ful subtle and ful queynte

and the wanton Aleyn and John of Cambridge in the Reeve's Tale, and yet another Oxford man, Jankin, the Wife of Bath's fifth husband, a professed misogynist and misogamist who delighted to read of wicked wives.

These two classes of scholars play their part in the medieval world long before Chaucer wrote of them. In the thirteenth-century *Morale Scholarium* of John of Garland,[1] the aid of Christ is invoked by the poor scholar, who is overcome by study, not deprived of virtue, who receives hee haws and even blows from the rich man who does not study and lives in his high house. This is the chant of the student:

> I eat sparingly in my little room, not high up in a castle. I have no silver money, nor do the Fates give me estates. Beets, beans and peas are here looked upon as fine dishes and we joke about meat, which is not in our menu for a very good reason. The size of the bottle of wine on the table depends on the burse which is never large.

And yet in a far higher sense than in Baudelaire's famous refrain, 'On est bien à vingt ans,' the lament becomes a chant of triumph:

> The scholastic life is the highest form of life. It gives boys such a cleansing of mind and body that these erstwhile dummies can explain the causes of eclipses of

[1] Edited by Louis John Paetow, Memoirs of the University of California, Vol. 4, No. 2 (1927), p. 162.

sun and moon, what keeps the sea in bounds, by what force the earth is rent asunder in earthquakes, whence come hail, snow, rain and lightning, and what makes the days long in summer and short in winter.

See the same eager spirit of the investigator, the industrious apprentice, in Laurence of Durham, who contrasts his own tastes and pursuits with those of the careless courtiers among whom he lived. To paraphrase the beginning of the ninth book of his most important work, the *Hypognosticon*,[2] in which he seeks to sustain somewhat labored parallels:

What must I do, having neither arms nor the shelter of ramparts
Sweating never for gain, sowing never a seed;
Masses and songs I love well, nor can ever the King's court
Take away wholly from me loving regard for the Muse.
Courtiers are casting the dice and the State in the balance is trembling,
While keen cavaliers fret, flinging their scorn and their hate.
Though grave graybeards now weigh heaviest matters of moment,
Mid all the stir I persist, playing as ever my game.
Mine not horses but muses and pens in place of the dicing:
My hawk, often a book, if not a verse in its stead.

So full is Laurence of his large subject that, when five books of his huge *Hypognosticon* are stolen from him, he is able to restore the lost 3,076 verses from memory. It is significant that Peter, who listens to his *Dialogues*, even today delightful reading, gives Laurence thanks for his rich instruction and closes the work with a chant of the love of God. Joy of scholarship is abroad in the land when men grow dithyrambic in its praise.

But, as always, blame is safer than praise. At least so it seemed to John of Salisbury, always sparing of applause, and having certainly little to bestow upon 'the leading teachers of philosophy, those who are most loudly acclaimed, surrounded by a noisy throng of disciples.'

In their lecture rooms they invite you to battle with them, become pressing and demand the clash of wit. If you hesitate to engage, if you delay but for a moment, they are upon you. If you advance and, though unwillingly, engage them and press them hard, they take refuge in subterfuge; they torture words; with tricks of magic they transform themselves until you marvel at the reappearance of the slippery changing Proteus. . . . He will finally be vanquished by his own meaning and be caught by the words of his mouth.[3]

---

[2] *Biographia Britannica Literaria*, II, 163.

[3] *Policraticus*, VII, ix. Pike's Translation (1938), pp. 244–245.

The attack of the moderns upon the ancients anticipates Swift's *Battle of the Books* by five hundred years when, as Raby points out,[4] John, who felt that the only sound basis is a thorough study of the ancients, makes the adherent of the new school of ready-made and self-taught scholars talk like this:[5]

For what is the old ass striving?
Why does he relate the words or deeds of the ancients?
We are wise from ourselves, our youth is self-instructive.
Our school does not receive the teachings of the ancients.
. . . .
Though a Petit-Pont adherent, of the very latest fashion,
The oldest of all teachings I swear was my own making.
A zealous crowd of youth surrounds me in adoration
And accepts as absolute truth most blatant of inventions.

The lines are significant in their irony, coming as they do from one in whom Manitius[6] finds 'the whole spiritual expression of his age, the incorporation of the collective culture of his time.'

To understand the scholarship and satire of the age, one must follow the struggle between arts and authors, between Paris, which deemed grammar the portal of the liberal arts, and Orleans, which had neglected the study of philosophy and insisted solely on the attainment of points of style through the direct study of such classical authors as Virgil and Lucan.[7]

The larger scholarship of the latter half of the twelfth century is happily illustrated in Alexander Neckham, student and later lecturer in the schools of Paris. Raby[8] proclaims him 'a humanist who attempted to master the whole of the learning of his age, theology, canon law, civil law and medicine.' Neckham wandered through the various fields of science with the same keen delight that was his when he visited the great cities of his world, whether at home or abroad. Heavens above, earth beneath, and

---

[4] *Secular Latin Poetry*, II, 90.

[5] *Entheticus*, Giles, VI, 240.

[6] *Geschichte der Lateinischen Literatur des Mittelalters*, III, 253.

[7] Sandys, *History of Classical Scholarship*, pp. 649–650, briefly summarizes Henri d'Andely's *Battle of the Seven Arts* (end of 13th century): "The Authors are aided by Ovid and Seneca and by Jean de Hauteville and Alain de l'Isle; yet they are worsted and Poetry buries herself out of sight somewhere between Orleans and Blois, never daring to show herself in that land. But she is honored still by the Britons and Germans."

[8] *S. L. P.*, II, 118.

the waters under the earth alike appealed to his insatiable curiosity.[9] It was natural that in his huge poem, *De Laudibus Divinae Sapientiae*, he should describe 'the chief seats of learning' in his day, summing up in a single couplet the four faculties of arts, theology, law, and medicine in the University of Paris, the *paradisus deliciarum:*

> Hic florent artes; coelestis pagina regnat;
> Stant leges; lucet jus; medicina viget.

And in Neckham's *De Naturis Rerum*, Sandys[10] notes that 'with its many anecdotes of animals he borrows much from Aristotle, Pliny, Solinus and Cassiodorus and also quotes Virgil, Horace, Ovid, Lucan, Juvenal, Martial and Claudian.'

Haskins in his valuable volume, *The Renaissance of the Twelfth Century* (p. 99), remarks that 'this classical revival manifested itself in the wide reading of Latin authors, especially the poets, and in commentaries thereon; in the active study and practice of grammar and rhetoric; and in the production of a large amount of excellent Latin prose and verse, some of which has the antique quality and feeling.'

Yet some of the great figures of this Renaissance found in their world much to criticize. John of Salisbury, *Metalogicus*, II, 10,[11] grieves that on revisiting his old companions on Mount Genevieve at Paris, 'I found them as before and where they were before, nor did they appear to have reached the goal in unravelling the old questions, nor had they added one jot of a proposition. The aims that once inspired them, inspired them still.' And John de Hauteville fills the third book of his *Architrenius* with 'the miseries of the poor scholars, the harsh discipline, the inadequate rewards when all is done, the immense and unrelenting labor, the broken health of the student, who pursues the shadow of his studies even in his dreams.' It has been remarked that 'these miseries are presented in the dark hues which Juvenal invented for his own inimitable pictures.'

---

[9] *See* his *De Naturis Rerum, passim.*

[10] *History of Classical Scholarship*, p. 526.

[11] Translated by R. L. Poole, *Illustrations of History of Medieval Thought and Learning* (1910), pp. 177 f.

Manitius (III, 806–807) has stressed de Hauteville's regard for detail in his weighty representation of the misery of students in Paris:

They dwell in a poor house with an old woman who cooks only vegetables and never prepares a sheep save on feast-days. A dirty fellow waits on the table and just such a person buys the wine in the city. After the meal the student sits on a rickety chair and uses a light, doubtless a candle which goes out continually and hurts the eyes. So he sits all night long and learns the seven liberal arts. Often he falls asleep at his work and is troubled by bad dreams until Aurora announces the day and he must hasten to college and stand before the teacher. And he wins in no way the mighty with his knowledge. But through the grace of Nature and Fortune he wins a bride at the end of the poem.

Nor is this all. As Wright notes in his introduction to *Anglo-Latin Satirical Poets* (I, xxviii),

the poet describes the poverty and wretched personal appearance of the students. He dwells on the meanness of their dress, on their bad lodging, spare nourishment, and hard beds and the baseness of those who served. He stresses the excessive labor it requires to become master of the seven arts; and pictures the students, after having spent a great part of the night in study, roused from their sleep before daylight to attend the lectures of the masters where they were treated with continual rudeness.

The philosophers themselves possess frequently a vain pride, although they know only the surface of wisdom. The hero's studies are the veriest hodgepodge, ranging from the ancient seers of Greece through the founding of Britain to the adventures of Arthur.

To the same Canterbury group as John of Salisbury belonged Nigel Wireker, who was a monk and perhaps Precentor of the Cathedral some time before the murder of Thomas à Becket (1170), with whom he seems to have been well acquainted, indeed, as he says, having eaten and drunk in his company. As he calls himself old in the introduction to his *Speculum Stultorum*, which, as Raby says, is directed against scholars, ecclesiastics, and monks, he must have been born about 1130. His chief work seems to have been written before the death of Louis VII (1180) and was dedicated to William de Longchamp, Bishop of Ely. Nigel certainly visited France as he refers to a stay in Normandy and shows a large knowledge of life in Paris. As Manitius remarks, the *Speculum Stultorum* leaves a cosmopolitan rather than a national impression. Nigel probably died before 1200.

Thomas Wright, in the introduction to his edition of the *Speculum Stultorum* in the *Anglo-Latin Satirical Poets of the Twelfth Century* (I, xx), remarks that 'Nigel Wireker's work is an exposure of the follies of the age and is directed especially against scholars and ecclesiastics. It throws great light on the character and history of medieval schools and universities and of medieval learning.' The ass, Burnellus or Brunellus (a diminutive of Brown, derived from scholastic logic of the day), who frequents the schools at Paris and in learning letters loses the labor that he has not spent because, at his departure, he was not able to remember the name of the city in which he had made a seven-year stay, signifies those who, since they have not senses trained or fit for understanding the heights of learning, yet, in order that they may seem learned in both testaments, read books which they do not understand, whose very names, after reading them through, they do not remember.

Of particular interest is the section (pp. 63 f.), 'How Burnel came to Paris and what he did there.' Going into the schools Burnel deliberates with himself whether these or those would profit him the more, and he associates himself with the English because he considers them subtle in sense, distinguished in manners, pleasing in face and speech, strong in mind and powerful in counsel; they rain gifts upon people and they hate the avaricious; they multiply their dishes and they drink without law, wassail and drinkhail. These last are the vices that accompany them. If you take these away, all else pleases. Nor, however, are these always to be blamed.

Speeding up his study, Burnel clings to the studious, so that he may learn to speak agreeably and grammatically. But because his sense is dull and his head very hard, he does not absorb the teachings of the master and his care and his toil go for nought and he is able to learn nothing but 'Ya.' From his boyhood he has learned 'Ya.' Nothing else than what nature has given him is he able to retain. And all his money and his labor are lost, and all hope of regaining his lost tail is gone.

After such self-communion Burnel decides to leave Paris early in the morning. Therefore, having bidden farewell to all his weep-ing companions, he hastens his step and, having reached the top of the mountain, he says in stupefaction when he looks down on Paris:

Sancta Maria, Deus, Crux Christi bless me! What is this place situated in the valley? This, I think, is Rome surrounded by its great wall. What else can this city of many towers be except Rome? And what is that if it isn't the Mount of Jupiter? Holy Virgin! Is Rome so near, the city in which I studied, whose name flees from my mouth and heart? Woe to me, what sort of fellow am I?

Then we have the sad anticipation of the reaction of his parents to his ignorance. They will think their money thrown away.

When a rustic whom he meets by chance reveals to him the right name 'Paris,' he is so afraid of losing it again that he decides to say nothing at all during the fifteen days of his journey except 'Paris,' whatever may happen or whoever may speak to him. And yet he loses the name when some one addresses him, and is plunged once more into sorrow which finds a vent in a long soliloquy, which oddly enough takes the form of a detailed recital of the various orders of monks and nuns, each of which receives little mercy. Burnel, not satisfied with any of the existing orders, decides to found a new order in which he proposes to blend the best in all the others—and the best is like the worst. His old adviser, Galien, is invited to join the new order, but Burnel's old master enters and claims him for his own and the poor ass is forced to end his days in his original humble position.

In the verse of the *Speculum Stultorum*, Nigel had traced the foolishly futile university career of Burnel, the type of the asinine. In the prose of his *Contra Curiales et Officiales Clericos*, he continues with constant irony his theme of twelfth-century academic training. Schools are avoided, ease is sought, the rod is put out of sight, baths and other means are offered by which new plantings are wont to be watered. Youths are sent to Paris to be trained in literary studies. There, after having dispensed with duty for a while lest they should be withered and worn by the effort of labor and study, they are introduced to dicing and gaming and other things which follow in proper course so that nature may breathe and so that the youths may not be thought ignoble on account of ignorance of pursuits of this kind. Those who preside over their work, making parental affection rather than the weakness of their age the criterion, seem to hearken unceasingly to the saying of David: 'Preserve for me my son Absalom!' Hence they grant the youths what they seek, and cover up what they do. After a bowing acquaintance with the elements of grammar and logic the boys return home and spend what remains of their time in hawking and hunting. Thus the period of life that they should give to implanting morals and acquiring virtues, they devote wholly to vanity and luxury. And, what is in youth a very bad sign, they become shameless and senseless with as bold a front as that of the Scarlet Woman.

Nigel now concerns his critical self with what we call graduate or professional study. He pictures the youths who go to Montpellier and apply themselves with a vim to the art and experiments of medicine. After a little time they come exultantly away carrying their pots and jars and busy themselves over sick beds. They attach themselves to the rich or certainly they are called by them in their need. Their returns are guaranteed by fixed taxes, and, when no church is vacant for the medical cleric, a certain sum must be raised from the revenues of the landowners until a church or prebend may be conferred upon him for his pay. It is difficult for a lord and not safe for a family to make these payments from income.

Having thus the means whence they may serve higher and climb higher, the aspirations of these doctors know no bounds. They are adorned with varied splendors, they are shod with striking footgear, they are clad in clashing colors. They win name and fame, conciliating other men by many gifts. When they see these approaching clothed in robes of state and clinging close to kings, those who have been lovers of the liberal arts deeming it ignominious to feel the pulses of rustics and to test the water of old women bid farewell to Paris and shift to Bologna. There they incorporate in themselves the whole corpus of the law, and after a reasonable time they return with a bound. They speak in new tongues and in sesquipedalian words, they teach men to carry on strife, to lay to rest old issues and to arouse those laid to rest. One should give these at once churches, even if by force. They are those without whom neither princes nor prelates can exist. They are feet to the lame and eyes to the blind. They have indeed these eyes for watching the way of justification in the law of God, but not for seeking it. They have these feet that may be called 'Romeseekers,' rather because they prosecute causes than because they direct them into the ways of peace. They are those who, having tried the perils of the way in remote regions and being often exposed to the inclemency of superheated air, have surrendered their bodies to punishments for the sake of their Lord.

By a close examination of the sermons and *exempla* of the period, Haskins has admirably illustrated the student life of the Middle Ages, particularly of the University of Paris in the thirteenth century.[12] It may not be superfluous to supplement his references with a few of those cited in the interesting volumes by Owst. Just as Christ has been proclaimed by a later poet, 'the first true gentleman that ever breathed,' so in a sermon by the Englishman, John of St. Giles,[13] he was hailed as 'a scholar who dismissed his mother on account of the schools and not his spouse'—that is, he was unwilling to dismiss church for the sake of the schools. 'Indeed,' continues the preacher, 'he loved her so much that although he saw the tears of his mother and John yet he suffered on account of his spouse.' A sermon of Bishop Brunton cited by Haskins and Owst shows that 'fatuous scholars sent by their parents to Paris at the greatest expense, to carry on their studies, may go to classes for the sake of appearances, they do not study in their books nor listen to the words of their teachers, but look far and wide out of the windows and point out the passers-by.'

Many of the *exempla* are aimed directly at the heads of clerks. In the *Alphabet of Tales*[14] translated from the *Alphabetum Narrationum* of Etienne de Besançon, a scholar after his death appears to his master clad in parchment with small letters written thereon

[12] *Studies in Medieval Culture* (1929), Ch. II, 36–71.

[13] Cited from an extant MS in the Bibl. Nat. at Paris by Haureau, *Quelques Manuscrits*, in Owst, *Preaching in Medieval England* (1926), pp. 34–35.

[14] *Early English Text Society*, Original Series 126, p. 104, No. CLI.

and disclosed to him that these were the sophistries and subtleties wherein he wasted all his days, and that he was now tormented with a great heat. A drop of sweat fell from his hand upon that of his master and pierced it as if the drop had been the sharp shot of an arrow and ever after there was a hole in his hand. 'And when the master saw this, he left the logic school and became a monk of the Cistercian order.' A dreadful warning to both teacher and student from which even a modern may profit. The second from the *Alphabet*, CCCXVII, is familiar to us all;

Valerius tells how that when Demosthenes might not easily bring forth certain letters, he labored so against a vice and an impediment in his mouth that no man might speak fairer than he. So on a time it happened to him to go to the seaside, where he heard great noise and dashing of the waves together; and he gave great heed thereto. And even when his mouth was full of sentence and reason, he would speak much and be long in speaking.

All this under the caption, 'Facundia necessaria est clerico.' Indeed, medieval teachers and preachers, for the sake of their hearers, would 'stoop to truth and moralize their song,' even if it were the song of Orpheus, as did John Waldeby when preaching upon the theme of clerics. Helen Waddell in *The Wandering Scholars* (Chapter V) cites from Haureau's *Notes et Extraits* (VI, 234) a sermon of Jean de St. Gilles to the university. 'It is to be observed that the Mother of the Lord suffered him not to be in the schools, save three days only, nor was he Magister save for three years and a half; and in this are those rebuked who dally forever in the schools.'

In reviewing twelfth-century clerical careers, one has frequent occasion to remember Tennyson's stanza in *In Memoriam:*

> How many a father have I seen,
> A sober man among his boys,
> Whose youth was full of foolish noise,
> Who wears his manhood hale and green.

Doubtless many a father not of youth but of the church, who wrote with stern disapproval of the wild life of the scholars, had in younger days heard the chimes at midnight in Paris of the twelfth century. Such was the Englishman, Serlo of Wilton, born about 1110, who took up his abode in Paris, became a teacher in the University, and despite his office wrote a mass of frivolous verse under the influence of Hugo Primas of Orleans. Later he was converted by the appearance of a departed friend who came to him from the fires of Purgatory. Serlo straightway forsook the world and joined the Order of Cluny on the Loire but later left them for the Cistercians and became Abbot of L'Aumône. The poems written before his conversion and those after provide a contrast not uncommon at this time.[15]

Nothing could better illustrate the taste of the young clerks of the Parisian classrooms than their delight in Serlo's poetic model, the dwarfish Hugo the Primate, not as a teacher in the chair that he dishonored but as a singer who took his life as the pattern of his poetry, and 'stamped his personality upon his work with the violence of a Juvenal or a Swift.' So confident is he of his appeal to his student audience that he pauses for a *plaudite* and wins the expected response:

Nos optamus hoc audire
Plus quam sonum dulcis lyre.

There are some who claim for Hugo Primas the authorship of the famous *Apocalypse of Golias*, so scurrilous and blasphemous, yet so indicative of academic taste or taint that men have claimed it for a better man, Walter Map; but there is little warrant for either attribution. To him that hath shall be given and both men had wide vogue. As Wright noted long ago,[16] 'Golias, the burlesque representative of the clerical order, the instrument through which their vices were satirized was also the representative of that jocular class which, by its unrestrained indulgence and satirical joviality, was the real burlesque of the clerical order with which it was connected.' The *familia Goliae* or Goliards were identified with 'Clerici *ribaldi*.' These ribalds abounded in the schools, where they turned to mirth all things of earth, and some of heaven, from Priscian to the Pope.

The chief delight of the Goliards was in song, in such rimes as those of the Arch Poet, a greater than Primas. Every one remembers the most notable stanza of his *Confessio:*

---

[15] *See* Raby, *S. L. P.*, II, 111–115; Manitius, 905–910.

[16] *Poems of Walter Mapes*, Camden Society (1841), p. xii.

Meum est propositum in taberna mori,
Ubi vina proxima morientis ori;
Tunc cantabunt letius angelorum chori,
'Deus sit propitius isti potatori.'

The idle apprentice is always lively in his abuse of scholars old and young, richly repaying their contempt: 'Only a fool would sit up all night to study arts and to yawn over Georgics. There is no advantage in being learned and as for the poets they may starve.' But the greybeards seem to have the better of the argument. Giraldus insists that, 'when the man of letters sits in his chimney corner with a book, he is his own best company.'[17] And John of Salisbury, ever authoritative, says the final word: 'Rare is the humility and lone the path of wisdom, that he may be taught himself or may teach others, for everything is referred to the shallow standards of filthy pleasure or futile utility: these are the aims of a soul astray.'[18]

Giraldus Cambrensis or Gerald of Wales, the consummate egotist of his time, delighted in many things but in nothing more than himself. In his *De Rebus a se Gestis* he tells us that he was born at Manorbeer in Pembrokeshire (1146), the son of William de Barri, a Norman baron, and Andgharad of a princely Welsh family, the sister of the Bishop of St. David's. From his uncle's instruction he went to Paris to pursue the higher branches of study, including jurisprudence and the canon law, and fared so well in his three sojourns that he was invited to lecture on the Trivium, particularly on rhetoric. He speaks of this in the second book of his work upon his favorite theme, *De Rebus a se Gestis*. So vivid, he tells us, was his presentation of his subject, so admirable indeed in form and color, so skillful in the adjustment of the sayings of philosophers and authors to his subject that the richer his hearers were in wisdom and training, so much the more eagerly did they give their ears and minds to hearing and to imprinting all upon the memory. Charmed by so great sweetness of words, the audience—although they were jaded by listening to the long and tedious discourses of other speakers, and although his own

[17] *Gemma Ecclesiastica*, II, 37, cited by Helen Waddell, *Wandering Scholars*, 113.

[18] *Policraticus*, Book VII, Ch. 15, in Pike's Translation, p. 275.

presentation was detailed, and was on a subject deemed tedious by many—could not be fatigued or satiated. The scholars began to write down his reasons (*causas*) one by one, as they fell from his lips, and to embrace them with a great longing. On a certain day, when a great concourse came from every side to hear his discourse, which was followed by murmurs of praise and favor from all, a certain illustrious doctor who had read in the arts at Paris and had long studied in the laws at Bologna (his name was Master Roger the Norman, afterwards deacon of the church at Rouen) burst forth in these words: 'There is no knowledge under the sun, which when taken to Paris would not be made to seem far more excellent there than elsewhere.' After giving the proem of his first lecture, 'Whether a judge ought to decide according to the evidence, or according to his own conscience,' Giraldus adds that all were in doubt whether greater praise ought to be given to the ornament of the speaker's words or the efficacy of his opinions and reasons. Giraldus, who deemed praise safer than blame, adds the tributes of other men particularly of his teacher in that subject who applauded the great success of his student in speaking so admirably in a meeting of scholars—for, as Jerome says, 'the success of students is the praise and glory of instructors.'

Giraldus vaunts another academic triumph—this time on English ground.[19]

He recited before a public audience of the University of Oxford on three successive days, and on each day he gave a sumptuous feast; on the first he entertained the poor people of the town, on the second the doctors and students of greatest celebrity, and on the third the other scholars and the burghers and soldiers of the place. He relates his doings on this occasion with much self-complacency, says that they were worthy of the classic ages of the poets of antiquity, and asserts that nothing like them had ever been witnessed on English ground.

And a third achievement still more surprising. When Archbishop Baldwin was sent to preach in Wales a new crusade, after the report of the capture of Jerusalem by Saladin, Giraldus assures us that 'the effects of his own eloquence were almost miraculous for, although the only languages he made use of were Latin and French of which the greater portion of his auditors were totally ignorant, they were so much affected by his discourse that

[19] *De Rebus a se Gestis*, II, 16 (Wright's paraphrase).

even the most illiterate of the multitude burst into tears and they hurried in crowds to take the cross.[20] Hence we draw the inference that, had Giraldus spoken in his native tongue, and that of his hearers, Wales would have been emptied of its male population. His friend, Walter Map, in a letter to Giraldus, suggests at once the power and limitations of that scholar's Latinity.[21]

You have written a great deal, Master Giraldus, and you will write much more: you have employed writing: I, speech. But, though your writings are far better, and much more likely to be handed down to future ages than my discourses, yet, as all the world could understand what I said, speaking as I did in the vulgar tongue, while your works, being written in Latin, are understood by only a few persons, I have reaped some advantage from my sermons; but you, addressing yourself to princes, who were doubtless, both learned and liberal but are now out of date and have passed from the world, have not been able to secure any sort of reward for your excellent works, which so richly merited it.

Walter Map, himself, had the strange fate of living through the centuries by works that he did not write. As I have said elsewhere,[22] 'to him, fine gentleman, polished courtier, reverent churchman, trusted friend of many good and great, coming ages lavishly ascribed the scurrilous indeed blasphemous mouthings of the sham bishop, Golias—the very ribaldries that Walter's close friend, Giraldus Cambrensis, held in such horror.' Walter himself had watched the clash of town and gown in Paris:[23]

While I was in Paris, there arose between clerks and laymen in the court of the King a quarrel, which soon grew into an open feud. The laymen got the upper hand and they handled roughly a great many of the clerks with fists and clubs; then fearful of the King's justice, they fled to their hiding-places. The King nevertheless 'heard the cry of the poor' and came and found one of the poorest of them, a mere youth in a black cloak with the blood flowing from his broken crown. His assailant proved to be the chief of the chamberlains of the Queen, the daughter of the King of Spain. He was arrested and, by the King's command, bound and led to the place of punishment. Then the Queen, with hair disheveled, cast herself down before the King's feet and pleaded for mercy—and the whole multitude of the court with loud wailings also besought the King. It was not strange that pity moved Louis to tears. None the less he was compelled by justice

---

[20] *Itinerarium Cambriae*, I, 11, *De Rebus a se Gestis*, II, 18.

[21] Giraldus, *Conquest of Ireland*, Last Preface.

[22] Introduction to Translation of *De Nugis Curialium* (1924), by Tupper and Ogle, p. x.

[23] *De Nugis Curialium*, V, 5.

to exact punishment and he ordered the man's right hand to be cut off, for this had broken the clerk's crown.

Truly 'mercy is enthroned in the hearts of kings.' Like Peter of Blois, whose life is also of large interest to the modern scholar, Walter Map was a student of the famous Paris professor, Girard la Pucelle.

'Say that England has taken me' was the chant of many a Frenchman during the century after the Conquest and their new country acknowledged their allegiance by linking their names with their homes. The monk Reginald whose lovely lines on his birthplace at Faye in Poitou have been long remembered[24] is always known as Reginald of Canterbury. But Peter of Blois, despite his archdeaconry of Bath, is, like his brother William, the author of the 'comedy' *Alda*, linked with the name of his native place. And this adopted son of England was worth the having, although there were some who failed to recognize his worth. In an oft cited letter (Epistle CLIX) he tells a friend at court that he had been called by King Henry to England and treated by him and his son with large grants and also honored by Archbishop and Bishop, and all the magnates of the land with all veneration and was thus exposed to the envy and malice of the time. By the use of certain letters won from the pope, he was 'violently deprived of every honor of his diaconate.'

He was certainly at school at Tours and he tells us in his later years that since the time of his youth he had been at schools and at court, and that during his youthful training he had taken the matter of his poems not from the world of fable, but from history, and that he had been compelled to learn by heart the letters of Hildebert of Le Mans. From Tours he went to the University of Paris, where, as we have seen, he sat in at least one lecture room with Walter Map. His historical lectures at Paris were on Justinian, Josephus, Suetonius, Hegesippus. It is doubtful whether Peter during these days at Paris was a scholar of John of Salisbury, but in his writings he shows great dependence upon John, particularly in his use of the ancients. After he had studied the arts at Paris he went to Bologna to study law and was greatly pleased to do so,

[24] Raby, *S. L. P.*, II, 103.

because in Paris, even while he was studying the law of God, he was giving his free time to the reading of the Codex and the Digest. We find him back in Paris devoting himself to theology, and to the teaching of children and younger students.[25]

Peter tells us that his ambition was to be a universal scholar, and he boasts of the vogue and vitality of his writings quite in 'Exegi monumentum aere perennius' fashion. His profound regard for his own scholarship is equaled only by his unmitigated contempt for the work of others outside of his own circle. This inveterate phrasemaker writes to a critical correspondent, one Ralph, Professor of Grammar at Beauvais: 'You have remained with the ass in the mire of a very dull intelligence. Priscian, Tully, Lucan, Persius, these are your gods, you schoolboy centenarian! But in the house of my lord, the Archbishop of Canterbury, there are men deeply versed in literature among whom are found all rectitude of justice, all prudence of foresight, every form of learning.' One infers that much of this was contributed by Peter himself. He boasts (Epistle 139) that from youth he had fought a good fight in schools and courts. This training, he felt, had stood him in stead because he learned, as a small boy, to gather his material not from fables, but from the facts of the history.

Peter has pointed out to us one key of knowledge, but a greater man than he, his master, John of Salisbury, has suggested[26] no less than six which he derived from another: 'The old man of Chartres' (Bernard) has briefly stated what the keys of knowledge are which open the traveler's way for those studying philosophy, with the hope of gazing upon the vision of truth:

> A humble mind, the zeal to learn, a life
> Of quiet, the silent search, a lack of wealth,
> A foreign land, these are the keys that open
> When we read, the doors to light our night
> Of ignorance.

One likes to quote this now, because no scholar of our day has better used these keys of knowledge than he to whom this volume of studies is dedicated, Carleton Brown.

---

[25] Wright, *Biographia Britannica Literaria*, II, 366–379.

[26] *Policraticus*, VII, 13 (Pike's Translation).

INTRODUCTION TO A STUDY OF THE MEDIAEVAL FRENCH DRAMA

GRACE FRANK

Bryn Mawr College

THAT the formal drama of ancient Rome disappeared and that Western Europe in the Middle Ages recreated its drama not from the dead debris of the extinct classical theatre, but from its own living faith, these are facts that usually awaken surprise when they are encountered for the first time and occasionally the initial skepticism persists. Somehow the posited hiatus between the ancient stage and that of the Middle Ages seems inexplicable when one remembers the many manuscripts of Terence copied in mediaeval scriptoria, the copious citations from these comedies in mediaeval literature, the Terentian plays of Hrotsvitha, and certain poetical works in Latin that bear the title of *comoedia;* when one remembers too that some of the ruins of ancient Roman theatres must have remained recognizable and not wholly pillaged during the Middle Ages, and that there are concrete references to both actors and acting in widely read ancient authors whose allusions could hardly have escaped the notice of mediaeval scholars.

Yet the classic Roman theatre had of course died before the fall of Rome. The last writer of tragedies whose works are known to have been produced is the consul, P. Pomponius Secundus, and he lived in the time of Claudius. Most dramatic works even in his day were destined for reading.[1] The only Roman comedy (*togata*) mentioned as having been played during the Empire is Afranius's *Incendium*, given at a festival sponsored by Nero, and references to performances of the so-called *palliata*, or new comedy of the Greeks, which are known to have been popular in the Empire, are relatively scarce.[2] It may be that some old plays were revamped, but all the evidence indicates that contributions to the stage in

[1] *See* Ludwig Friedländer, *Darstellungen aus der Sittengeschichte Roms*, II (1922), 119.
[2] *Op. cit.*, 119 ff.

the late Empire took the form of farces—the Atellan farce and the mime—and pantomimes, types of entertainment that respectively replaced the comedies and tragedies of the Republic.

The Atellan farce, like the modern Punch and Judy show or the Italian *commedia dell'arte*, centered about certain fixed characters (usually four: Pappus, Dossennus, Bucco, and Maccus), and its development was necessarily limited.[3] The mimes, on the other hand, which long survived,[4] had a broader range of characters and wider interests; in fact, from the testimony of ancient writers, it is apparent that the word *mimus* covered performances of diverse forms, ranging from extemporaneous fooling of the lightest sort to more serious types of comedy that might, at least in part, be committed to writing.[5] The pantomimes consisted essentially of solo dances performed to the accompaniment of singing and musical instruments, and their charm, like that of the Russian ballets, depended largely upon the union of dancing, music, and scenic effects. Such texts as formed the basis of the pantomimes have disappeared, although Lucan is said to have

---

[3] These characters appear frequently in art. Cf. the illustrations in Allardyce Nicoll's *Masks, Mimes and Miracles* (London, 1931). Late references to the Atellan farces are cited there, pp. 138 ff.

[4] Reich, *Der Mimus* (1903), pp. 778 ff., quotes passages from Salvianus of Marseilles who, in his *De Gubernatione Dei* (dated between 439 and 451), protests that the churches of Marseilles were neglected while the theatres were visited ("nos altaria spernimus et theatra honoramus"; cf. Migne, *P. L.*, LIII, 116). There were performances of some sort in the sixth century at Rome, but, although the words of Isidore of Seville in the seventh century imply that the theatres of Spain were still standing then, he speaks of dramatic performances in the past tense (Reich, *op. cit.*, pp. 785 f.). Nicoll, *op. cit.*, p. 146, thinks that Isidore "knew of theatres only as disused buildings," but "was personally acquainted with the activities of the *histriones* and the *mimi*." That such entertainers performed plays is, however, uncertain. The terms came to be applied loosely during the Middle Ages to various types of entertainers.

[5] Plutarch, *Quaest. Conv.*, VIII, 8, 4, distinguishes between *paegnion* and *hypothesis* (παίγνιον; ὑπόθεσις). The Oxyrhynchos mime discussed by S. Sudhaus, in *Hermes*, XLI (1906), 247 ff., was of course written down, but apparently served merely as the basis for further dialogue and action. Conceivably, a written scenario would be more important to certain types of mimes than to others. At least two mimographs of the second century A. D., Marullus and Lentulus, are referred to in such a way in the fourth and fifth centuries as to indicate that their works had been written down and preserved (Reich, *op. cit.*, p. 746).

written fourteen *fabulae salticae*, and the themes of many others are known to us.[6] In any case no performances of farces, mimes, or pantomimes are heard of in the West after the sixth century, and no texts, so far as we know, survived into the Middle Ages. In fact, despite the Herculean efforts of Reich to establish a continuity of tradition between the ancient mime and mediaeval dramatic traditions, all records of any sort fail us in the West between the sixth and ninth centuries.[7]

In the East,[8] when the capital of the Empire was transferred to Constantinople, the theatre moved with it. There are records of at least four theatres in Constantinople, and, although no texts of plays performed in them survive, it is evident that the same types of entertainment—mime and pantomime—prevailed there as in the West. It has been suggested that Byzantium created a new drama through the influence of such performances upon the Church, but the suggestion lacks supporting evidence. The curious Greek play, *Christos Paschon*, variously dated from the fourth to the eleventh or twelfth centuries (it is more probably late than early), a mosaic composed of tesserae from the writings of Euripides and other classical Greek dramatists, would be an interesting link between the ancient and mediaeval theatres, were it not in all probability an example of a literary, closet drama. It seems more likely that in the East as in the West drama latent

[6] Ancient references to pantomimes and modern discussions of the subject are cited in Friedländer, *op. cit.*, II (1922), 125 ff., and by Nicoll, *op. cit.*, 131 ff.

[7] Reich, *op. cit.*, pp. 788–793, admits bridging this gap with pure hypothesis. Cf. also P. S. Allen, *The Romanesque Lyric* (Chapel Hill, 1928), pp. 253 ff., who, however, in the process of destroying some of Reich's theories is apt to cast aside too much of the ancient evidence that has survived. The passages cited by Nicoll from the seventh and eighth centuries (pp. 145–146) are inconclusive for our purposes: Isidore's mention of *histriones* and *mimi* implies no knowledge of stage performances. That the different terms used to designate various types of entertainers (*scenici*, *histriones*, *mimi*, *saltatores*) lived on cannot of course be questioned. We are concerned here with the possible survival of the more formal types of dramatic performances, not with the existence of entertainers.

[8] La Piana, *Speculum*, XI (1936), 171–211, gives convenient references to useful, earlier works on the Byzantine theatre by Krumbacher (1897), himself (1912), V. Cottas (1931), and Vogt (1931). Cf. also J. S. Tunison, *Dramatic Traditions of the Dark Ages* (Chicago, 1907), and M. S. De Vito, "Origine del dramma liturgico," *Biblioteca della 'Rassegna'* (1938), 69–120.

in the Church emerged independently and eventually created recognizable forms. At Byzantium the sermon appears to have been more potent than the ritual in this process; at any rate dramatic homilies are known there from as early as the fifth century. However, it is uncertain what relation, if any, exists between these and the scenario of a true Greek Passion play preserved in a Vatican manuscript of the thirteenth century.

Attempts to link the Western mediaeval stage with the Roman through Byzantium have met with little success. That Eastern and Western dramatic forms may have influenced one another in the Middle Ages exists as a possibility, though nothing more. An ultimate Byzantine origin has been suggested for the Prophets' Procession; similarities in the dramatic development of certain Biblical scenes have been ascribed to direct contacts; the Greek Passion play of the Vatican manuscript is thought by some to have influenced Western plays on this subject, by others to be itself derived from occidental models. Indeed, how far in each of these cases we are dealing with fortuitous analogues, how far resemblances may be due to independent use of the same sources, and how far we are justified in positing direct borrowings remains conjectural.

With the disappearance of the ancient theatre, what became of those who had performed there?[9] We know that during the Empire the old word for actor, *histrio*, was gradually replaced by *pantomimus*, and that the profession itself, which had been amiably regarded in Cicero's day when the drama was in good standing and men like Roscius and Aesopus were highly esteemed, fell upon evil times with the corrresponding decline in the quality of the performances.[10] Cicero considered Roscius worthy of being a senator, and Aesopus's son married into the Roman aristocracy, but during the last century of the Republic the censorial stigma of *infamia* rested upon actors who took part in lower class performances (*ars ludicra*), and later in the Empire all actors were branded with civic disqualifications. As time went on, both

---

[9] On the mediaeval entertainer, see E. K. Chambers, *The Mediaeval Stage* (Oxford, 1903), I, chap. ii; E. Faral, *Les Jongleurs en France* (1910); P. S. Allen, *op. cit.*, chap. xiii.

[10] See T. Frank, "The Status of Actors at Rome," *Class. Phil.*, XXVI (1931), 11.

histrio and *pantomimus* were associated with the *mimus*, and these terms were indiscriminately applied to various types of entertainers who, by the fifth and sixth centuries, included even jugglers, buffoons, dancers, musicians, and bear tamers.

The Church quite consistently opposed the profession and in various decrees forbade actors and actresses to become Christians or to marry Christians unless they abandoned their calling. The Christian emperors, to be sure, did not suppress the spectacles, merely preventing their performance on Sundays and holy days, but the popes were irreconcilable and forbade them at all times.

Did the professional entertainer disappear? Both *mimus* and *pantomimus* must have lost their professions when the theatres fell, and it is possible that those of them who could not turn to some other calling used their talents for a time in performances of an inferior order. The word *mimus* in any case continues to be used in the general sense of entertainer; up to the ninth century it is the regular term applied to the jongleur and thereafter is one of several terms used to denote him.

Chambers believes that the *mimus* somehow merged with the Germanic entertainers—the scops, gleemen, and minstrels—to produce the jongleur, an idea vigorously opposed by P. S. Allen who contends that, although some sort of entertainer survived, he was neither a *mimus*, i.e., a player in mimes, nor a scop, i.e., a creative artist.[11] There seems to be some confusion of definitions involved in this argument, due perhaps to the modern use of the term jongleur to denote both performer and composer and especially to Allen's insistence—plausible in itself, but beside the point here—that the creative impulses of the Middle Ages emanated from monks and churchmen. Whether or not we should speak of 'merging,' a none too happy conception, all we need assume, I think, is that there were entertainers of some sort during the Dark Ages: men sang songs, told tales, performed tricks, imitated each other, travestied the world and its ways in various fashions. These men, however, did not preserve the continuity of the formal theatre of ancient Rome nor create the formal theatre of the Middle Ages; they merely gave evidence in some of their exhibitions of the perpetuity of the dramatic instinct.

---

[11] Chambers, *op. cit.*, p. 25; Allen, *op. cit.*, pp. 257 ff.

Manuscripts of the Terentian and Plautine comedies, to be sure, remained in existence. Indeed the scriptoria of France, especially those of Corbie, Fleury, Rheims, and Limoges, produced many of our early manuscripts of Terence, and other Terentian manuscripts are localized less specifically as having been written in Touraine and the south of France.[12] Only eight of the twenty comedies now ascribed to Plautus were generally known before the fifteenth century (although the other twelve were copied at least three times during the eleventh and twelfth centuries), and references to his works are relatively scarce in France. Yet the Palatine recension of Plautus, according to Traube (*Vorlesungen u. Abhandlungen*, III, 68), goes back to Orléans, and two Frenchmen of the middle of the ninth century, Helperic of Auxerre and Smaragdus of Saint Mihiel, cite him (Manitius, I, 448 and 465). However, it is evident from the testimony of countless mediaeval writers[13] that the works of Terence and Plautus were not connected in their minds with any idea of the impersonation of actors speaking upon a stage, that the very meaning of the word 'drama' was misunderstood, and that the terms 'comedy' and 'tragedy' were regularly misapplied throughout the Middle Ages to narrative and even to lyrical forms of literature, 'comedy' being reserved primarily for works ending happily and 'tragedy' for those with an unhappy conclusion.[14]

Servius seems to have been responsible, in part at least, for this misconception. Commenting on Vergil's third Eclogue (*Servii*

---

[12] Cf. Leslie Webber Jones and C. R. Morey, *The Miniatures of the Manuscripts of Terence* (Princeton University Press, 1930–1931).

[13] For mediaeval references *see* Manitius, *Geschichte d. latein. Lit. d. Mittelalters*, indices of the three volumes, s.v. *Terenz* and *Plautus*. It must be remembered, however, that many mediaeval citations of "Plautus" refer to the *Querolus*, a "continuation" of the *Aulularia*, which was mistakenly attributed to Plautus in the Middle Ages. Havet in his edition of the *Querolus* (pp. 2–4) assigns it without much evidence to Gaul and dates it *ca.* 420–430. Others have placed it in the third or fourth century.

[14] Comedy was further defined as concerned with lowly folk and written in ordinary language, whereas tragedy had to do with the mighty and was written in lofty style. For instance, Placidus defines *comoedia* as "quae res privatorum et humilium personarum comprehendit, non tam alto ut tragoedia stilo, sed mediocri et dulci." Cf. W. Cloetta, *Beitraege zur Litteraturgeschichte des Mittelalters*, I, 14 ff.; W. Creizenach, *Geschichte des neueren Dramas*, I, 9 ff.; Chambers, *op. cit.*, II, 208 ff.

Gram. in Virg. Bucolica Com., ed. Thilo and Hagen, 1887, III, p. 29), he points out its dramatic character, stating that there are three styles of writing, one in which the poet speaks alone; another 'dramaticum, in quo nusquam poeta loquitur, ut est in comoediis et tragoediis; tertium, mixtum.' He says that all three are represented in the Bucolics, and places the first and third eclogues in the second, or 'dramatic,' category. Diomedes, another writer of the second half of the fourth century, follows Servius in general, but more definitely classes certain eclogues with tragedies and comedies (*Art. Gram.*, Lib. III, ed. H. Keil, *Gram. lat.*, I, 482): 'dramaticon est vel activum in quo personae agunt solae sine ullius poetae interlocutione, ut se habent tragicae et comicae fabulae; quo genere scripta est prima bucolicon et ea cuius initium est "quo te, Moeri, pedes?" ' (that is, *Ec.* IX). Isidore of Seville (*Etymol.* VIII, 7 in *P.L.*, LXXXII, 309) copies Servius almost literally; Bede follows Diomedes closely (*De Arte Metrica* §25, ed. Giles, VI, 78), but adds to Diomedes's examples of 'drama' the Song of Songs, saying, 'Quo apud nos genere Cantica canticorum scripta sunt, ubi vox alternans Christi, et ecclesiae, tametsi non hoc interloquente scriptore manifeste reperitur.'

After the conception of drama as allied to the stage had been lost, the terms comedy and tragedy readily became disassociated from the idea of drama. Not only narrative and lyric works containing much dialogue, but others also were thus mislabeled. Boethius, who employed the word 'tragedy' in his *Consolatio* in the general sense of tragic happening, unwittingly led his commentator, Notker, to define *tragoedia* as *luctuosa carmina*,[15] and mediaeval glossaries regularly define both terms without regard to any dramatic connotations.[16] The non-dramatic works both of antiquity and of contemporaneous writers came to be classified as 'comedies' and 'tragedies' on the basis of their style and contents

---

[15] Cf. Isidore, *Etymol.*, XVIII, 45, De tragoedis (*P. L.*, LXXXII, 658): "tragoedi sunt qui antiqua gesta atque facinora sceleratorum regum luctuoso carmine, spectante populo, concinebant."

[16] In the lexicons of the thirteenth and fourteenth centuries published by Roques, "Recueil général des lexiques franç. du m. â." in *Bibliothèque de l'École des Hautes Études*, 264 (1936), *comedia* is glossed by *chançon de poète*, *comicus* by *poète*, *hystrio* by *glouton vel guglour*, *scenices* by *foles fames*, etc. Cf. pp. 128, 12, 287, 352, 468.

alone: Horace, Persius, and Juvenal wrote *comoediae*, whereas Lucan's *Pharsalia* and Dracontius's epic *Orestes* (of the end of the fifth century) are called *tragoediae*. Dante speaks of comedy as a kind of poetic narrative ('est comoedia genus quoddam poeticae narrationis') and the title of his great work—chosen because it begins amid troublesome and bitter things and ends in paradise, treats of ordinary people, and is written in the vulgar speech—reflects the definitions of his own day.

Several factors apparently contributed in some measure to the misconceptions that became current. In the first place it was quite generally thought that the plays of Terence had been recited in ancient times by the author himself or by a *recitator* reading from a pulpit, while pantomimists stood below and acted out the scenes. Livy's description of the beginnings of the drama at Rome (VII, 2, followed in part by Valerius Maximus, II, 4), with its references to players from Etruria who danced to the strains of the flute, its mention of actors who used singers to accompany their gesticulations, and its anecdote about Livius Andronicus who, after overstraining his voice, was obliged to call upon a boy to sing the monody while he himself acted his role in silence, probably had something to do with mediaeval ideas about how the classical drama was performed. It may well be also that writers like Isidore of Seville and vague legends about the mimes and pantomimes of the Empire played some part in the formation of the misconceptions. Isidore, for example, says of the ancient orchestra: 'orchestra autem pulpitum erat scenae, ubi saltator agere posset, aut duo inter se disputare' (*P.L.*, LXXXII, 658). It seems possible, too, that the early confusion of the editor, Calliopius, whose recension of Terence is now dated in the fifth century,[17] with a reader or reciter of Terence's works fortified the erroneous notions current. The Calliopian recension is usually signed 'Ego Calliopius recensui' and it has been plausibly suggested that a manuscript abbreviation of *recensui* (rec), resolved as *recitavi*, was originally responsible for the confusion.[18] In any case, early commentators of

[17] See John Douglas Craig, *Ancient Editions of Terence* (Oxford, 1929) and Jones and Morey, *op. cit.*

[18] Creizenach, *op. cit.*, p. 6; cf. Jahn, *Berichte üb. d. Ver. d. k. sächsischen Ges. d. Wiss.* (Leipzig, III, 1851), 362 f.

Terence[19] and early miniaturists[20] indicate Calliopius in the role of narrator.

Yet Terence, however misunderstood, was very much alive throughout the Middle Ages; not Terence the writer of comedies, but Terence the sage who took his place among the philosophers.[21] From Charlemagne's time on his works served as schoolbooks. Few read him as poetry, to be sure—his meters seem to have been ignored or misunderstood—but his neat phrases, which were liked for their compactness and quotability, appear and reappear in countless florilegia. Moreover, although his influence upon the mediaeval drama cannot be posited, it was exercised upon various works of potential dramatic import.

A curious fragment of unknown origin, date, and purpose, which has survived in a unique manuscript of the late tenth or early eleventh century, presents in its scant 64 lines a dialogue between Terence and a Persona Delusoris (probably Scoffer here).[22] The Persona Delusoris informs the ancient poet that he has little use for his work; he doesn't know whether it is prose or poetry; and what's the good of it anyway? 'You are old and outworn; I am new and fertile,' he boasts. Terence asks him whether he in his vaunted youth has produced anything comparable, upon which the Delusor in a kind of aside admits that the old poet has the best of the argument, but says that he intends to maintain the contrary. The conversation continues in similar

---

[19] Cloetta, *op. cit.*, p. 35; Creizenach, *op. cit.*, p. 6; J. P. Jacobsen, *Essai sur les origines de la comédie* (Paris, 1910), p. 4. According to one recension, Eugraphius (who probably lived in the fifth or sixth century) in his comment to the ending of Terence's *Andria* wrote: "verba sunt Calliopii eius recitatoris, qui dum fabulam terminasset, elevabat auleam scaenae, et alloquebatur populum 'vos valete,' 'vos plaudite,' sive 'favete.'" Cf. Donatus, ed. Wessner (Teubner, 1908), III, 85.

[20] Three early Terence MSS from the south and west of France—the earliest of the tenth century—have miniatures picturing Calliopius; one shows him enthroned in the center, reading to the assembled Romans, with Terence at his right, and the rivals (*adversarii*) of Terence at his left. Cf. Jones and Morey, *op. cit.*, I, 165, and Plates 10, 166, 329. A later miniature is in P. Lacroix, *Sciences et lettres au m. â.* (1877), p. 534.

[21] References to Terence may be found in J. D. Craig, Jones and Morey, Manitius's indices, *op. cit.*

[22] Chambers, *op. cit.*, II, 326; the translation in Allen, *The Romanesque Lyric*, p. 244, is free and somewhat misleading.

vein until presently the fragment breaks off, but it would appear that in the end Terence triumphed. Some have conjectured that this poem served as a prologue to a Terentian recitation, others that it may be merely a clerkly exercise written for the amusement of the author and his friends; Allen believes it a young clerk's jest, the parody of some monastic mind on the tendency to substitute nonsense for art. Is it not rather a defense of Terence penned by a conservative master to warn the young that their desire for innovation is understood, but that the old classics still have their uses? However this may be, the fragment has no parallel and has exerted no traceable influence.

Upon Hrotsvitha,[23] the famous Benedictine nun of Gandersheim who lived in the tenth century, Terence made so fruitful an impression that she wrote what she called a *dramatica series*, i.e., six dramatic pieces in prose, claiming Terence as her model, though carefully explaining that while his subjects too often involve the frailty of women, hers turn on the heroic adherence of saintly women to their vows of chastity. In the various prefaces to her works, Hrotsvitha reveals herself as an eager, vivid, original woman, cognizant of her own ability, who, though she realizes the limitations imposed upon her by reason of her sex and her life in a convent, is none the less determined not to waste the gifts that God has bestowed upon her. Perhaps she felt the quickening effects of the revival of culture in the Saxony of her day, for Gerberga, her abbess at Gandersheim, was a niece of that Otto the Great who attempted to reëstablish the Empire of Charlemagne and all that it symbolized. In any case, Hrotsvitha's dramatic pieces show that she was bound by no precedent, that her imagination was likewise untrammeled, and that her feeling for situation, both material and psychological, could be sensitive and sure.

Whether these works, written in dialogue and frequently swift

[23] Hrotsvitha's works have been edited by Winterfeld (1902) and Strecker (2d ed., 1930). An English translation was made of the plays by Christopher St. John for the Mediaeval Library (ed. Gollancz) in 1923. Cf. also G. R. Coffman, *MP*, XXII (1925), 239 ff.; Manitius, III (1931), 1064; K. Young, *The Drama of the Medieval Church*, I (1933), 543. The relative paucity of the MSS of Hrotsvitha and the fact that none has come to light outside of Germany suggest a restricted public for her works.

of action, were designed for recitation, representation, or for private reading, we do not know, though the author's two prefaces to them suggest the last. They turn upon such themes as the conversion of Thais, the courtesan, rescued from her wicked life and led to enter a nunnery by a hermit who approaches her in the guise of a lover (*Pafnutius*), the guilty love of a pagan for a consecrated virgin (*Gallicanus*), or for a holy Christian woman vowed to chastity (*Calimachus*). Mediaeval in spirit, the product of the cultural environment of a convent, not unrelated in subject matter to certain saints' lives, these pieces, for all their holiness of purpose, are nevertheless so romantic in the exuberance of their expressions, the erotic overtones in them at times become so insistent, that it is difficult to conceive of their actual performance before a conventual audience even in a day of intellectual renascence. Indeed Hrotsvitha herself refers to her blushes in writing of themes not fit for 'our hearing.'

It has been suggested that the Saint Nicholas plays later produced in Germany and elsewhere came out of a similar environment, that perhaps seventy-five years after Hrotsvitha's time an imaginative man reading her dialogues and knowing the liturgical drama of his own day may have been inspired thereby to honor some special saint by writing the first of our miracle plays. However, the step from narrative saints' lives to miracle plays is so short that it hardly seems necessary to assume the interposition of the nun of Gandersheim, and the influence of her remarkable achievement upon the mediaeval stage, if any, remains entirely conjectural.

Other works that have been assumed by various scholars to have had some formative effect upon the mediaeval theatre are the so-called 'elegiac comedies.'[24] These are Latin poems written in elegiac verse which, although partly narrative and partly dia-

[24] On these "comedies" see Cloetta, *op. cit.;* Chambers, II, 213; Creizenach, I, 20; Faral, *Romania*, L (1924), 321; Manitius, III (1931), 1015 ff. They are conveniently consulted in G. Cohen, *La "Comédie" latine en France au XIIe siècle* (Paris, 1931), 2 vols., with important individual prefaces (sometimes contradicting the general introduction) to the various poems. Cf. also W. B. Sedgwick, "Notes, chiefly textual, on Cohen's 'la com. lat.'" in *Bulletin du Cange*, VIII (1933), 164, and H. Hagendahl, "La 'com.' lat. au xiie s. et ses modèles antiques," ΔΡΑΓΜΑ *Martino P. Nilsson dedicatum* (Lund, 1939), p. 222.

logued, sometimes refer to themselves, both in the manuscripts and in the texts, as *comoediae*. Their themes and characters derive in some instances from classical authors (Terence, Ovid, etc.), in others from mediaeval anecdotes. A number of them have been connected with a region bounded by Orléans, Blois, Vendôme, and Chartres—that is, roughly, with a region in which many manuscripts of Terence were copied and in which the liturgical drama flourished—but, since none of them is dated earlier than the twelfth century and some may belong to the thirteenth, the surviving examples at any rate are all posterior to our earliest liturgical plays.

Among the best known of these works are two attributed to Vitalis of Blois, the *Geta* and the *Aulularia*, both probably of the twelfth century. The *Geta* must have been immensely popular in its own day, for it was used as a schoolbook and made the names of Geta and his fellow servant, Birria, proverbial in the Middle Ages. It survives in over forty manuscripts. Its theme (probably acquired indirectly) is that of Plautus's *Amphitruo*, the perennially pungent theme of the attempt of Jupiter and his servant (Geta) to seduce Amphitruo's wife. Some lively satire on the sophistries of pseudo-logicians must have evoked smiles from students of the trivium. (For example, the real Geta upon meeting his double, Archas [i.e. Mercury], remarks: 'All that exists is one, but I who speak am not one. Ergo, Geta is nothing.' And later, to himself: 'Perish dialectic by which I am so completely destroyed! Now I am learned, but learning is harmful. When Geta learned logic, he ceased to exist.') The *Aulularia*, derived not from the Plautine original but from the *Querolus*, tells again of the miser whose story is familiar to modern audiences from Molière's *L'Avare*. Nearly if not quite as famous as the *Geta* was the poem called *Pamphilus* that concerns itself with the manner in which the hero, helped by an old *entremetteuse*, overcomes the none too active resistance of the girl he loves.

The question naturally arises: how were these elegiac comedies performed, if performed at all? Cloetta believes them to have been designed for the half-dramatic recitation of minstrels; Faral regards them as a transitional form between Latin comedy and mediaeval farce. Chambers calls them school pieces, and Cohen suggests the possibility of recitations in public by one or more persons, or of representations by scholars before their comrades with the assistance of a *meneur de jeu*, perhaps their professor of rhetoric.

A few manuscripts of these pieces seem to show by their rubrics that the poems were intended for representation, and certain passages in the texts would doubtless be enlivened if the full implications of their humorous situations were made manifest by some sort of action. In most of the poems, however, narrative and dialogue are so tightly interwoven (each sharing parts of verses with the other and both needing to be spoken if the metrical scheme is to be observed) that it is difficult to see how such pieces could have been performed as plays. Moreover, in many of them the narrative portions are inordinately developed, the individual speeches are excessively long, and there is nothing to suggest dramatic action. One may reasonably conclude, I think, that these Latin *comoediae* belong to the learned traditions of the Middle Ages, that they were written to be read or studied in schools, and that their vivacious form and content made some few of them adaptable for recitation—perhaps for presentation—by ambitious masters and their pupils. Those few manuscripts (of the *Geta*, *Aulularia*, and *Babio*) in which the names of the suppositious speakers and a few stage directions have been added—apparently in glosses later than the texts—would seem to preserve versions of the poems that were thus adapted. Most of the manuscripts, however, contain no such rubrics, and one must not be misled by modern editors who frequently supply them.

Similar to the elegiac comedies, closely related to them and products of the same environment, are the so-called 'Horatian comedies.'[25] These are monologues that narrate in the first person the experiences of a single speaker: how he used trickery to gain his love, how he instigated a song contest among three girls and awarded a prize, together with himself, to the fairest, etc. Neither the elegiac nor the Horatian comedies, potential progenitors of

[25] As Dain well says (in Cohen, *op. cit.*, II, 115, n. 1), they form a separate genre only for modern scholars.

the drama though they were, seem to have exercised any influence upon the theatre. Cohen posits likenesses between the *Babio*, the *Garçon et l'Aveugle*, a fifteenth-century Resurrection play, *Pathelin*, and Molière's *Les Fourberies de Scapin*, or again between the *Babio*, the *Baucis et Traso*, and Molière's *l'Étourdi* (*op. cit.*, I, xiii–xiv), but the similarities suggested are too few, too tenuous, and too readily explainable by the universality of their themes to detain us. These Latin pieces are obviously not dramatic in intention, not written to be spoken and acted before an audience by actors suitably equipped to give visible embodiment to their roles. They merely testify to the narrow borderline that separated narrative from dramatic literature in the Middle Ages and to the ease with which, once the impulse had come from elsewhere, narrative poetry could be turned into drama.

It has occasionally been suggested that vestiges of the ancient buildings in which classical plays had been performed must have preserved for posterity some tradition as to the methods of their performance.[26] We hear indeed of 'an extraordinary number of theatres' in Gaul in the second century.[27] Sidonius Apollinaris described the theatre as still flourishing at Narbonne *ca.* 460.[28] We also learn of mimes, pantomimes, and acrobats at Narbonne *ca.* 470. Among the Roman theatres of Gaul that survived, at least in part, well into the Middle Ages were those of Arles, Autun, Narbonne, Orange, and Paris. But it is clear that the original functions of both theatres and amphitheatres were early lost to memory. The remains of the theatre at Arles came to be known as the 'tour de Roland.' Many amphitheatres were used as forts, some passing into the hands of the Arabic invaders. Later these were dismantled (as at Fréjus where, in the tenth century, the stones of the ancient amphitheatre were used in building a church), or were occupied by military orders (as at Nîmes where the amphitheatre was thus occupied till the fourteenth century), or were adopted for tourneys, dwelling houses, etc. The amphi-

---

[26] See Friedländer, *op. cit.*, IV (1921 ed.), 250–253 (cf. also pp. 218 ff. and 223 ff.).

[27] A. Grenier in T. Frank, *An Economic Survey of Ancient Rome*, III (1937), 540.

[28] *Carmina*, XXIII, 263; cf. S. Dill, *Roman Society in the Last Century of the Western Empire*, p. 117; Friedländer, *op. cit.*, IV ,251, and Chambers, I, 19.

theatres of Bordeaux and Poitiers both received the name 'Palais Gallienne.'

When plays were no longer performed in the theatre, when the amphitheatres were abandoned, when the Church began linking theatre, circus, and amphitheatre together as works of the devil and suggesting that Christians who desired *spectacula* would find them at hand in the Return of the Lord and the Day of Judgment,[29] when alien invaders introduced new customs and frequent battles obliterated old ones, when the buildings remaining unrazed were devoted to novel functions and received strange names, it is perhaps not so difficult to understand why the ruined remnants of the ancient theatres and amphitheatres failed to enlighten later generations as to their original purposes.

But what of classical authors who refer in no uncertain terms to the ancient theatres? What of Cicero's *De Oratore* with its references to Roscius (III, 26, 102), his *Pro Sestio* with its descriptions of acting (LV–LVII), his *De Officiis* which implies that some actors excel in voice, others by their skill in acting, and that they choose their roles accordingly (I, 114)—and so on?[30] Unfortunately, of the many early mediaeval authors who reveal a knowledge of Cicero, none, so far as I know, happens to mention any of the passages that refer to the theatre. This is true, for instance, of Isidore of Seville. Most of these men, like the West Frank Hadoard,[31] who was the most widely read student of Cicero of the ninth century and who generously excerpted his works, care chiefly for the moral teachings of antiquity. Others, like Lupus of Ferrières[32] (as well as Hadoard), reveal that they possessed only mutilated copies of Cicero, or that, like Alcuin, they cite

---

[29] Tertullian, *De Spectaculis*, written *ca.* 200 A.D. Cf. Loeb Library edition (1931), Ch. xxix–xxx.

[30] See references in T. Frank, "The Decline of Roman Tragedy," *Class. Journ.*, XII (1916), 177–178, and in Merguet's two lexicons to Cicero's works, s.v. *histrio*, *mimus*, *theatrum*, etc.

[31] Cf. Paul Schwenke's ed. of Hadoard in *Philologus*, *Supplementband*, V (1889), 399 ff., and in general on Cicero's "Fortlebung" see Manitius, I, 478 ff., and the indices, s. v. *Cicero*.

[32] Manitius, I, 486; C. H. Beeson, *Lupus of Ferrières* (Cambridge, 1930), esp. p. 7 on defective MSS.

a number of his works only at second hand.[33] The so-called commentary on Terence, which went by the name of Donatus in the Middle Ages, especially the section attributed to Evanthius,[34] would have proved enlightening, if read intelligently. Unfortunately, that section seems either to have been neglected or misunderstood.

It is evident, however, that here and there students of the classics existcd who reconstructed from their reading a fair idea of what the ancient theatre had been like. Thus, John of Salisbury (*ca.* 1115–1180), who knew Cicero well, betrays such knowledge in his *Polycraticus* when he writes: 'And there were actors who by bodily gesture, by the art of words and by modulation of the voice publicly represented tales true and feigned. You find them in Plautus and Menander and by them the art of our Terence became known. After the comic and tragic poets disappeared, when frivolity conquered all, their clients, the comedians and tragedians, were driven away.'[35] So, too, Honorius of Autun:[36] 'sciendum quod hi qui tragoedias in theatris recitabant, actus pugnantium gestibus populo repraesentabant.'

But this knowledge seems to have remained sterile so far as any attempt to reproduce the ancient type of theatre was concerned. Nor, except in three instances, havewe any evidence that scholars equated the classical theatre with the contemporary liturgical plays (which in the manuscripts are variously called *officium*, *ordo*, *processio*, *ludus*, *repraesentatio*, *historia*, *similitudo*, *miraculum*, *misterium*).[37] These three quite different instances are therefore the more significant. One occurs in a commentary on Horace's *Ars Poetica*, a scholium preserved in a manuscript of the eleventh or twelfth century. In explaining Horace's statement that movement on the stage can be accomplished by action or by narration of action, the scholiast says that in the Feast of Herod both action and narration appear. A second instance occurs in a prophet play of 1204 from Riga. This play

[33] Schwenke, *op. cit.*, pp. 404–406.

[34] Ed. P. Wessner (Teubner, 1902).

[35] Lib. I, cap. viii in *P. L.*, CXCIX, 405.

[36] In Young, *op. cit.*, I, 83. Honorius flourished in the first half of the twelfth century.

[37] Cf. Young, *op. cit.*, II, 407 ff.

is surprisingly referred to as a 'ludus prophetarum ordinatissimus, quem Latini Comoediam vocant.' The third appears in a late twelfth-century commentary by Arnulfus of Orleans on Ovid's *Fasti* (I, 47): 'Romani singulis annis conveniebant in Martium Campum et ibi representabant illam interfectionem a Silla (apparently an imaginary slaughter of Marians by Sullans) olim factam, sicut nos modo representamus interfectionem innocentum.'[38]

Sporadic knowledge of the ancient theatre in the Middle Ages can be posited, therefore, but knowledge productive of any continuity of tradition cannot. Before the age of printing, when manuscripts were rare and costly, literary works had to depend largely upon the human voice to gain an audience. Poets recited their verses or others did this for them; the epics and romances of the Middle Ages were chanted, declaimed, or read aloud. In many instances attempts at impersonation, with appropriate gestures and voice changes, must have enhanced the recital of non-dramatic works. But one must distinguish clearly between such non-dramatic works—however dramatically presented—and true drama, written for production by a group of actors who would incarnate their roles, use suitable speech, mimetic action, and vestments, and play their parts to the accompaniment of pertinent scenic effects. Whatever the Middle Ages knew or did not know about the comedies and tragedies of antiquity, they fashioned their own drama, the only drama that flourished potently before the Renaissance, not from the ashes of the past, but from the warmth of their faith and the desire to give it a visible, dynamic expression.

---

[38] The first two instances are cited by Creizenach, I, p. 7. Cf. Young, *op. cit.*, II, 542. For the third, and its interpretation, I am indebted to Jean Holzworth's forthcoming Bryn Mawr dissertation, *An Unpublished Commentary on Ovid's* Fasti by Arnulfus of Orleans.

'MEDITATIONS ON THE LIFE AND PASSION OF CHRIST': A NOTE ON ITS LITERARY RELATIONSHIPS

CHARLOTTE D'EVELYN
Mount Holyoke College

IN a valuable note in *The Modern Language Review* for July 1935,[1] Mr. F. J. E. Raby records the fact that John of Hoveden's Latin poem, *Philomena*, is the direct and only source of the Middle English poem published under the title, *Meditations on the Life and Passion of Christ*.[2] Mr. Raby's discovery, together with the publication of a modern edition of *Philomena*,[3] offers the present writer the opportunity—or rather the duty—of comparing the two texts in detail. This identification of its Latin source makes possible the correction of some doubtful passages in the English text and clears up also the relation of the *Meditations* to a second English poem, the *Orison of the Passion*. All three poems are unusually interesting examples of medieval devotional literature and the modifications which have taken place in the theme of the Passion as it passes from *Philomena* to the *Meditations* and again to the *Orison* offer an excellent illustration of literary adaptation.

Mr. Raby characterizes the *Meditations* in its relation to *Philomena* as 'a free version, sometimes expanded, more often compressed,' and as 'a poem of great charm, reproducing for [its] English readers the devotional quality of the original.'[4] This characterization is essentially just, though, in fact, expansions in the *Meditations* are exceedingly rare, compressions multitudinous, and the resulting devotional quality marked by a simplicity and directness not often attained in *Philomena*. As he worked over the fervent and unflagging Latin text, this fourteenth-century para-

[1] *MLR*, XXX, 339–343.

[2] *EETS*, 158 (1921).

[3] Clemens Blume, *Johannis de Hovedene* "Philomena," in *Hymnologische Beiträge*, IV (Leipzig, 1930). The poem had not been published in full since the Luxemburg edition of 1603; *op. cit.*, p. v.

[4] *MLR*, XXX, 340.

phraser seems to have thought with its modern editor that *Philomena* might best be enjoyed 'piecemeal.'[5] The selections which the English poet has chosen to translate and paraphrase are the measure of his own poetic powers and devotional preferences.

This fact of condensation is the first and most obvious basis of comparison between the two poems. *Philomena* runs to 4,524 lines; the *Meditations*, to 2,254 lines. The theme of *Philomena*, lyrical meditations on the power of love as exemplified in the life and passion of Christ,[6] lends itself easily to condensation and omission. There is neither story nor argument to be kept in strict order and intact. Consequently the *Meditations*, though but half the length of *Philomena*, does not give the effect either of incompleteness or of disproportion in its paraphrase of the original.

The omissions extend throughout the poem and vary in length from a couplet to forty-four consecutive quatrains.[7] As typical of these omissions one may note in detail one instance which occurs in an elaborate eulogy of the Virgin. Between ll. 2158 and 2159 of the *Meditations*, nineteen quatrains, 1082–1100, of *Philomena* have been dropped. In content these omitted lines present an ingenious and artificial series of comparisons. First the surpassing excellence of the Virgin in all things is matched victoriously against the specific excellences of those familiar Biblical and classical examples, Solomon, Maccabeus, Alexander, Virgil, Scipio, Caesar, Livy, Tullius, Job, and Jeremiah, to name no others on the roll. Then shifting the basis of comparison the Latin poem introduces a list of contradictions and impossibilities which must come to pass before Mary's praise can be sung adequately. Again these are drawn from classical and Biblical tradition with saints and martyrs, early fathers, and natural objects added. It is an astonishing array of paradoxes: Judas no traitor, Cain no murderer, Herod no infanticide, Dacian no persecutor, and the mole a basker in sunlight. All these elaborations the author of the *Medita-*

---

[5] Blume, *op. cit.*, p. xiv.

[6] *See* Blume, *op. cit.*, pp. xi f. for an elaborate analytical table of contents of *Philomena;* for a summary of the *Meditations*, see *EETS*, 158, pp. xv f.

[7] Between ll. 1810–1811 of *Meditations*, quatrains 719–763 of *Philomena* are omitted.

tions disregards, picking up his thread again exactly where the Latin poet, exhausted by eloquence,[8] returns to simpler language.

The English poem, one should note, is by no means without all such colors of rhetoric. A paradoxical description of earthly love, for example, is retained almost in its entirety.[9] But in this instance the paradoxes, commonplaces most of them of secular and religious love poetry, are themselves the subject of discussion, not merely illustrations of the subject. Moreover, in this passage book-learned references are altogether missing. In general the English poem refrains from following *Philomena* in its more original and bookish flights of rhetoric. Its omissions are not of subject matter, but rather of the elaboration of subject matter.

If rigorous condensation of material is the first and most striking difference between the two poems, the second is deliberate simplification of subject matter and expression. This is achieved by preferring direct statement to indirect allusion and by avoiding verbal intricacies both of sound and sense. Where the Latin is simple, the English follows it closely; where the Latin is ornate, the English strips it down. *Philomena* is a consciously elaborated effort in which learned language and highly wrought rhetoric are part, one feels, of the poet's offering of praise. In the changes which the English poet has made, the distinctive quality of each poem is brought out. For example, the author of the *Meditations* frequently supplies a proper name in place of the allusion made in the Latin text: *latronis scelera* (*Phil.* 516:3) becomes *Baraban, þe*

[8] *Phil.* 1101: 1, Et quid dicam elinguis copiâ?

[9] Compare *Phil.* 464–474 and *Medit.* 1295–1322. This pasage in the *Meditations* is one which the present writer had referred to Rolle's *Incendium Amoris* (ed. Deanesly, Manchester, 1915) as its direct source; see *EETS*, 158, pp. xxvi f. The close similarity of the *Incendium* and the *Meditations* results rather from their common use of *Philomena.* Verbal parallels in the *Incendium* and *Philomena* are unmistakable.

Compare *Phil.* 470:1–2. Philomena plus bove mugiens,
Merulina vox melos nesciens

with *Incendium*, p. 259 f. Habet et philomenam magis uacca mugientem; merulinam uocem, melum nescientem. But Rolle, unlike the author of the *Meditations*, rejects the next comparison, Pellem turtur vulpinam vestiens (*Phil.* 470: 3) in favor of the more orthodox, ouem uulpinam pellem induentem (*Incendium*, p. 260). The whole subject of Rolle's relation to Hoveden, as Mr. Raby has already remarked (*op. cit.*, p. 340), should be worked out in detail. The materials, however, are not yet fully available. *See* below p. 87, n. 14.

stronge þef (*Medit.* 1439); *Hoc testatur levitae lectio* (*Phil.* 828:1) becomes *þat witnesset wel seynt Steuene* (*Medit.* 1939); *Praeco penna praecinctus aquilae* (*Phil.* 832:2) becomes *Also Iohan euangelyst* (*Medit.* 1951); and *Te palpandum donas discipulo* (*Phil.* 1043:2) becomes *þou bad seint Thomas to gropon* (*Medit.* 2062).

These identifications lie on the surface and involve only a simple change. That it is a characteristic change is well illustrated by what may be called a misuse of the practice. In *Philomena*, in a meditation on the crucifixion expressed in a series of contrasts of 'yesterday' and 'today,' occur the lines:

Heri solem accinxit radio,
Nunc suspirat pressus sudario. (*Phil.* 710: 1–2)

This couplet reappears in the *Meditations* as follows:

ȝesterday he sente þe sonne his lyȝt;
To-day þey han hud al his syȝt. (*Medit.* 1771–1772)

But the poet does not leave it at that. Apparently *pressus sudario* recalled to his mind a specific incident and he makes the reference explicit in the following lines:

Þanne comeþ *þer* forþ a good wo*m*man
And reuþe haþ of þ*a*t ryȝtful man.
Wiþ a cloþ his face sho wipte,
Þe forme þ*er*-of þe cloþ him clipte. (*Medit.* 1775–1778)

This addition breaks the 'yesterday' and 'today' formula and introduces straightforward narrative into the midst of involved exposition. It is an extreme and, therefore, a revealing instance of the writer's preference for direct to allusive statement.

Philomena is full of verbal ingenuities which range from alliteration applied to every word in the line to intricate plays on the sound and meaning of words. Rare words, some of them perhaps his own invention, are summoned to the poet's aid.[10] Whether such virtuosities could be reproduced in the vernacular is an unanswer-

[10] Without attempting an exhaustive list one may note such words as allator (12: 3), caelicida (852: 4), figuratrix (456: 3), frangibile (298: 4), fugabilis (791: 1), laboratrix (418: 4), manabilis (938: 2), mutatrix (1030: 1), pernoctescit (773: 4), praemagnifice (838: 2), proceleuma (366: 3), relevatrix (996: 2), sagittabile (659: 2), serratio (324: 1), sitularem (736: 2), spongiale (609: 2), vinescit (55: 1). These words are not found in Lewis and Short's classical Latin dictionary, in Du Cange, or in Baxter and Johnson, *Medieval Latin Word-List.*

able question. It is evident, at least, that the author of the *Meditations* did not make the attempt. The obvious verbal play, for instance, in the second line of the following couplet is ignored in its English paraphrase.

Phil. 169: 1–2	*Medit.* 633–634
Virgis caedunt manus spurcitiae Carnem caram carentem carie.	His swete sydes fair and clene I-bete weron wiþ scories kene.

Similarly, the English poem does not attempt to reproduce the echoing of words, such as *stell-*, *still*-forms, which is a favorite device in *Philomena*. As for example:

Phil. 525: 1–2	*Medit.* 1467–1468
Scribe carnem stellatam stillulis Instar caeli stellati stellulis.	Writ his body *with* blod y-spreynt As is þe welkene *with* sterres y-peynt.

The Latin text often calls for close reading not only to get the sense of the passage but to catch the cunning arrangement of word and letters. The following quatrain is an example in point:

Ecce, migrat, qui per clementiam
Deicidis precatur veniam;
Caeli sidus passum iniuriam,
Caelicidis procurat gratiam. (*Phil.* 851)

Here the meaning is not obscure but the meaning is not the sole interest. One is intended to note as well the balance of the second and fourth lines in arrangement of words, and in alliteration of the verbs; and one suspects also that a play on sound in *Caeli sidus* and *Caelicidis* is intentional.[11] The author of the English poem sacrifices this cleverness of the Latin and is content to express the simple meaning simply:

Lo, now he goþ þ*at* haþ pyte
On hem þ*at* dedon him on þe tre. (*Medit.* 2003–2004)

Even where curiosities of word and letter are not conspicuous, the Latin text tends to general, abstract statements. These the author of the *Meditations* reduces to more concrete, direct expression, often with happy effect.

---

[11] The repetition of *caeli-* forms is continued through the next quatrain, which is omitted in *Meditations*.

Phil. 476: 1 f.	*Medit.* 1331–1334
Insit mihi. . . .	Mak me, Ihesu, glad to be
Paupertatis laeta possessio,	Simple and pore for loue of þe,
Retentorum hucusque datio.	And let me neuere for more nor lasse
	Loue god to wel þat sone shal passe.

It is obvious from these comparisons that the two authors were working in different styles. One might suggest pertinently if uncharitably that the simplification of the English poem was due primarily to its author's inability to understand or cope with the intricacies of his Latin model. Did he frankly omit what he could not construe and make use of simple words because he was 'a burel man'? One cannot judge by what is not there. But it is notable that in the passages from the Latin poem which *were* translated into English, actual mistakes are hard to find. For example, in translating 'Quare pendet, qui montes ponderat' (*Phil.* 782:2) by

> Whi hangeþ he vpon an helle
> þat hangeþ helles at his wille? (*Medit.* 1843–1844)

the English poet has not kept the distinction between the verbs *pendeo* and *pondero*. Possibly his Latin text was at fault or carelessly read.[12] In any case the mistake is a slight one. In another dubious instance the English poem, perhaps purposely, turns the thought of the Latin in a different direction:

Phil. 244	*Medit.* 759–762
Rosam veris ortam rosario,	þe beaute of þi louely lere
Quam sol mane rubricat radio,	Passeþ alle roses clere,
Plus transcendit tua laudatio,	Ryȝt as þe flour fair in felde
Quam flos foenum in veris medio.	Passeþ heþen and weykeþ for elde.[13]

Philomena makes a progressive comparison: Christ in his beauty is more praiseworthy than the rose, as the flower is more praiseworthy than dry grass. But *flos* and *foenum* have suggested to the English poet another and more familiar comparison, that of man's life withering as the grass of the field. This comparison he uses as a transition to the next, but not immediately succeeding, lines of *Philomena* which he translates, namely,

[12] No variant readings for this line are recorded by Fr. Blume.

[13] Comparison with the Latin shows that the full stop belongs at the end of l. 762 and not at the end of l. 760, as originally printed.

> Quis non planget carnis virgineae
> Florem fractum flagello frameae? (*Phil.* 247: 1–2)

The 'mistake,' then, may have been intentional. Such aberrations from the strict meaning of the Latin text are so few that, whether intentional or not, they give one no reason to think that the English poet could not deal adequately with his Latin source. The differences in style in the two poems are not explicable merely as the difference between 'lered' and 'lewed.'

As for additions, one can say that only a handful of lines in the *Meditations* have no counterpart in *Philomena*. These rare additions are of some interest. One of the longer examples occurs early in the text in a passage contrasting the majesty and might of Christ, as he is Lord of the Universe, with his humility and helplessness, as he is Son of Mary. Nine quatrains of *Philomena* (13–21) are condensed into ten lines of the *Meditations* (49–58) and then the English text adds ten lines of its own:

> But by-leue we may haue
> He cam not to spille but to saue;
> For he cam not on stedes proude,
> With hidous cry ne w*ith* trompes loude,
> Wiþ sheldes, pauyes, ne wyþ targe,
> Wiþ plates, helmes brode and large,
> Wiþ sharpe swerdes ne w*ith* lang spere,
> Ne wiþ non other grisly gere,
> W*ith* no pride no w*ith* no pres,
> But mekely as a prynce of pees. (*Medit.* 59–68)

The introduction in these lines of a touch of narrative and a simple statement of orthodox belief are in contrast with the persistent balancing of 'might' and 'weakness' in *Philomena*. Among the additions, also, realistic details are occasionally included. In a meditation on the march to Calvary, *Philomena* has the lines:

> Scribe . . .
> Carne caesa cor evanescere
> Ut flos arens in veris vespere. (*Phil.* 582: 1 f.)

These reappear in *Meditations* with additions:

> He wex feynt and gan to felde
> And wente not faste al as þey wolde.
> Þanne weron his fon redy and prest
> And shouon him forþ w*ith*outon rest;

With punches and strokes þey dedon him go;
Sore wep þat lord for wo. (*Medit.* 1555–1560)

Similarly, the savagery of the Jews is contrasted, with new details of bestiary origin, with the mild restraint of the lion:

Phil. 135	*Medit.* 517–526
Leo non sic iras exacuit Fame pressus, cum cervum circuit, Ut tu, quando Rex laesus siluit Et ut agnus os non aperuit.	Þe lion whan him hongreþ sore, He gynneþ for to crye and rore; But whan he haþ his preie founde, And it falleth to þe grounde, He hath mercy þer-of also blyue, And let it gon away a-lyue. But þou haddest mercy non Of him þat stod stille as ston; But feller þan þe lioun wod Þou were to spillon þat lombes blod.

Both *Philomena* (632) and the *Meditations* (ll. 1665 f.), in paraphrasing a passage from the Song of Songs, describe the soul, Christ's spouse, as singing for joy; but in the *Meditations* she also weeps.

Sho syngeþ to him a loue-song
And wepeþ also euer among.
Syngyng he mot teres lete
ffor ioye of him þat is so swete. (*Medit.* 1665–1668)

All these examples—and *not* many others could be cited—are typical of the additions found in the *Meditations*. They might more properly be called expansions, for they grow out of the subject matter of *Philomena*. And the additions, like the paraphrase as a whole, are marked by simplicity and directness.

Mr. Raby's identification of the source of the *Meditations* makes possible a few corrections and clarifications in the English text where the scribe—or the modern editor—had gone astray. Emendations should be made in the following cases:

(1) *Phil.* 264: 1–2	*Medit.* 817–818
Patres pascens pane placentiae Da mendico vel micam hodie.	Siþþe þou art loue and bred of lyf, Send down a corun to þi caytyf.

The manuscript of the *Meditations* distinctly has four minims in the word printed as *corun*. It is clear now that this word is not a variant of *corone*, but translates the Latin *micam*. *Corun* is therefore a scribal error for *crom*, due perhaps to confusion with *corn* or *corone*. Correcting a modern error at the same time, the line should be emended to read 'Send doun a c[r]o[m] to þi caytyf.'

(2) *Phil.* 468: 3	*Medit.* 1310
limosum lilium	[Bl]od-red lilie

The phrase *limosum lilium* occurs in a list of paradoxes descriptive of earthly love. The manuscript of the *Meditations* reads *Sod red lilie*, which the Latin shows to be correct. The manuscript recording should therefore be restored. *Sod red* is apparently a unique formation, not recorded elsewhere.[14]

In several places doubtful words and passages in the *Meditations* are clarified, if not wholly explained, by the Latin text.

(1) *Phil.* 97: 3	*Medit.* 371
Flos odoris, quo mors perimitur	þe flour so swete *þat* þet haþ shent

Comparison of the two lines shows that the English word *þet* is a scribal variant for *deþ*, as the editor had suggested in the glossary. Substitutions of *þ* for *d* and *t* for *th* are fairly frequent throughout the manuscript[15] and no emendation is necessary.

(2) *Phil.* 219	*Medit.* 663–666
Rogo, scutum te mihi facias Sensituro mortis molestias, Te complexus eius insidias Non verebor sed nec versutias.	Whan deþ shal come me to asayle þanne wolde muche þis sheld avayle. Vnder þi sheld, Lord, *þo*u me couere ffor dynt of deþ at fendes oeuere.

The Latin words *insidias* and *versutias* indicate the meaning to be given to the word *oeuere*, which, as far as the writer knows, is not found elsewhere in an English text.

---

[14] This list of paradoxes was incorporated, as already noted (*see* above, n. 9), into Rolle's *Incendium Amoris* and hence translated for the second time into English by Richard Misyn in his 15th-century version. But in Rolle's text the phrase *limosum lilium* appears as *lilium liuorem*. (Deanesly, p. 259.) This Misyn translates *of lillis blaknes* (*EETS*, 106, p. 89). Other differences occur in this passage between the text of the *Incendium* and that of *Philomena*, which suggest that Rolle's copy of the latter may not have been like the text now printed. Fr. Blume, among his variants, does not record any for the phrase *limosum lilium*.

[15] See *EETS*, 158, p. ix.

(3) *Phil.* 275	*Medit.* 853–856
Fons est vivus sciens effluere	He is a flour þat welkeþ noȝt—
Et arentes fauces reficere.	In- to oure hertes wiþ loue- þoȝt—
Numquid gaudes hunc interimere,	Or þ*o*u be glad swich on to shende
Cuius virtus dat tibi vivere?	Þ*a*t ȝeueth þe lyf withouten ende.

The text of the *Meditations* is obviously confused. First of all, line 853 is a careless repetition of an earlier line, 849, which paraphrases *Phil.* 274:2, *Flos est iuges fundens fragrantias*. No doubt the author of the *Meditations* followed the figures in the Latin text from *flos* to *fons*. Line 853, therefore, probably began, 'He is a fount . . . ,' and possibly for *welkeþ* the text originally read *welleþ;* but what the rime-word was is uncertain. The reading *Or* in the third line is still an unsatisfactory connective and one is left in doubt whether the English, like the Latin, intended a question. The present state of the text in this passage is due, one feels sure, to some scribe and not to the author.

(4) *Phil.* 287	*Medit.* 889–892
Adhuc, Amor, audi sequentia!	But ȝit lesteneþ a litel more:
Eius certe sola memoria	Þ*a*t lord þ*a*t þou tormentedest sore,
Revirescunt corda marcentia	Wiþ herte þenketh on him aryȝt,
Velut rore vernali lilia.	He maketh it lych þe lilie bryȝt.

The reading *Wiþ herte* in the third line had already been queried by the editor as a mistake for *wan herte* or *what herte*.[16] The construction of the corresponding Latin, which is a statement rather than a command, favors reading *thenketh* also as in the indicative rather than the imperative mood. In that case *Wiþ* is a mistake and either one of the suggested emendations brings the line into closer agreement with its source.

(5) *Phil.* 326: 1–2	*Medit.* 1005–1006
Cum clauduntur manus clavigerae,	Þe nailes in his hondes to
Reserantur caelestes camerae.	Þe gates of hay to vs un-do.

Here again, the Latin text makes clear the general meaning of the phrase, *þe gates of hay*. But whether *hay* is a variant of *high* or a corruption of *heaven* is still undecided.

From a comparison of the *Meditations* with its source, one would

[16] See *EETS*, 158, p. 24, note on l. 891.

say that, on the whole, the author understood his text and that the unique fifteenth-century manuscript which has survived preserves a comparatively satisfactory copy of the original.

There remains to be considered, briefly, the relation of the *Meditations* to the so-called *Orison of the Passion*. The *Orison*, as Mr. Raby noted, is not a source of the *Meditations;* rather the *Orison* itself is derived from the longer poem. As the *Meditations* has shortened and simplified its Latin original, so the *Orison* picks and chooses and changes lines in the English poem to suit its own purpose. The cutting is drastic, 154 lines in the *Orison* for 2254 in the *Meditations*. In the *Orison* the incidents of the Passion form the chief subject matter and scattered lines from the more simple treatments of that theme in the *Meditations* are brought together not unskillfully.[17]

It is clear for several reasons that the *Orison* was intended for practical devotions. Its brevity, for one thing, and its concentration on the subject of the Passion. Again, while most of the lines are taken over from the *Meditations* without change, the few alterations which do occur make the poem more direct and personal in its appeal. Notable is the substitution throughout the *Orison* of the name *Iesu* for the personification *Love* and of second personal pronouns for third. As a single example one may cite the following:

Medit. 1483–1484	*Orison* 49–50
Loue, ȝet writ wel in myn herte, How blod out of his woundes sterte.	Ih*es*u, ȝite write in myne herte How bloode oute of þi wond*is* sterte.

The few lines added in the *Orison*[18] point in the same direction: they represent a petitioner's desire to share more fully in the experiences he has been rehearsing. Furthermore, in some manuscripts, the *Orison* is marked by crosses and preceded by a rubric such as one finds in Bodl. Add. E 4: 'In seyinge of þis orisone stinteþ *and* abideþ at eu*ery* crose and þinkeþ whate ȝe haue seide; ffor a more deuout prayer fonde y neu*er* of þe passione, who-so wolde abidingly sey it.'

[17] *See* text of *Orison* printed in *EETS*, 158, pp. 60 f., where the correspondence of lines is noted.

[18] Lines in the *Orison* for which no satisfactory equivalents are found in the *Meditations* are 1–4, 15–20, 74, 79–83, a total of 19 lines.

Finally, the number of extant manuscripts of the *Orison* is an indication that it must have been fairly popular in the fourteenth and fifteenth centuries. Its popularity, one may assume, was due to its usability as a private prayer. Eleven copies are extant,[19] a large number compared with the single text of the *Meditations*. In spite, then, of its complete dependence for its substance on the *Meditations*, the *Orison* may claim an independent existence and even a different function. And this popularity, one may note, continues. For one printed text of the *Meditations* there are four of the *Orison*[20] and the latest has been modernized for the general reader of devotional verse.

This interrelationship of *Philomena*, the *Meditations*, and the *Orison* is a notable example of the shifting and shaping of material to suit individual purposes and abilities. The theme of the Passion has produced three poems, different in spite of their interdependence, alike in their sincerity of feeling. Of these three devout offerings of prayer and praise, *Philomena* is by far the most learned, the most highly wrought, the most brilliant achievement. The *Meditations*, for all its simplification, is still rich in imagery, sustained and vigorous in its devotional appeal. In comparison with these rich offerings the *Orison* is a widow's mite. But, like the widow's mite, it is by no means the least effective in its expression of simple piety.

---

[19] Ten MSS are listed in Carleton Brown, *Register of Middle English Religious and Didactic Verse*, II, 164, No. 1082. An eleventh copy in the Bement MS, now in the Huntington Library, is recorded by R. H. Robbins, in *PMLA*, LIV, 374, note on No. VI.

[20] The *Orison* is printed from the Wheatley MS (B.M. Addit. 39574) in *EETS*, 155 (1921), 1 f.; from Bodl. 29110 (b) in *EETS*, 158 (1921), 60 f.; from Longleat MS 29 by Carleton Brown in *Religious Lyrics of the Fourteenth Century* (1924), p. 114, No. 91; and by Frances M. M. Comper in *Spiritual Songs from English MSS of Fourteenth to Sixteenth Centuries* (1936), pp. 216 f.

THREE CHAUCER NOTES

HALDEEN BRADDY
Texas Christian University

I. SYMBOLIC COLORS

AMONG such decorative poetic devices as anagrams, palindromes, and acrostics,[1] mediaeval writers often sought to embellish their styles by the employment of symbolic colors. Interestingly enough, this formula was not infrequently adopted by Geoffrey Chaucer, especially in passages concerning courtly love where he describes the diverse emotional conditions of the lover. In fact, there are several important passages which seem to show that Chaucer was applying a single, unalterable pattern.

By his own statement Chaucer uses blue to indicate a lover's loyalty or fidelity, for in the Squire's Tale (644 f.) he says that 'veluettes blewe' are the 'signe of trouthe that is in wommen sene.'[2] Moreover, in *Anelida and Arcite* (330 ff.) when 'clad in asure,' the beloved proves 'For to be trewe.' Further, in *Troilus and Criseyde* (III, 885 ff.) the 'blewe ryng' sent to Troilus assures him of Criseyde's fidelity.

In addition, the colors black, red, and white appear to have the respective meanings of sorrowful, ardent, and joyful. In the *Book of the Duchess* (445, 457) Chaucer twice refers to the knight who mourns for his lately deceased mistress as garbed in black, and the company of ladies in the Knight's Tale (899) who weep for their husbands killed in the war are 'clad in clothes blake.' Finally, red for ardent may easily have been designed in the description of the Wife of Bath in the General Prologue (A 456, A 458) and of Absolon in the Miller's Tale (3317, 3319)—the Wife's 'hosen weren of fyn scarlet reed' and she was herself 'reed of hewe,' and Absolon's 'rode was reed' also and likewise 'In hoses rede he wente fetisly.' Obviously more than coincidence is suggested by the al-

---

[1] *See* examples noted by A. Brusendorff, *The Chaucer Tradition* (Oxford, 1925), p. 48.

[2] Unless otherwise observed, all quotations are from *The Complete Works of Geoffrey Chaucer*, ed. F. N. Robinson (Boston, 1933).

most identical depictions of these two similarly amorous characters.

There is a passage in the rhetorical *Anelida and Arcite* which is especially interesting: here (146 f.) several colors are grouped together so that there appears white for joyful, red for ardent, and green for disloyalty ('newefangelnesse'). In stating that Arcite has seen another lady and has 'cladde him in her hewe—Wot I not whethir in white, rede, or grene?' Anelida seems careful to avoid any mention of blue inasmuch as this color would imply that Arcite was loyal. White and red have already been discussed, and the symbolism of green is evident from Chaucer's statement in the Squire's Tale (646 f.) that 'the mewe is peynted grene' to depict 'all thise false fowles.' According to the color symbolism observed in Chaucer's practice, Anelida's statement may now be interpreted as meaning that her rival's 'hewe' is 'carefree (joyful), ardent, or false.'

These examples of color symbolism definitely establish that Chaucer was consistent in the meanings he attached to certain colors when describing the diverse emotional conditions of the lover. How should this treatment be accounted for?

One possibility is that the poet's knowledge derived from proverbial lore.[3] The colors black, red, and blue do have proverbially the respective meanings in their eulogistic significance of mournful, fervent, and constant; but neither the eulogistic nor the dyslogistic significance of both green (lively, hopeful, or envious, jealous) and white (triumphant, innocent, or blank, ghostly) accords with the poet's use of green for disloyal and white for carefree, joyful.

However, if proverbial meaning does not altogether explain Chaucer's practice, there remains the possibility of literary tradition. For in seeking to explain the cult of a poetic device, the weighty influence of literary tradition clearly cannot be excluded.

In this connection, it is arresting that in *Le Remede de Fortune* Guillaume de Machaut explicitly treats color symbolism according to the formula observed in Chaucer. That is, with Machaut, blue

[3] On the proverbial meaning of these colors, *see* Walter Sargent, *The Enjoyment and Use of Color* (New York, 1924), pp. 50–59.

stands for loyalty, red for ardency, black for grief, white for joy, green for novelty, and yellow for falsity. The French passage reads as follows:

> Or te vueil ces couleurs aprendre,
> Comme en Amours les dois entendre:
> Saches que le pers signefie
> Loiauté qui het tricherie,
> Et le rouge amoureuse ardure
> Naissant d'amour loial et pure;
> Le noir te moustre en sa couleur
> Signefiance de douleur,
> Blanc joie, vert nouveleté,
> Et la jaune, c'est fausseté (vv. 1901–10).[4]

Now 'in view of Chaucer's fondness for Machaut,' as Professor Kittredge expresses it,[5] there is apparently nothing to disagree with the suggestion that the English poet was following the practice of Machaut. Chaucer unquestionably knew *Le Remede* itself, because in the *Book of the Duchess* he several times[6] translates or paraphrases verses of this French poem.[7] Instead, then, of relying solely on proverbial lore as the source of his information, Chaucer gives every evidence of awareness to literary tradition in following closely the particular system of color symbolism cultivated by Machaut. Chaucer's adoption of the formula in *Le Remede* is thus at once a commentary upon the decorative style of his lyrical passages and a testimonial as to the deep infiltration into his works of mediaeval French influences.

Moreover, it seems important to observe that the identical meanings of loyalty and disloyalty attach to blue and green, respectively, in *Against Women Unconstant* where all three stanzas conclude with the same line: 'In stede of blew, thus may ye were al grene.' The appearance of this line in Machaut's *Le Voir Dit*, 'Qu'en lieu de bleu, dame, vous vestez vert,' immediately suggests

[4] *SATF* (Paris, 1911), II, 68–69.—There seems to be no allusion to this passage in Robinson's edition, and although *Le Remede* is mentioned by Skeat, he does not quote these verses nor attempt to show that Chaucer followed Machaut's scheme; see *The Works of Geoffrey Chaucer*, 2d ed. (Oxford, 1899), I, 565.

[5] *MP*, VII (1910), 472.

[6] *See* Robinson's notes, esp. pp. 885–886.

[7] L. Cipriani, *PMLA*, XXII (1907), 554; *see* esp. Kittredge, *PMLA*, XXX (1915), 4–23.

that the Frenchman was again the model, especially since the general idea in the two poems is also similar.[8] And these two facts, it seems evident, constitute strong arguments together with the Chaucerian language of the text in favor of Chaucer's authorship of the balade *Against Women Unconstant.*

To sum up, since there appears no indication that the two writers were dealing independently with a body of proverbial lore, it seems reasonably safe to conclude that Machaut here as elsewhere served as Chaucer's example.[9] Finally, Chaucer's use of Machaut's formula should not be regarded lightly inasmuch as this color symbolism appears to furnish the key to at least two interesting passages. First, the statement in the *Complaint of Mars* (8) that the birds departed 'Wyth teres blewe' Professor Robinson[10] explains by reading 'blewe' as 'livid, pale,' connecting the word with *blo* (ON. *bla*[*r*]). Color symbolism here seems to afford a better reading of this passage, for Chaucer appears plainly to imply by blue that, in harmony with the spirit of Saint Valentine's Day, the 'foules' were faithful, loyal, and true. Secondly, in *Troilus and Criseyde* (III, 900 f.) Pandarus advises Criseyde: 'I nolde setten at his sorwe a myte, / But feffe hym with a fewe wordes white.' Professor Robinson[11] glosses white as 'specious' or 'plausible.' But it should be noted that white as joyful is very probably the correct reading, as elsewhere in *Troilus and Cressida* (I, 640 ff.) there is a passage which seems to imply that joy is to sorrow as white is to black. Moreover, white as joyful not only makes excellent sense but appears here also intentionally contrasted with the word 'sorwe.' Chaucer, it would thus appear, may be read with no

---

[8] The French balade containing the above-mentioned refrain is a part of *Le Voir Dit* (*Société des Bibliophiles François* (Paris, 1875), p. 309, vv. 7544–7664; this line also occurs separately on p. 213, v. 4929), itself a collection of letters and replies, balades, lays, and rondeaux (G. Hanf, *Über Guillaume de Machauts "Voir Dit"* [Halle, 1898], p. 1); but the balade may also have circulated in another form as it appears to be a song and is included among Machaut's musical compositions (F. Ludwig, *Guillaume de Machaut, Musikalische Werke* [Leipzig, 1926], No. 36, pp. 44–45); thus the verse may have enjoyed popularity equivalent to that of a proverb.

[9] For a recent interesting discussion of and bibliographical references to color symbolism, *see* Don Cameron Allen, *PQ*, XV (1936), 81–92.

[10] Page 972.

[11] Page 937.

abatement of zest and with what seems more perfect understanding if the French formula for color symbolism is only remembered.

II. CEYS AND ALCIONE

In the 'Introduction' to his Tale, the Man of Law says of Chaucer that 'In youthe he made of Ceys and Alcione' (v. 57).[12] The story of Seys and Alcione is of course included in the *Book of the Duchess*, but the form of the title given by the Man of Law (Ceys, not Seys as in *Book of the Duchess*) has often been construed as evidence that Chaucer wrote an independent poem on the subject.[13] In a recent discussion of what he considers a somewhat analogous literary situation, Professor Lowes, however, would interpret this statement as a reference to the *Book of the Duchess:* he contends that in mentioning his 'trettiés amoureus de Pynotëus et de Neptisphele' or his '*livret* de Pynotëus et de Neptisphele,' Froissart is not alluding to an independent work on this theme but only to a single episode in the *Prison Amoureuse* where these citations occur. But Professor Lowes seems to draw entirely the wrong inference, for Froissart is clearly not identifying the *livret* with the whole *livre*. Instead, at the conclusion of his long work, Froissart explicitly states that all 'chils livres fust appellés la *Prison Amoureuse*.'[14] Indeed, so far as this evidence is concerned, the situation in Chaucer and Froissart is obviously not parallel.

The question as to the Man of Law's reference is further complicated by Lydgate's statement in the *Fall of Princes* that Chaucer wrote 'The pitous story of Ceix and Alcione, / / And the deth eek of Blaunche the Duchesse' (vv. 303–04).[15] But now inasmuch as it seems quite unlikely that Lydgate should describe the brief incident of Ceix and Alcione on an equal basis with the central theme of the death of Blanche as an allusion to the *Book of the Duchess*, it appears altogether possible that Chaucer may have

---

[12] Robinson, *op. cit.*, p. 74.

[13] *See* esp. F. J. Furnivall, *Trial-Forewords* (London, 1871), p. 115; and W. W. Skeat, ed., *The Works of Geoffrey Chaucer* (Oxford, 1894, 1900), I, 63; V, 105; but cf. J. M. Manly, ed., *Canterbury Tales* (New York, 1928), p. 564.

[14] J. L. Lowes, *PMLA*, XX (1905), 769 ff., esp. 826, n. 3. For the quotations, *see* Aug. Scheler, ed., *Œuvres de Froissart* (Brussels, 1870), I, 211–347, esp. 343.

[15] *Fall of Princes*, ed. by Henry Bergen, Carnegie Institute (Washington, 1923).

treated this episode independently. No poem answering this description seems to be extant, but Chaucer appears to have written a number of works that are now lost, as, for example, 'the book of the Leoun' mentioned in the 'retraccioun s,'[16] a lost poem thought to have been a redaction of Machaut's *Dit dou Lyon*.[17]

In this connection, it may be observed that in the fourteenth century the subject of Ceys and Alcione was treated separately in a balade by Deschamps,[18] one of Chaucer's favorite French writers.[19] Chaucer's version of this theme is based principally on Ovid,[20] but it is generally believed that he may also have used a French account. In at least one passage, however, there seems to be no French parallel, for Professor Robinson notes that 'The storm and ship-wreck are described at length in Ovid (ll. 480–557). Machaut does not mention them.'[21] Accordingly, it may be important that in the second stanza of Deschamps's balade the storm at sea and the subsequent shipwreck are both narrated.[22] In any case, the 'Ceix et Alcyone' written by Deschamps is a contemporary illustration of the independent treatment of this episode and thus affords evidence by way of analogy that Lydgate's reference may not apply to the *Book of the Duchess* but to a separate poem composed, as the Man of Law says, in Chaucer's 'youthe.'

If *Ceys and Alcione* may now be regarded as having first existed in separate form, it is not at all difficult to determine why Chaucer decided to include this episode in the *Book of the Duchess*. First of all, the account of a loving king and queen balances appropriately with the narrative of a faithful knight and lady. More significantly, the tragedy of Seys and Alcione (as it has now become

[16] Robinson, *op. cit.*, p. 314.

[17] *Ibid.*, p. 881; F. M. Dear, *Medium Ævum*, VII (1938), 105, suggests that Chaucer's *Book of the Lion* was an occasional piece for Lionel, Duke of Clarence, whom Froissart called "monseigneur Lion."

[18] Le Marquis de Saint-Hilaire, ed., *Œuvres complètes . . .* , *SATF* (Paris, 1878), No. XXXV, I, 118–119.

[19] J. L. Lowes, *op. cit.*

[20] F. J. Miller, ed., *Ovid's Metamorphoses*, Loeb Classical Library (London, 1916), II, 384 ff.

[21] Robinson, *op. cit.*, p. 882.

[22] There seem to be no verbal agreements between Deschamps's account and the version of Chaucer as it appears in the *Book of the Duchess*.

spelled) sets the whole tone of the elegy and foreshadows perfectly the central motive of a grief-stricken lover (in one case Alcione, in the other the Black Knight) lamenting the decease of one greatly beloved. Thus, although the episode is by no means indispensable to the exposition of the main plot, it looms, most probably as a result of revision,[23] as one of the most moving sections of Chaucer's elegy.

III. SIR GUICHARD D'ANGLE, A POITEVINE FRIEND

The place of Guichard d'Angle of Poitou in the Chaucerian circle is well established by Froissart's reference to him as one of Geoffrey's associates in the embassy to France in the spring of 1377.[24] As I have elsewhere[25] recently attempted briefly to sketch the life of Sir Guichard, my present purpose is not so much to review these materials as it is to assemble some further data to illustrate his connections with Chaucer and some of the poet's friends.

First, it seems important to observe that Guichard was so highly regarded by his compatriots that his partisanship of the Black Prince influenced if not occasioned a Poitevine immigration to England.[26] As he first strongly sponsored the French cause,[27] Guichard's shift in allegiance must accordingly be traced briefly. In fact, one of the earliest records connects him with a patriotic demonstration, for on August 17, 1346, he figured prominently in Jean Larcheveque's company which was on parade in Poitiers.[28] Moreover, he shortly thereafter distinguished himself by successfully defending Niort, of which fort he was captain, against three successive assaults by English forces under the Count of Derby. Froissart states that there Guichard established himself, not unlike Chaucer's Knight, as *uns très gentilz*

---

[23] According to Skeat (I, 63): "The original 'Ceys and Alcion' evidently ended at l. 220; where it began, we cannot say, for the poem was doubtless revised and somewhat altered. Ll. 215, 216 hint that a part of it was suppressed."

[24] *Chroniques de J. Froissart*, ed. S. Luce (Paris, 1888), VIII, 225–226.

[25] *Three Chaucer Studies* (Oxford, 1932), No. II, pp. 34 ff.

[26] J. H. Gaillard, *Le Moyen Age*, XLII (1932), 135 f.

[27] H. Beauchet-Filleau, *Dictionnaire Historiques et Généalogique des Familles du Poitou* (Poitiers, 1891), I, 79–80.

[28] *Ibid.*

chevaliers.[29] Exploits like this perhaps led Philippe de Valois to appoint him in 1351 Seneschal of Saintonge, the functions of which office he exercised until September 24, 1354.[30] His most heroic exploit, however, appears to have occurred in 1356 at the battle of Maupertuis where he was left for dead *aux pieds au roi Jean*, whom he had come forward to defend.[31] In October 1360, the French King finally commissioned Sir Guichard to surrender to the Black Prince the keys to La Rochelle.[32]

In the years immediately following Guichard seems to have become a partisan of the king of England, apparently largely out of admiration for the military achievements of the Black Prince.[33] During the years 1370–1372, Charles V completed the confiscation of d'Angle's goods and properties,[34] but he straightway began seemingly to prosper under English sovereignty as King Edward in 1374 appointed him his personal representative to treat with the French.[35] On September 29, 1375, King Edward also granted him for life or until further order, in consideration of loss of lands taken by the French, the sum of 26s. 8d. at the Exchequer,[36] and on January 1, 1376, he was further granted, in compensation for damages sustained in wars and for services in the king's cause, the keeping of the manor of Caversham until the full age of the heir of the king's kinsman, Edward le Despenser.[37] Indeed, throughout the closing years of Edward's reign Guichard figured in prominent circles, often being provided by the king's order along with such notables as Lord Latimer, John of Gaunt, and the Black Prince with suitable robes for celebrating festive occasions.[38] It was only natural that he should be favorably regarded by the new sovereign since the Black Prince in 1376 had

[29] *Op. cit.*, IV, 13.

[30] Paul Guérin, *Recueil des Documents concernant le Poitou* (Oudin, 1886), XVII, 258.

[31] Beauchet-Filleau, *op. cit.*

[32] Paul Guérin, *op. cit.*

[33] G. F. Beltz, *Memorials of the Order of the Garter* (London, 1841), pp. 182 ff.

[34] Paul Guérin, *op. cit.*

[35] Beauchet-Filleau, *op. cit.*

[36] *Calendar of the Patent Rolls*, 1374–77, p. 177.

[37] *Ibid.*, pp. 206, 214, 442.

[38] Sir Harris Nicholas, *History of the Orders of Knighthood of the British Empire* (London, 1842), II, xx–xxi.

appointed him guardian of the youthful Richard.[39] Accordingly, on December 10, 1378, King Richard II made an allowance of £1,000 yearly to 'Guychard Dangle,' Earl of Huntingdon, having on July 16 already advanced him to this earldom.[40] On the death of d'Angle in 1380, two of Chaucer's intimate friends, Sir Lewis Clifford and Sir John Clanvowe, officiated as executors of Sir Guichard's will.[41]

Finally, it remains to be noted that Guichard's unusual rôle in politics enabled him to associate with more than one literary figure of the time. For example, he became acquainted in 1360 with the Marshall Boucicault at La Rochelle.[42] Boucicault, as Professor Kittredge has shown,[43] was a friend of the Clifford family, and thus Chaucer may have heard of the valiant Boucicault[44] from either Sir Lewis Clifford or Sir Guichard. At La Rochelle, d'Angle also first met Sir John Chandos, for it was in December 1360 that he was obliged to surrender this city into the custody of Chandos.[45] Nine years later he was to become the compatriot of Sir John Chandos, under whose command he served at Montauban.[46] The Herald of Chandos, moreover, gives in his narrative poem a graphic account of d'Angle's part in the Spanish campaign.[47] Since Sir Guichard also knew Froissart,[48] Oton de Graunson,[49] Ayala,[50] and Enguerrand de Coucy,[51] his literary acquaintance was fairly extensive. These brief biographical notations thus serve to show how numerous and how significantly interwoven were the connections of the friends within Chaucer's circle.

---

39 *Chroniques de J. Froissart*, ed. S. Luce (Paris, 1888), VIII, cxxxviii.

40 *Cal. Pat. Rolls*, 1377–81, p. 314.

41 Sir Harris Nicholas, *Testamenta Vetusta* (London, 1826), I, 109.

42 R. Delachenal, *Histoire de Charles V* (Paris, 1909), II, 332.

43 *MP*, I (1903), 1 ff.

44 Cf. Édouard Guillon, *La Nouvelle Revue*, XXXVI (1918), 243 ff.

45 Beauchet-Filleau, *op. cit.*

46 Paul Guérin, *op. cit.*, XIX, 90.

47 *The Life of the Black Prince*, ed. M. K. Pope and E. C. Lodge (Oxford, 1910), vv. 3239 ff., 4197 ff.

48 G. L. Kittredge, *Englische Studien*, XXVI (1899), 321 ff.

49 *See* my article *SP*, XXXV (1938), 515 ff.

50 *See* my article, *PMLA*, L (1935), 69 ff.

51 On whose connections with the Chaucerian circle, *see* H. L. Savage's brilliant paper, *Speculum*, XIV (1939), 423 ff.

THE TALE OF MELIBEUS

WILLIAM WITHERLE LAWRENCE

Columbia University

IN the brilliant sisterhood of the stories of Canterbury the *Tale of Melibeus* is certainly the neglected stepchild. Today we seldom glance at her, and, if we do, it is with pity and disdain. The appreciative critics will have none of her. The late Mr. Chesterton and Mr. H. D. Sedgwick, for example, have not so much as mentioned the *Melibee* in their substantial volumes. Even the specialists are frequently condemnatory. Professor R. D. French, in his excellent *Chaucer Handbook*, speaks of the translation as 'Chaucer's literary sin.' The late Professor W. P. Ker, whose sagacity need not be emphasized, has told us that 'the *Tale of Melibeus* is perhaps the worst example that could be found of all the intellectual and literary vices of the Middle Ages—bathos, forced allegory, spiritless and interminable moralizing . . . beyond rivalry for its enjoyment of the rankest commonplaces. There is glow and unction about its mediocrity; the intolerable arguments of Dame Prudence are a masterpiece, as though written in an orgy and enthusiasm of flatness and insipidity.'[1]

To the question why Chaucer should have busied himself with this sort of thing the answers have been varied. No doubt the sudden drop from verse, which the poet employed with such mastery, to prose, which was even in his hands awkward and undistinguished, accounts in part for our feeling that the *Melibeus* is dull, though I do not recall having seen this emphasized. Professor Hotson's theory that 'the *Melibeus* is a political tract, designed to dissuade John of Gaunt from launching on the invasion of Castile, in 1386,' must certainly be rejected. To conclude that John of Gaunt would have been moved by a close translation of

[1] G. K. Chesterton, *Chaucer* (New York, 1932); H. D. Sedgwick, *Dan Chaucer* (New York, 1934). The *Melibeus* is not listed in the index to either volume. R. D. French, *A Chaucer Handbook* (New York, 1929), p. 246. W. P. Ker, in *English Prose Selections*, ed. Henry Craik (London, 1893), I, 42 ff.

a popular and well-known work, written in the preceding century, and containing nothing pointing directly to the invasion of Castile, is to attribute to that robust hero a supernormal sensitiveness. The suggestion has been made that the tale is revenge upon the Host for interrupting *Sir Thopas;* and Professor Ker even toyed with the idea, which his good sense rejected, that it is a satire on heavy moral writing, as the piece preceding is on the doggerel romances. Certainly the poet was not punishing his readers for the sins of the Host, and he knew that a travesty is best if short. Ker went on, however, to put the matter in its true light: the *Melibeus* was dull neither to Chaucer nor to his contemporaries. 'The peculiarity of Chaucer is that with all his progress in his art he kept close to the general sense of his age, and had always, in some corner of his being, the average mind of the fourteenth century. To that part of him belong all his prose works. The *Tale of Melibeus* is representative of the ideas and tastes of millions of good souls. Being representative, it could not be alien from Chaucer.' The interest of the tale for the Middle Ages has also been emphasized by another distinguished scholar. Indeed, if this story is a Cinderella, Professor Tatlock may almost be called her fairy godmother, who discerns her true virtues beneath her russet dress, transforms her before our eyes, and sends her off to the ball to dance in company with her gayer sisters.[2]

The truth is that just those qualities in this long piece which we find tedious were highly esteemed in the Middle Ages. If we imagine it freed from all that bores us, there would not be much left. But, since it affected our forefathers so differently, it offers an unrivaled opportunity for studying changes in literary taste, for contrasting mediaeval and modern conceptions of what makes profitable reading. To this even the elementary student and the 'general reader' should give some attention today. They cannot be expected to plow through the whole of the *Melibeus*, but they

[2] J. Leslie Hotson, "The *Tale of Melibeus* and John of Gaunt," *SP*, XVIII (1921), 429–452. F. J. Mather, edition of Chaucer's *Prologue*, etc. (Riverside Literature Series, Boston, etc., 1899), p. xxxi. I have endeavored to show the fallacy of the theory that *Sir Thopas* is a satire on the Flemings, *PMLA*, L (1935), 81–91. W. P. Ker, *loc. cit.*, 42 f. J. S. P. Tatlock, *Development and Chronology of Chaucer's Works* (Chaucer Society, London, 1907), pp. 188–197.

should be reminded that they must read not only what diverts them, but what does not, if they really wish to know Chaucer and to understand the significance of his work for the days in which it was written. The very fact that the *Melibeus* lacks interest should stimulate interest to find out why this is so.

This pursuit would be more entertaining, though less instructive, if Chaucer had put something of himself into the tale. His version is a close translation of a French condensation of the *Liber Consolationis et Consilii* of Albertanus of Brescia, written in 1246, but he was also familiar with the Latin. How highly the work was esteemed is shown by its translations into Italian, German, and Dutch, and its inclusion in the *Ménagier de Paris,* a fourteenth-century manual of domestic economy, and in the sixteenth century in a French treatise on chess, and an edition of the *Livre du Chevalier de la Tour Landry.* Chaucer's rendering was no task of his salad days; as Professor Robinson remarks, 'all the literary associations favor an assignment to the Canterbury period.' He knew two other works by Albertanus, and there is every reason to suppose that he valued the *Melibeus* not merely because it would appeal to his readers, but for its own sake, and that it was mainly on this latter account that he gave himself the very considerable labor of translating it.[3]

Much of the fascination which the *Melibeus* held for mediaeval readers lay, of course, in its pervading didacticism, and its wise saws drawn from past authorities and from current tradition. Times have changed; sustained moralizing is repellent to us today. We are absorbed in concrete issues; we believe that we enjoy an advanced civilization, and yet that the world is changing so rapidly that the past is no guide for its problems. The Middle Ages, as every one knows, felt otherwise. Where we look forward to new ideologies, new 'deals,' new principles of government and justice, they looked backward in the confident trust that earlier

[3] For the details of Chaucer's relationship to his sources, and the popularity of the *Melibeus,* see F. N. Robinson, *Complete Works of Geoffrey Chaucer* (Cambridge, Mass., The Riverside Press, 1933), pp. 846 ff.; Tatlock, *loc. cit.;* Thor Sundby, *Albertani Brixiensis Liber Consolationis et Consilii* (Chaucer Society, Copenhagen, 1873), valuable as an edition and for its excellent introduction; W. W. Skeat, *Complete Works of Geoffrey Chaucer* (Oxford, 1894), III, 426–427.

and happier times could best teach them how to live. They were conscious of being in a world not yet reduced to order, and were eager to get it arranged according to the most approved moral principles. In criticizing the *Melibeus*, Professor Tatlock has emphasized their 'perpetual relish in the gnomic style,' and pointed out how frequently Chaucer employed it and how much he obviously enjoyed it. Furthermore, 'the interest of the earlier Middle Ages in creative literature had been chiefly for lyric feeling and for action; they had produced little analysis of human motive and shown little knowledge of the human heart. At a certain stage in the intellectual development of a people, these become intelligible and attractive; witness the rise of literary allegory into popularity in the thirteenth century. Now *Melibeus* offers both; strange as the statement may seem at first, *Melibeus* really shows insight.'[4] With this I am quite in agreement, and I wish that Professor Tatlock had further developed this point. But I think that another and more important feature of the tale has been strangely neglected—its repeated and earnest pleading for peace rather than war, for mediation and law rather than private revenge. Compared with this, its moral lessons, its psychologizing, and its elegant extracts seem of secondary significance.

First of all it is well to understand clearly the course of the story. For the *Melibeus* is a story, thus contrasting sharply with the Parson's Tale. The Parson does not give his hearers narrative, but a typical mediaeval sermon, into which has been inserted a tract on the Seven Deadly Sins. Omitting the loquacities of Dame Prudence as far as possible, the outline of the action and the discussion may run something as follows.

There was a young man named Melibeus, rich and powerful, who had a wife Prudence and a daughter Sophie. In his absence, three enemies entered his house and beat his wife, and inflicted five wounds on his daughter, leaving her for dead. Upon his return he gave himself over to grief, but his wife advised him to have patience, to call his friends and relatives together, and to ask their advice. This he did. Many thought it best for him to take vengeance on his foes, but the wiser ones counseled caution. Melibeus determined upon revenge, but Dame Prudence admonished him not to be overhasty. He answered that he would not be guided by her, especially on account of the dangers in following the counsels of women.

[4] *Loc. cit.*, pp. 189–190.

Prudence replied at length, defending her sex, and finally persuaded him to be governed by her. She also bade him heed the precepts of God, not to give himself over to anger, to keep his own counsel, and to distinguish between good and bad advisers. Melibeus asserted that vengeance is right, but she rejoined that one wrong does not cure another, that the strongest defence a man may have is to be beloved by his friends and neighbors, that vengeance is a mistake, that he had sinned against the Lord, and that the judge who had jurisdiction over his enemies should punish them. These points she argued in detail, also warning him not to put dependence upon his wealth, or to give himself over to his passions. Melibeus promised to follow her counsels absolutely. Thereupon she sent for his enemies, pointed out to them the evils of war and the blessings of peace, and converted them so that they promised to make amends. Her action was confirmed by her kinsmen and friends. The enemies of Melibeus came to him, and promised to give him such satisfaction as he thought best. At first he was minded to deprive them of their goods, and send them into exile, but was dissuaded by Prudence, so that he forgave them completely, as God forgives sinners.[5]

As narrative, this is thin stuff, stiff and conventional, poor in description, lacking in suspense, and too obviously a mere vehicle for moralizing. The chief characters have no life or individuality, save Dame Prudence, who is a canny soul, knowing how to manage a husband, letting him weep to relieve his feelings, soothing his vanity, and making 'semblant of wratthe' when necessary. There is interminable talk, and little action. But the shortcomings of the story as a story bothered the Middle Ages very little. The important thing for them was that it was allegory, from which they could draw valuable moral lessons. This form of literature charmed them like a wizard's spell, and its influence was never more potent than in the thirteenth and fourteenth centuries. Even when in prose, it had something of the emotional stimulus of poetry. As Henry Osborn Taylor remarks, 'allegory became the chief field for the mediaeval imagination.'[6] Modern times have ceased completely to feel its fascination. As a living force in literature it is dead today, surviving only when the story has become the main interest, as in *Gulliver's Travels*, or when it commands attention for the perfection of its artistry, as in the *Divine Comedy*, or as a social document, in *Piers Plowman*.

What is the chief message of the *Melibeus?* At first sight, the

---

[5] Robinson, pp. 201–224.

[6] *A Historian's Creed* (Cambridge, Mass., 1939), p. 126.

tale seems to be that of a man sorely tried under adversity and at length, by the exercise of virtue, restored to happiness, like Job. Indeed, there is reason to suppose that the Book of Job may have influenced the invention of the simple plot. The author quotes from it; the question why God allows man to suffer cruel affliction is touched upon, and the symposium of the friends of Melibeus reminds us of the discourses of Eliphaz the Temanite and Bildad the Shuhite and Zophar the Naamathite. The Book of Job had of course been a favorite allegory in the Middle Ages ever since Pope Gregory the Great wrote his famous commentary. But Melibeus is not, like Job, a good man tested by the Lord (and Satan);[7] he is a man who has sinned. The allegory is clumsy enough, but its significance is clear from the words of Dame Prudence, who is at once an actor in the tale, and its expositor. Melibeus is the 'honey-drinker' who has tasted so much of temporal riches and delights that he is drunken; he has forgotten Christ, against whom he has sinned, so that the three enemies of man, the world, the flesh, and the devil, have wounded his soul (his daughter Sophie) in five places, that is, through the five senses (Robinson, 213–214). So Dame Prudence says 'I conseille yow . . . aboven alle thynges, that ye make pees bitwene God and yow; and beth reconsiled unto hym and to his grace' (221). The allegory creaks a good deal at the end, when the goodwife sends for the three enemies and converts them to such sweet reasonableness that they are willing to make humble amends, and submit themselves to Melibeus. That is not the way the world, the flesh, and the devil usually treat a sinner, no matter how much prudence and wisdom he may display. However, the mediaeval man was not censorious; he took allegory as he found it, and thanked God for what it taught him.

Much more striking than the significance of the *Melibeus* as an allegory of sin and God's forgiveness is its constant insistence that peace is better than war, and composition or legal punishment better than private vengeance. This, I believe, interested

[7] I do not forget that the motivation of the underlying folk tale has been much obscured by the processes of growth in the Book of Job. See Morris Jastrow, Jr., *The Book of Job; its Origin, Growth and Interpretation* (Philadelphia and London, 1920).

Albertanus chiefly, which was perhaps the reason why his allegory stumbled at the end. At first, Melibeus is all for violent measures: 'it semed that in herte he baar a crueel ire, redy to doon vengeaunce upon his foes, and sodeynly desired that the werre sholde bigynne' (Robinson, 202). Then follows the best scene in the story, vividly set forth, and not overloaded with quotations until Dame Prudence begins to speak. Were it in verse, I venture to think that it would have been admired; as it is, real conviction and eloquence occasionally break through the crabbed prose. Melibeus has called together his friends, and asked their counsel. The physicians advise vengeance, and so do envious neighbors and feigned friends and flatterers. But 'an advocat that was wys' reminds them that to begin war and execute vengeance is not lightly to be undertaken. But most of those present, especially the young folk, cried out 'War! War!'

> Up roos tho oon of thise olde wise, and with his hand made contenaunce that men sholde holden hem stille and yeven hym audience. 'Lordynges,' quod he, 'ther is ful many a man that crieth "Werre! werre!" that woot ful litel what werre amounteth. Werre at his bigynnyng hath so greet and entryng and so large, that every wight may entre whan hym liketh, and lightly fynde werre; but certes, what ende that shal therof bifalle, it is nat light to knowe. For soothly, whan that werre is ones bigonne, ther is ful many a child unborn of his mooder that shal sterve yong by cause of thilke werre, or elles lyve in sorwe and dye in wrecchednesse. And therfore, er that any werre bigynne, men moste have greet conseil and greet deliberacion.' (Robinson, 203)

It is plain that Melibeus, even after a long discourse from Dame Prudence, still stands for the principle of an eye for an eye and a tooth for a tooth.

> 'Certes,' quod Melibeus, 'I understonde it in this wise: that right as they han doon me a contrarie, right so sholde I doon hem another. For right as they han venged hem on me and doon me wrong, right so shal I venge me upon hem and doon hem wrong; and thanne have I cured oon contrarie by another.' (Robinson, 210)

But after much more eloquence from his spouse he is converted to a better way of thinking, so that at the end he is reconciled to his enemies and they to him, and he gives up all thought of vengeance. The importance of this general point was clearly seen by Sundby, in his excellent edition of the Latin text. He noted that

Albertanus 'safely leads his readers to the goal he had proposed: condemnation of feuds and wilful wars, and submission to law. *This is the principal tendency of his book*, and very remarkable for the time when it was written.'[8] It is a pity that Sundby did not develop this further, and that its significance has not been seen by those who have endeavored to explain the English *Melibeus*. In order to understand it fully we must consider the contemporary administration of justice, and the career of Albertanus.

Precisely the conflict which we trace in the *Melibeus* between private revenge and organized justice marks the development of law in the later Middle Ages. The earlier centuries had striven chiefly for the regulation of private vengeance, the systematization of penalties, and the termination of long-standing feuds. As time went on, and the power of the state increased, and the practical features of Roman law were better understood, the old Germanic concept of vengeance as the recognized method of inflicting punishment and gaining redress was gradually abandoned. The influence of the Church was particularly important; specifically through the 'Peace of God,' which exempted certain parts of the community from warfare, and the 'Truce of God,' which restricted times and seasons when war might be waged. In the thirteenth century, especially in the reign of Louis IX in France, these humanizing and liberalizing tendencies were marked in lay authority in the so-called *asseurement*, or suspension of hostilities by mutual consent of the contending parties, and in the *quarantaine du roi*, which set up a truce of forty days, and protected relatives not directly concerned in the original criminal action. Religion, ethics, and law are mingled in the arguments of Dame Prudence, as they were in mediaeval attempts to organize justice at this time. Reform of judicial procedure was especially affected by Christian teaching in the administration of a man of the deep and sincere piety of St. Louis. He was far more powerful than many of his predecessors—he was really King of France, not

[8] Sundby, p. xvii. Italics mine. I did not notice Sundby's remarks until after the first draft of this article was written. How they have escaped the attention of readers of the English text for so long I do not see. Possibly they have received attention in criticism which I have overlooked.

merely an important noble among other contentious nobles. His influence and example spread far beyond the boundaries of his own kingdom. In 1258 he endeavored to interdict private warfare altogether in France, but without complete success. The old custom of private vengeance was not to be abolished so quickly. Not until well into the fourteenth century was it effectively replaced by punishment at the hands of duly constituted authorities. Justice was often administered in a strange way, alternating between cruel severity and complete forgiveness—as we may observe in the closing pages of the *Melibeus*.[9]

That Albertanus of Brescia was fully aware of these changes and greatly interested in them there is every reason to suppose. He was a judge, and consequently forced to face the practical realities of punishment. Some of the best advice against hasty vengeance in the *Melibeus* is put into the mouth of 'an advocat that was wys' (Robinson, 202). Though the exact dates of his birth and death are not known, Albertanus was certainly a contemporary of Louis IX, and he must have been affected by what was going on in jurisprudence in France, a country which was then in so many ways exercising a predominating influence in Western Europe. His home was in Northern Italy, where such influence might be expected. He was a bookish man, familiar with a wide range of authors, including writers on law. Besides five extant Latin *sermones* and the *Melibeus* allegory, he wrote two Latin treatises, *De Amore et Dilectione Dei* and *De Arte Loquendi et Tacendi*. Furthermore, he was active in public affairs. It is noticeable in the *Melibeus* that little distinction is made between 'werre' and 'vengeaunce,' and indeed in those days they were much alike. Of what we should call 'war' today he had ample experience in the struggles between the North Italian cities and the Holy Roman Emperor; he appears at a conference as a delegate from a Brescian borough, and in 1238 commanded the castle of Gavarno. His *De Amore* was composed in prison.[10]

---

[9] For the legal situation in mediaeval France, and its reflection in imaginative literature, *see* F. Carl Riedel, *Crime and Punishment in the Old French Romances* (New York, 1938), esp. 11–43.

[10] For biographical details in regard to Albertanus, see Sundby's Introduction.

Viewed against this background, the *Melibeus* takes on, I think, a new significance. To men wearied of continual strife, in countries exhausted by internal struggle and foreign invasion, this parable, written by no monkish idealist but by an active citizen, judge, and military leader, expressed the hope of something better and finer in the administration of justice and the settlement of wars. We may recoil at its prolixity, we may yawn at its trite aphorisms, we may smile at its crude allegory, but we cannot deny that it shows a wisdom and a vision of which the thirteenth century stood sadly in need. It was no less timely in the age of Chaucer. The exhaustion and depression in England in the reign of Richard II are too familiar to need emphasis. How deeply the evils of war and the perversion of justice impressed Gower and Langland we know; can they have been absent from Chaucer's mind when he translated the *Melibeus?* May they not, indeed, have been one of the chief reasons why he made the translation? The allegory was popular for other reasons, of course, but we may well doubt whether it would have attained such vogue had it been merely, like thousands of other works, a Christian manual or a didactic floralegium.

Whether the *Melibeus* was translated expressly for the *Canterbury Tales* it is impossible to say. I believe that Chaucer valued it mainly for its own sake, not because it would fit a given situation. With it and the Tale of Sir Thopas, however, he solved very neatly the problem of not seeming to compete himself for the dinner given at the common cost at the end of the journey. Obviously, the prize could be awarded neither to a parody nor to a piece so little of a real 'tale' as the *Melibeus*. With it, moreover, Chaucer secured that happy mingling of the grave and gay which is so clear a part of his design. No serious comment follows it; on the contrary, the Host seizes on a minor feature—the submission of Melibeus to Dame Prudence—and gloomily compares her patience with the tantrums of his own helpmeet. In the emphasis on the 'maistrye' which Melibeus allows his wife eventually, though of a different mind in the beginning ('certes, if I governed me by thy conseil, it sholde seme that I hadde yeve to thee over me the maistrye,' Robinson, 204), lies the germ of the later discussion of supremacy in marriage among the pilgrims. This rankles in the breast of the Nun's Priest, who is subject to petticoat rule, and whose tale is a curious parallel to the *Melibeus*, with the roles of husband and wife reversed. The cock 'tok his conseil of his wyf, with sorwe' and would have lost his life but for his own adroitness; he could quote authorities far more copiously than she, whereas Prudence snows Melibeus quite under with her citations; the 'Mulier est hominis confusio' and 'Wommennes conseils been ful ofte colde' are the direct opposite of the exaltation of woman and her help in trouble in the *Melibeus*. All this leads on, in turn, to the Wife of Bath's prologue ('He yaf me al the bridel in myn hond') and tale ('Thanne have I gete of yow maistrye') and so to the later discussions and tales. We shall be clearer in our minds about the sequence in which it is best to read the tales after the publication of Professor Manly's forthcoming studies, and the discussion which will no doubt ensue. It seems plain, however, that the order in the Ellesmere MS is not satisfactory, and that much is to be said for reading the tales in the sequence determined by internal evidence of time, stages of the journey, etc., of the sort employed by Furnivall and followed by Skeat in the Oxford Chaucer.

Upon the position of the *Melibeus* in the drama of the pilgrimage I do not wish to dwell, especially as I have discussed this fully elsewhere,[11] but rather to point out that it is primarily a humanitarian document, very much in the taste of its own time, and for that very reason more powerful in its appeal than an argument in more modern terms would have been. A good deal in the preceding pages will be familiar to specialists in the mediaeval field, but it has been set down in the hope that it will help those less familiar with that field to see clearly why the *Melibeus* was reckoned, in its own day, an integral and important part of the 'sentence and solas' of the *Canterbury Tales*.

---

[11] "The Marriage Group in the *Canterbury Tales*," *MP*, XI (1913), 247–258.

CHAUCER AND THE AUCHINLECK MS: 'THOPAS' AND 'GUY OF WARWICK'

LAURA HIBBARD LOOMIS

Wellesley College

CHAUCER names *Guy of Warwick* among the 'romances of prys' of which he makes such delightful fun in *Sir Thopas*. No one questions that he knew this romance and knew it well. Years ago Miss Caroline Strong[1] showed how extensively he was indebted to it for phrasings and details and even incidents of his burlesque. Though most of her forty odd quotations were taken from the Auchinleck *Guy*, she avoided, as scholars generally do, all discussion of Chaucer's actual manuscript source.

It is with this phase of the matter that the present inquiry has to do. My concern is primarily with the Auchinleck MS itself and the interesting question whether Chaucer ever had this manuscript, to us so famous and so venerable, in his hands. Quite apart from *Guy of Warwick* there is, I believe, evidence of his use of other Auchinleck romances, but in no other case is the evidence so ample, the possible tests so various, as in connection with the long-winded *Guy*. The question must, therefore, be decided on the basis of the one romance of which he made the fullest use. 'Auntrous' as the attempt may seem to be, I venture with some confidence to present certain new considerations, and especially to present a new method for giving us, in this matter, an 'approximation to certainty' that Chaucer did read *Guy of Warwick* in this particular manuscript.

The idea will, no doubt, at the outset encounter that instinctive opposition which, as Professor R. W. Chambers has observed apropos of a Shakespearean autograph, meets things that are too good to be true. It will seem fundamentally improbable and impossible to prove that to this 'olde boke,' in which there is no clue to aid us except the internal evidence of certain texts, the poet

[1] Strong, "Sir Thopas and Sir Guy," *MLN*, XXIII (1908), 73 ff. and 102 ff. Except for certain essential instances, I have avoided duplicating Miss Strong's material.

himself had access. The pleasure of believing that what he once handled we too can touch recoils upon itself in disbelief. Yet indubitably he read some English manuscript and the most zealous skeptic must admit that in this one rare instance, at least, there is no reason against the possibility of Chaucer's having seen the volume.

In the first place, there is the matter of date. Unlike the majority of our extant Middle English manuscripts, this one does not date from the fifteenth century. The Auchinleck MS, it is all but unanimously agreed, was written in the second quarter of the fourteenth century. Not only does the writing suggest a date before 1350, but the whole volume contains no allusion to anything later than the death of Edward II (1327) and a prayer for the next 'ȝong kyng,' Edward III.[2] In the second place, this book, though invaluable today, cannot, in its own time, have been of great cost and so beyond the reach of a booklover of comfortable means. Like nearly all contemporary manuscripts written in English, its appeal and its value were both of popular character. Its miniatures alone, even the few that vandals have left, tell the tale; they are neither large nor of that expert workmanship which distinguishes more costly books. At a glance any one can see that this book is in a different category altogether from that finely illuminated vellum Missal, which is still in Westminster Library, and for which in 1384 the Abbot Lytlington paid the equivalent of $2,200.[3] The Auchinleck MS now numbers 334 leaves, but, though large and well written, it was, assuredly, never designed for a prince's pleasure, but only for some prosperous citizen. Finally, it would appear from recent investigations that most of the manuscript was written by London scribes, a fact which gives us some basis for believing that it still remained, in Chaucer's

---

[2] E. Zettl, *An Anonymous Short Eng. Metrical Chronicle*, *EETS*, 196 (1935), xvi. For the date and a good list of authorities dealing with the Auchinleck MS, *see* J. M. Booker, *A Middle English Bibliography* (Heidelberg, 1912), p. 54. For the date alone, *see* also *Amis and Amiloun*, ed. MacEdward Leach, *EETS*, 203 (1937), p. xc, n. 1.

[3] For Lytlington's Missal *see* Eric Millar, *Eng. Illuminated MSS, XIV–XV Centuries* (Paris, 1928), p. 28, Pl. 71–72. For an illuminated page from the Auchinleck MS, *see* the Maitland Club edition of *Beves of Hamtoun* (Edinburgh, 1838).

day, in the city where it was written. According to Kölbing's[4] old but outstanding study, five scribes wrote the text; the first and most important of these scribes, the *a*-man, wrote 35 of the 44 extant items. Among these was his copy of the *Seven Masters (Sages) of Rome*, ff. 65–99. In Brunner's[5] edition of this poem, published in 1933, the London origin of this scribe was authoritatively established, but the significance of the fact for the largest part of the whole manuscript has been strangely overlooked. In 1935 the London origin of Kölbing's third scribe, the *y*-man, was established by Zettl.[6] This scribe wrote the couplet version of *Guy of Warwick* and also the *Short Metrical Chronicle* which Zettl edited. No adequate linguistic studies for the other three scribes are available,[7] but if the two who wrote more than three fourths of the whole compilation were of London, the manuscript itself may justly be called a London production.

The lack of any chronological, economic, or geographical reason against Chaucer's having seen this special volume is, of course, no argument; it merely establishes a pleasant possibility. About the history of the manuscript itself we have no information before the day in 1744 when it was given by Alexander Boswell, father of the famous James, to the Faculty of Advocates of the University of Edinburgh.[8] Since then the book has been repeatedly examined, and a wealth of fine scholarship has gone into the editing of single texts. With the exception, however, of such

---

[4] Kölbing, "Vier Romanzen-Handschriften," *Englische Studien*, VII (1884), 177–191 (The Auchinleck MS).

[5] Karl Brunner, *The Seven Sages of Rome*, *EETS*, 191 (1933), xxv–vii.

[6] Zettl, *op. cit.*, p. cxxi.

[7] Carr, "Notes on a Middle Eng. Scribe's Methods," *Univ. of Wis.*, *Studies in Lang. and Lit.*, II (1918), 153 ff. In this study of the Auchinleck *a*-scribe, Miss Carr rightly complained (pp. 153, 157, n. 10) of the fact that in editions of twelve of the thirty-five poems copied by this scribe, no single editor referred to other editions for pertinent facts or theories about *a*'s dialect, or even betrayed knowledge that these and other poems were written by him.

[8] Kölbing, *Eng. Stud.*, VII, 178; W. H. Hulme, *The ME. Harrowing of Hell*, *EETS,ES*, 100 (1907), xi–xiv. The MS is still in Edinburgh in the National Library (Adv. MS 19. 2. 1). It is a pleasure to acknowledge the helpful courtesy of M. R. Dobie, Keeper of MSS, in replying to questions and in facilitating my use of the MS.

early editors as Laing and Scott,[9] who gave comprehensive accounts of the whole manuscript, or of Kölbing, whose description is still the best in print, few people have concerned themselves with the manuscript as a whole. In only one instance, so far as I know, has it ever been really discussed in connection with Chaucer. It was then briefly, and as I believe wrongly, dismissed with the observation that for his quotation in *Thopas* from *Beves of Hamtoun*, Chaucer must have used not the Auchinleck text of *Beves*, but some lost manuscript.[10]

Before turning to a new analysis of the material in the Auchinleck volume, we may well pause to ask the means by which, in any such case, we might hope to establish that a medieval author used one, rather than another, manuscript. One advantage, for such an inquiry, the medieval book had over the modern—no two were ever exactly alike. Of one hundred and thirty-five manuscripts, for instance, which have recently been collated by Professor Jacob Hammer for his projected edition of Geoffrey of Monmouth's *Historia Regum Britanniae*, no two were found to

---

[9] David Laing, *A Penniworth of Witte* (Edinburgh, 1857), pp. xiii–xxxi; Sir Walter Scott, *Sir Tristrem* (Edinburgh, 1819, 4th ed.), pp. lxxxii and cvii–cxxvi.

[10] E. Kölbing, *Beues of Hamtoun*, *EETSES*, 46, 48, 65 (1885–1886, 1894), 219, l. 12 n.; *see* also *Eng. Stud.*, XI (1888), 504. Kölbing's collation of the MSS in his edition of *Beves* (p. 1) showed that Chaucer must have used the Auchinleck *Beves* or the lost source of a 15th-century MS C (Cbg., Univ. Lib., Ff. II. 38). The Auchinleck *Beves* reads:

*Lord*inges, herkneþ *to me tale!* 1(1–4)
Is *merier þan þe niȝtingale.* . . .
Of a kniȝt *ich wile ȝow roune.*

The italicized words appear also and in the same order in *Thopas*, st. 19. But Kölbing accepted C as Chaucer's source because, like *Thopas*, it has *lystniþ* for *herkneþ* and omits the *is* of l. 2; he did not consider the unimportance of *is*, nor the fact that in *Thopas*, ll. 712, 833, *listeth*, l. 893, *herkneth*, Chaucer used these words at will and not by rote. The fact that Chaucer kept twelve out of seventeen words including the important riming phrase, *to me tale*, seems decisive evidence for his use of the Auchinleck *Beves*.

Yet listeth, lordes, to my tale *Thopas*, l. 833
Lordinges, lysteniþ, grete and smale. *Beves*, C, l. 1

For this variation in C Kölbing offered no explanation save the possibility of a "lost version." The evidence that follows of Chaucer's use of the Auchinleck versions of *Guy of Warwick* still further confirms his use of the Auchinleck *Beves*.

All quotations from Chaucer are from F. N. Robinson's invaluable edition, *The Complete Works of Geoffrey Chaucer* (Boston, 1933).

be exact duplicates. The medieval book was not made for or by mass production; it was written, as we all know, by individual scribes who varied, to greater or less extent, the text they copied. Even in the matter of compilation no two volumes, at least of romances extant in Middle English, are ever of exactly the same content. For these obvious reasons, then, it is less hopeless than might at first appear to say with some confidence that a medieval author who shows himself aware of certain texts read them in a particular manuscript. Ideally, before making such an assertion, we might demand that the following conditions be fulfilled. Granting that the manuscript in question be of such origin that the later author might have known it, we would say that it must have:

1. A unique combination of texts
2. One or more unique texts
3. Unique readings in one or more of its texts

In other words, if a medieval author shows himself aware *of texts found together only in one manuscript*, and *of texts that are found nowhere else*, and *of readings that occur nowhere else*, we may feel that in all human probability this was the manuscript that he read. Though we cannot, in view of all the manuscripts known to be lost, give too much importance to the fact that today a manuscript text is unique, still we cannot refuse to credit the converging evidence of unique combinations of texts and of unique readings in those texts. For we have, after all, the positive evidence of all our still extant manuscripts to establish their essential individuality. Manuscripts can be grouped by families, relationships can be traced, but in Middle English at least it is certain that no compilation of romances exists which is an exact copy of any other. It is, therefore, fundamentally improbable that a manuscript satisfying not one but all of the exact and peculiar conditions noted above should ever have been duplicated. It must have been the actual manuscript known to the medieval author.

The first presumptive piece of evidence that Chaucer once had the Auchinleck MS in hand comes from *Thopas*, st. 29, where he names together three 'Matter of England' romances:

> Men speken of romances of prys
> Of Horn child and of Ypotys,
> Of Beves and of sir Gy.

The crux of the matter here is the allusion, for it is the only known allusion, to *Horn Child*,[11] a romance which exists *only* in the Auchinleck MS. Beves of Hampton and Guy of Warwick were, to be sure, popular heroes whose names were commonly coupled together and whose stories still appear together in a Cambridge manuscript, University Library, Ff. II. 38, but in no other instance are they conjoined with *Horn Child*. That Chaucer's association of the three together was not a matter of chance is proved by the Auchinleck MS.

It may be remarked to the skeptic, who recalls that the four other poems[12] named in *Thopas* are not found in this volume, that on this point no argument can be based. For one thing, it is certainly not my intention to maintain that the Auchinleck MS was the only English book known to our English poet; but, for another, it is worth pointing out that every one of these four English poems and certain others, which it is probable that Chaucer knew, may once have been included in this very volume. Bulky as it still is, it is a mutilated book. The original numbering shows that at least fourteen items have been lost from it, to say nothing of whole pages torn out here and there. Five of these lost original items came at the very beginning of the manuscript. In this varied assortment of English verse, nearly all contemporary types of poetry were represented; the didactic *Ypotys*[13] may have been there, along with the romances, since *Owain Miles*,

---

[11] *Horn Child*, ed. by J. Hall in *King Horn* (Oxford, 1901), pp. 179–192. Cf. L. A. Hibbard, *Medieval Romance in England* (New York, 1924), pp. 97 ff.; Trounce, "The English Tail-Rhyme Romances," *Medium Aevum*, I (1932), p. 93, n. 18. Trounce strangely urges that Chaucer was derisively alluding to the older, better romance, *King Horn*, and not to its tail-rime sequel, *Horn Child*. Since Chaucer borrowed nothing but the name from either poem, our only certainty is the fact that, for some reason, he associated the name with those of Guy and Beves. For this the Auchinleck MS alone offers a concrete explanation. In this MS the title of *Horn Child* is written in red and had originally a miniature below it, facts which may have attracted Chaucer's attention. Cf. *Eng. Stud.*, VII, p. 190, no. 41.

[12] The didactic *Ypotys* and the romances of *Pleyndamour* (now lost), *Libeaus Desconus*, and *Perceval of Galles*. For MSS and editions of these and other romances here mentioned, *see* J. E. Wells, *Manual of Writings in Middle English* (New Haven, 1916), and later supplements.

[13] Early fourteenth-century fragments of *Ypotys* were published by Miss Sutton, *PMLA*, XXXI (1936), 114 ff. I owe much to the suggestion of Miss Everett, *Rev. Eng. Studies*, VI

ff. 25–31, and the long didactic English poem, the *Speculum Gy de Warwyke*, ff. 39–48, still are there. Equally, of course, these other texts may never have been included. About that, in all probability, we shall never know. Our only certainty is that the otherwise unknown *Horn Child* is here found with *Beves* and *Guy*, and that Chaucer mentions the three together.

It is to this particular matter of combination, now to be illustrated in a variety of ways, that I would direct attention as a new means, in this connection, of testing Chaucer's use of a particular text. In literary scholarship we are all inclined, it would appear, to give large credence to the possible workings of chance, of coincidence, and to distrust almost wholly, so far as Middle English romances are concerned, the possibility of ever proving that any particular phrase or detail ever came from one particular source. In view of the conventional character of the romances, this sense of impossibility is not surprising. The 'parallel phrase' method is now without honor as a method of establishing either source or common authorship. But the case is different, we must all admit, when we have to do with *a large number of particular and peculiar combinations*. It is inconceivable, even with the most conventionalized materials, that either chance or convention should account for a whole series of combinations, and combinations of different kinds, which are peculiar to Chaucer and this one manuscript alone. Coincidence has a long arm but is not Briareus.

We have already noted one combination of different texts which the Auchinleck MS alone preserves, and which Chaucer alone mentions. A second similar combination occurs in *Guy of Warwick* itself, for in this one manuscript the romance is presented in two different versions, a couplet version, ff. 108–146, written by the *y*-scribe, and a twelve-line, tail-rime stanzaic version, ff. 146–167, written by the *a*-scribe. The first is known in other manuscripts;[14] the latter only in the Auchinleck MS. The story is presented in these two Auchinleck versions in almost continuous form. The unexplained change from the couplet to the stanzaic

(1930), 447, who first called attention to two collections which alike contained *Ypotys* and *Libeaus* in texts copied by one scribe.

[14] Cf. Wells, *Manual*, pp. 16, 764; Hibbard, *Medieval Romance in Eng.*, p. 138.

form may, though I base no argument on the possibility, represent no new source but only a deliberate shifting, in the work of a hack-author, after 7,306 lines in couplets, to another metrical form. A similar shifting is to be observed in *Beves of Hamtoun*, ff. 176–221, in this same manuscript. The fourth or *y*-scribe, who copied this romance, wrote lines 1–474 in six-line, tail-rime stanzas; the remaining 4,212 lines in couplets.[15] But whether this interpretation be true or not, that the Auchinleck authors and scribes sometimes themselves shifted, *in medias res*, from one verse form to another, there is no question but that the stanzaic *Guy of Warwick* is unique and that in this one manuscript alone it is combined with the couplet version of *Guy*. This is a matter of vital importance to our inquiry. That Chaucer used the two versions conjointly, that he sometimes neatly dovetailed them together, as in the peculiar account of Thopas's amorous charms, st. 6, his bird-inspired love-longing, st. 10, his complaint of being bound by love, st. 13, his vow to forsake all women, his seeking a *pryve* place and going by *dale and downe*, st. 14–15—these things are susceptible of proof. It is impossible to account for Chaucer's use of *Guy of Warwick* except on the basis of these two versions. It is this combination which points most urgently to his use of the Auchinleck MS.

The proof of this statement lies in the large number of small but specific combinations, largely but not entirely verbal, which we can trace throughout the two versions of this one manuscript, but not in any other manuscript of *Guy*. The individual elements of these combinations are, admittedly, often slight and almost wholly conventional. Chaucer used them with such merry and matchless skill, so ordering and transforming and varying them, that the full measure of his imitation has, even under close scrutiny, escaped detection.[16] Readers of *Thopas* get an amusing sense of general rather than specific imitation, but there can be no final

[15] Kölbing, *Beves*, p. xi, remarked in connection with these and other instances of metrical changes in the romances: "the reason is altogether unknown."

[16] Cf. Chaucer, ed. Robinson, p. 842; "No particular romance seems to have been singled out by Chaucer for imitation or attack." This was my own opinion, four years ago, even after concluding a prolonged study of *Sir Thopas* for the volume of *Sources and Analogues* to be published (sometime) for the Chaucer group of the Modern Language Association.

question, after we have traced out the combinations given below, of their cumulative significance. No matter how the identical words or phrases or rimes, the specific details and concepts are manipulated by a master wit to produce an effect at once so like and yet so different in *Thopas*, the little linked groups of these elements in the parody have a recognizable pattern which betrays the source in some specific passage in the Auchinleck romance.

In checking the statement that these passages are peculiar for the most part to these two texts, we can turn to other manuscripts of *Guy*. Of these the closest by all odds to the Auchinleck MS is the fifteenth-century manuscript, C, Cambridge, Caius College, 107, a text which Zupitza edited in the same volume with the Auchinleck *Guy* (*EETSES*, 42, 49, 59). This C MS, indeed, so largely parallels the Auchinleck MS (henceforth to be referred to as *Guy*, *A*) that Weyrauch[17] thought it copied from the same source. Thousands of lines are approximately the same, but whereever essential variation does occur, through different wordings or omission, it appears that the Auchinleck text invariably, in the test cases noted below, has the crucial combination of words, phrases, rimes, details, etc., which identifies Chaucer's borrowing. This, I take it, is as plain proof as we can ever ask that Chaucer used this particular manuscript for all that he borrowed from *Guy of Warwick*. Whatever we may think, in a particular instance, of the possibility that he might, by chance or natural association, have achieved the same combination, it is inconceivable, in so large a series, that all these same combinations should have been a matter of chance. He must have used *Guy*, *A*, or an identical copy. This conjecture, in the venerable presence of the Auchinleck volume, is needless; it is, moreover, offset by the evidence that the manuscript closest to *Guy*, *A*, is, in these test instances, so different from it, and by the fact, already noted, that the Auchinleck MS alone contains that unique combination of romances which is alluded to by Chaucer.

In the following citations I have used an asterisk to indicate that the passage in question is to be found *only in Guy*, *A*. In other manuscripts it is either omitted or so changed as to offer no paral-

[17] Weyrauch, *Die me. Fassungen der Guy of Warwick* (Breslau, 1901), pp. 43, 52–53.

lel to Chaucer's phrasing. Passages are quoted to show through combinations of identical elements, through exceptional elements, through the special order or the special repetitions of this one text some precise cause for Chaucer's parodistic imitation. Words common to *Guy*, *A*, and *Thopas* are italicized, but since this means does not always serve, especially in the case of altogether exceptional rimes or meanings, I have, even at the risk of overspecific statement, ventured to analyze, in the footnotes, the significance of many of these passages. What cannot be realized by any one who has not slowly sieved through the stylized sea of Middle English romance is the important fact that nearly all the combinations of elements here noted are, in themselves, unique. Individually, the elements may occur anywhere, everywhere; together, in these specific combinations, these particular patterns, they belong exclusively to *Guy*, *A*, and to Chaucer's deliberate and delicious parody.

SIR THOPAS	GUY OF WARWICK
st. 1	
Listeth, *lordes*, in *good entent*,	*lord*inges alle, 238(5–9)*
and *I* wol telle *verrayment*	Mine men ȝe ben, *verrament* . . .
	Ich biseche ȝou wiþ *gode entent*[18]
Al of a knyght was fair and gent . . .	*Al of a* gentil *kniȝt* . . . 1(3, 11)*
His name was sire Thopas.	*His name was* hoten *sir* Gij.
st. 2	
Yborn he was in *fer contree*	Þurch mani diuers *cuntray*, 2(5–12)*
In Flaundres, al *biyonde the see*, . . .	Þat was *biȝond þe see*. . . .
His fader *was* a man ful *fre*	Þe king . . . / Þat *was* boþe hende & *fre*, . . .
	Ful fer in þe norþ *cuntre*.[19]

[18] *Thopas* and *Guy* alike combine the exceptional rime, *entent: verrayment*, with the phrase *gode entent* and the *I* appeal to *lordinges*. Chaucer's form is almost invariably *entente* (Robinson, p. 843, l. 742). In *Guy*, though *verrayment* in all MSS is a frequent rime word, and though *gode entent*(*e*) occurs several times in a Cbg. MS of *Guy* (Univ. Lib. Ff. II, 38, ed. Zupitza, *EETSES*, XXV–VI, ll. 1761, 2134, 3818), *Guy*, *A*, alone rimes this phrase with *verrament*.

Chaucer's first stanza thus combines four elements from *Guy*, *A*, st. 238, with two remarkably similar lines from st. 1. The endlessly repeated minstrel phrase, *I wol telle*, is combined with *His name was* in *Isumbras*, st. 1, in *Ipomydon*, B, 1, 15, in the *Seven Sages*, 3, 6, but only in *Guy* is this last phrase combined with the exceptional *Al of a kniȝt*.

[19] The second stanzas of *Guy*, *A*, and of *Thopas* contain the same four rime words, alike repeating *cuntre*. Each stanza speaks of a hero who was born or adventured afar, and of

And *lord he was of that contree* . . .	Þer he *was lord of þat cuntre.*[20] 71(5)*, 278(5)*
st. 3–4	
Sire Thopas wax a *doghty* swayn . . .	Þat *douhti* man of dede.[21] 10(6, 12)*, 74(6)*
His *rode* is lyk scarlet . . .	Oysel sche . . . wiþ þe *rode* so rede . . . 5688
His heer, his berd was lyk saffroun,	*His here*, þat was ȝalu and briȝt[22] . . . 6107
Of Brugges were his hosen broun.	(See below, *Thopas*, st. 26, *hosen* in *Guy*)
	Of cloth of Tars & riche cendel, . . . 709–712
	Þe mantels weren of michel priis.
His robe was of *syklatoun*,	Gode cloþes of *sikelatoun*[23] & Alisaundrinis. 2835*
That coste many a jane.	
st. 5	him lerd 171–175
	Of wodes & *riuer* & oþer game; . . .
He koude hunte at *wilde deer*,	Michel *he couþe* of *hauk* & hounde.
	In þat on half orn þe *riuer*, 6341–6342*
And ride an *hauk*yng for *river* . . .	In þat oþer half forest wiþ *wilde dere.*[24]

another noble person. No better illustration can be given of Chaucer's power to vary the effect of his original while preserving its essential ideas and its riming pattern. The phrase *in fer contre* is also found in *Guy, A*, 1617, 1635, 6117, st. 33(7), 170(7).

[20] The repetition of this line in the stanzaic section of *Guy, A*,* is noteworthy, for repetitions of this sort seem particularly to have attracted Chaucer's derisive attention. For this line in other romances, *see* Robinson, p. 843, l. 722, n.

[21] This line appears twice in *Guy, A*,* st. 10. Its overemphatic *douhti* may have inspired the *doghty* of *Thopas*, st. 3; likewise from *Guy, A*, st. 10–11, Chaucer took other details. *See* below, n. 26.

[22] The first 122 lines, now lost, of *Guy, A*, undoubtedly contained, as the closely related Caius MS (C) still does, details from which Chaucer may have borrowed suggestions for Thopas's physiognomy. Cf. C, 65, *Hir* (i.e., Felice's) *skynne was white;* C, 68, *nose wel sittyng*. Though Chaucer may equally well have transferred to Thopas the whiteness, the nose, the *rede rode*, which are combined in the description of a single lady in *Libeaus* (ed. Kaluza, st. 79), instead of the two ladies in *Guy, A*, still it is certain that only the latter combines these same physical details with additional reference to the hero's yellow hair and to "gode clothes" of *sikelatoun*. *See* n. 23.

[23] *Guy, A*, alone combines mention of materials from far-off places, their great cost, and specific mention of *sikelatoun*. This unusual word appears elsewhere in ME romance only in *Richard Coeur de Lion*, l. 5268, once contained in the Auchinleck MS, ed. K. Brunner, and in *Florence of Rome*, ed. Vietor, l. 177. There is no evidence that Chaucer knew this last romance.

[24] Chaucer's rime, *wilde deer: riveer*, is noted by Robinson, p. 843, l. 712, as exceptional. It is matched in *Guy, A*, 6341–6342.* Chaucer's meaning *waterfowl* for *riveer*, as suggested

	on *hunt*ing þai gun ride, 4(10), 20(6) him rode on *dere* hunting 11(2)
Of wrastlynge *was* there *noon his peer.*	In þe world *was non his pere.*[25] 256(12)
st. 6	
Ful *many* a *mayde, bright in bour,* They moorne for hym *paramour,* . . .	Þat day Gij dede his miȝt 237–241 To serue þritti *maidens briȝt;* Al an-*amourd* on him þai were. . . .
But he was chaast and no lechour	Þer of no ȝaf he riȝt nouȝt.
	He haþ ben desired of *mani* woman 10(6–7)*
(See below, st. 14, *forsake*)	& he haþ forsaken hem euerilcan
	Of leuedis *briȝt in bour,* . . . 11(6, 9)* Y pray þe *par amoure.*[26]
st. 7–8	
And so bifel up*on a day,*	*On a day* . . . 5(1), 8(1), 11(1) *for soþe* to say[27] . . . 2(1), 3(1, 4), Alle *for soþe y ȝou telle.* 3440
For sothe, as *I yow telle may* Sire Thopas wolde out ride.	*For soþe y ȝou telle may* 7292*, 152(3)*.
He worth upon *his steede* gray, And *in his hand a* launcegay, A long *swerd* by his side.	Gij anon asked *his stede* þo, 4129–4131 His spere, & his *swerd* also; *In his hond a* gode *swerd* he bar.
	Sir Gij opon þat *stede* wond 251(4–6)* Wiþ a gode glaive *in hond,*
He *priketh* thurgh *a fair forest,*	& *priked* him forþ his way.[28] Þai comen into *a fair forest,* 6719–6720*

by Robinson, p. 843, l. 737, is precisely matched in *Guy, A*, 171. There are many references to hunting throughout *Guy, A*, but the three references concentrated in st. 4–20 seem particularly worthy of note since they are immediately connected with Guy's love affair as was also Thopas's hunting and love.

[25] This line occurs also in *Guy, C*, 9140, in an episode from which, in this Caius MS, it could not be shown that Chaucer took anything else. In *Guy, A*, it occurs in the Colbrand episode, st. 238–269, from which Chaucer may have taken hints. Cf. citations from these stanzas in connection with *Thopas*, st. 1, 7–8, 16–17, 24–26.

[26] The couplet and the stanzaic versions of *Guy, A*, combine to explain the *many* lovelorn *maidens* in *Thopas*, also that hero's indifference, and the identical riming phrases, *briȝt in bour: paramour*, used in connection with just these same matters. *See* also the *forsake* parallel, *Thopas*, st. 14.

[27] The numerous repetitions of these common tag phrases in the early stanzas of *Guy, A*, seem specifically to account for their early appearance in *Thopas*.

[28] The two series of combinations in *Guy, A*, are to be noted, the *steed-sword-in his hond*

*Ther*inne is many *a wilde best.*	*Þer* þai fond a bore, *a wilde best.*
st. 10–11	
The briddes synge, it is no nay, . . .	So michel he herd þo foules *sing,* 4519–4537*
Sire Thopas fil in love-*longynge,*	Þat him þouȝt he was in gret *longing* . . .
Al whan he herde the thrustel *synge,*	
And *pryked as he were wood.*	Þat hors he *prikeþ* . . . [29]
	Þai *priked* þe stedes . . . 97(4–6)*
	& ferd *as* þai *wer wode.*
	& priked riȝt as he wer wode. 181(10)*
st. 13–14 (Thopas about his love)	(Guy about his love)
'O seinte *Marie,* benedicite!	God graunte þe . . . 26(11–12)*
	And *Marie,* his moder swete.
What eyleth this *love* at me	'*Leman,*' seyd Gij oȝain, . . . 24(1–6)*
To *bynde* me so soore?	'Þi *loue* me haþ so y-*bounde*[30]
An elf-queene shal my *lemman* be.	
For in this world no *womman* is	Y no schal neuer spouse *wiman* 5(11)*
Worthy to be my make . . .	Y nil neuer spouse *wiman* . . .' 12(5)*
Alle othere wommen I *forsake*	& he haþ *forsaken* hem euerilcan . . . 10(8)*
And to an elf-queene I me take	(ie., Guy has forsaken all women)
By dale and eek by *downe!*'	Y schal walk / *bi doun & dale.*[31] 29(9)*

-*spear,* of the couplet, the *steed-glaive-in hond-priked* of the stanzaic version. Between them they account for these elements in *Thopas,* st. 7–8. Because of the naturalness of the association, however, these are to be considered the least convincing of the combinations here noted.

29 The combination of the rime *sing*:*longing* with the bird-inspired hero and reference to his *pricking* is to be found only in the couplet version of *Guy, A,* and in *Thopas.* Miss Strong, *MLN,* XXIII, 103, noted that over forty times in *Guy, A,* a knight comes *pricking.* Chaucer uses the word eight times in eighty-four lines.

30 *Thopas,* st. 13–14, combines references to *Marie, leman,* and to being *bound-by-love;* among the *Guy* MSS these are likewise combined only in *A,* st. 24, 26. In *Guy, C,* 7413, the corresponding passage has only the reference to *leman.*

31 Thopas's vow, *alle wommen I forsake, / . . . an elf-queene I me take,* seems to come directly from Chestre's *Launfal* (ed. French and Hale, *Middle Eng. Met. Romances,* 1930), where there is the same theme of the fairy lady (*Here fadyr was kyng of fayrye,* l. 280), and where we find the same promise in rime, *Yf þou wylt truly to me take, / And alle wemen for me forsake,* ll. 316–317. But Chaucer must have had *Guy, A,* equally in mind since this contains, in common with *Thopas,* not only the elements noted above, n. 29–30, but also, in connection with Guy's love affair, the stress on his vow to wed no woman (but one), his vow to walk by *doun and dale,* a phrase rarely found in the romances, though common enough in ballads, and finally his coming to a *prive* place.

st. 15 Into his sadel he clamb anon, And *priketh* over . . .	On hors þai lopen fot hot[32] 97(2, 4)* Þai *priked* þe stedes . . . Sir Gij lepe on his stede fot hot 259(1)*
he foona, in a *pryve* woon . . . For *in* that contre was ther *noon* That to *him durste* ride or *goon* Neither wyf ne childe.	In *prive* stede stode Gij . . . 4518* *In* þis warld is man *non* 148(7–9)* Þat oȝaines him *durst gon*, Herl, baroun, no kniȝt.[33]
st. 16 Til that ther cam a greet geaunt, His name was sire Oli*faunt*,	(The Giant Amoraunt) For he is so michel of bodi y-piȝt, 63(1–6) Oȝains him tvelue men haue no miȝt, . . . So wonderliche he is long.
	(The giant Colbrand) He was so michel & so vnrede, Þat non hors miȝt him lede. . . . 255(4–5) He was so michel & so strong, & þer-to so wonderliche long. . . . 256(10–11)
A perilous man *of dede*, He *seyde*, 'Child, by *Termagaunt!*	So strong he is *of dede*. 96(3)* 'Hold þi pes,' *seyd* Amor*aunt*, 121(1–2)* 'For, *bi* mi lord sir *Teruagaunt*,[34]

[32] These repeated *fot-hot** mountings of Guy in the stanzaic version probably best account for the parodistic leisure of *he clamb* in *Thopas*. All texts of *Guy* contain numerous references to leaping on horseback.

[33] The stanzaic version alone combines the same rime, approximately the same rhythm, the same *durst*, as *Thopas*, st. 15. *Guy*, *C*, 9138–9189, reads, *And so proud, and so fell, / That no man myȝt with hym dwell.* For the specific reference to *wyf ne childe* in *Thopas* Chaucer probably drew on the Auchinleck copy of the *Seven Sages* (ed. Brunner, *EETS*, 191, p. 32):

and sent him forht al barfot 711
Wiȝ outen leue of *wif* and *child*
And wente into a forest *wild*.

[34] The huge size of the two giants, Amoraunt and Colbrand, is emphasized in all texts of *Guy*. *Guy*, *A*, not only provides similar elephantine suggestions of size, but alone rimes the *-aunt* syllable of the giant's name with the oath, *bi Teruagant* (st. 121), alone uses *of dede* and *seyde* in connection with the giant. (Cf. C, 8414, *Quod Ameraunte.*) The oath by the giant recurs in A, 126(8).

Anon I sle thy *steede*'	Þe *stedes* nek he dede also . . . 101(2) Þat sadel & hors atvo he smot[35] 260(10)
st. 17 The *child seyde*, 'Al*so moote I thee*,	As a *child* he stode him vnder[36] . . . 263(3)* 'Tel me,' he *seyd*, . . . *so mot y the*, . . . 110(1–2)
Tomorwe wol I meete with thee	When he seye Amoraunt so grim . . . 64(7–10)* Þan asked he respite til a day[37]
st. 18 But faire escapeth child Thopas	(Guy's escape) & nou3t of flesche atamed is 117(11–12)*
And al it was thurgh *Goddes grace*	Þurch *grace of god* almi3t. þurch goddes help 73(9), 86(5), etc.
st. 19 listeth, lordes, to my *tale* . . .	Heraud so trewe in *tale* 42(1, 3)*
How sir Thopas . . . Prikyng *over* hill *and dale*	He 3ede *ouer* alle bi doun *&* *dale*.
st. 16, 20, 21 With harpe and pipe and symphonye	(Guy's wedding feast) Þer was mirþe & melody, . . . 16(10)* Þer was trumpes & tabour, 17(1–2)* Fiþel, croude, & harpour, . . .
To make hym bothe *game and glee*	Þe bridal hold wiþ *gamen & gle* 14(5)*
'Do come,' he seyde, 'my *mynstrales*,	An al maner menstracie . . . 16(11)*
And geestours for to tellen tales	*Minstrels* of mouþe, & mani dysour 17(5)* To glade þo bernes bliþe.[38]

[35] The duplication in *Guy*, st. 101, 260, of the incident of the horse-slain-by-the-giant is to be noted. Magoun, "The Source of Sir Thopas," *PMLA*, XLII (1927), 833 ff., in arguing for the direct influence of *Libeaus Desconus* on *Thopas*, emphasized the likenesses between the giant combats, the giant's horse-killing, his threats, etc. Undoubtedly Chaucer knew *Libeaus*, but, as *Guy*, *A*, accounts for much more than *Libeaus*, we must believe that it was *Guy*, not the other romance, which exercised the primary influence on *Thopas*. Thopas's love affair is fully accounted for by *Launfal* and *Guy*, *A*, and not by the evil *dame d'amour* of *Libeaus*. (*See* above, n. 31.) The giant in *Guy*, *A*, 126(8)* has a *leman*, a reference which may have served to suggest to Chaucer a connection between the elf-queen and Olifaunt.

[36] This unique reference to a child is supplemented, again only in A, st. 95(1), by the line, *Þis litel kni3t þat stont me by*. Both references appear in connection with a giant combat. Did they suggest Chaucer's humorous use of the appellation *Child?*

[37] Only A, st. 64* and st. 110*, combines in a giant combat story, just as in *Thopas*, st. 17, the familiar phrase, *mot y the*, with the unusual idea of deferring combat.

[38] The stanzaic version fully describes Guy's wedding feast. Like *Thopas*, it combines *game and gle*, *minstrels*, and a list of musical instruments.

st. 24	
And over that a fyn *hawberk*	Þe *hauberk* he hadde was *reuis*[39] . . . 91(4, 6)
Was al ywroght of *Jewes werk*,	In Ierusalem when he was þare.
	Of mailes was nouȝt his *hauberk:* 256(1–2) It was al of anoþer *werk*.
Ful strong *it was of* plate;	*Ful* clere *it was of* mayle[40] 92(3–4)*
As whit *as* is a lilye flour	*As* briȝt *as* ani siluer it was
st. 25	
His sheeld was al of *gold* so reed,	A targe listed wiþ *gold* 93(8), 250(9)*
And therinne was a bores heed,	
A *charbocle* by his syde.	In the frunt stode a *char-bukel* ston. 249(10)
st. 26	
His jambeux were of quyrboilly, . . .	Hose & gambisoun so gode kniȝt schold, 93(6)* Gloues, & gambisoun, & hosen of mayle 250(5) As gode kniȝt haue scholde.
His *helm* of latoun *bright*	(His hauberk) As *briȝt* as ani siluer 92(4–7)*
His brydel *as* the *sonne shoon*,	Þe halle *schon* þerof *as sonne* of glas,. . . His *helme* was of so michel miȝt.
	An *helme* he hadde of michel miȝt 249(7–11)*

[39] This ghost word *reuis* (for *ievis*) was due to the Auchinleck scribe's error in writing an *r* for an *i*, just as in the next line he miswrote *Clarels* for *Charles* (Charlemagne). Cf. my article, "Chaucer's Jewes Werk," *PQ*, XIV (1935), 371 f. I believe that Chaucer, accustomed to the mistakes of Adam Scriveyn and others, perceived the true significance of the word (a not difficult feat in view of the immediately following reference to Ierusalem), and so took over the corrected word into his own text. No other MS of *Guy* uses the word *ieuis*, nor did the source of the Auchinleck MS, if we accept the reading of C, presumably derived from that same source:

On he had a good *hawberke:* C, 8093–94
Hit was of a full good *werke* . . .
When hit com to Ierusalem. 8096

Though the C text here has Chaucer's rime, *hawberk*:*werk*, he could have found this in A, 256 (1–2) in a second account of Guy's arming, and nothing is more certain than the fact that Chaucer blended these two accounts in his parody. *See* n. 41.

[40] Cf. C, 8107, *Hit was so clere and so bryght*, which altogether misses the Chaucerian parallel of A, st. 92(3).

	With a cercle of gold, þat *schon briȝt* As briȝt *as* ani *sonne* it *schon.*[41]
st. 27–28	
Loo, lordes myne, heere is a fit! *If ye wol* any moore of it, . . . *Now* holde youre mouth, *par charitee,*	*Now herken,* & ȝe may here 44(1–2)* In gest, *ȝif ȝe wil* listen & lere . . . *par charitee,* 8(10), 11(8), 30(1), 226(10) etc.
	Listeneþ *now* & sitteþ stille . . . 3997 More ȝe schul here *ȝif ȝe wille* 4790
And *herkneth* to my *spelle.*	*Now* wende we oȝain *to* our *spelle* 4819–4820
Anon I wol yow *telle.*	Þat ȝe me herd er þan *telle*[42] Y schal now *tellen* þe. 246(3)
st. 29	
But sir Thopas, he *bereth the flour*	In warld þai *bere þe flour* 67(12)*
st. 30	
His goode steede al *he bistrood*	*His gode stede he bi-strod* 6411 Þe best / Þat euer miȝt *bistriden stede* 1(5)*
Upon his creest . . . a lilie flour	On þe helme stode *a flour* 250(1) On þe helm . . . þe floures 105(5), 208(5)

The long, foregoing list of quotations needs no further commentary; the individual and the cumulative effect can hardly be denied. By taking account not of merely similar isolated elements, but of *identical elements used in similar combinations* throughout the Auchinleck *Guy of Warwick* and *Sir Thopas,* we are able to trace the specific influence of the one text upon the other. The combinations in question, with few exceptions, occur within the space of a few lines in *Guy, A,* or within such closely allied passages as the two accounts of the hero's love, his two armings, his

[41] Like *Thopas,* st. 24–26, the two accounts of Guy's arming alone combine in A, st. 91–93 and A, 249–250, 256, mention of a Jewish *hauberk, ful . . . it was of plate* (*mayle*), *as whit* (*briȝt*) *as,* a golden *shield,* a charbuncle, *jambeux* (*gambisoun*), a bright *helm, as the sonne shoon.*

Though this decisive list indicates Chaucer's associated borrowings from *Guy, A,* he also borrowed, for *Thopas,* st. 26, certain details from *Thomas of Erceldoune.*

[42] *See* above, n. 27. The insistent repetition of tag phrases in *Guy, A,* is notable. I have given only a few examples of those closest to Chaucer's imitation.

two giant combats.[43] By comparison with all the other extant texts of *Guy* we are able to say that they invariably omit or change some significant element in these combinations,[44] a fact which proves that Chaucer did not use these texts, or rather their fourteenth-century prototypes. From the evidence of *Thopas* alone,[45] it appears that Chaucer made use of the unique Auchinleck *Horn Child*,[46] of the Auchinleck text of *Beves of Hamtoun*,[47] and of the two versions in this volume, one of them unique, of *Guy of Warwick*. He could have found them all together in this one manuscript written by London scribes before 1350. I regret to say that I do not think Chaucer held this medieval omnibus volume in any great 'reverence.' He had read too long, too critically, in one of its longest and most tedious romances. If we recall the Host's rude condemnation of *Sir Thopas:*

> Now swich a rym *the devel I biteche!* 921
> Thy drasty ryming is *nat worth a toord!* 930

we may, for once, feel fairly sure that the comment represents Chaucer's own feeling about *Guy of Warwick* at least. Because, for this condemnation of the parody that is more full of this romance than of any other, he borrows these two phrases straight from the Auchinleck *Guy:*

> *þe deuel biteche* ich ȝou ichon! 5834*[48]
> Þou *nart* nouȝt *worþ a tord!* 3704

---

[43] The chief exceptions are the parallels given for *Thopas*, st. 1, 3, 5. The two accounts of Guy's love are in *Guy, A*, 235–245, 4519–4537, and st. 5–19; the two armings, st. 91–93, 249–252, the two combats, st. 95–134, 255–270.

[44] To save space I have quoted in only a few instances the readings of other MSS, but any one with the various editions of *Guy* in hand and the method in mind that here serves to check MS readings can verify for himself the truth of the assertion. *See* above, n. 10.

[45] In another article I shall consider Chaucer's use of the "Breton Lays of the Auchinleck MS."

[46] *See* above, n. 11.

[47] *See* above, n. 10.

[48] It is characteristic that C omits A, 5834, and for A, 3704, has *nouȝt worthe a mouse tord!*

WAS CHAUCER A LAODICEAN?

ROGER S. LOOMIS
Columbia University

IN an essay on Chaucer and Wyclif published in 1916, Professor Tatlock remarks of the poet, 'He was not such stuff as martyrs are made of, but something of a Laodicean.'[1] With this statement and with the substance of Mr. Tatlock's article as a whole I agree; no one nowadays would present the portly poet, pensioner of three orthodox but far from immaculate kings, composer of love allegories and racy fabliaux, as a zealot, a reformer, a devotee of causes. *Something* of the Laodicean there is about him, but was he wholly lukewarm, wholly neutral in the warfare of principles which went on in his day as it does in ours? Can it be said of him, as it was said of the Laodiceans, 'I know thy works that thou art neither cold nor hot'?

The question is a real one since some of the most eminent of Chaucer scholars and literary critics have expressed the conviction that the poet was wholly indifferent or noncommittal as to moral, social, and religious issues. The authority of Lounsbury lies behind the following statements: 'He looks upon all social and political phenomena of his time from the comparatively passionless position of a man of letters who happened to be also a man of genius.'[2] It was not religious sympathy but intellectual clearness 'that led him to draw his famous portrait of the Parson.'[3] 'For his religious rascals he seems, in fact, to have had a sort of liking.'[4] 'Many of the tenets of Wycliffe found favor with the class with which he had become affiliated. . . . It is certainly only in this way that Chaucer can be characterized as a follower of Wyc-

---

[1] *MP*, XIV (1916), 67.

[2] T. R. Lounsbury, *Studies in Chaucer* (New York, 1892), II, 469.

[3] *Ibid.*, 482.

[4] *Ibid.*, 470.—Lounsbury seems to be deaf to the ironic undertones in "a noble ecclesiast," "a gentil harlot and a kynde."

liffe.'[5] 'He speaks with contempt of the gentility that is based upon position and descent, and not upon character. But his contempt is invariably good-humored and little calculated to provoke resentment.'[6]

Professor Coulton writes in similar vein. 'Where Gower sees an England more hopelessly given over to the Devil than even in Carlyle's most dyspeptic nightmares—where the robuster Langland sees an impending religious Armageddon . . . there Chaucer with incredible optimism sees chiefly a merry England to which the horrors of the Hundred Years' War and the Black Death and Tyler's revolt are but a foil. The man seems to have gone through life in the tranquil conviction that this was a pleasant world, and his own land a particularly privileged spot.'[7]

Professor Root has much the same to say: 'Chaucer is never touched by the spirit of the reformer. . . . He sees the corruption of the Church and clearly recognizes the evil of it; but who is he to set the crooked straight? . . . The good is always admirable; and the evil, though deplorable, is so very amusing. . . . Let us cleave to what is good and laugh goodnaturedly at what is evil.'[8]

Mr. Christopher Dawson observes that Chaucer 'is a courtier and a scholar who looks at the English scene with the humorous detachment of a man of the great world. . . . Chaucer took the world as he found it, and found it good.'[9] Miss Hadow remarks that Chaucer's 'object is to paint life as he sees it, to hold the mirror up to nature, and as has justly been said, "a mirror has no tendency." '[10] Professor Kuhl asserts: 'Chaucer's rollicking humor and his apparent indifference towards existing conditions give point to his philosophy in *Vache* [*Balade de Bon Conseil*].'[11]

In that indispensable and judicious guide to Middle English literature, Professor Wells's *Manual*, we find the following pronouncements: 'His [Chaucer's] work is always the product of

---

[5] *Ibid.*, 479.

[6] *Ibid.*, 473.

[7] G. G. Coulton, *Chaucer and His England*, 2d ed. (London, 1909), p. 11.

[8] R. K. Root, *The Poetry of Chaucer* (Boston, 1906), pp. 28 f.

[9] C. Dawson, *Mediaeval Religion* (New York, 1934), pp. 160 f.

[10] G. Hadow, *Chaucer and His Times* (New York, 1914), p. 156.

[11] *MLN*, XL (1925), 338, n. 90.

poise and control; it is tolerant; it is cool; it is the utterance of an amused spectator, not a participant.'[12] 'Among a nation of writers who had been and were concerned especially for the welfare of their fellows and society, in a period when the literature was responding particularly to the impulse of great political and religious and social needs and movements, Chaucer exhibits scarcely a sign of any reforming spirit, or indeed any direct reflection of those needs and movements.'[13] The dependence of the poet's fortunes on royal and noble patrons may have made wise a diplomatic silence in regard to contemporary conditions; but the silence remains.'[14] 'Slyly he exposed the worldliness and hypocrisy of monk and friar and pardoner and summoner. But it is the individuals that he exposed, not what fostered and lived by such agents. He did not take the matter to heart. . . . He expresses no indignation.'[15] 'As regards religious views Chaucer is as non-committal as he is regarding most others. . . . Much vain effort was formerly expended in arguing that he was a Lollard, or at least of strong Lollard leanings.'[16]

This conception of Chaucer's bland unconcern with the great issues of his day, thus expressed by eminent scholars, is also to be met with in the work of modern critics who, though making no pretense to specialized knowledge, are deservedly influential. Miss Eleanor Chilton writes: 'There is no conviction in reading him . . . that he was ever more than an amused bystander at the comedy.'[17] Aldous Huxley speaks of Chaucer's 'serenity of detachment, this placid acceptance of things and people as they are.'[18] 'Peasants may revolt, priests break their vows, lawyers lie and cheat, and the world in general indulge its sensual appetites; why try and prevent them, why protest? After all, they are simply being natural, they are all following the law of kind. A rea-

---

[12] J. E. Wells, *Manual of Writings in Middle English* (New Haven, 1916), p. 602.

[13] *Ibid.*

[14] *Ibid.*, p. 603.

[15] *Ibid.*, pp. 603 f.

[16] *Ibid.*, pp. 604 f.

[17] E. Chilton, H. Agar, *The Garment of Praise* (New York, 1929), p. 121.

[18] A. Huxley, *Essays New and Old* (New York, 1927), p. 252.

sonable man, like himself, "flees fro the pres and dwelles with soothfastnesse." '[19]

Here, then, is an array of testimony from some of the best critical minds united in the belief that Geoffrey Chaucer looked upon the stormy spectacle of English life with a smiling tolerance, was merely amused by abuses in church and state, was inclined to believe that this was the best of all possible worlds. If cross-examined, he would doubtless be, like Calvin Coolidge's minister, against sin; he would also be in favor of virtue; he pitied suffering in remote times and places; he doubtless expressed with sincerity the more sentimental forms of religious emotion. But, according to this view of his nature, he never was moved to indignation by any contemporary evil, never took sides on any issue of moment, never lifted a finger to set the crooked straight. Lounsbury frankly concedes that the influence of environment and an eye to the main chance controlled Chaucer's pen; Coulton lays the major emphasis on his congenital optimism; Root attributes this unruffled surface to his serene Boethian philosophy; while Huxley finds the explanation in an attitude of fatalistic naturalism. But though these critics disagree widely as to why Chaucer remained a neutral observer of the events of his day, they agree that he was neutral, that he must have seemed to those involved in the struggle a sitter on the fence, a Laodicean.

In this paper I am not at all concerned with rendering a moral judgment on a great genius; I am but slightly concerned with probing into the obscure matter of motives; I am mainly concerned with a question of fact. Did Chaucer show an amiable and universal tolerance in dealing with contemporary men and affairs; or did he on more than one occasion make it quite clear on which side he stood?

There would, of course, be no debate if there were not some evidence to support the view that the poet was a neutral by temperament, or by philosophical conviction, or from a discreet regard for his personal fortunes. He was in daily contact with men on opposite sides of the bitter struggle for power between King Richard and his uncles, and yet, as Professor Hulbert has brought out,[20]

---

[19] *Ibid.*, p. 254.

[20] J. R. Hulbert, *Chaucer's Official Life* (Menasha, 1912), pp. 70 f.

he seems to have kept the friendship of both factions. Professor Kuhl has suggested that Chaucer's selection of the five guildsmen in the General Prolog was dictated by the consideration that these guilds were neutral in the conflict between the victualers and the nonvictualers, and so gave no offense to either party.[21] To retain, as Chaucer did, his pensions and perquisites during the last years of Richard's reign and to have them immediately confirmed by Richard's foe and conqueror implies a prudent neutrality and superlative tact. But, when all this has been said, does Chaucer's character suffer? Was there any reason why in any of these quarrels a man was bound to declare himself? In a conflict of interests, not of principles, a man of sense will try to keep out of trouble and is not to be censured if he can keep on good terms with both sides. If Chaucer accepted favors from men as little admirable as King Richard and John of Gaunt, he might well plead in extenuation that even a man of stern principle, John Wyclif, owed much of his early power and influence to these same questionable supporters. We can hardly expect the poet to be squeamish where the reformer was not. We may be sure that Wyclif's relations to Richard and his uncle involved no downright betrayal of his principles, and, if the question be raised as to Chaucer, we may well give him the benefit of the doubt. There is no evidence that in his public career or in his relationships with public men he was guilty of dishonorable conduct. If, in the midst of these factional struggles and personal rivalries, the diplomat in Chaucer prescribed for him the unheroic role of a friend to both sides, that is all to his credit as a man of sense.

When we consider his attitude on matters of greater moment, there is still some confirmation for the view that he avoided controversy and played safe. His references to the Hundred Years' War and to the Peasants' Revolt are purely casual, and indicate no attitude whatsoever.[22] Here are two topics on which, we may be sure, every tongue was loosed. Chaucer twice served as a soldier in the war, and twice acted as ambassador to bring it to a termination. During the Peasants' Revolt he must have counted

---

[21] *Transactions of the Wisconsin Academy of Sciences*, XVIII, 652 ff.

[22] Like Professor Tatlock, I cannot detect a slurring allusion to the Peasants' Revolt in *Troilus*, IV, vv. 183 f. Cf. *MLN*, L (1935), 277 f.

some of his fellow students at the Inner Temple among the victims, the palace of his friend John of Gaunt was sacked, and the Princess Joan of Kent, who, Miss Galway has given us some reason to believe,[23] was the object of his Platonic devotion, was insulted by the mob. But scholars have repeatedly observed that there is not one serious and specific comment on either the great war or the revolt in all his extant work. Though Minot had written his jingoistic jingles to celebrate the early triumphs of King Edward, and though Gower had loosed his invectives against the insurgent peasantry, Chaucer maintained a neutrality which was certainly not dictated by his personal interests.

In regard to the events of 1381 it is not possible to interpret that silence with certainty. But is it not probable that his failure to match the violent denunciations of his friend Gower is to be explained by the fact that, as a humanitarian and a just man, he knew too well that Jack Straw and his 'meynie' had serious grievances and that the revolt had been crushed only because Richard had broken his solemnly pledged word to the people? On the other hand, the mob had beheaded the innocent archbishop and massacred the harmless Flemings. May not Chaucer have reasoned that, where there was much wrong on both sides, there was no obligation to offer his career as a vain sacrifice to the cause of the oppressed? Once more it is arguable that Chaucer's neutral attitude, even on a great public question, was dictated not by artistic detachment or cowardice, but by a feeling that right and wrong were so mixed that to tell the whole truth would merely bring down on his head the curses of both sides. At any rate, his reticence on the matter proves that he was not one of those gentlemen of property who become more voluble on the sins of the unemployed and the arrogance of labor than on any other subject. And surely it is little short of amazing that, writing the General Prolog within six years of the Peasants' Revolt, this poet of the court should sketch for us a representative peasant, the Plowman, not as a loafer, a scamp, a bolshevik, a sower of class hatred, but as a model of all the social and Christian virtues.

This interpretation of Chaucer's attitude toward the great

[23] *MLR*, XXXIII (1938), 145–199.

rising becomes the more plausible when one realizes that one of his favorite topics is the responsibility of the gentleman to behave like one. As Chesterton has acutely remarked, 'Though Chaucer is called a courtier, it is Chaucer, much more than Langland, who is always saying that true nobility is not in noble birth but in noble behaviour; that men are to be judged by worth rather than rank; and generally that all men are equal in the sight of God. And similarly, though Langland is treated as a revolutionary, it is Langland much more than Chaucer who is always saying that upstarts have seized power to which their birth does not entitle them; that the claims of family have been disregarded through the insolence of novelty, and that men are bragging and boasting above their station.'[24] Not to mention the passage which Chaucer translated from Boethius and the evidence that he had also carefully noted what Dante and Jean de Meun had to say on the subject,[25] he inserted in his Parson's Tale, as Professor Patch has observed in his discerning article on 'Chaucer and the Common People,'[26] remarks not found in Peraldus to the effect that 'of swich seed as cherles spryngen, of swich seed spryngen lordes.'[27] He dragged into the Wife of Bath's Tale a long and vigorous discourse on the text that he is 'gentil that dooth gentil dedis.' He wrote one of his best balades on the same theme. It is, of course, true, as Professor Robinson asserts,[28] that these ideas were official doctrines of the Church. But surely the poet did not reiterate them and go out of his way to introduce them because they were harmless platitudes, but rather because he thought that, if repeated often enough, they might make some impression on the snobs and titled cads whom he counted among his readers. After all, the sentiment is precisely that of Burns's *A Man's a Man for A' That,* which critics have not been wont to treat as a rhetorical commonplace. Was Chaucer less revolutionary than Burns because he harped on the same theme in the fourteenth instead of the eighteenth century?

[24] G. K. Chesterton, *Chaucer* (London, 1932), p. 247.

[25] J. L. Lowes, "Chaucer and Dante's Convivio," *MP*, XIII (1915), 19–27.

[26] *JEGP*, XXIX (1930), 379.

[27] *The Complete Works of Geoffrey Chaucer*, ed. F. N. Robinson (Boston, 1933), p. 300.

[28] *Ibid.*, p. 808.

As for the Great War, though he voiced no judgment on it specifically, he does have a good deal to say about war in general. We must discount the lines in *The Former Age* which proclaim among the blessings of an ideal society that 'No flesh ne wiste offence of egge or spere,' 'No trompes for the werres folk ne knewe.' For other blessings of the Golden Age enumerated in the same poem are a diet of mast, haws, and water of the cold well, and the enthusiasm of the vintner's paunchy son for a vegetable and teetotal diet is open to grave suspicion. But we may take far more seriously the Melibeus. True, Chaucer introduces it jestingly as a little thing in prose. But it is incredible that he should have deliberately set himself at his desk and spent good days and weeks translating a work of edification only in order that he might bore himself and his readers. He did not translate the *Rose* or the *Boethius* or the *Astrolabe* or the Parson's Tale with any such ponderously subtle effort at humor. Chaucer, the humorist, like Mark Twain, Dickens, Thackeray, and many another master jester, had his grave aspect, and was capable of translating a work of instruction for no more recondite a purpose than instruction. Professor Robinson rightly avers[29] that for the poet and his age the Melibeus was an interesting treatment of a very live topic—the practical futility of force, the wickedness of revenge, the beatitude of the peacemaker. We may agree with Professor Cowling that 'its appearance amongst the *Canterbury Tales* seems to indicate that the strain and loss in blood and treasure due to the Hundred Years' War with France had caused the prudence and pacifism of this allegory to appeal to others besides Chaucer.'[30]

The portrait of the Knight in the General Prolog also carries its meaning. As the late M. Legouis has remarked, 'The virtues of his [Chaucer's] Knight, of his Clerk, of his Parson are in fact so many hidden sermons.'[31] In all these we have obviously ideal portraits, and it is noteworthy that the ideal knight as depicted by Chaucer had devoted his military career, incidentally perhaps to

[29] *Ibid.*, p. 13.

[30] G. H. Cowling, *Chaucer* (London, 1927), p. 162.

[31] E. Legouis, *Geoffrey Chaucer*, trans. L. Lailavoix (London, 1913), p. 155.

'his lordes werre,' wherever that may have been, but mainly and specifically to fighting for our faith against the heathen on all fronts. This emphasis was probably deliberate. In the single volume of Wyclifite writings collected by Matthew there are seven direct attacks on war waged by Christians on Christians.[32] Of Wyclif himself, Workman writes that he maintained that wars waged for 'God's justice,' 'in the cause of the Church or for the honour of Christ,' are right, and no other.[33] If Chaucer's listing of the campaigns of the Knight, if the phrases 'foughten for oure feith' and 'again another hethen' are a part of the doctrine implied in the description of the Knight, that doctrine coincides with the doctrine of Wyclif on the subject of war.

Chaucer's attitude toward the Hundred Years' War may also be inferred from his silences. M. Legouis makes the statement, startling but true: 'There is not a single patriotic line in his work.'[34] There is no disparaging reference to Frenchman or Italian or German as such. He was a better Wyclifite, a better Catholic, a better internationalist than the great majority in his day. He believed that Christendom must at least defend itself by the sword against Islam—and what agnostic of today would deplore the victory of Charles Martel at Tours?—but within the bounds of Christendom Chaucer believed profoundly in peace. The mature Chaucer of 1387 must have been convinced of the futility of war, except for some high cause far transcending the territorial pretensions of monarchs, and must have deplored the waste and destruction and barbarity that characterized the conflict between his own people and a people whom he had all the reasons of a poet to admire. His protest he put into the Melibeus and the portrait of the Knight, where his contemporaries, I feel sure, caught his drift more easily than do most of his interpreters today.

Readers or hearers of the General Prolog in the year 1387 would also have felt that on another vital controversy of the time Chau-

---

[32] *English Works of Wyclif*, ed. F. D. Matthew, *EETS* (London, 1890), pp. 73, 91, 99, 100, 132, 152, 176.—The view is not, of course, exclusively Wyclifite. Cf. Gower, *Vox Clamantis*, Bk. III, vv. 663–666, 945–947; Bk. VII, vv. 491 f.

[33] H. B. Workman, *John Wyclif* (Oxford, 1926), II, 28.

[34] Legouis, *op. cit.*, p. 31.

cer was deliberately taking sides and shaping the evidence. Three years after Wyclif's death Lollardy was still powerful and popular in London; though partially suppressed at Oxford, it was still alive there; it found favor with a party of the lesser nobility and knights, including Sir Lewis Clifford, Sir Richard Stury, and other friends of Chaucer's. Now if Chaucer displays any bias in his selection of characters for idealization or satiric treatment, it is in this very matter. I am not going to revive the legend that Chaucer was an avowed Wyclifite and propagandist,[35] nor am I proposing that his attacks on the vices of the clergy proclaim him unorthodox. It has not been brought out, however, so far as I am aware, how heavily the scales are weighted in the General Prolog in favor of the supporters of Wyclif and against the classes who opposed him. Who are the ideal types depicted?

There is the Knight, who has already stood for Chaucer's protest against warfare between Christians. But he was also a member of a class notorious at this time for their support of Lollard preachers and anticlerical doctrines. Under date of 1382 we read that Sir Thomas Latimer, Sir Lewis Clifford, and Sir Richard Stury forced their tenantry to attend Lollard sermons and stood by armed to see that the evangelists were unmolested.[36] In the very year of the General Prolog, 1387, the attack of Pateshull on the morals of the friars pleased, we are told, these same knights, as well as Sir John Clanvowe, Sir William Neville, and Sir John Montague.[37] This group was called the *milites capuciati*, or

---

[35] H. Simon, *Chaucer a Wycliffite, Essays on Chaucer*, Ser. 2, Chaucer Society (1876).

[36] Henry Knighton, *Chronicle* (Rolls Series), II, 181. On the Lollard Knights, cf. Workman, *op. cit.*, II, 380–404, and W. T. Waugh, "The Lollard Knights," *Scottish Historical Review*, XI, 55 ff. Mr. Waugh seems unduly skeptical of the genuine Lollard feeling among these knights. Yet the testimony of contemporary chroniclers, the fact that four of them risked the anger of the king by their support of the radical *XII Conclusions*, the self-accusation in the wills of Clifford and Latimer supply a firm foundation for belief in their sincerity. Montague sheltered Lollards at Shenley, including probably Nicholas Hereford, and removed images from the chapel. Latimer's manor of Braybrook seems to have been a center for the copying of Lollard literature. Such an accumulation of evidence is not to be offset by the fact that some of these men went on crusade or were executors of the wills of the orthodox.

[37] *Chronicon Angliae, 1328–88*, ed. E. M. Thompson (London, 1874), II, 377. Cf. G. M. Trevelyan, *England in the Age of Wycliffe* (London, 1925), p. 327.

'hooded knights,' because they did not doff their hoods at the sacrament of the altar. 'Fuerunt et alii multi milites male scientes de fide catholica.'[38] The Lollard document of 1388 known as the *XXV Points* concludes with the prayer that God will light the hearts of lords to know and destroy the heresies of the official church.[39] The protest to the pope in 1390 against the corruption of the clergy and the usurpations of the papacy might be construed as an answer to this prayer, since it was signed by John of Gaunt, the Earl of Salisbury, and the knights, Clifford and Stury.[40] Clifford, Stury, Latimer, and Montague formed a group of knights who in 1395 attempted to bring the whole issue before open parliament.[41] As late as 1399 Archbishop Arundel warned convocation against certain knights in parliament[42] whose identity is obscured since all the knights formerly prominent had been by this time reduced to silence by royal and ecclesiastical pressure.

There is a special significance in these facts, for five of these most conspicuous Lollard knights were at one time or another members of Richard's privy council: Clifford, Stury, Neville, Clanvowe, and Montague. They were not humble country gentlemen or mere soldiers; they were powers in the land. Moreover, of these five knights all but Montague were Chaucer's close friends.[43] The witness of their contemporaries makes it abundantly clear that knights as a class were suspected of anticlericalism and some were regarded as outstanding supporters of Lollardy during the decade after Wyclif's death. We know that the poet was linked by ties of friendship to leaders of this group. In idealizing the Knight he was not only flattering a class with which he had close associations, but he may have deliberately held up to admiration a class which because of certain prominent members was popularly identified with the cause of Lollardy.

It is, of course, fair to object that Chaucer's Knight had been on a crusade and was going on a pilgrimage—both practices of

---

[38] *Ibid.*

[39] Workman, *op. cit.*, II, 390.

[40] *MLN*, XL (1925), 322 f.

[41] *Annales Ricardi II* (Rolls Series), 173 ff. Workman, *op. cit.*, II, 390 f.

[42] *Annales Henrici IV* (Rolls Series), 290.

[43] Chaucer, *Canterbury Tales*, ed. J. M. Manly (New York, 1928), pp. 40 f.

which Lollards disapproved, and that therefore his author could not have conceived him as in any sense a representative of the cause. It is true, nevertheless, that four conspicuous Lollard knights fought for the faith against the infidel in Tunis in 1390: Clifford, Montague, Neville, and Clanvowe.[44] Montague, it would seem, continued his crusading career in 1391 by service in 'Lettow' and in 'Pruce.'[45] In 1394 or 1395 Clifford joined the Order of the Passion founded for the recovery of the holy places.[46] All these crusading activities, it is important to note, took place while Clifford and Montague were still prominently identified with the Lollard cause and before there were any signs of defection among the other knights. Wyclif himself, we remember, had declared that wars waged in the cause of the Church and for the honor of Christ were right. The crusading career of Chaucer's Knight, though it might have been denounced by Lollard extremists,[47] does not remove from him the associations with Lollardy that attached to his class. On the other hand, that he should promptly on his return from his 'viage' seek the shrine of 'the hooly blisful martir' does disqualify him as a good Wyclifite. For the Reformer and his disciples were consistently opposed to pilgrimages.[48] It cannot be maintained—and I do not maintain—that the Knight was a Lollard. Nevertheless, no matter how orthodox the individual, knights as a class were in the public mind of 1387 tinctured with Wyclifite sympathies; just as in the public mind of today professors as a class are regarded as reds, no matter how large a percentage votes the straight Republican ticket. Chaucer's unrestrained laudation of the Knight might be taken as an expression of sympathy with a suspect class.

This supposition is reinforced by the fact that Chaucer next chooses for serious and unqualified laudation a secular clerk of Oxford. Though nothing identifies him individually as a disciple

---

[44] Workman, *op. cit.*, II, 382, 385. *Scottish Historical Review*, XI, 77.

[45] *Scottish Historical Review*, XI, 73. *DNB* (1921–22), XIII, 652. A. S. Cook in *Transactions of the Connecticut Academy*, XX (1916), 207.

[46] Workman, *op. cit.*, II, 382. *MP*, I (1903), 12. N. Jorga, "Philippe de Mézières," *Bibl. de l'Ecole des Hautes Etudes* (1896), 491.

[47] Wyclif, *Select English Works*, ed. T. Arnold, III (1871), 140 f.

[48] Workman, *op. cit.*, II, 18.

of Wyclif, yet it was the secular clerks of Oxford who till 1382 had been open supporters of his teachings.[49] Though the University in that year condemned the heretical doctrines, and they were studied henceforth surreptitiously, in the western counties in the year 1387 three of Wyclif's foremost disciples, all secular clerks who had been associated with the master at Oxford, Purvey, Hereford, and Aston, were active in propaganda.[50] It is reasonable to suppose that in 1387 a secular clerk of Oxford would still, in spite of all appearance to the contrary, belong to a highly suspect group. And Chaucer portrays for us such a man as a wholly admirable type.

The third idealized figure is the Parson. He is not labeled a Wyclifite; he is not one of the itinerant poor priests; but not only his fellow pilgrims, the Host and the Shipman, smell a 'loller' in the wind, but many a modern scholar as well. Moreover, he never denies the accusation. If there was one fundamental thought characteristic of Wyclif, it was the authority of the Bible and especially the gospels as opposed to the Fathers, philosophers, councils, and all commentators and canonists whatsoever. Dr. Workman writes: 'Wyclif's insistence on the supreme authority of Scripture was not less than that of Luther and won for him at an early date the proud title of 'doctor evangelicus,' while he desired that the title of 'viri evangelici,' 'men of the Gospel,' should be given to his adherents.'[51] How close was the association in orthodox circles between reference to the gospel's authority and heresy, we know from the witness of Margery Kempe, who, when she pleaded before the Archbishop of York that 'the Gospel giveth me leave to speak of God,' was promptly answered by one of the Archbishop's clerks, 'Here wot we well that she hath a devil within her, for she speaketh of the Gospel.'[52] Now three times Chaucer hammers home the point that the Parson took his doctrine from the gospel. He 'Cristes gospel trewely wolde preche.'

---

[49] *Ibid.*, 141 ff.

[50] *Ibid.*, 136, 162, 336.

[51] *Ibid.*, 149 f.

[52] *The Book of Margery Kempe*, ed. W. Butler-Bowdon (London, 1936), p. 189. Cf. Workman, *op. cit.*, II, 150, n. 2, 198.

'Out of the gospel he tho wordes caughte.' 'Cristes loore and his apostles twelve/He taughte, but first he folwed it hymselve.'

In this final couplet there is a further hint that Chaucer intended his ideal priest to be recognized as a Lollard—a hint which no one seems to have publicly exposed though doubtless some scholars have realized its significance. If there is one phrase which occurs inevitably and often monotonously in the English writings of Wyclif and his followers, it is the phrase 'Crist and his apostles.' It is a phrase notably absent from the contemporary writings of the orthodox, though a diligent search would presumably turn up a few examples. But in the literature of Lollardy it is to be found, with variations, as a familiar leitmotif. In the *De Papa* of 1380 Wyclif wrote, for example, in the space of two paragraphs: 'Thes prelatis blasfemen in Crist and in His hooly apostlis'; 'Crist forsok it in word and dede, and bi His lore His apostlis'; 'Crist ordeynede that His apostlis . . . shulden be scaterid'; 'thus may Cristen men lerne bothe of Crist and His apostles.'[53] The so-called *Complaint* of 1382 is full of references to Christ and the apostles.[54] In *The Church and Her Members*, written by Wyclif in the last year of his life, we find: 'Crist . . . movede apostlis to do his dedes'; 'apostlis of Crist'; 'Crist or his apostlis'; 'thus lyvede Crist with his apostlis'; 'so diden Cristis apostlis.'[55] In the anonymous English *De Officio Pastorali* we read: 'Crist and his apostlis never cursiden ne pletiden for ther dette'; 'Crist and his apostlis weren not gredy of worldly godis.'[56] In the anonymous declaration of 1388 the same motif recurs: 'Anticrist, adversary of Jesus Crist and of his apostlis'; 'That Crist and his apostlis durste never do'; 'contrarie ageyne Crist and his apostlis';[57] and so forth and so forth. The same document contains passages describing the perfect priest not unlike Chaucer's: 'Hit is not leefful to a preste for to sette to hire his bysynes of werkis. . . . Lete prestis lif wele that thai be ly3t of worldly men by holy ensaumple, . . . techynge tho gospel, . . . as Seint Jon Crisostome

[53] Wyclif, *Select English Writings*, ed. Winn, pp. 72 f.

[54] Wyclif, ed. Arnold, III, 509–522.

[55] Wyclif, *Select English Writings*, ed. Winn, pp. 121 f., 130, 133, 138.

[56] Wyclif, ed. Matthew, pp. 415, 423.

[57] Wyclif, ed. Arnold, III, 457–459.

wittenessys by techynge taken of Cristis apostilis.'[58] The phrase reëchoes through the Lollard tract *Of Clerks Possessioners.*[59] The text of the *XII Conclusions* put forth by the Poor Priests in 1395 begins thus: 'We, poor men, tresoreris of Christ and his apostles.'[60] In the Lollard tract of 1402, *Jack Upland*, the author sharply demands of the friars, 'Why make ye you so many maisters among you; sith it is agaynst the techinge of Christ and his apostels?'[61] In 1407 Sir William Thorpe, when examined for heresy, declared: 'This foresaid learning of Master John Wycliffe is yet holden of full many men and women the most agreeable learning unto the living and teaching of Christ and his Apostles.'[62] The quotations from this and other documents could be extended to many pages. It is safe to say that when Chaucer spoke of the Parson as teaching Christ's lore and that of his apostles, he left no doubt in the minds of contemporary readers that here was the ideal parish priest conceived according to the Lollard view.

The Parson's later reproof to the Host in the matter of swearing confirms this interpretation.[63] Wyclifite opposition to this practice was notorious.[64] It was, for instance, one of the accusations of heresy against Margaret Backster in 1428 that she warned her neighbor to abstain from all swearing, either by God or by any saint.[65] The Parson's Prolog, probably composed after the

[58] *Ibid.*, 492.

[59] Wyclif, ed. Matthew, pp. 121–139.

[60] Workman, *op. cit.*, II, 391.

[61] Chaucer, *Complete Works*, ed. W. W. Skeat, supplementary vol., *Chaucerian and Other Pieces* (Oxford, 1897), p. 196.

[62] A. W. Pollard, *Fifteenth Century Prose and Verse* (Westminster, 1903), p. 119.

[63] Chaucer, ed. F. N. Robinson, p. 90. Cf. Workman, *op. cit.*, II, 28; G. G. Coulton, *Medieval Panorama* (Cambridge, New York, 1938), p. 466. Tatlock seems to be doubly mistaken when he asserts that the Shipman's calling the Parson a "loller" because of this reproof has no significance, for it is not the Shipman but the Host who uses the word, and the Lollard objection to swearing, as the following notes indicate, was notorious. (*MP*, XIV, 259, n. 2.)

[64] Workman, *op. cit.*, II, 27 f. Pollard, *op. cit.*, pp. 149–153. Wyclif, ed. Arnold, III, 332, 483. The objection to swearing was, of course, not confined to Lollards. Cf. Chaucer, ed. Robinson, p. 183; Coulton, *Medieval Panorama*, pp. 465 f.; *The Book of Margery Kempe*, ed. W. Butler-Bowdon, pp. 64, 150, 186, 189; G. R. Owst, *Literature and Pulpit in Medieval England* (Cambridge, 1933), pp. 414–425.

[65] Coulton, *Medieval Panorama*, p. 707.

disintegration of the Lollard party in 1395, still contains two suggestions of Lollard puritanism. Bluntly, the priest declares in response to the Host's invitation, 'Thou getest fable noon ytoold for me'; and later, 'I kan not geeste "rum, ram, ruf," by lettre, / Ne, God woot, rym holde I but litel bettre.'[66] Both these views regarding the use of 'fables' and of rime in sermons can be matched in the Lollard *De Officio Pastorali*, in which we read: 'Certis that prest is to blame that shulde so frely haue the gospel, and leeueth the preching therof and turnyth hym to mannus fablis. . . God axith not dyuysiouns ne rymes of hym that shulde preche.'[67] But though Chaucer consistently maintains the definitely evangelical coloring of his Parson through the Parson's Prolog, the Tale one must acknowledge is wholly conventional and orthodox. Here is no talk of 'Cristes lore and his apostles twelve,' but much concerning the seven deadly sins and the formalities of confession—topics sanctioned, even specifically prescribed, by the hierarchy.[68] Unfortunately, there is no clue to the date of the Parson's Tale, and we are left to conjecture for an explanation of the incongruity between all Chaucer had led us to expect of the man and all that finds expression in the sermon. One conjecture which may be as good as any other is that the sermon belongs to the last years of the century, when Lollardy was patently a lost cause. Chaucer was approaching the mood in which he arranged for his interment in Westminster Abbey and wrote his *Retractions*.[69] This was no time for him to round off his *magnum opus* with a heretical sermon, which would, even if he felt inclined, get him into trouble and might rouse an indignant hierarchy to burn every copy of the *Canterbury Tales*.

If Chaucer's relation to Lollardy followed the evolution thus outlined, it would parallel that of two of his oldest friends, Sir Richard Stury and Sir Lewis Clifford. As has been noted above, under the date of 1382 they are named as active supporters of the

---

[66] Chaucer, ed. Robinson, p. 272.

[67] Wyclif, ed. Matthew, pp. 438, 532. Cf. Wyclif, ed. Arnold, III, 147.

[68] D. Wilkins, *Concilia Magnae Britanniae et Hiberniae*, III (London, 1737), 59.

[69] G. G. Coulton, *Chaucer and His England*, 2d ed. (London, 1909), pp. 71–73. Tatlock in *PMLA*, XXVIII (1913), 521 ff.

poor priests; and thirteen years later, in 1395, they are still listed as advocates of the extremist *XII Conclusions*. But Stury was promptly forced to recant under royal pressure, and soon after died.[70] Clifford in 1402 not only recanted but also informed on his associates in the movement; and in his will, two years later, spoke of himself as a false traitor to God, unworthy to be called a Christian man, and directed that his body be buried in the furthest corner of the churchyard, unmarked by any stone whereby one might know where his stinking carrion lay.[71] These two intimates of the poet fell away after 1395 from a movement that had become dangerous. Their motives we do not know and cannot judge. The difference between the decidedly free-spoken Chaucer of the General Prolog and the entirely correct Chaucer of the Parson's Tale and the *Retractions* may be attributable likewise to the ebb of the Wyclifite tide. But he who would apportion the degree of policy and the degree of sincere contrition which motivated Chaucer's change of front would be a bold man.

The General Prolog of the *Canterbury Tales*, then, furnishes three wholly ideal portraits; of these one is plainly sketched in accordance with Wyclif's ideas, and the other two represent members of classes known to be sympathetic to his program. On the other hand, the Prolog furnishes portraits of several rascals. The rascality of the Miller and the Merchant is briefly and lightly touched upon; that of the Shipman is offset by admiration for his hardihood and seamanship; and that of the Reeve and the Manciple is offset by admiration for the cleverness with which they cheated their wealthy masters. But there are three rascals whom Chaucer seems to have labored to make morally repulsive—the Friar, the Summoner, and the Pardoner—and the two latter he made physically loathsome as well. The Friar would cajole a farthing out of a widow in barefoot penury. The Summoner's face was covered with white-headed pustules, and he was so generous that he would let a man keep his doxie for a whole year in return for a quart of wine. The Pardoner sold sham relics of Our Lady and St. Peter, was a pompous hypocrite, had glaring eyes,

---

[70] Workman, *op. cit.*, II, 400.

[71] *Ibid.*, 402 f. Chaucer, *Canterbury Tales*, ed. Manly, p. 657.

and a goatlike voice; 'I trowe he were a geldyng or a mare.' If contempt and loathing can be expressed in words, they are found in these three portraits. Now, of course, satire on clerical scoundrels was no monopoly of the Lollards; Catholics in good standing were loud in their denunciation of these same traitors to the faith.[72] But the fact remains that Wyclifite literature is full of attacks on the mendicant orders, ecclesiastical courts, and the veneration of relics. As Professor Tatlock puts it: 'Everybody assailed the clergy, but the reformer's club and the poet's rapier made for the same points; there is a striking resemblance in what they say, and they clearly thought much the same.'[73]

The impression made by the General Prolog on the public of Chaucer's day may perhaps be appreciated if we imagine a novel published in 1936, say, in which three characters were idealized—a Middle Western farmer, a college professor, a Democratic politician of liberal views—and three characters were pilloried—a journalist in the employ of Hearst, a syphilitic banker, a homosexual stockbroker. Though the novel contained no downright New Deal propaganda, would a modern reader have any doubt as to where the author's sympathies lay? Neither can there be much doubt as to where Chaucer's sympathies lay when he wrote the Prolog of the *Canterbury Tales*.

Finally, there is a subject which Chaucer thrice treats in passages for which he has no source and in which he seems to be expressing his own mind. That subject is the use and the abuse of the royal power. The balade, *Lack of Steadfastness*, which is undeniably a humble remonstrance on the part of the poet to his sovereign, Richard II, depicts in general terms the lawlessness and confusion of the times, and calls on the king to show forth his sword of castigation, dread God, do law, and wed his folk again to steadfastness. Again, since in the Prolog to the *Legend of Good Women* we find Alceste urging a course of mercy and

[72] G. R. Owst, *Literature and Pulpit in Medieval England* (Cambridge, 1933), pp. 216–286. G. G. Coulton, *Five Centuries of Religion* (Cambridge, 1927), II, 504–660. D. Chadwick, *Social Life in the Days of Piers Plowman* (Cambridge, 1922), pp. 7–37. J. Gower, *Confessio Amantis*, Prolog. C. Dawson, *Mediaeval Religion* (New York, 1934), pp. 185–189. J. B. Fletcher in *PMLA*, LIII (1938), 971–988.

[73] *MP*, XIV, 264.

justice on the God of Love, who is also a king, many scholars have been inclined to see here another tactful reminder to Richard. Such an interpretation does not necessarily involve any complete identification of the God of Love with Richard or of Alceste with any queen or princess. When we note that Alceste recommends to the god-king some courses of action which seem to have little to do with the immediate situation—for example, to keep his lords in their rank, to do right to both poor and rich, not to listen to envious tattlers[74]—then we may reasonably surmise that the poet had in mind not only the fantastic and half-humorous situation of his dream, but also the real situation of the realm. The poem was to be sent to Queen Anne; doubtless her husband would see it too, and it is quite like Chaucer to offer a little advice to his king in a form which might prove palatable and which could surely not give offence.

A few years before, in what was to be the Knight's Tale, Chaucer had created a situation which had marked analogies with the scene of Alceste's intercession for the poet.[75] Theseus, it will be remembered, discovers Palamon and Arcite in mortal combat, is resolved to execute them, is swayed to clemency by the entreaties of his queen and Emelye, and then reflects, 'Fy / Upon a lord that wol have no mercy. . . . That lord hath litel of discrecioun / That in swich cas kan no divisioun, / But weyeth pride and humblesse after oon.'[76] Here it is possible that Chaucer is gently hinting that Richard is doing well to heed the pleas of Queen Anne for a policy of magnanimity and mercy. We know, then, that Chaucer undertook to advise his sovereign openly once; and it is more than likely that in these two other passages he sought in more indirect ways to guide the royal will into the right channels.

The facts and the inferences I have adduced in this paper justify our rejecting any notion of Chaucer as either a sycophantic timeserver, who merely echoed the sentiments of his patrons and associates, or of a cheerful philosopher who looked upon the follies

---

[74] Chaucer, ed. Robinson, pp. 578 f. Cf. H. R. Patch in *JEGP*, XXIX (1930), 380 f.

[75] Tatlock in *Studies in Philology*, XVIII (1921), 419 f.

[76] Chaucer, ed. Robinson, p. 40.

and struggles of mankind with an amused detachment. Needless to say, he was no martyr for any cause; he never, in modern parlance, 'stuck his neck out' too far or kept it out after it became dangerous. Perhaps it was his modesty which led him to feel that nobody would be much concerned or much the better if he sacrificed his pensions or his person for a principle. In the *Balade de Bon Conseil*, addressed to the son-in-law of his Lollard friend, Clifford, a poem in which he seems to have distilled the essence of his practical philosophy, he frankly advises Vache not to meddle in situations where he can only harm himself and achieve nothing. 'Stryve not as doth the crokke with the wal. . . . Be war also to sporne ayeyns an al.' But Chaucer does not counsel his younger friend to remain a detached spectator of life if we are to judge by his own practice. He did speak out, we have seen, on various controversial subjects more than once, presumably when he thought his efforts would not prove vain. The line in the same balade, 'Tempest thee noght al croked to redresse,' should therefore be read with some stress on the 'al.' For certainly on some occasions Chaucer did exert himself to set the crooked straight.

If in the light of the foregoing facts any one chooses to point the finger of scorn at Chaucer as something of a Laodicean and a trimmer, if any one living in a country where speech on political and religious questions is still free chooses to adopt an attitude of moral superiority to a poet of the Middle Ages who observed for the most part a politic discretion in his utterances, 'lordynges, by your leve, that am not I.'

SOME ENGLISH WORDS FROM THE 'FASCICULUS MORUM'

FRANCES A. FOSTER
Vassar College

THE Franciscan collection of sermon material known as the *Fasciculus Morum*[1] gives evidence of the popular acceptance in the early fourteenth century of a score or so of words, some not found elsewhere so early, and others recorded only once in the first half of the century. They are largely colloquial English, such as would be readily intelligible to unlearned audiences in provincial towns of England, for the friar author was adapting his matter to the poor and ignorant, both in the verses that he occasionally introduced and in the phrases that sometimes translate a Latin term and sometimes round out an anecdote. Although all the manuscripts are late, only Bodley 332 being of the fourteenth century,[2] the treatise was, I think, composed in Edward the Second's reign, as Dr. Little indicated: the king's shield with three leopards would not be so described after Edward III assumed the lilies of France in 1337; the mention of St. Thomas Aquinas without the Saint would have been normal before his canonization in 1323; and the new words *schavaldours* and *riflouris* are used, not with the generalized meaning familiar to Wyclif and Langland, but specifically pointing to the gentleman brigandage of the decade after Bannockburn as a new and deplorable situation.[3] The evidence as to authorship is of no great

[1] The treatise is described by Dr. A. G. Little in *Studies in English Franciscan History* (Manchester, 1917), pp. 139–157.

[2] To Dr. Little's list of manuscripts (*op. cit.*, pp. 139–141) should be added the following: Magdalen College Oxford 13 (extracts); Cambridge University Dd. 10. 15; Harley 1316 (beginning and end missing); Lincoln Cathedral A. 2. 13, and A. 6. 19 (extracts); Edinburgh University 82; Cardiff Public Library 3. 174 (formerly Phillipps 9419, sermons only); and Madrid University, Faculty of Law 110, now shelved as 116^{30}.3.

Corrections in the list are: Rawl. C. 670 and Corpus Christi are after 1400; British Museum Additional 6716 and Durham University contain extracts; Vatican Ottoboni is no. 626. The Würzburg MS is now in the J. Pierpont Morgan Library, New York, no. 298.

[3] *Ibid.*, pp. 142–144, and *see* below, pp. 154–156.

help in establishing the date: Robertus Selke or Silke is named as compiler at the end of five MSS;[4] one of these, Laud Misc. 213, also has at the top of the first folio in a later hand an ascription to Johannis Spiser; and the Madrid MS reads: 'Explicit fasciculus morum quem composuit frater Ricardus de pissis magister in theologia de conuentu salopie custodie Vigorniensis prouincie anglie.'[5] It is not clear whether the author was Robert or John or Richard, but the Madrid MS ascription to a Shrewsbury friar agrees with the place names Coventry and Shrewsbury in the *exempla*, and confirms Dr. Little's suggestion that it came from the custody of Worcester.[6] Perhaps Richard of Pisa composed the treatise and Robert Selke, who might be the Robert Sulks or Sellack O. F. M. ordained acolyte and subdeacon in 1371,[7] prepared the Table.

The words listed below are sparsely represented by fourteenth-century quotations in the Oxford Dictionary. They are cited from Rawlinson Poetry C. 670, with modern capitals and punctuation. Although the approximate date and provenance of the author are known, the form of the English words, modified by the scribes of later manuscripts, cannot be accepted as original; but we can feel confident that these words were already familiarly current in the west of England during the first quarter of the fourteenth century. Those from the English verses are likely to be earlier, since many of the verses are probably thirteenth-century material incorporated in treatise.

BABEWEIS (v.r., babways, babaues)

Sicut vbi pictores formant aliquas ymagines qui dicuntur *Babeweis* in parietibus; aliquos enim illorum formant cum facie hominis et cum corpore leonis, aliquos eciam cum facie hominis et residuo corporis asini, et alios cum capite hominis et cum parte posteriori vrsi, et sic de singulis (f. 109r).

This word is from Old French *baboye*, a grimace (Godefroi), with a meaning nearer 'baboynes,' *Purity* 1409; *NED* cites mediaeval Latin *babuinare*, 'to paint marginal figures in MSS.'

---

4 Laud Misc. 213 and 568, Corpus Christi, Durham University, Linc. Cath. A. 2. 13.

5 Miss Ruth Dean kindly sent me notes on this MS.

6 Little, *op. cit.*, p. 146.

7 *Ibid.*, p. 141.

BYLE, face

Dum enim aliquis talis mundanus fictus amicus ab aliquo desiderat dileccionem, similat, blanditur, adulatur, sed habito optento dicunt illud anglice:

Now ich haue þat I wyle,
Goddus grame on þy byle (f. 40v).

Compare the contemporary line: 'Ne triste no man to hem, so false theih beth in the bile' (*Poem temp. Edw. II*, line 353, cited in *NED* under *bill*, sb² 2).

ELUENLONDE

. . . dicunt se videre reginas pulcherimas et alias puellas tripudiantes cum domina Diana choreas ducente, dea paganorum, que in nostro vulgari dicuntur *elues*. Et credunt quod tales possunt tam homines quam mulieres in alias transformare naturas et secum ducere in *eluenlonde*, vbi iam, vt dicunt, manent illi athlete fortissimi, sicut Onewyne et Wade (f. 121v; printed from Eton MS 34 by Dr. Little, *op. cit.*, p. 230).

This reference to Eluenlonde is a little later than *Guy of Warwick* (A) 3862 (*NED*). Dr. Little, who printed this passage from Eton MS 34 in *Studies in English Franciscan History*, pp. 230–231, was uncertain about *Onewyne* (the reading of six MSS; others read Onwyn, Vnwyn(e, Onewone, Onewene, Oweyn, Euelkine, Queywne); it may be a misreading for Oweyn of *St. Patrick's Purgatory*, though no reliance can be placed on Caius College MS 71, which is the only MS with that reading; or it may be a name suggested by Annwvyn (Hades) in the story of Pwyll, Prince of Dyved (*Mabinogion*, Everyman edition, pp. 14–17). Onewene is named as a tavern keeper in E. Powell's *The Rising in East Anglia* (1896), p. 11. In a fifteenth-century expanded version of the *Fasciculus*, Onewyne and Wade are omitted and 'Rex Arturus cum suis militibus' substituted (Corpus Christi Oxford 218, Lincoln College 52, and Edinburgh University 82).

FARE-WELLE ÞOU HADDEST

Distributor autem elemosynorum inferius in cista ponit delicata et pinguia et superius grossiora. Ribaldi autem ex auiditate discrecionem non habentes precurrunt et de grosso pane porcionem accipiunt. Senes vero et humiles quorum est rex exitus ex prouidencia metiri gratis se subtrahunt expectantes in fine dulciora acceptura; quod videntes alii dolent quod ita auidi fuerunt sed supervacue quia si iterum petant beneficium, vacui tamen recedunt et eis dicetur: 'Fare welle þou haddest' (f. 85v).

FOR-SKYPPERS, *see* Over-hyppers

FREDAY

Et nota quod dies passionis fuit sexta feria, que anglice dicitur *Fryday:* et merito mutatur *i* in *e* vt ita dicatur *Freday*, quia in illa die vt dictum est, de seruitute diaboli nos eripuit et liberos ad celestia regna reddidit (f. 45r).

Compare the thirteenth-century Franciscan sermon treatise in Rawlinson MS. C. 534: 'et hec pena inflicta fuit die ueneris qui anglice dicitur *Fryday*, quia in illo die liberalis fuit et nos liberos fecit' (f. 18v).

FYCHES

. . . per vestes (v.r. vesces) anglice *fyches* (v.r. fetchys) intelligvntur illi quibus dicitur 'In carcere fui.' Nam sicut istud granum est intollerabilius ad gustandum, sic carcer ad sustinendum (f. 40v).

Wyclif translates Isaiah xxviii, 25: 'Barly, and myle, and ficche (1388 fetchis) in ther coestes.' (*NED*)

GLODIER

Inuidus . . . bene comparatur cuidam reparatori vasorum qui dicitur *Tynker* (v.r. tynkeler) vel *glodier*, qui transiens per domos et villas hinc et inde [vbi] pulcra vasa aurea et argentea, enea et lignea aspicit, de illis non curat nec sibi de aliquo placent, sed cum viderit ollam, cacabum, patellam, ciphum aut discum laceratum et confractum, statim gaudet et inde sperat sibi aliquid lucrari (f. 33r).

Tynekere is cited in the *NED* from a tax assessment of 1265, and not again till *Piers Plowman*. *Glodier* is, as Professor R. J. Peebles suggested to me, probably an error for *glewer* which occurs in the *Cath. Angl.*, 160/1, Latin 'glutinarius.'

GOBYLYN

. . . hominibus qui solebant ire de nocte pro suis amasiis querendis complendis, quod vt pluries accidit casus iste: quando enim inceperunt iter suum versus aliquem locum precogitatum quod quasi subito quasi acrisia seducti circuierunt erratice per totam noctem quoddam nemus vel manerium, semper credentes in recto itinere transire. . . . Sed tandem lucente aurora diei perpendebant se nichil perfecisse in via quam principaliter intendebant. Vnde cum sic quasi attoniti et cogitati considerabant se esse delusos, audierunt iuxta se quendam strepitum ac si esset derisio cuiusdam inuisibilis, qui secundum aliquos est quidam demon qui vulgariter dicitur *gobylyn* (f. 144r).

The *Gobelinus* appears in France as early as the twelfth century (Du Cange); in England he is mentioned in *A Song against the Retinues of the Great People* (Camden Soc., 1839), p. 238.

GOULES

Accipite scutum fidei in quo scuto non incongrue possunt depingi arma illustrissimi regis Anglie: ipse enim vt videtis gestat scutum de minio, *goules*, cum tribus leopardis transeuntibus de auro puro et bene. Nam per illud scutum in *goules* intelligo ardentem amorem et caritatem . . . (f. 119^{v}) Scutum autum in se erit purpureum cum leone argenteo rampante in medio cum corona aurea, ac in pectore eius vnam rosam habebit de minio, id est *goules* gestante (f. 149^{r}).

Goules was of course familiar in French; (see another shield of Christ: 'Son esku fu blaunk, estencellé de goules,' in *An Allegorical Romance on the Death of Christ*, printed by Wright as an appendix to his edition of Pierre de Langtoft's *Chronicle* [Rolls, II, 430]); but it is not till the time of *Gawayn and the Green Knight* that the term was again recorded in English: 'þe schelde, þat was of schyr goulez' (619).

MARL

. . . diligens preparacio terre . . . Debet primo comburi igne contricionis et postea arari vomere confessionis . . . postea debent trunci et male herbe eradicari, et tunc apponi alia terra fertilis et pinguis, anglice *marl* (f. 115^{v}).

NED does not record the word before 1372.

MOWE ON THE MONE

Sicut talis tirannus semel cuidam simplici dixit propter terram suam: 'Voueo,' inquit, 'deo terram illam mihi vendes, dabis aut permutabis, vel tu facies *a mowe on the mone*, hoc est, tu eris suspensus per collum immediate (f. 31^{v}).

The French expression 'E me firent trestuit la moe' (*Roman de la Rose*, 8077, Littré) was familiar in fourteenth-century England: 'He makketh the a mouwe' (*Political Songs*, Camden Soc., p. 339). The *Fasciculus* phrase is different in effect, and seems to be an early example of the jesting references to hanging so frequent in Shakespeare.

OVER-HYPPERS AND OVER-LEPERS

Longe-slepers and ouer-lepers
For-skyppers and ouer-hyppers
I holde luþer hyne,
I am noȝt heren ne þey ben myne;
But þey sone amende thay shullen to helle pyne (f. 90^{r}).

The Rawlinson text is better than that printed by Dr. Little (*Studies in English Franciscan History*, p. 153). The three compounds *over-lepers*, *for-skyppers*, *over-hyppers* refer not, as Dr.

Little's note would imply, to dancing, but to the garbling of the liturgy by lazy priests:

de mane nimis dormire et ad ecclesiam indissolute venire, ibique indistincte officium psallere, sincopando, et festinando. . . . (*Ibid.*)

The verb *overhippen* is similarly used in Robert of Brunne's *Chronicle:*

For Mayster Wace þe Latyn alle rymeś
Þat Pers ouerhippis many tymes (Rolls, 64).

The other two words occur in a fifteenth-century manuscript quoted by Skeat in his note to *Piers Plowman*, C, XIV, 123. The lines are not original with the author, for Mr. R. H. Robbins informs me that they are found in the thirteenth-century Trin. Coll. Camb. MS 323, f. 28r.

POKET

. . . quidam frater tali fornicarie respondit: 'Vere, filia,' dixit, 'ipse qui formauit istud sacculum hoc modo supra ventrem tuum pessimus scissor fuit, *for schamely hyt poket*' (f. 101v and repeated with little change 139r).

Poket is a later occurrence of the verb *powȝe* found in Robert of Gloucester: 'þe tailors corue so moni peces uor is robe ne ssolde powȝe,' where the XV century Digby MS 205 reads 'poke' (Rolls, 6394). It is a different word from Chaucer's 'He poked John' (Reeve's Tale, 249).

POKORELLI

De isto ergo lapide beloculo . . . facit sibi diabolus lapidem molarem quo scilicet vtuntur fabri . . . sed illi qui hunc lapidem vertunt sunt tales pokorelle (v.r. pokorelli), semper ad malum instigantes dicendo: 'Expelle talem de domo aut ciuitatem' (f. 32v).

Bromyard calls Pokerellus the sacristan of hell; *see* G. R. Owst, *Literature and Pulpit in Medieval England* (Cambridge, 1933), p. 394.

RYFLOURS

See the passage quoted under *Schavaldours*. The earliest *NED* reference is in 1326 (*Annales Paulini* Rolls, I, 321), when *Rifflinge* and *Riffleres* are recognized as new terms for the London lawlessness which paralleled that in the North. Godefroi cites the verb *riffler* from thirteenth-century French. Half a century later the word was so perfectly naturalized in England that the upcountry Coveytise says:

'I wende ryflynge were restitucioun' quod he 'for I lerned neuere rede on boke,
And I can no Frenche in feith' but of the ferthest ende of Norfolke.'
(*Piers Plowman*, B-text, V, 238).

SCHAVALDOURS

Et nota quod inter omnes homines Anglici possunt deo regraciari propter speciale priuilegium quod habent. Dicitur enim quod in Hibernia et Wallia bene inueniuntur latrones qui vaccas, boues et alia pecora vicinorum furantur, propter quod latrones aperte dicuntur. Sed in Anglia laudetur deus non sic: sed quod reuera generosi inter nos dicuntur Schaildors, ryflors; tales enim frangunt thesauros magnorum, asportant bona, abigant pecora, spoliant religiosos, nec inde conscienciam habent, sed summe gaudent quando abbatem priorem vel alium monachum spoliare possunt et dicunt: 'Certe voluntas dei fuit quod talis rusticus monachus aut frater hodie nobis occurrit.' Vnde illis videtur quod quicquid fecerunt iuste faciunt et cum ratione (f. 73ᵛ).

As Dr. Little notes (*op. cit.*, pp. 143–144) in pointing out the importance of *schavaldours* for dating the *Fasciculus*, the word first comes into prominence about 1317 with reference to border raiders in the northern counties. Actually it is first recorded in a complaint against the acts of Andrew de Harcla (or Harclay) and his brother at Carlisle in 1319 (*Cal. Doc. Scotland*, III, 127). But Robert de Graystanes, a monk of Durham, writing some time before 1336 recalls the murder in 1312 of 'quendam schavaldum vel praedonem, Johannem de Wardal nomine, sel Regi familiarem' (*Historia Dunelmensis*, Surtees Soc. [1839], p. 94; and *Calendar of the Patent Rolls*, 1307–1313, p. 542); and Sir Thomas Grey, whose father held the castle of Norham in these troublous times, writes of *schavaldours* in connection with the abduction of the Lady Clifford in 1315 (*Scalacronica*, tr. Maxwell [Glasgow, 1907], p. 65; *CPR*, 1313–1317, p. 422). Probably the most famous band was that headed by Sir Gilbert de Middleton and Walter de Seleby, which robbed two cardinal delegates and the bishop-elect of Durham on September 1, 1317. Sir Thomas Grey attributes the act to the anger of Gilbert because the king had arrested his cousin Adam de Swynbourne for too frank speech about conditions on the Marches, supposedly after February 22, 1317 (*Scalacronica*, p. 60; *CPR*, 1313–1317, p. 687). Both Sir Thomas Grey's father and the monk of Durham were in a position to know the circumstances, but complaints of Gilbert's violence go back to October, 1313, when he was with the garrison of Berwick (*Cal. Doc. Scotland*, III, 65). He must have been at least tolerated by the Earl of Pembroke, since he was custodian of Mitford Castle under him (*Hist. Dun.*, p. 100; *CPR*, 1313–1317, p. 254); but he seems to have been of the Earl of Lancaster's party, since he went into the Cathedral of Durham to confer with him after the robbery (*Hist. Dun.*, p. 101; and T. F. Tout, *The Place of the Reign of Edward II in English History* [1914], p. 114). Among Gilbert's followers were many adherents of Lancaster (*CPR*, 1317–1321, pp. 233–235); four men who owed their pardon to Pembroke (*ibid.*, p. 117), and one to Sir Thomas Grey (*CPR*, 1321–1324, p. 209). When Gilbert was captured at Mitford Castle in 1318, his comrade Walter de Seleby escaped to the Scots and fought under Robert Bruce; with the accession of Edward III, he returned to England and was employed in responsible posts (*Walsingham*, Rolls, I, 152–153; *CPR*, 1327–1330, p. 36; *Cal. Doc. Scotland*, 1329, p. 177; 1346, p. 265; 1357, p. 308).

From these details, to which others might be added, it is clear that *schavaldours* before the time of Wyclif referred not to wasters in general, but to groups of landed gentry in the north of England who made flagrant raids in the years 1313–1319. And the *Fasciculus* with its ironic reference to contemporary conditions seems to be close to those years. Half a century later the word had lost its local associations, as in Wyclif's 'mynstralis or shaualdours' (*Wks.* [1880], p. 210, cited in *NED*).

The origin of the word is not clear; its most common form is *schavald(o)urs* (the French petition of 1319, *Scalacronica*, and many MSS of the *Fasciculus*); Knighton uses *shavaldres*, and two MSS of the *Fasciculus* have the shortened forms *shaldours* and *schaildors*. The Latin chroniclers read *savaldores* (Trokelowe), *schavaldos* (*Hist. Dun.*), and *schaveldarios* (Murimuth). Perhaps it is from old French *cheveler*, *caveler*, depilare (Godefroi).

SMACKYNG

Ronde in schapynge,
  þynne in þe bakynge
Whyte in the seynge
Swete in the smackyng (f. 88r).

The meaning 'tasting' is established by the Latin that follows: 'Per gustus dulcedinem denotatur . . . '

TELSTERS, TILESTERRIS, etc.

. . . incantores qui artem suam verbis exercent, anglice *telsters*, quicum carminibus et aliis miseriis suis sanitatem promittunt (f. 121r; printed in Little, *op. cit.*, p. 228, from Eton MS 34).

NED cites from a fifteenth-century list in Wright-Wülcker, 582/22: '*Fascennina, i. femina que novit incantare*, a tylyester'; and *see* 582/4.

VNBOLDESTE

When þou þy lyfe vp-holdeste
þynke wan þou arte oldyste
And do gode at þe ȝate;
When þou with deth vnboldeste
[Thou shalt not they thow woldest]
For þan is al to late (f. 114r).

The first line should read 'Man þat lyfe etc.'; and the missing fifth line is supplied from Laud Misc. 213. *NED* cites the adjective *unbeald* 897, and *vnbalde* 1205. The vb. occurs twice in *Le Regret de Maximian:* ' . . . keldeþ / mi bodi ounbeldeþ,' and ' . . . helde / þat makeþ me forto ounbelde' (*English Lyrics of the Thirteenth Century*, ed. Carleton Brown [1932], pp. 94–95); and in *The Seven Sages of Rome:* 'Seþþe þe elde / Biginneȝ so to vnbelde' (Auchinleck MS, line 606, *EETS*, Or. Ser., 191, 1933).

THE DRAMATIC UNITY OF THE 'SECUNDA PASTORUM'

HOMER A. WATT
New York University

CONSIDERED as effective drama many of the English miracle plays are, it must be admitted, pretty sorry stuff. Indeed, they could hardly be otherwise. The essential story was dictated by biblical material that did not always offer a dramatic conflict. In transferring this material from Bible to play the anonymous authors were concerned primarily with the task of putting brief episodes into dialogue form and not with that of developing action, conflict, characters. Where they tried to season the playlet with contemporary elements, they found themselves cramped by the necessity of sticking essentially to the biblical episodes. As a result there is often a lack of unity and economy in the plays, and the added bits of contemporary realism are foreign to story and mood. The entire effect, in brief, is agglutinative, as though the authors were torn between a responsibility to reproduce the biblical originals and a desire to entertain the audience by odd items of bickering among characters, monologue acts, and occasional slapstick stuff wedged into the play to provide entertainment but totally unrelated to the main biblical action. So Cain's boy in the Towneley play of *The Killing of Abel* is an obvious intruder, as is also Iak Garcio of the first shepherds' play of the same cycle. When, therefore, one of the miracle plays appears on analysis to be an exception, it is a pleasure to demonstrate the extent to which it anticipates those dramatic techniques that emerge in the best work of the Tudor dramatists. Not all of the Tudor playwrights, as a matter of fact, in spite of their acquaintance with classical models, have displayed the technical ability of the 'Wakefield Master,' anonymous author of the justly praised *Secunda Pastorum* of the Towneley cycle.

Like his dramatic descendants, the Tudor playwrights, the Wakefield Master was under the pressure of tradition, but, like the best of them, he succeeded in subduing the tradition to his dramatic needs. What, in a nativity play, was his dramatic problem? He was committed, certainly, to a dramatic representation of the shepherd story from the second chapter of Luke, and this commitment he fulfilled as charmingly as has been done in any nativity play. But the Bible story occupies only a climax of one hundred and seventeen lines of a total of seven hundred and fifty-four, and the rest of the play seems to be, at first sight, an unrelated comic interlude. Actually, as will be shown, it is far from being only this. Another traditional pressure upon the Wakefield playwright was that of using not Palestinian shepherds but English contemporary types. But here too he succeeds in merging these diverse elements so as to secure essential dramatic unity. The *Secunda Pastorum*, indeed, will stand up under the strictest structural analysis.

The play has a traditional beginning in which each shepherd comes in grumbling. In these "complaints" there is little that is new. Coll, Gyb, and Daw all complain about the weather; Coll, the old shepherd, sighs about hard times and about the oppression of the poor by the rich; Gyb, the second shepherd, is henpecked, and advises the young men in the audience against marrying in haste lest they repent at leisure; Daw, the boy, has in him the seeds of youthful rebellion, and believes that apprentices are exploited by their masters. The grumblings of the three herdsmen are more effusive and detailed than are those of the shepherds in the *Prima Pastorum* but are not different in kind. In the first nativity play of the cycle the second shepherd complains that "poore men ar in the dyke' (l. 93) and that in the conflict between master and apprentice he wots not 'wheder is gretter, the lad or the master' (ll. 70–71); and the first shepherd, henpecked like Gyb in the second play, quotes with approval the proverb that

> A man may not wyfe
> And also thryfee,
> And all in a yere. (ll. 97–99)

This differs little from Gyb's advice to young men in the *Secunda Pastorum:*

> These men that ar wed / haue not all thare wyll;
> When they ar full hard sted, / thay sygh full styll; (ll. 73–74)
> . . . .

Bot, yong men, of wowyng, / for God that you boght,
Be well war of wedyng . . . . (ll. 91–92)

Such plaints, and especially those against social and economic conditions, are probably the expressions in drama of the same verbal rebellion of those who swink which may be found in other contemporary literary forms, such as the debates and the dream allegories. It is just possible, however, that the author of the *Secunda Pastorum* was aware of the foil which they provided for expressions of joy over the golden age that came with the birth of Jesus. His play, certainly, begins on a note of sorrow but ends on a contrasting note of joy.

It is not as I wold, /for I am al lappyd
In sorow, (ll. 4–5)

mourns Primus Pastor when he first appears. And the exploited shepherd boy expresses at the end of the play the thought of all three that the nativity of Jesus brings better days,

Lord, well were me / for ones and for ay,
Myght I knele on my kne / som word for to say
To that chylde. (ll. 685–687)

Such a formula has the flavor of the typical Elizabethan comedy —sad, unstable beginning and happy ending.

But the dramatic unity of the play is determined by elements even more marked. Of these the most striking appears in the skill with which the author has bound together in a single theme episodes that seem superficially to be unrelated. He does not show, of course, all of Shakespeare's genius in using the dream motif as the flux for diverse elements in *A Midsummer Night's Dream*, but he possessed very evidently some sense of the dramatic value of a single theme to give unity to a play. In the *Secunda Pastorum* his unifying theme is, of course, that of the birth of a child. When the play is so considered, it becomes at once apparent that the Mak-Gyll episode is no unrelated part but is very definitely connected in theme with the conventional nativity scene that follows it. Indeed, Mak's special complaint, upon his first appearance, is that he is like the old woman in the shoe:

Now wold God I were in heuen, / for there wepe no barnes
So styll. (ll. 193–194)

Moreover, his conversation with the shepherds in his first encounter with them contains frequent allusions to his wife's unhappy and inconvenient power of reproduction, which keeps him poor in body and in pocket:

> *I. Pastor.* How fayrs thi wyff? by my hoode, / how farys sho?
> *Mak.* Lyys walteryng, by the roode, / by the fyere, lo!
> And a howse full of brude / she drynkys well to;
> Yll spede othere good / that she wyll do
> Bot so!
> Etys as fast as she can,
> And ilk yere that commys to man
> She bryngys furth a lakan,
> And som yeres two. (ll. 235–243)

The mind of Gyll, too, runs in the same direction. Indeed, in her plot for hiding the stolen sheep she makes capital of her known reputation for reproduction:

> *Vxor.* A good bowrde haue I spied, / syn thou can none;
> Here shall we hym hyde / to thay be gone,—
> In my credyll abyde,— / lett me alone,
> And I shall lyg besyde / in chyldbed, and grone. (ll. 332–335)

Later the entire stage business of the pseudonativity shows on the part of both Mak and Gyll considerable practice in playing childbed and nursing roles. After Mak first enters, in short, the theme of a childbirth dominates the play to the very conclusion.

The unity of the play that arises out of the nativity theme is enhanced still further by a most remarkable foreshadowing of that contrast of burlesque and serious which is so frequent a device in Elizabethan comedies. It is not to be supposed, of course, that the Wakefield Master knew anything about that juxtaposition of masque and antimasque which created such unity and contrast in the English comedies of two centuries later. It would seem certain, however, that he would have understood and appreciated this device fully, for in the Mak interlude and the conventional nativity scene which follows, the contrast is as well marked as in many of the best of the Elizabethan comedies. In the Mak episode, in fact, it is not the sheep-stealing but the sheep-hiding details which are the more essential to the play, for in these latter appears a perfect burlesque of the charming Christ-child scene that concludes the play. Between the burlesque and the religious episodes the three shepherds provide the character links. Twice a birth is announced to them, and twice they go seeking—once to unearth a fraud, and a second time to worship the new-born Lord. The comparative details are so obvious, once the key is apparent, that pointing them out should hardly be necessary. However, such a comparison reveals the amazing extent to which the Wakefield Master kept in mind throughout his composition of the play the dual episodes of the burlesque and the conventional nativity.

It has been said already that Mak's complaint of his wife's perennial fertility prepares the minds of the three shepherds for his more specific announcement of her latest gift to him. This preparation is not entirely unlike their foreknowledge of the coming of the Christ child:

> *II. Pastor.* We fynde by the prophecy— / let be youre dyn—
> Of Dauid and Isay / and mo then I myn,
> Thay prophecyed by clergy / that in a vyrgyn
> Shuld be lyght and ly, / to slokyn oure syn
>   And slake it,
> Oure kynde from wo;
> ffor Isay sayd so:
> *Ecce virgo*
>   *Concipiet* a chylde that is nakyd. (ll. 674–682)

But no prophets foretell the coming of Mak's heir, and no angel announces his arrival. Mak had planned with his rascally wife to say that she

> . . . was lyght
> Of a knaue childe this nyght (ll. 337–338),

and he tell the shepherds that the news has come to him in a dream—or rather in a nightmare, for it makes him quite unhappy—:

> Now, by Sant Strevyn,
> I was flayd with a swevyn,
>   My hart out of-sloghe:
>
> I thoght Gyll began to crok / and trauell full sad,
> Welner at the fyrst cok, / of a yong lad
> ffor to mend oure flok. / Then be I neuer glad; (ll. 383–388)

In both the burlesque and the conventional nativity scenes the news of the child's birth comes to the shepherds just after they have slept. In this respect the two scenes are identical; but the arrival of the sheep-baby is absurdly reported by his putative father, whereas the announcement in the Bethlehem scene is in the simple biblical tradition:

Angelus cantat 'Gloria in exelsis'; postea dicat:
Angelus. Ryse, hyrd-men heynd! / for now is he borne
That shall take fro the feynd / that Adam had lorne: (ll. 638–639)

In the two sleep episodes, incidentally, one is irresistibly reminded of the burlesque dream of Bottom and the romantic ones of the lovers in *A Midsummer Night's Dream*, and of the similarly contrasting sleep scenes in Lyly's *Endymion*. The sleeping shepherds of Bethlehem the Wakefield Master did not have to invent; his cleverness is apparent in his creation for his Yorkshire trio of a burlesque parallel nap.

The succeeding parallel detail comes with the journeying from the plain where the herdsmen slept to the birthplace. The Yorkshire shepherds are not, to be sure, drawn to Mak's hut by his announcement that his wife has given birth to a man-child, although on their arrival they are at once plunged into a nativity situation. It is to be supposed that the journey to the manger of Jesus at the end of the play is a serious duplication of the burlesque journey to the hut of Mak. Says Daw, after the loss of the sheep has been discovered, and Mak has been suspected of having stolen it:

Go we theder, I rede, / and ryn on oure feete.
Shall I neuer ete brede / the sothe to I wytt. (ll. 467–468)

And his master, after the angel's announcement, begs for similar haste:

To Bedlem he bad / that we shuld gang;
I am full fard / that we tary to lang. (ll. 665–666)

Thus twice the three shepherds make a journey to the crib of a newly-born child, probably measuring the distance to their goal in both instances by parading around the pageant-wagon.

There is no indication in the Towneley manuscript that the Bethlehem shepherds were drawn to the stable where the Christ-child lay by a song of the Virgin to her child. But since songs were often sung at a production but not subsequently written in the manuscripts, there is, on the other hand, no certainty that, as the herdsmen approached the holy site, the boy who played Mary did not sing one of the lullabies of Our Lady of the kind that Carleton Brown has put into his volumes of medieval religious lyrics. The Wakefield Master was evidently a trained musician, for not only in the *Secunda Pastorum* but in the *Prima Pastorum* as well (ll. 656–659 and 413–414, respectively), he has put into the mouths of the shepherds technical comments on the singing of the angels. It is doubtful if he would have overlooked an opportunity to include a sacred lullaby, especially since it would have provided an excellent foil for Mak's fearful cradle song in the sheep-hiding scene. For in their Yorkshire phase, as it may be called, the music-loving shepherds are almost repelled from Mak's hut by a lullaby that no longer exists, unfortunately, but that was very evidently a hideous and unmelodious burlesque. The gloss of the Early English Text Society edition of the play alludes to this effusion as a 'noise,' but it was without doubt a song by Mak with his wife groaning a stiff burden from her childbed. For so they had planned it:

> *Vxor.* Harken ay when thay call; / thay will com onone.
> Com and make redy all / and syng by thyn oone;
> Syng lullay thou shall, / for I must grone
> And cry outt by the wall / on Mary and Iohn,
> ffor sore. (ll. 440–444)

But the shepherds are quick to recognize Mak's deficiencies as a singer:

> *III. Pastor.* Will ye here how thay hak? / Oure syre lyst croyne.
> *I. Pastor.* Hard I neuer none crak / so clere out of toyne; (ll. 476–477)

With so many contrasts in the play it is difficult to think that the author would fail to use this harsh lullaby as a burlesque opposite a sweet song by the Virgin. Incidentally, Gyll's crying out on Mary and John effects an excellent forward link with the conventional nativity.

The Yorkshire shepherds, like the Bethlehem shepherds, find the babe in swaddling clothes (ll. 433, 598–599), but warned away by the 'parents' they hesitate to approach the cradle. The scene in Mak's hut is divided between the comic business of hunting for the stolen sheep and the fencing with Mak and Gyll over

. . . this chylde
That lygys in this credyll. (ll. 537–538)

Failing to find their sheep the herdsmen actually leave the hut but return at the suggestion of the aged Coll:

I. Pastor. Gaf ye the chyld any-thyng?
II. Pastor. I trow, not oone farthyng.
III. Pastor. ffast agane will I flyng,
Abyde ye me there. (ll. 571–574)

It is the boy Daw's attempt to press 'bot sex pence' into the hand of the 'lytyll day-starne' that leads to the discovery of the fraud and the punishment of the rascally Mak. The link with the nativity episode here is, of course, the gift-giving, in the Mak scene burlesque, in the later episode simple and touching. Daw's term of endearment to Mak's swaddled 'infant'—'lytyll day-starne'—is applied, incidentally, by Gyb, the second shepherd, to the Christ-child (l. 727).

One final device employed by the Wakefield Master to give structural unity to the play and also to divide the little drama into definite scenes is the introduction of song. Reference has already been made to the possible contrast of Mak's lullaby and the song of the Virgin, and the biblical original forces the introduction of the '*Gloria in exelsis*' of the Angelus. The three other songs are sung by the shepherds. Of these the second is their attempt to imitate the angel's '*gloria*'—a device employed also in the *Prima Pastorum* (ll. 413 ff.). The first is a three-part song—'tenory,' 'tryble,' and 'meyne' (ll. 182–189)—used to mark the conclusion of the first scene and the coming of Mak. Finally, the play closes with a 'going-out' song by the shepherds, a device exactly similar to that used frequently by the Elizabethan playwrights to mark the ending of a comedy and to clear the stage. The song that the shepherds sang as they left the stable of the Christ-child and brought both burlesque and conventional nativity episodes to an end does not appear in the Towneley manuscript. But Mary's command to the shepherds—'Tell, furth as ye go' (l. 744)—and their own feeling—'To syng ar we bun' (l. 753)—indicate clearly that it was no jolly shepherd song that they sang but one of an angel, a star, three simple shepherds, and a babe in a manger.

It may have been not unlike the song which the shepherds of the Coventry Corpus Christi nativity play sang as they left Joseph and Mary and the Christ-child:

> Doune from heaven, from heaven so hie,
> Of angeles ther came a great companie,
> With mirthe and ioy and great solemnitye,
>   They sange terly terlow,
> So mereli the sheppards ther pipes can blow.

And thus '*Explicit pagina Pastorum.*'

RICHARD SELLYNG

ALBERT C. BAUGH

University of Pennsylvania

IT is seldom that an author of a single poem of 172 lines, a man otherwise unknown to fame, finds a place in the pages of the *DNB*. Yet such is the case of Richard Sellyng. What is more, his *Evidens to Beware and Gode Counsayle* was and still remains in manuscript. In the ten lines which Mary Bateson devotes to him in the *Dictionary* there are no biographical data. She merely notes that he 'fl. 1450' and 'may be the Richard Sellyng who in 1432–1433 conveyed Bernham's Manor, Norfolk, to Sir J. Fastolf and John Paston (cf. *Paston Letters*, ed. Gairdner, i. 164, 228).' It is my purpose here to publish the poem and to offer a conjecture concerning its author.

In *Evidens to Beware* the author looks back upon his youth, now past, and contemplates life as one who knows not how much longer it will last. When he could stretch himself in the stirrups he exulted in bodily strength; age now reminds him that youth should be a time in which to lay up store for the future, as in summer man provides for the winter. The young man's heart stands 'on a jolly pin'; the old man has a slack, rivelled skin. Since age is now come upon him he will seek the help of Our Lady. There follows 'An Uracion til oure lady' occupying three stanzas. The 'Gode Counsayle' takes the form of a reflection on man's good resolves in time of danger, resolutions too often forgotten when the emergency which inspired them is past. Death spares no man. Preachers warn us to think of our end. Consider the parable of the wise and foolish virgins. Christ turned the water into wine at Cana—but he will leave it to those that preach and expound their texts to tell how Christ saves. May he bring us to everlasting 'nupcias.'

The whole is written in rime royal except for twelve lines at the end in which Sellyng disparages his 'symple tragedie,' not at all like those of Lombardy that 'storax' wrote, and sends his poem to John Shirley to correct it and perchance to derive some pleasure from the perusal of it. He alludes to their old acquaintance, now happily capable of being renewed, since chance has made it possible for them again to 'mete daylye in on place.' The only text of the poem that has come down to us is in one of Shirley's MSS (Harl. 7333). Its date is therefore before 1456, the date of Shirley's death.

A Richard Sellyng appears under three different circumstances in documents of the period. Sellyng is not a common name, judging from the rather infrequent occurrence of it in the records. When it does occur in the fifteenth century the individual usually has the given name Richard. While it is possible that there was more than one Richard Sellyng, esquire, in the period during which the author of the poem must have lived, I believe with such conviction as is justified short of proof that the references are to a single man, that his social status makes him a suitable person to have written the poem in question, and that in the absence of any other claimant we may accept him tentatively as the author.

We may begin by noting the Richard Sellyng mentioned by Miss Bateson, who in 1432–1433 had dealings with Sir John Fastolf in Norfolk.[1] The earliest reference I have found to him[1a] is in the third year of the reign of Henry VI (1424–1425), where he appears as the husband of Joan, the widow of Sir William Bardolf. Since Bardolf had died only the year before, the marriage could not have taken place long before the date mentioned. The transaction involves the release of the lordship of Castor Bardolph's in Norfolk.[2] Joan did not enjoy many years of married life with her new husband, for in 1435 Richard appears as the

---

[1] Her reference to the *Paston Letters* (ed. Gairdner, I. 164) is an error. The letter there printed, although referring to Sellyng, is dated 1450 and has to do with another matter. Her authority is probably Blomefield's *History of Norfolk* (1805–1810), X. 426, where it appears that he transferred the manor she mentions (Bernham's Manor, Norfolk) to Fastolf. It was later in John Paston's possession.

[1a] Unless he is also the Richard Sellynge who is one of a group of ten that acknowledges a recognizance for £100 on December 10, 1423 (*CCR*, 1422–1429, p. 127).

[2] Blomefield, *History of Norfolk*, XI. 203.

executor of his wife's will.[3] The final settlement must have been delayed, for by 1429–1430 he is again married, this time to Alice, late widow of Sir John Wiltshire.[4] In 1432–1433, the year in which Richard and Alice conveyed Burnham's Manor to Sir John Fastolf, they also conveyed by fine to Fastolf the manor of Drayton (co. Norfolk).[5] On February 18, 1432, Sellyng acknowledges a recognizance for £200 to Fastolf and a John Kyrtelynge, clerk.[6] Here he is described as 'Richard Sellynge lately dwelling in Baconsthorp co. Norfolk esquire.' The debt was cancelled upon Fastolf's acknowledgment. Many years later (November 11, 1450) Fastolf writes to Sir Thomas Howys, his parson at Castlecombe: 'I thank you for the quittance of Richard Sellyng you have sent me by Worcester [his secretary, William Wyrcester] . . . . Ask my cousin Herry Sturmer's wife to search for an indenture and other writings between me and Sellyng or Lady Wiltshire.'[7] And again, a year later (September 23, 1451), he writes to Howys: 'Item, send me the value of Cooke ys tenement in Drayton, wyth xx. acres lond therto, what it was worth yeerly when it stode hoole; for Sellyng seith it was worth but j. noble a yeer.'[8] The tense of the verb here suggests that Sellyng is still alive. Unless this Richard Sellyng is to be identified with the person or persons to be mentioned next, I find no further trace of him. The name Sellyng is rare in Norfolk records. I have found only one other occurrence of it, the record of a John Sellyng, esquire, who was a commissioner in 1431 to assess a grant in Norfolk.[9]

Shortly after the date at which the Richard Sellyng just discussed is described as 'lately dwellyng in Baconsthorp co. Norfolk'

---

[3] Md' q*uo*d xx° die Februar' anno r' R' Henr' sexti t*er*ciodecimo Ric*ar*dus Sellyng' Armiger' excec' testi' Johanne nup*er* ux*or*is ac executricis testi' Will*elm*i Bardolf Militis. . . . (Sir F. Palgrave, *Antient Kalendars and Inventories of the . . . Exchequer* (3v, [London], 1835), II. 153.

[4] In that year Richard and Alice conveyed Wilkin's Manor, Norfolk, which Alice held for life. Cf. Blomefield's *History of Norfolk*, VII. 45.

[5] Blomefield, *op. cit.*, X. 411, 426.

[6] *CCR*, 1429–1435, p. 173.

[7] *Paston Letters*, ed. J. Gairdner (1872), I. 164.

[8] *Ibid.*, I. 228.

[9] *CPR*, 1429–1436, p. 137.

(1432) and, except for the settlement of his wife's estate, drops out of sight until 1450, a Richard Sellyng, esquire, turns up in the records as engaged in military service at Calais. On June 18, 1434, he is commissioned along with two others to take the muster of certain forces on their arrival at that town.[10] Early in the following year (February 14, 1435) he is given power, along with John Stokes and Stephen Wilton, to treat with Louis, Duke of Bavaria, concerning the money due him from the king.[11] He is still abroad on July 18, when he is again commissioned (with others) to take the muster of certain men-at-arms and archers 'when they come to Calais, before they leave the marches thereof.'[12] One of the three others serving with him on this commission (Richard Bokeland) had been associated with the Richard Sellynge of the recognizance of 1423.[13] It is significant that the Richard Sellyng of Norfolk who acts as executor of his wife's will made settlement at just this time (February 20, 1435) and delivered to the Exchequer of Receipt (probably through an attorney) a receipt for £300 completing the payment of the king for Bardolf's wages at Calais 'ut p*er* ii billas de debent*ura* Ric*ardo* Bukland' lib*er*at*as* apparet.'[14] Bukland was a prominent person, for a time treasurer of Calais, and the occurrence of his name in these three transactions may have no significance. But it does not lessen the possibility that the Richard Sellyng who is engaged in military service at Calais is identical with the Norfolk Richard Sellyng who was married to Joanna Bardolf. In any case, he was further empowered on December 17, 1435, with Richard Wodevyle, lieutenant of Calais, John Stokes, Richard Bokeland, and Thomas Borowe to treat with the Master of Prussia and of the Hanse for redress of injuries.'[15] He is apparently back in England on November 17, 1436, probably some months before that date. According to an entry in the *Patent Rolls* the castle of Banelyngham in the marches of Picardy, which had lately been committed to his

---

[10] *CPR*, 1429–1436, p. 359.

[11] *Syllabus of Rymer's Foedera*, II. 659.

[12] *CPR*, 1429–1436, p. 476.

[13] Cf. note 1a.

[14] Palgrave, *op. cit.*

[15] *Syllabus of Rymer's Foedera*, II. 660.

keeping, had been captured by the king's enemies, and for this 'misfortune and betrayal of the said castle his goods were taken unto the king's hands, until the king considered thereof.' Sellyng apparently gave a satisfactory account of his conduct, alleging 'that he and those with him were forced to retire with great pain and damage, as was proved on examination before certain lords and other notable men of the realm at Calais,' and he offered 'letters testimonial under the seal of the mayor of the town' in support of his statements. Accordingly the king directed 'that by writs under the Great Seal order be given to deliver his goods to him.'[16] This apparently ended Sellyng's military experience.

It will be seen that from the middle of 1434 till the latter part of 1436 a Richard Sellyng, esquire, was at Calais on military service. None of the documents cited furnishes definite evidence of his identity with the man previously discussed, the Richard Sellyng, esquire, who had been living in Norfolk and who was married for a short time to the widow of Sir William Wiltshire. Such slight indications as are furnished by the association with other people point to their identity, and I believe these Richard Sellyngs are one person. The chronology of events makes this assumption altogether reasonable. We turn now to the third Richard Sellyng who has left his traces in the record.

By June 10, 1438, a Richard Sellyng, esquire, appears as the husband of a Kentish woman, Elizabeth Brockhill, only daughter and heir of Thomas Brockhill, a man of considerable means. The family seat was at Brockhill (Brockhull, *alias* Thorne), within sight of the coast at Saltwood, where the murderers of Becket met before proceeding to Canterbury. There the couple seem to have lived. At the beginning of the nineteenth century enough of the house or castle was left to show 'both the antiquity and great extent of this mansion.'[17] Elizabeth's father died in 1437, and the following year she and her husband entered into an agreement with Nicholas Brockhill, her father's brother, for the partition of

[16] *CPR*, 1436–1441, p. 27. This as well as the two commissions for taking musters was noted by Miss Helen P. South (*PMLA*, L. 371).

[17] Hasted, *History of Kent*, III. 406.

property which descended to them according to the 'tenure of gavelkynde.' As a result of the agreement it was settled 'that the said Richard and Elizabeth in her right shall have the manse or dwelling house of the said manor with the garden adjacent and other parcels of the manor, lands, rent and service, namely . . . ' and then follows a detailed description of the property.[18] Elizabeth inherited other land as well, such as Bredmer or Broadmarsh in the parish of Folkstone.[19] From this time on Richard Sellyng appears as a typical member of the landed gentry. As 'Richard Sellyng of the county of Kent, esquire' he is one of the mainpernors for Sir John Styward when taking over certain manors in Norfolk and Bucks at a yearly farm of some £70.[20] On November 10, 1438, he obtains an order from the king to the sheriff of Kent 'to give Richard Sellynge and Elizabeth his wife seisin of five acres of meadow at "Stevyntonysforde"' lately forfeited by the tenant who 'held them of the said Richard and Elizabeth in the right of the said Elizabeth.'[21] Everything seems to indicate that this Richard Sellyng owed his position as a man of property mainly to his wife.

Sellyng had one son, John, born about 1441. How long his wife lived is not known, but she died before he did. There is record of a bond which Richard Sellyng entered into in 1442,[22] but he does not otherwise appear in the records until 1455 when he is old and infirm. On May 21 of that year there is entered a pardon 'to the king's esquire, Richard Sellyng,' of £10 forfeit for not appearing on a jury in which he was empanelled. He was forgiven the fine 'on his petition shewing that he has long served the king's pro-

---

[18] *CCR*, 1435–1441, pp. 275–276.

[19] Hasted, *History of Kent*, III. 376. The Brockhill (Brockhull) family is traced in Hasted (III. 406–407). The steps are Sir Warren de Brockhull (*temp.* Edw. I)—Sir William—Sir Thomas (*temp.* Edw. III, a prominent person, several times sheriff of the county and knight of the shire)—Sir John—William—the brothers Nicholas and Thomas. Thomas's daughter Elizabeth is the person with whom we are concerned.

[20] *Cal. Fine Rolls*, XVII. 49 (July 12, 1438). In 1439 Styward was made keeper of the Kentish castle of Rochester.

[21] *CCR*, 1435–1441, p. 202.

[22] *CCR*, 1441–1447, p. 72.

genitors[23] and the king, is broken with age and totally blind, and that he was not summoned or warned by his body or lands.'[24] Thus 'broken with age and totally blind' he lived on for another twelve years. According to the inquisition post mortem[25] his death occurred May 16, 1467.

There would be nothing unusual in the situation if the Richard Sellyng here traced were identical with the person previously found serving at Calais. The latter returned from Calais in 1436. Two years later he could then be married to the Kentish heiress. Assuming the probability that the Calais esquire is the Richard Sellyng first noted in Norfolk, it would mean that his second wife had died and he had now married again. The problem is complicated, however, by the fact that there were two places named Sellyng in Kent, one in the immediate neighborhood of the Brockhill manor, the other in the northern part of the county, a few miles from Ospring and Chaucer's Boughton-under-Blee in the union of Faversham. It might seem natural for Elizabeth Brockhill to marry a man from her own neighborhood.

However, although a Sellyng family is found in Kent from fairly early times,[26] it seems always to be associated with the Faversham district. I find none in the Brockhill (Saltwood) area, and I have searched in vain for a Richard Sellyng in Kent in the first half of the fifteenth century with whom the husband of Elizabeth Brockhill might be identified.

---

[23] Interpreted literally, this would take us back to Henry IV.

[24] *CPR*, 1452–1461, p. 242.

[25] Taken at Eltham, October 31, 1468, where it is recorded that his wife is dead, that he is seized of the manor of Thorne, and that John, his son and heir, is 27 (Chanc. Inq. P. M., 8 Edw. IV, No. 46). The list of his manors is given in *Cal. Inq. post Mortem*, IV. 344.

[26] I find Sellyngs in Kent, located in Selling and Faversham, from the reign of John. In 1206 a plea of warranty of a charter shows that Nicholas de Selling and Hawise, his wife, had two sons, Simon and Ralph (*Arch. Cant.*, IV. 308). In the same year Simon transfers to his brother lands in Faversham and Selling (*ibid.*, XIV. 204). Ralph is a juror in an inquisition between 1216 and 1219 (*ibid.*, II. 315). A generation later there is a John, son of Nicholas de Sellinge, who (1253–1263) has property in Wodnesberghe, Godwinestone, and one and three-quarters fees in the hundred of Calehill (cf. *ibid.*, XII. 209, 218, 219; IV. 314). An Adrian de Selling testifies in an extent of the manor of Folkestone in 1271 (*ibid.*, VI. 240).

A century before the period in which we are interested, that is, at the beginning of the fourteenth century, a John de Sellyng and his descendants for four generations are found in Selling and the Faversham district, and in Pluckley, fifteen miles southwest. There is a John de Sellyng whose wife is named Idonea. He is the son of a John Sellyng, about whom I know nothing. John and Idonea had three sons: John, Ralph, and Richard.[27] The elder John (husband of Idonea) was dead by 1323, and for some time after his death his widow and his younger sons Ralph and Richard make an effort to get possession of some of his property, which they claim is being wrongfully withheld by Bartholomew de Badlesmere.[28] The eldest son (John), although owning property in this region, is also an apothecary in London.[29] By his wife Joanna he had four sons.[30] The youngest, Edmund, had a daughter

---

[27] The earliest record of John Sellyng that I know is a fine of 1308 in which he is described as the son of John Sellyng and disposes of the manor of Sherland in Pluckley to his son John and his wife Joanna for £100 (*Arch. Cant.*, XI. 312). Two years later he transfers another messuage in Sellynge, Seldwyht, and Badlesmere to his three sons, John, Ralph, and Richard (*ibid.*, XI. 331). A fine of 1313 in which John, son of Richard de Senglyngge, and Alice his wife dispose of land in Ancrise near Branddrede I take to refer to a grandson (*ibid.*, XII. 299).

[28] The Inq. post Mortem for the elder John Sellyng is in Chancery File 77, No. 6, dated 16 Edw. II, in which he is said to have placed his wife Idonea in dower with respect to a messuage in Sheldwich and Sellingge. The moiety of this messuage was in the king's hands among the lands of Bartholomew de Badlesmere by forfeiture and the means by which it came into Badlesmere's possession are noted. Among the *Ancient Petitions* there are several in which Idonea and her two younger sons seek to recover possession of the property (cf. File 267, No. 13, 325, and File 74, No. 3659 [Idonea]; File 74, No. 3656 [Richard]; File 74, No. 3659 [Ralph]. *See* also *Cal. Inq. post Mortem*, VI. 262). Badlesmere apparently still had the property at his death (cf. *ibid.*, VII. 300). The *Inq. post Mortem* for Idonea was held 17 Edw. II (*Cal. Inq. post Mortem*, IV. 433).

[29] There is no doubt about the identity of this man. In 1 Edward II (1307–1308) he is paid 50 marks as "John de Sellyngg, apothecary, of London, for various drugs purchased from the same John in divers years, for the use of the Lord the King, whilst he was Prince of Wales." Cf. F. Devon, *Issues of the Exchequer* (London, 1837), p. 123. In 1308, a deed of William, son of John de Pluckley, gives to John Malmains land adjoining the lands of John de Selling, apothecary of London. Five years later this same William de Pluckley acquires a messuage in Pluckley, and the witnesses are John de Sellyng, John and Robert, his sons, etc. (*Arch. Cant.*, XV. 26). In a fine of 1308 John de Sellyngg' and Joanna his wife acquired from John, son of John de Sellyngg and Idonea his wife, the manor of Sherland in Plukele for £100, as already noted (*ibid.*, XI. 312).

[30] By a fine of 1315 John de Sellynge, spicer, and Joanna his wife acquire other land with

Margaret, married to a John de Surrender.[31] After this I cannot trace the line. I find a John, Joanna, and Nicholas de Sellyng, all assessed on property in Calhulle in 1346 in connection with the knighting of the Black Prince.[32] A John Selyng senior and junior, of Maidstone, were involved in the Peasants' Revolt of 1381.[33] There is a Richard de Selling who is admitted Vicar of St. Mary's, Minster (Isle of Thanet), August 30, 1361,[34] and a 'Richard Sellyng, donsel, of the diocese of Canterbury' who was granted an indult to have a portable altar in 1423.[35]

From this brief survey of the Kentish Sellyngs it is apparent that there is no record of a Richard Sellyng who could have married Elizabeth Brockhill. In the absence of conclusive evidence to link this Kentish esquire with the Richard Sellyng who ten or twelve years earlier had dealings with Sir John Fastolf in Norfolk, I recognize that the identification of the two must be tentative, but I consider it highly probable that in the Richard Sellyng, esquire, who appears as a party to some small transactions involving money and land in Norfolk, soon after as a soldier at Calais, and shortly thereafter as the husband of a Kentish heiress of modest fortune we have to do with one man. The Richard Sellyng who held, through his wife, the manor of Brockhill or Thorne at the time of his death handed on to his descendants a coat of arms described as 'Vert, a chevron between three griffins heads erased, or.'[36] If it is ever shown that our Norfolk Richard Sellyng bore these arms, the identity of the Richard Sellyngs of the records could be considered established. In the meantime, it may be noted that in 4 Henry V (1416–1417) Sir William Bardolf, whose widow married the Richard Sellyng of the Norfolk records, was granted for life the keeping of the castle and lordship of Sandgate, in Picardy, with all the profits thereof during peace or war.

remainder to their four sons, John, Robert, Thomas, and Edmund (*ibid.*, XIII. 302). In 1317 John de Sellyng, spicer, acquires lands in Sellyng with remainder to the same four sons (*ibid.*, XIII. 312). For other transactions see *ibid.*, XI. 350 and XIV. 186.

[31] *Arch. Cant.*, XV. 26.

[32] *Feudal Aids*, III. 32, 36, and *Arch. Cant.*, X. 138.

[33] *Arch. Cant.*, IV. 75–76, from Coram Rege Roll, Mich. Term, 5 Ric. II.

[34] Hasted, *History of Kent*, IV. 331; *Arch. Cant.*, XXVII. 99.

[35] *Cal. Papal Reg.*, *Papal Letters*, VII. 305.

[36] Hasted, *History of Kent*, III. 407.

Some years after his death it was in the keeping of Richard Sellyng, who enjoyed it for at least fifteen years. How much longer I do not know. When in 22 Henry VI (1444–1445) Sellyng filed an accounting in connection with the ten years, 10–20 Henry VI, of his stewardship, the account is headed 'Kent.'[37] A link connecting the same Richard Sellyng with Norfolk, Calais, and Kent thus seems discernible.

Evidens to Beware is just such a poem as a country gentleman in later life might write and submit modestly to his friend, John Shirley, for correction. Until some better claimant for the honor is forthcoming, I think we may tentatively attribute it to the Kentish gentleman whose social position is so consonant with Shirley's designation of the poet as 'that honurable squier.'

Evidens to be ware and gode covnsayle made nowe late
by that honurable squier Richard Sellyng.

Whilist I hade youþe I wist nouȝt what it was [Harl. MS 7333, fol. 36
And yete þer-of hade I aye grete plentee
By whos conduyt my desyrous pourchas
Now have I ffounde age by whos Auctorite
I leve as al men done w^t^oute surtee
Of yeere of daye. of saysoun or of tyde
How long þ^t^ age wil w^t^ me here abyde

And youþe abode als long as ever he myght
Nouȝt as I wold so longe god knowith al.

---

[37] L. T. R., Foreign Accounts, 22 Henry VI (abstract): Kent: Account of Richard Sellyng, esquire, executor of the will of Joan, late the wife and executrix of the will of William Bardolf, knight, deceased, to whom King Henry V, the father of the now king, by his letters patent given at the town of Calais on 9 October, 4 Henry V, granted the custody of the castle of Sandgate in Picardy for term of his life with such money as well in time of war as of peace with such fees, etc. as the Captain of that castle took and received, etc. The issues and profits of the same from 9 October, 10 Henry VI, to 9 October, 20 Henry VI, Richard Sellyng and John Ricroft, the other executor of the will of Joan the wife of William Bardolf, computed as £540 16*s.* 5*d.*—For Sellyng's keeping of the castle and lordship see *Lists and Indexes*, XI. 47 (Enrolled Accountes, Calais, Various). Here Bardolf is listed as keeper for the period 4 Henry V—3 Henry VI and 3–9 Henry VI, although he was dead at the time covered by the second entry. Sellyng is listed as Keeper in 10–20 Henry VI and again 20–25 Henry VI. Just when the transfer to Sellyng occurred is not entirely clear. The tenure did not imply residence. It was a grant from which the grantee derived certain profits. Presumably an occasional visit would have been desirable.

Whan age was co*mm*yn he be-gan to fyght
Youþe fledde als faste as shadow on þe walle
Þus be we Rulid be oure lorde Eternall
To whome him listiþe youþe on lenkþe he sendeþe
And al oure ages as he wolle he endeþe[1]

I wold be gladde & lusti wist I howe
And besy me a medecine for to fecche
I knewe neuere what yowþe was or nowe
For whan I myght me in my stiropis streche
Me thowte myselfe þt I was þoo noo wrecche
And al made youþe and my bodyly helthe
Weoch is þe Richesse of this worldly welthe

Whan age was Come helþe bygan to wane
Than luste and delyght be-ganne for to shrinke
þoo wanne I nought but wastide as a draane
Yitte for al þt I most Remembre and thynke
How þt habarowe cloþe mete and drinke
In yowthe men gete þeire age for to susteyne
Vn-to þe wise / þis is þeire labour and peyne

In somer saysoun / men laboure with-oute
In ffeld and woode wt Right grete besynesse
By-cause of wynter wiche þei sore dovte
þat eche man wille as he best canne gesse
For man and beste his vitaille for to dresse
Tendure þe wynter withe his stormis colde
þis hathe men vsid by thes dayes olde

Somoure is to wynter his pourveioure
Of al man*er* stoffis and eke vetaile
And wynt*er* to som*er* is els harboroure[2]
þus he yeldithe som*er* his aquitayle
From yer*e* ⟨to yer*e*⟩[3] ffor þt shall neu*er* fayle
Ryght so farithe age whan yowþe ne may not dure
Takeþe al in gouernaunce / and in his cure.

Eu*er*ye weyght desirithe long for to leve
Wherfore thei praye and þei wishe also
Vnto hym þt al may dispose & geve
It is owre Right þt we al do soo
For of þis worldes eonde þe Ioye is woo

---

[1] MS. ondoþe.

[2] MS. harborowe.

[3] Insertion.

As to the body þat is of Erthe ewrought
W^{t} oute þe soule / it is worthe Right noute

þe younge manis herte / stondithe on a ioly pynne
Ful lustely he tredithe on þ^{e} stonis
þe old man haþe / a slakke Ryvelid skynne
Wherin be wrappid his olde feoble bonjs
I trow þ^{t} in this worlde ful many on is
þat cane not holden him Ryght hertly plesid
þowghe þat god w^{t} long lyfe haþe him esed

As for my parte I thanke mich god of al
þat of youþe I am passed my freelte
W^{t} age I swelle nowe and ever shalle
Ful longe have I desired so to be
Of vertue have I but litille propurtee
Of meryte or grace ful scarsly for to wynne
But pray to ow*re* lady & thus I wolle be-gynne

An Uracion til oure lady by Sellyng.

O excellent qvene of þe heuenes alle
Of eorþly worlde / also hye Empresse
Whom þ^{t} I clepe mayde moder & call
[. . . . .]
Gretteste of Estate and suche humblesse
Was neuer yitte founde / in heght ne lowe degree
Resceyve my prayer*e* þ^{t} I now make to þee

Of the see thow art þe lode sterre
Euer clere & never pale ne waane
Thorouhe wham was eonded all þe mortall were
þat sum tyme was by-twene god & man
By yowe ladye oure final pes bygan
Whanne god from hevene sent his sone adowne
Whome thowe conceyvid for oure Redempcion

Nowght only pees but helthe & medecyne
To all þat liven in woo or distresse
Vowche-sauff / ladye þyne eris to encline
O. mayde. O modir. O. eternall goddes
⟨for þi gret myght & þi gret prowe[s]⟩[4]
Wiche of alle wymmen arte þe soverayn
My prayere ne me þat þow neu*er* disdeyne

Whanne men haue parell oþer in shippe or in barge
þanne vowen they fastynge or pylgrymage
þe feloune syþe were he frome presoune large

---

[4] Inserted in margin.

He wolde amend and neu*er* do ovtrages[5]
þe seeke man thenkethe / yf god wolde aswage
His peyne and of his lyf do hym Respite
To serve god ay he wolde his herte delite

þe shippe in haven is by grace arrevyed
And al þe men & goodis in savetee
þe ffeloun is at large vnstokkid or ongyved [fol. 36^{v}.
þe seke is hole and in prosp*er*itee
Boþe al þe forsaide men and also he
þeire old rule nowe ageine nuwe þei be-gynne
And have forgote / þe parell þ^{t} thei were Inne

The marinar sayliþe and doutiþe not þe wawe.
The marchaunt wold Recouer þat he hathe lorne
þe felovne Robbithe and is a stronge outlawe
More crewelle and worse þan he was to-forene
þe man þt is hole haþe in his hert esworene
þat seyth fully / nowe in his fulsum age
He wolle give almes and do pilgrymage

He cane w^{t} good wille bargayne & eke dele
þat canne endente. w^{t} hym to have longe lyfe
Wherw^{t} shall he þ^{t} endento*ur* ensele
I trowe w^{t} buttre / wryten on a borcyff[6]
To be þ^{e} more fetyse & portatyff
Deþe þat vnder god is his mynister
Makeþe[7] none suche evidense in his Registre

Whanne þe shepe have pastured vpon þ^{e} grene
þe herde hem dryveþe a-geyne in-to þ^{e} folde
And þene departight þe fatte from þe lene
þe fatte ben than to[8] þ^{e} bocher solde
The remenaunt of hem bein rekenid & tolde
And shaule lyve longer tille a-noþer yeere
Tille þei be wexsen fatte al at leyseure

This saumple is kouþe and lyght to vndirstonde
But deþe worchethe al in an-oþer wyse
He sparithe no-thyng what þ^{t} Comythe to hande
Riche man ne poore old younge fole ne wyse
He passithe not his p*er*sonne be mainpryse

---

[5] MS. ovtragee.

[6] So in MS.; I cannot explain the word.

[7] *ke* inserted.

[8] Written above; *from* crossed out.

Suche statuyt and proces ben in his lawe
Wheþ*er* he shalle leng*er* liue or ell*es* be slawe

What neodeþe me of þis mater to telle
But for þat slouþe shoulde thynke no tyme elore
Þer is no thing / by-twene hevene & helle
Þat it naþe beo spoken of ffful yoore
So diuerse matiers þei may not be bore
In no mans remembraunce ne in his mynde
Seche olde storyes and þer ye shull hem fynde

Prechovres have taught vs. ofte in many a place
Þat to god shulde man ay be Redy
And thynk howe shorte and brutill is liuis space
To hem þat of þe worlde · been moste gredy
Þer for do thynke on poure and nedye
Vpon almiti god entende & kepe
Þat whan he comythe þow. beo not founde on slepe

Whane youre Spouse co*m*me[9] to þe gate be Rennynge
Þat yee be redye to entre yn þer*e*-ate
As did þe maydenis wt laumpis brynnynge
ffor þey were Redy & prudent algate
Þe Remenaunt of þe maydenis cam to late
Yitte cam thei in þey knockyd all be Rowe
Þe spouse wolde hem neyþ*er* here ne knowe

Weddyng was made in þe cane of galalye
Þe spouse þer of was[10] Archedeckyne
Ther was of vitaille leve welle grete plente
But at þe laste þei lacked of þeire wyne
þane Ihesus þer of his power devyne
As he was neuer of his grace straunge
Made sixse water pott*es* into weyne chaunge

In this mater I wolle noo depper wade
Lest myn vnknowyng make me to drowne
Clerkis þt beon of ki*n*nyng ffull elade[11]
Lete hem so preche and þeire texstes expounde
Þat by his mercy of thornis þat bare þe croune
He bryng vs to þeeverlasting nupcias
And gyffe vs g*r*ace to amend *our* trespase[12]

---

[9] Inserted.

[10] Inserted.

[11] MS. eloode.

[12] The whole line is inserted in the margin.

Loo þis is but a symple tragedie
No-thing lyche vn-to hem of Lumbardye
Wiche þat storax wrote vnto þemp[er]ere[13]
Sellyng makithe þis in hes manere
And to Iohn shirley . nowe sent it[14] is
For to amende where it is a-misse
And also for plesaunce and for desporte
And for olde acqueintance & newe Resorte
That is fallen til vs boþe nowe by grace
Þat we may mete daylye in on place
And assemble to speke of thyng*es* trewe
Off fern yeeris alsoo . oure talis renuwe

---

[13] I cannot explain this allusion.

[14] MS. is.

WYNKYN DE WORDE AND A SECOND FRENCH COMPILATION FROM THE 'ANCREN RIWLE' WITH A DESCRIPTION OF THE FIRST

(TRINITY COLL. CAMB. MS 883)

HOPE EMILY ALLEN

THE 'first' French compilation from the *Ancren Riwle* mentioned in my title occurs in the volume which I made known, for its relations to the *Riwle*, in a letter to the *London Times Literary Supplement* of October 24, 1936.[1] The time has not come for me to discuss textual variants in the Trinity version which seem to go back to a manuscript different from and probably superior to any other extant. Minute textual problems do not, however, concern the Early Modern English derivative of the *Riwle* which makes the primary subject of this paper. Other facts concerning the Trinity compilation are given in a later section of this article, as they are of general interest for a considerable range of *Ancren Riwle* studies.

Both my letter on the Trinity MS and the present paper should be taken as making one series with four earlier short contributions to *Ancren Riwle* scholarship,[2] each of which also recorded one or more facts giving definite evidence of the wide circulation in

[1] The Trinity MS came to light during the period when my research on feminine piety in medieval England was being made possible through grants from the American Council of Learned Societies. I have incidentally used in this paper much of the material collected at that time. I am particularly grateful to Professor Brown for his having guided me to his own interest, medieval religious literature. In collecting the materials used here I have had valuable assistance from Mr. J. A. Herbert, a particular well-wisher of Professor Brown.

[2] *See* "A New Latin Manuscript of the 'Ancren Riwle' " (of the early fourteenth century), *MLR*, xiv (1919), 209; "Another Latin Manuscript of the 'Ancren Riwle' " (of the early sixteenth century), *ibid.*, xvii (1922), 403; "Some Fourteenth Century Borrowings from 'Ancren Riwle,' " *ibid.*, xviii (1923), 1–8 (corrected at one point, *ibid.*, xix (1924), 95); "Further Borrowings from 'Ancren Riwle' " (from *ca.*1140–1215 to the early sixteenth century), *ibid.*, xxiv (1929), 1–15.

medieval England of the devotional masterpiece written sometime in the Angevin period.[3] Professor Chambers, in his momentous study "On the Continuity of English Prose,"[4] brought out a general significance, of which I had been unaware, in scattered facts accruing during my study of the history and influence of the *Ancren Riwle;* these facts proved a circulation spanning three hundred years, and Professor Chambers showed that this length of continuity was unique in Middle English literature, and he used it as a basic factor in his demonstration of the continuity of English prose. Since then two more derivatives of the *Ancren Riwle* have come to light. In the last section of this paper I comment briefly on the fact (which cannot alter his general conclusions) that one is French and the other founded on a French source; as also on some others of the broad scholarly problems raised by the English early edition and the French compilation. Throughout this paper, I mark for emphasis whatever, in either of the derivatives treated, gives evidence as to the degree and kind of circulation which they gave to the *Ancren Riwle.* Each of these two works has a double interest for my study of the history and influence of the *Ancren Riwle* (to quote the title of my 'project' for ACLS). Neither work could have been directly derived from the *Riwle;* through the summary investigation here described, details have come to light as to their direct sources respectively; it is evident that such texts (of which no copies are known to exist) also gave interesting evidence as to the continued popularity of the *Riwle* among influential English persons.

I

The book printed by Wynkyn de Worde, which I shall now identify as a derivative, is that entitled by the bibliographers the *Treatise of Love,* and dated by them in 1493. (I append to this

[3] The most extensive of the "borrowings" came to my attention through a quotation identified as from the *Riwle* by Dr. Owst in the first of his two wonderfully documented works on medieval English preaching; see *MLR* (1929), p. 13, and G. R. Owst, *Preaching in Medieval England* (Cambridge, 1926), p. 111.

[4] Cp. R. W. Chambers, "On the Continuity of English Prose from Alfred to More and his School," an introduction to *EETS,* 186 (1931), reprinted separately (Oxford, 1932), pp. xcvii–xcix, *et passim.*

section of my paper quotations from this work, arranged consecutively, so that the reader can at once look up my source for the statements made, with references to the pages, in the summary description now to be given.)

The *Treatise of Love* is one of the rarer English incunabula; neither the British Museum nor the Bodleian possesses a copy.[5] It is a folio of 48 leaves (eight quires, sig. A-H), in two columns, of 36 lines. It makes one of the group of six volumes which were printed by Wynkyn in the years immediately following Caxton's death. Caxton's name, rather than Wynkyn's, was given in these books, and for the time covered by their publication they seem to make a small output for the Westminster press. The confusing character of these editions, to a scholar new to the problems of bibliography, may be judged by the fact that in my publication of 1929 already cited I referred to one of them, the *Chastising of God's Children* (which takes its title and some scattered sentences from the *Riwle*),[6] as a publication by Caxton, being misled by the presence of Caxton's device accompanying the book. A plausible explanation for this group of transitional publications by Wynkyn has been given by Plomer. We know that legal difficulties were encountered in the settlement of Caxton's estate, and Plomer suggested that all these books may have 'been paid for before

[5] *See* Pollard and Redgrave, *Short-title Catalogue* (London, 1926), No. 24234: "This tretyse is of loue, etc. fol. [W. de Worde, 1493]"; E. Gordon Duff, *Fifteenth Century English Books*, printed for the Bibliographical Society (Oxford, 1917), p. 110, where the whole of the incipit is given; S. de Ricci, *A Census of Caxtons*, printed for the Bibliog. Soc. (Oxford, 1909), p. 112. My study of the *Treatise* was originally made from the copy in the Cambridge University Library, but has been supplemented by a film, which I was kindly permitted to have made, of that at the Henry Huntingdon Library. I wish to express my gratitude to Miss Anne Pratt of the Yale University Library and to Miss Pafort of the Pierpont Morgan Library for facilitating my research for this paper. In a description of the Morgan *Treatise*, Miss Pafort had noted that the work had not been studied for subject-matter. In the second section of this paper Professor W. H. Tretheway has given me invaluable assistance (cf. *ibid.*).

[6] The borrowing was made before 1401 (*see* my *op. cit.*, 1929). I traced a German source of one section, in my *Writings Ascribed to Richard Rolle* (New York, 1927), p. 335, to be referred to in future as *Rolle*. In my part of the apparatus to the edition of the *Book of Margery Kempe* for the Early English Text Society, I carry further my study of the sources, and the great significance for medieval English piety, of the *Chastising*.

Caxton's death, or were on order at that time, and perhaps partly printed.'[7]

If this explanation is applied to the *Treatise of Love*, no action—beyond an order for a book projected but not yet written—can be dated before the death of Caxton (1491). For we are distinctly told in the heading (A[1] c. 1) that the work to follow was translated from French into English in the year 1493, which is that given by the bibliographers for the printing. We might naturally suppose that it cannot have been published before the end of 1493. Thus it is likely to have been at press still when Wynkyn was beginning to print the first work which he brought out under his own name. This is Walter Hilton's long classic of mystical literature, the *Scale of Perfection*, which came out in 1494 and must have marked the triumphant end to any legal difficulties which Wynkyn may have had in taking control of Caxton's press. For this highly influential monument of medieval English piety owed its first edition to a direct command conveyed to Wynkyn by the king's mother, the 'Lady Margaret'; Plomer prints the verses describing the circumstances of the publication (*op. cit.*, p. 52). The explicit details given as to the production of the *Scale* increase the curiosity felt by the reader as to the identity of the anonymous translator of the *Treatise*. He was also the patron of the publication, as the conclusion makes clear. He calls himself, in the heading, 'imperfect in such work.' Nothing makes certain whether he is a cleric or layman. This was, of course, a period when secular persons became authors—even a nobleman like Lord Rivers, and the Lady Margaret herself (who translated a pious work from French).[8]

The final summing up, in Wynkyn's *Treatise of Love*, enumerates various treatises making up the book. For complete accuracy this print should be called 'Treatise of Love and Other Religious Treatises'; several of the series of tracts included treat 'Love,' and among them the most extensive one in the collection, which is the first. This work (as the summing up makes clear) actually

---

[7] H. R. Plomer, *Wynkyn de Worde and his Contemporaries* (London, 1925), pp. 46–47.

[8] This was printed by Pynson in 1504 (C. H. Cooper, *The Lady Margaret*, Cambridge 1874, p. 95).

gives most of its first pages to the Passion; much Latin and stereotyped discussion is given here, with a good deal of reference to St. Bernard—perhaps indicating a source (which I have not attempted to trace). Possibly the compilation had been amplified after it left the hands of the first compiler. Though the heading does link the discussion of Love (to follow) to the Passion, yet the primary subject announced in the heading is not reached until A^{5v} c. 1. If the source is ever found, it may turn out to be less diffuse in the first sections.

The primary subject, according to the heading, is 'the four most special loves in the world,' which comes from the *Ancren Riwle*, pp. 392 sq.[9] So do the passages immediately preceding (A^{3} c. 2, sq., A^{5} c. 1), as well as the texts on Love with which the *Treatise* opens (A^{1} c. 1 sq.^{v}). The book has thus at least begun with a borrowing from the *Riwle*, even though that which the heading has led us to expect is postponed. The texts taken from the *Ancren Riwle*, pp. 382–386, are rearranged, with one change of imagery which may be intended to make the work more cogent to a feminine reader. Altogether, nearly the whole treatment of Love in the *Riwle* (Bk. vii, through pp. 384–400) is embodied in the *Treatise of Love*; it runs all through quires B–E, often with influence on the material which is added. In spite of the late date and dependence on a French source, the context is well preserved (as my quotations illustrate) in all the borrowings from the *Riwle* on Love. But the compilation also contains later treatises; in one on 'Remedies against the Seven Deadly Sins' (F^{3} c. 2–G^{1v} c. 2), borrowings occur from the portion of the *Riwle* on the same subject (Bk. iv), which are more freely treated.

[9] *The Ancren Riwle*, ed. J. Morton, Camden Soc. (1853). The fact that the edition of the *Riwle* now available prints only the Nero MS (with some variants) tremendously handicaps all study of the work. The study of all manuscripts and versions by Mr. G. C. Macaulay (the only such exhaustive study ever made) resulted in an extremely valuable publication in 1914 (*MLR passim*). This was, however, presented, as he makes clear, only with selected textual variants and illustrations of his grounds for his opinions. Through Mrs. J. A. Herbert and Dr. Coulton I have learned that Mr. Macaulay left a cupboard-full of notes on the *Riwle*, which were unfortunately later lost. The parallel texts printed by Dr. Hall for selected sections of the *Riwle* are of great value; see *Selections from Early Middle English* (Oxford, 1920).

Traces of French vocabulary occasionally remain to support the statement that the direct source is French (cf. B^{4v} c. 2, also A^{5v} c. 1 [*surmounteth*], and E^{6} c. 1 [*reames*]). The transmutation of *Giwerie* into *vsurye* (sig. A^{5v} c. 1, cf. p. 392) might signify a date for the compilation after the expulsion of the Jews in 1290—if textual corruption did not sometimes bring alterations of a similar sort. I comment later on another textual revision.

In an 'intermediate' conclusion (G^{1v} c. 1), that part which seems to go back to the French compiler is addressed to a 'sister,' as has been the tract on the Remedies (F^{4} c. 2) and the first long piece, the 'Treatise of Love.' In the latter, two references seem to make clear that the 'sister' is a secular great lady (A^{6} c. 1, B^{2} c. 1). Not only are all the parts using the *Riwle* addressed to a lady, but also the treatise on 'Three Signs of Love' which follows the 'intermediate' conclusion. In this work a reference to the devotion of St. Francis to the Holy Name (G^{1v} c. 2) may be noted; its interpretation is uncertain, in view of the wide veneration of this great saint outside his own order. Tracts which follow, on the 'Branches of the Appletree' (expounding contemplation, etc., by imagery of birds and flowers) and the 'Seven Signs of Love,' may give a clue some time to the origin of the collection; the English translator seems to have found all his treatises in one miscellany. The short pieces with which the whole book ends (H^{4v} c. 2–H^{6} c. 1) were possibly inserted by the printer to fill up a quire. Of these, the last two are the well-known *Nine Words* and *Six Masters*, of foreign origin (see my *Rolle*, pp. 317–319). The former has here an unusual heading. This text was printed by Dibdin (*Typographical Antiquities*, London, 1812, II, pp. 301–302, pointed out by Miss Pafort). The two last pieces are of the sort found as late insertions in manuscripts as well as in incunabula (cf. *infra*). The former is often dated at 1345.

At all times during the Middle Ages theological compilations were of course common. Many were probably made in French, for secular great ladies, as this was. We have no information leading us to believe that the *Ancren Riwle* would be generally accessible to compilers abroad. In my next section I shall describe an Anglo-Norman compilation (for another kind of public) from *ca.*1300 (or earlier), when most of the English upper classes probably still used French, and English ladies are recorded as literary patrons of French works. A pious work was compiled in French as late as 1354 by the great English nobleman, Henry, Duke of Lancaster.[10] And I conjecture that in the latter part of the fifteenth century (before 1493), there is likely to have been a reinforcement, from Burgundy, of the influence of French pious literature in English court circles. Marguerite of York, Duchess of Burgundy (the sister of Edward IV), herself brought about the establishment in England of the Franciscans of the Strict Observance (who were special propagandists of the cult of the Holy Name of Jesus, which was then particularly strong in the Low Countries and also in England).[11] At the Greenwich house, founded (1481) under her influence, and adjacent to the royal palace, all of the first and most of the later friars were aliens. I cite the Burgundian relations of English court circles at this time as an agency possibly bringing about combinations of English and Continental religious treatises. Religious compilations must then have been peculiarly popular at the Burgundian court, for a professional compiler—who worked for the English-born duchess—enjoyed a curiously professional status by favor of the duke. I have described Douce MS 365, 'written in 1465 for Marguerite of York. . . . The scribe is the famous David Aubert, copyist and "grossoyeur" of the Duke of Burgundy' (*Rolle*. p. 338).[12] This volume contains a copy of the French version of the *Abbey of the Holy Ghost*, with such continual inflations as the borrowings from *Ancren Riwle* have received from the compiler of the French source of the *Treatise of Love*. Special links bound the English court to Burgundy at this time; printing itself came to England from the Low Countries; the duchess was the patron of Caxton

[10] An edition of this work by M. Arnould is announced by the Anglo-Norman Text Society. For an interesting description at length by M. Arnould, see *Bulletin of the John Rylands Library*, October 1937, pp. 352 sq.

[11] *See* A. G. Little, "Introduction of the Observant Friars into England," *Proceed. Brit. Acad.*, xi (address delivered, July 11, 1923). *See* also *Rolle*, pp. 314–317.

[12] On Aubert *see* P. Paris, *Les MSS françois de la Bibliothèque du Roi* (Paris, 1836), I, 106.

(*The Library*, Bibliog. Soc., 4th Ser. VII (1927), pp. 391–392; de Ricci, *op. cit.*, frontispiece).

Thus the somewhat unusual tracts included in the latter part of this collection should be searched for in Continental French manuscripts of the late fifteenth century, as well as in Anglo-Norman manuscripts of the thirteenth. It is an example of the confusing international literary influences of the Middle Ages that the *Nine Words*, cited as included in English in Wynkyn's volume, occurs in French as a (mid-xiv cent.) insertion in an important Anglo-Norman manuscript (Arundel 288), and was also very prevalent in the Low Countries and in Germany (in German, French, and Latin). Thus this work and the often associated *Six Masters*, though of foreign origin, give no clue to the origin of the French compilation used in the *Treatise of Love* or (since a later insertion may have been used) to the date. The very rich lady for whom the French compiler adapted the *Ancren Riwle* may have been a contemporary of Maud de Clare, Countess of Gloucester (wife of the head of the English baronage), who owned the Cleopatra MS *ca.* 1280, of the two pious royal ladies of a century later, the duchess of Burgundy and the Lady Margaret, or of any of the pious English ladies who drank from 'cups of gold' during the intervening generations (cf. B^2 c. 1).

But whereas the date of the source is thus uncertain, the date of the translation is explicit. Though not based on English this is actually the latest derivative of the *Ancren Riwle* now known in English. The next latest is the *Five Senses* of probably almost a half-century earlier (of which the provenance is uncertain since the ascription to "Lichfield" cited by Dr. Owst is postmedieval). Though the English derivative the *Chastising* was printed by Wynkyn in the same group with the *Treatise*, the 'borrowings' here were made at least a century earlier (as extant manuscripts prove). It is a fact which (so far as I know) has not been accounted for by bibliographers that of the twelve copies recorded of the latter, all those which have been traced (nine) are bound with the *Chastising* except one, which is presumed to have once been so accompanied (de Ricci, *op. cit.*, p. 112). Such physical association of the two derivatives of the *Ancren Riwle* honored by Wynkyn de Worde immediately after the death of Caxton is of sentimental interest; it would be of historical interest if we could suppose that some one attached to the Westminster press recognized the link between these two works, created by their borrowing from the *Riwle* (to which each owes the passage giving its title).

The passages in the *Treatise of Love* on which I base the remarks just made (here supplied with a minimum of modern punctuation), and the sources of any borrowings which they give from the *Riwle*, are as follows:

A[1] c. 1 [opening]: This tretyse is of loue and spekyth of iiij of the most specyall louys that ben in the worlde and shewyth veryly and perfitely bi gret resons and Causis how the meruelous & bounteuous loue that our lord Jhesu cryste had to mannys soule exceedyth to ferre alle other loues, as apperith well by the paynful passion . . . whiche tretyse was translatid out of frenshe Into englyshe the yere of our Lord Mccccl xxxxiij by a persone that is vnperfight in suche werke . . . of their charyte to pray for . . . the sayde translatour. / *Canticum beate marie de dolore suo in passione filii sui: plenitudo legis est-dilectio.* [Large initial.] The apostel seinte poule seyth the fulfillyng of the lawe ys loue & Seynte gregory seyth. . . . All thys that ys commanded in þ[e] olde lawe and in the newe is one[c. 2]ly in loue (cf. *A. R.* pp. 386, 384) . . . as seyth the holi abbot moyses. . . . If a nedill sowe[A[1v] c. 1]yd not nor sherid [*sic*] clipped not, who wold holde them in ther hau*n*dys? [Cf. *A. R.* p. 384: ase þe holi abbod Moises seide . . . 'ȝif eax ne kurue, ne þe spade ne dulue, ne þe suluh ne erede, hwo kepte ham uorte holden?']

A[3] c. 2. Ryght dere beloued frende in god, now take hede ententyfly and wyth grete deuocyon to thys ensample that folowyth, wherfor and ye shuld loue thys swete ihesu cryst; therin shall ye fynde delicious matyr, for thys hath doon ihesu þ[e] kyng of glorie be your sowle, that is hys loue, as doth a kynge of farre contreys, that louyth a strange lady & sendeth his masse*n*gers before wyth hys lettyrs of loue. In the same maner dyde our lorde Jh*e*su sente hys patryarkis & hys prophetis of the olde testamente wyth letters. These ware the swete prophecys, of hys gracyous comynge into erthe . . . she all poore was besegid in an olde castell wyth hym [*sic*] rounde abowte, & thys cas-

A. R., p. 388: Nimeð god ȝeme, mine leoue sustren, uor hwi we ouh him to luuien. Erest, ase a mon þet woweð—ase a king þet luuede one lefdi of feorrene londe, and sende hire his sondesmen biforen, þet weren þe patriarkes & þe prophetes of þe Olde Testament, mid lettres isealed. . . . A lefdi was þet was mid hire uoan biset al abuten, and hire lond al destrued, & heo al poure, wiðinnen one eorðene castle. . . . Heo underueng al ase on unrecheleas þing þet was so herd iheorted þet hire luue ne mihte he neuer beon þe neorre.

tell was weyke and made of full febyll mater. . . . And she receyued alle these thynge as a vyleyne þt vnnethys cowde yelde hym a gramercy for alle these grete welys, so rude & harde was hyr herte.

A5v c. 1: Ther be four special louys in this worlde. þe one is betwene ij good felawes. The tother between mother and chylde. The thyrde betwene body and sowle. And the fourth betwene ma*n* and wyf. But the dere loue that Jh*esu* cryste louyth vs and also that we shulde loue hym passeth and surmounteth alle other louys. Men myght say that thys were a right good felaw that wolde laye hys plegge in place for to aquite hys felaw owte of dette and of vsurye, but the swete Jh*esu* put hymself in place and leyd hys tendyr body to aquyte hys loue, whyche is our sowle, owte of the pryson of helle and of alle vsuryes.

A. R., p. 392 sq.: Uour heaued luuen me iuint iðisse worlde-bitweonen gode iueren þe uormeste is; bitweonen mon & wummon þe oðer is; bitweonen wif & hire child þe þridde is; bitweonen licome & soule. Þeo luue þet Jesu Crist haueð to his deore leofmon ouergeð ham alle uoure, & passeð ham alle. Ne telleð me him god feolawe þet leið his wed ine Giwerie uorto acwiten ut his fere? God Almihti leide himsulf uor us ine Giwerie, and dude his deorewurðe bodi uorto acwiten ut his leofmon of Giwene honden.

A6 c. 1: Now I pray yow, ryght dere sustyr, remembyr yow stedfastly whan*ne* ye lye in your large softe bed, wel arayed wyth ryche clothys and warme couerynge and hote furrys, so well at ese, and your Jentylwoman so redy to serue yow; than*ne* thynke ye often wyth gret pyte how she that was the quene of angellys . . . how hyr bed was streyght and harde and arayed wyth pore clothys.

B2 c. 1. Whan*ne* ye beholde your ryche clothis & other fayr Jewellis, [c. 2] your gret horses & fayr harneys, than*ne* bethynke yow of the poor clothyng that your lorde and loue ihesu cryst & hys dyscyplys hadde . . . also often whan*ne* ye sytte at þe tabyll, so rychly arayd & serued, & goodly Jentylme*n* abowte yow, so well araied & well seruinge, þt serue yow so nobely wyth cuppys of gold, & syluer vessell, wyth so many & dyuerse & good metys, wyth delycyous sawses, & pleysau*n*t wynes, Thanne remembyr yow, wyth gret compasc*io*n, how poorely the ryche kyng of heuene was serued, your spowsethe, swete Jh*es*us.

B4v c. 2: yf þe chylde . . . myght neuyr be helid but hyt were bayned in the mothyrs blood and, yff the mother wolde make thys bayne, thys shewed well a gret and specyall loue.

A. R., p. 394: Child þet heued swuche vuel þet him bihouede beð of blode er hit were iheled, muchel luuede þe moðer hit þet wolde him þis beð makien.

E6 c. 1: Now and ye will not gyue your loue, I wyll bye it. Wyll ye selle it for mi loue or for ony other thinge? It is moost resonable marchandyse, loue for loue. And yf it be to selle for that

A. R., p. 398: Ȝif þi luue nis nout forto ȝiuen, auh wult allegate þet me bugge hire, do seie hwui. Oðer mid oðer luue, oðer mid sumhwat elles? Me sulleð wel luue uor luue; and so me ouh forto

pryce, I haue truly boughte it with a nother loue. And that loue that I haue shewed you passeth all the louys of the world. And though they were al togider, yet is it gretter. And yf ye say that ye wyll not gyue it me so good chepe, name how moche ye wyll haue. And ye can not name so moche but I wyll gyue you as moche. Wyll ye castelles? Wyll ye reames? Or wyll ye aske al the worlde? Yet shall I make you a better couenaunt.

sullen luue, & for none þinge elles. Ȝif þin luue is so to sullen, ich habbe ibouht hire mid luue ouer alle oðre. Vor, of þe uour meste luuen ich habbe ikud toward þe þe meste of ham alle. And ȝif þu seist þet tu nult nout leten þeron so liht cheap, auh wultu ȝet more, nem hwat hit schule beon. Sete feor o ðine luue. Þu ne schalt siggen so muchel þet ich nulle ȝiuen þe, uor þine luue, muchele more. Wultu kastles and kinedomes? Wultu welden al þene world? Ich chulle don þe betere.

E6v c. 1: *Quomodo est istud: sine modo a nobis deus amari meruit* [a text quoted from St Bernard, which serves as a link to the subject of the Seven Hours].

F3 c. 2. *A solis ortu* [etc.] Here endeth the lamentac*i*on of our lady, whiche she had in þe passion of our sauyour. / Here begynneth a treatyse moche prouffitable for reformac*i*on of soules defoyled wyth ony of the vij dedely synnes. To his riht dere suster, salute and helthe of soule and of body in hi*m* that is true sauyour....

F5v c. 2: Another remedie there is ayenst slouth and ayenst euery euyll, and a mene to purchace euery wele. This is oryson, and therfore the fende dredeth moche þe charytable prayer, for this cause, þe prayer entreth so moche in the court of ihesu cryst ayenst the fende that it doth two thi*n*gis. It byndeth hym and brenneth hym. We rede that a holy man was in his prayers....

A. R., p. 244: Inward, & meðlease, & angresfule bonen biwinneð sone sucurs & help & ure Louerd aȝean flesches fondunges; and ne beon heo neuer so angresfule, ne so fulitowune, þe deouel of helle duteð ham swuðe; vor teken þet heo draweð sone adun sucurs aȝean him, and Godes hond of heouene, doð him two hermes- bindeð him, & berneð. Lo! her preoue of boðe. Pupplius, on holi mon was in his bonen....

F6v c. 1: But who that by true fayth beholde well the poure petaunce that our lorde Jhesu cryst had the day þt he was lete blood on the crosse, they sholde haue lityll appetyte to that glotenie. There ben two maner of folkes that haue grete nede of good and comfortable meters, this is to knowe, they that traueyle, and they þt blede....

A. R., p. 260: Aȝean glutunie is his poure pitaunce, þet he hefde o rode. Two maner men habbeð neode uorte eten wel, & forto drinken wel-swinkinde men, & blod-letene.

G1v c. 1. Blessyd be the clene of herte . . . the holy company of heuen. My dere suster, there I trust we shall be togyder, bothe body & sowle, at the grete daye of Jugement. And this grau*n*t vs almighti god of his Infinite mercy. Amen. And all ye that rede or here this, pray ye for hym that made it, and for theym that wrote it, and for hir that was the cause that it was made, and of your charite for [c. 2] theym that translatid it and wrote it out of frenssh in to e*n*glissh, one pater noster and one avee, that god haue mercy on vs and that we may come to hym, [etc.] [an 'intermediate' cinclusion, probably intended to cover all the works included up to this point.] As wyse folkes sayen there ben thre signes of very loue and frenshypp. . . . And this dyde saynt Frau*n*ceys, of whom pope Gregory wytnessith by his bull, þ[t] he sawe often wyth his eyen that whan men named the name of ihesu before saynt fraunceys, he was soo rauysshyd wyth that blessid name, that he had nother the herynge nor the sight of ony persone or thinge that was done aboute him for a tyme.

G3ᵛ c. 2. Here foloweth a Treatise that spekyth of the vertu & of the brau*n*ches of the appultree, whiche is expouned morally, as foloweth hereafter. / The Prophete saith thise wordes: 'I shall mount to the appultree & take of the frute.' Somtyme is vnderstonde by the appultree the crosse, And somtyme penaunce, Somtyme contemplacyon.

H2ᵛ c. 1 [after treatises on the Branches of the Appletree and Seven Signs of Love]. How fayth exhorteth the persone to eschewe & haue in contempt all euyll thoughtes. . . . Grete awayte ought eueri bodi to haue vpon theymself þ[t] they retorne not ayen vnto those synnes that they haue ben reconsiled of [the last work noted in the final summing up].

H4ᵛ c. 2. Here begynneth a techynge by manere of predycacyon, made to the peple by master Alberte, conteynyng ix artycles. / Mayster Alberte Archbysshop of Coleyne sayd thyse wordes in the persone of Jhesu cryst.

H6 c. 1. Thus endeth this present boke, whiche treateth fyrst of the gloryous passion of our Sauyour and of the compascyon that his blessyd moder had therof. And also sheweth in another treatyse folowynge . . . [details follow] [c. 2.] Whiche boke was lately translated oute of frensh in to englisshe by a Right well dysposed persone, for by cause the sayd persone thoughte it necessary to al deuoute peple to rede or to here it redde. And also caused the sayd boke to be enprynted [probably supplied by the printer, as the heading had been supplied by the translator].

II

A series of French religious tracts run through the volume now bound as Part II, ff. 1–54, Trinity Coll. Camb. MS. 883 (R.14.7). The items were described in considerable detail by Dr. James in his *Western MSS. in the Library of Trinity College Cambridge* (Cambridge, 1901), and, in more general terms, in Vising's comprehensive but very brief survey, *Anglo-Norman Language and Literature* (Oxford, 1923). Dr. James did not recognize the *Riwle* in this volume, because the incipit of the main block of text is altered, and the work appears as 'Uie de gent de religion' (f. 124ᵛ). However, the incipit retains the opening text of the *Riwle:*

'*Recti diligunt te.*' A clue was thus given, and I was able to make general statements, in the letter to *LTLS* already cited, as follows:

[the volume] is found to contain most of the *Ancren Riwle*, in Anglo-Norman. This is not the version found in the Cotton MS, hitherto the only French copy known. Mr. J. A. Herbert would date the Trinity hand [in the late thirteenth or early fourteenth century] a little earlier than the Cotton. The Trinity text is more altered than the Cotton, yet it gives readings of great interest. Only about half is consecutive; the rest is embedded in other treatises.

The series of tracts in the Trinity MS run to a very great length, for they fill a large number of folios, and the format of the volume is large (James calls it $10\frac{1}{2}$ by $6\frac{5}{8}$ in.); the works are written in two columns. To examine with complete finality a compilation of such length would demand a prolonged period of close study. At the same time, the features of the collection pertinent to this paper are such as can probably be described with general accuracy from a rapid survey like that which I have given. (As in my first section, I again append a series of quotations to give the grounds for my summary statements. In making these statements, I shall add references '*cf. infra*' to numbered quotations (A, B, etc.), grouped together *infra*, pp. 209–212. The quotations are arranged in order of my use of them, rather than according to their own order, except in the case of the last, which owes its position to its length.)

The large 'consecutive borrowing' from the *Riwle*, 'Uie de gent de religion' (ff. 124^v–154^v), gives: the *A. R.*, pp. 2, l.1–15, l.23; 49, l.5–198, l.6. It had been preceded by three principal treatises: on the Seven Deadly Sins, on Penance, and on the Ten Commandments. That on the Sins includes the 'de generaus medicines' cited separately by James, as the prefatory summary proves (f. 1^vc.2). All four items seem to be here presented as making part of one whole, due to the same compiler, or, possibly, to a group of compilers working in unison. The opening address quoted by Dr. James from the first treatise of the collection is reproduced with trifling changes for all the other three (cf. *infra*, Quot. A), as also for some of their subdivisions; it sounds to me individual, and thus seems—to me at least—to betray a basic unity in the whole series of tracts. Moreover, I have noted in the *Uie* cross references explicitly backward to the first treatise (the *Sins*). In the original

Riwle at one point a cross reference also occurs, but it is not explicit, and is forward (cf. *infra*, Quot. B). A dichotomy has been made of the text of the *Ancren Riwle* by 'the compiler' (thus to cite a person who *may* be *any* member of a group); what is of general application in the *Riwle* is given first, in the tracts on the Sins and Penance. The more esoteric residue (the 'Uie de gent de religion') follows after an interval—for no 'borrowings' have been traced in the *Commandments*.[13] Since the two parts of the *Riwle* appear in reverse order, when the compiler carried over the cross reference into the compilation, the reference had to be altered to fit the order there followed. This somewhat meticulous adaptation seems to indicate a very deliberate intention of presenting the *Uie* as making part of the same 'compileison' as had opened the volume. No less significant is a final addition. The compiler carries his 'consecutive borrowing' through the summary mention of the seven sins as animals on p. 198 (to l.6); he then concludes the *Uie* with a reference back to the first tract, for the rest of this discussion. French expositions of the Creed and Lord's Prayer follow, with an imperfect copy of St. Edmund's *Mirror*.

The *Uie* in the Trinity MS is not, as Dr. James thought, "unfinished," yet it gives only the first four parts of a work announced in the preface as of nine. Professor Trethewey has provided me with a text of the prefatory table of contents (Quot. G), which greatly increases the historical interest of the Trinity MS. This table can be compared with that prefaced to the *Riwle*, and with Dr. James's rough index to the compilation; I will summarize the results of such comparisions, so far as they concern my interests in this paper: (1) The direct source of the *Uie* was a version of

[13] My own rough notes have been supplemented by a table of "correspondances" supplied by Mr. Herbert. This shows that the first borrowings, in ff. 7–34ᵛ of the *Sins*, give the *Riwle*, pp. 240–296, "embedded" in the tract in twelve separate sections, most of them out of sequence. The tract ends with a large borrowing (pp. 198–216, on the sins as beasts, and the devil's court). The borrowings in the treatise on Penance are two very long ones (pp. 298, l.12–346, l.27, in ff. 51–66ᵛ; pp. 348, l.3–410, l.18, in ff. 100ᵛ–111ᵛ), and one very short (the conclusion, the only part of Bk. viii here used, which is partly repeated. Cf. *infra*, Quot. D). Mr. Herbert's references follow a foliation added after my photostats were made. Since the older foliation (not consistent) is, I am told, still legible, I have not adjusted a few incidental references, in the body of this article, to the old foliation.

the *Riwle* already much expanded. This lost derivative of the *Ancren Riwle* I shall in this paper call 'the expansion,' in distinction to its own derivative, 'the compilation'; (2) In the expansion all the eight books of the *Riwle* were present except the first (liturgical). The preface of the *Riwle* served as Part I in the expansion, the opening address (in Quot. A), with the table (Quot. G), as the preface; Parts II–IV coincided with Bks. ii–iv (as they do with Parts II–IV of the *Uie*). But Parts V–VIII reproduced the three tracts which open the compilation; the long section on Pains of Purgatory (etc.) making part of the extant *Penance* was separate (as Part VIII), the *Commandments* (which follow Penance, with no 'borrowings' from the *Riwle*) preceded, as Part VII. Part IX of the lost text was the *Riwle*, Bk. viii (on domestic matters); this is the only portion of the expansion not somewhere present in the compilation (at least in the main outlines, for, without a copy of the former, we cannot be sure of its *minutiae*); I note in *Penance* an 'embedded borrowing' from the conclusion of the missing portion of the expansion (cf. Quot. D); (3) In the expansion, Bks. v, vi, vii, of the *Riwle* had evidently been conflated and expanded to make a systematized treatment of Penance (Part VI); the treatment of the Sins had been detached from Bk. iv to make the separate Part V (leading up naturally to what amounted to a penitential); (4) Thus evidently not only did 'the dichotomy' merely shift the order of items already present in the expansion, it also merely carried further a process already begun of making more prominent those parts of the *Riwle* which were of practical utility to any devout person preparing for confession (a Sacrament of which the use had been widely extended in 1215); (5) We must waive all judgment as to the alterations that may have been made at the time of the dichotomy; both the tracts and the *Uie* may, in the *minutiae* of their text, have then been subject to addition and abridgement. But since it is clear that laborious interweaving of parts of the *Riwle* with new material had gone to the making of the expansion, it seems altogether likely that the 'embedded' borrowings in the tracts had originated in the expansion, of which the *Uie* (the 'consecutive borrowing') seems to give a partial text.

But it should be repeated that without a copy of the lost expansion we can never be sure of its relation to the extant compilation. Notable features of the latter which (in view of the two stages of revision which it represents) arouse curiosity as to their origin are: some lengthy digressions in the tracts (I shall later cite those on alms and *disciplines*); the stereotyped *exordia* (Quot. A); the inflation in the *Uie* of all addresses to recluses. I shall review such signs of provenance as have been noted in the compilation; for my discussions it is important that they offer no positive obstacle to the supposition that 'the compiler' (a person or a group) *may* have been responsible both for expanding the *Riwle* and for later—for a different public—making the dichotomy which (with whatever alterations then accomplished) created the compilation. It should be said emphatically that of course 'Compiler I,' 'Compiler II,' etc., may have developed this derivative of the *Riwle;* but to give a comprehensive pioneer description with allowance made for all conceivable complexities does not seem likely to further sound study of the problems. I shall, in the interest of clarity, continue to refer to 'the compiler' as a sort of algebraic *x* or John Doe; my reader can easily determine to which of the two parts of the compilation—that of the 'embedded borrowings,' or of the 'consecutive'—any passage under discussion belongs, and make his generalization for himself. The editor will later bring new evidence of provenance. But the evidence which I adduce now can hardly have its historical interest for my studies destroyed, whatever conclusions are later reached as to 'the compiler.'

The Trinity treatise on the Sins is preceded by a long comment and summary (ff. 1-1v). Here an explicit statement of the purpose for which the work is written makes clear that though the work here begun may be useful to a wide public, it (like the *Uie*) is intended for 'hommes et femmes de religion' (cf. *infra*, Quot. C). This statement is couched in the plural; it is uncertain whether this is a 'we' of authority, formality, or conventual unity.

In any case, in the conclusion to the eighth part of the same treatise, the compiler combines a reminiscence from the conclusion of the *Riwle*, in the first person (carried over from his source), with the statement that he has made his compilation 'al hon*or* deu tut puissa*n*t e de ma douce dame seinte marie e de seint franceys e al salu des almes . . . ' (cf. *infra*, Quot. D). The most natural explanation for this passage (though, as I shall repeat later, I think perhaps not the only possible one) is that the writer is himself a Franciscan. What he is, his group is likely to be (if a group prepared this compilation). The interweaving of the reference to St. Francis with a fragment of the *Riwle* suggests an origin in 'the expansion.'

In a long discussion of *disciplines*, the practice is cited of such exercises on the part of St. Jerome, St. Benedict, 'seint domenik fundeour de freres p*re*cheours,' and 'seint franceis fondeour des freres menours'; this whole section is repeated in Latin, hence has probably been enlarged by the compiler from a source (cf. ff. 86ᵛ–87: 'beatus dominicus . . . beatus franciscus'). This impersonal reference to St. Dominic and St. Francis—in this order—at first seems at variance with the Franciscan passage (*supra*). Works on St. Francis were written by persons outside his Order (see A. G. Little, *A Guide to Franciscan Studies*, London, 1920, p. 12). Early Dominicans and Franciscans shared the favor of important secular persons, lay and clerical, and were themselves friends; a friar of either Order might refer respectfully to the founder of the other.

Special interest in the mendicant ideals may explain the presence of a large section on alms (ff. 76–81), in which the life of 'St Johan le aumoner' is cited (f. 80). The Anglo-Norman legend of this saint found by M. Paul Meyer should be compared with this part of the tract on Penance.[14] Franciscan influence may explain what appears to be a reminiscence of the opening of Bishop Grosseteste's *Château d'Amour*,[15] as for the fact that the ninth section of the treatise on Penance is identical with the French version of the tract on the Pains of Purgatory often ascribed to Grosseteste (a widely known piece which I encountered in my re-

---

[14] P. Meyer, *Notices et Extraits des Manuscrits de la Bibliothèque Nationale*, 38 (1903), pp. 294 sq.

[15] "Ki bien pense, il creit bien" (f. 37ᵛ). Cf. "Ki bien pense bien poet dire; / sanz penser ne poet suffire / De nul bien fet comencer" (J. Murray, *Le Chateau d'Amour de Robert Grosseteste*, Paris, 1918, p. 89).

search on the *Manuel des Pechiez*, and in that on the *Prick of Conscience*).[16] In the Arundel MS 288 (already cited for its text of the *Nine Words*), I find that this tract of 'Grosseteste' opens (f. 84) with the same heading addressed to 'treschiers freres et soers en deu' which it bears in the Trinity compilation. Apparently the well-known tract is merely a detached segment of that work. Miss Ruth J. Dean, who is editing the French versions of 'Grosseteste,' in 1936 kindly examined this section of the Trinity MS and will use it in her forthcoming edition. It should be repeated that this piece made Part VIII of the expanded *Riwle*. Grosseteste was, of course, a reforming bishop, a secular priest who gave to the new Minorite order (and in lesser degree to the Preachers)[17] a very enthusiastic admiration.

Certainly the compiler of the *Uie* shows exceptional nonsectarianism. He amplifies every reference to recluses in the 'Uie de gent de religion,' so as to apply to all classes of those 'who live under rule,' men as well as women (thus amplifying, with historical allusions of great interest, 'his' initial reference to the work being intended for 'hommes et femmes de religion'). I quote two of the amplifications in question (cf. *infra*, Quots. F and E). It will be seen that one includes a reference to 'friars of the sack,' which (if original) would seem to date the compilation after *ca.*1257, and before *ca.*1307.[18] The compiler seems to subdivide the friars in a way probably hard to interpret by extant English records. Conspicuous subdivisions of monks and canons (especially of canons) existed, but pass unnoted here. If it be argued that these classifications merely render sects known to exist abroad, or have been carried over from a source, even so mention of *seven* mendicant orders seems significant. As a matter of fact, I note in an earlier treatise (f. 63) a reference to 'le liuere de concordances de reules de gent de religion,' from which some of these curious enumerations of religious sects may have been derived. Identification of

[16] Cf. my "Manuel des Pechiez and the Scholastic Prologue," *RR*, viii (1917), 445; *Rolle*, pp. 378–379.

[17] His patronage of both orders is sometimes ignored. *See* his letter to Adam Marsh (1236?), Rolls Series 25, 1861, *Letters of Grosseteste*, ed. Luard, p. 71.

[18] *See* A. G. Little, *Eng. Hist. Rev.*, ix (1894), pp. 121–7; though the order was abolished in 1274, some of its friars survived till 1307 in Norwich (cf. n. 25).

this work might test this conjecture—which, if supported, would demonstrate a common hand in *Penance* and the *Uie*. If the 'Grosseteste' can be taken as associated with the group of the bishop, its presence in the 'expansion' would seem to indicate the same Franciscan influence as can be traced in the earlier part of the 'compilation.' That such influence means Franciscan authorship on the whole seems likely but not certain.

Though this compilation must have come from at least the sphere of influence of the Franciscan order, the Trinity copy was owned by the oldest type of 'hommes de religion'—by Benedictines. Thus it was used, as 'the author' intended, by persons under vows, though outside the limits of his own especial affiliations—a fulfillment of his nonsectarian intentions that he might find gratifying. The provenance of this volume is extremely interesting for my studies, from various points of view (not all of which I can mention here). It seems clear from such a corrected passage as the rubric of the *Uie* (Qhot. A) that the Trinity MS is not an archetype. (I use the title, 'Trinity compilation' for the sake of clarity.)

There is an inscription (early fourteenth century) on the top of the first page: 'I.ix.Galfridi de Wroxham m*onachi*.' Dr. James here recognized the pressmark of the library of Norwich Cathedral, and Dean Beeching identified the monk-owner with the refectorer of Norwich Priory in 1311.[19] Dr. Saunders's recent researches on the priory rolls show that the name of the refectorer is not given with his rolls immediately preceding that date; that 'G. de Wroxham' was refectorer, also, at least 1313–1314, and died in 1322.[20]

As Dean Beeching pointed out (*op. cit.*, p. 76), it was the Lenten custom in Benedictine houses for books to be distributed among the monks (a regulation which, as Dom Wilmart has pointed out to me, did much to keep medieval libraries alive). As in the case of other books bearing the names of Norwich monks, this volume may have been assigned for private devotional reading. But Dr. Saunders shows that the Norwich refectorer procured certain

---

[19] H. C. Beeching and M. R. James, "The Library of the Cathedral Church of Norwich," "*Norfolk and Norwich Archaeol. Soc.*, xix (1915), p. 75.

[20] H. W. Saunders, *An Introduction to the Rolls of Norwich Cathedral Priory* (Norwich, 1930), p. 69.

books of a type which, to me at least, suggest that a small reference library may have been kept in the refectory (*op. cit.*, p. 143). Probably (though here I speak a priori) the Norwich refectorer had some responsibility for the provision of books to be read at meals (according to the explicit prescription of the Rule of St. Benedict).[21]

Mr. Herbert points out to me that the Egerton MS of the pious tales of Adgar (also Anglo-Norman) is marked for refectory reading (and represents the kind of volume which he thinks was usually chosen for such use).[22] In all the incipits to the parts of the Trinity compilation quoted (cf. *infra*, Quot. A), the possibility that the work may be read aloud is put prominently; but a reference to the illiteracy which was probably so frequent at this period may, of course, be all that is indicated. I note that there is perhaps an unusual amount of subdivision in some parts,[23] though on the whole the segments are not uniform. Evidently nothing can be proved, in the present state of our information, as to what use Dom Wroxham made of this book. But his ownership has suggested to me a possible practical utility, in monastic circles, for the spritely expositions of the *Ancren Riwle*, which I had not

---

[21] I find of interest for my study of the feminine piety of medieval England the form in which this regulation appears in the *Winteney Rule*, ed. M. M. Arnold Schröer (Halle, 1888), p. 83. Dr. James believed that a Norwich volume had "added to it, the name of the monk who procured it for the house" (*The Wanderings and Homes of Manuscripts*, London, 1928, p. 65). The problem is complicated, but the actual inscriptions and monastic custom seem to me to support Canon Beeching's interpretation (*supra*) for at least some cases. Dr. James notes the possible effect, on the library of Norwich Cathedral Priory, of the fire of 1272 (wrongly dated by him at 1286, *op. cit.*, p. 66, cf. Beeching, p. 68). The Trinity MS was probably written during the period of replenishing the library after the fire. One of the few extant early MSS from Norwich is marked 'ad colacionem,' for conventual reading (Goulburn and Symonds, *Bishop Herbert de Losinga*, Oxford, 1878, II, pp. iii–iv, and Beeching and James, MS 26).

[22] For a valuable article by Mr. Herbert on Adgar, see *Romania*, xxxii (1903), pp. 394–421.

[23] Cf.: "Isci commence li qu*a*rt chapitle de la secunde p*a*rtie de la tierce partie de confession" (from a rotograph of the Paris MS (f. 57[v]), kindly given me, as a specimen of that copy, by Mrs. Dempster; see *infra*, p. 208). Frequent subdivision into chapters and paragraphs characterizes the *Uie* as well as the tracts.

thought of before, and which—a priori—we might expect that this widely circulated work sometimes fulfilled.

The Trinity volume is well written, and Dr. James notes its 'border of beautiful pen-ornament.' Experts in medieval palaeography may later pronounce on the chance that the manuscript might have been written at Norwich; there still exist a large number of Norwich Priory manuscripts to give a basis for study of the Norwich scriptorium (Beeching and James, *op. cit.*). In the same way, linguists may later be able to determine the affiliations of the Trinity text of the *Riwle* in a way to aid its localization. A quotation which I shall give in conclusion will show a certain affinity to the Titus MS (which also seems nearer than any other copy to the midfifteenth-century English derivative, the *Five Senses*, first brought to light by Dr. Owst); *see* my *op. cit.*, 1929, pp. 13–15.

It is at least certain that the compilation was made somewhere in England. I have noted references (by way of imagery) to the 'King of England' at ff. 43^{v}, 94^{v}. And, though nothing proves that the 'Franciscan compiler' worked at Norwich, it should be pointed out that conditions recorded in this city *ca.*1300 would offer as congenial a background for his enterprise as any of which we have record in England at the same time. It would seem altogether likely that copies of the *Ancren Riwle* were owned in Norwich during the middle and late thirteenth century, for an exceptional number of parish churches there then had reclusories attached.[24] Among them was St. Ethelred's, appropriated to the refectory at the Cathedral. The St. Ethelred's reclusory was torn down in 1305, though the 'anachorita' had paid rent to the refectorer (at that time nameless) in the same year. Blomefield says that the anchorage was rebuilt in 1305, though without giving his authority; also that *ca.*1300 the Norwich Franciscans acquired land and established a reclusory with a garden in which they put an 'anker.'[25] If Blomefield can be trusted here, a male recluse (probably a friar) would be indicated. But it has not always been

---

[24] *See* R. M. Clay, *The Hermits and Anchorites of England* (London, 1914), pp. 233–235. I wish to express my indebtedness to Miss Clay and Miss D. M. B. Ellis for my access to unprinted notes on the recluse life, by each of these authorities, which were of great value.

[25] *See* Saunders, *op. cit.*, p. 142; F. Blomefield, *Norwich* (Norwich, 1806), ii, 75, and 102 (a reprint of his *Norfolk*, vol. iv). For 'friars of the sack' see *ibid.*, pp. 334–335.

recognized that *anachorita* can apply to either sex (in Lat. and Fr., only the inflected *inclusa*, *reclusa*, and derivatives, respectively, can make the sex of an 'anchorite' certain). Anchoresses were sometimes taken informally under the protection of convents of men. Not knowing Blomefield's source we cannot verify his 'anker.' But from the point of view of the early history of reclusion in England his reference, though ambiguous, is of interest.

I have noted from the Trinity compilation (cf. *infra*, Quot. E) a reference to 'recluse noire ou grise' of historical interest. I do not know whether the 'black anchoress' is Benedictine or Dominican. No records of early Dominican recluses in England of either sex are extant, though there are various records of anchorites in Benedictine houses—as at Westminster.[26] It seems doubtful whether the St. Ethelred's 'anchorite' paying rent to the Benedictine refectorer (who to some degree must have been responsible for the cell) might be called 'black' if not Benedictine. But certainly the 'grey recluse' at this period is Franciscan.[27] It should be emphasized that, so far as extant records go, the Norwich Franciscan reclusory was the first recorded in England from any friary, of any mendicant Order. But in 1296 one Emma, an anchoress near Shrewsbury, 'wore the Franciscan habit' (being apparently, like the 'anchorite' at St. Ethelred's, enclosed next a parish church).[28] Our information as to this first 'grey recluse' comes from the Lanercost Chronicle; it is possible that some of the anchoresses of the early period known only from wills might also have 'worn the habit' of a mendicant Order; in the early fifteenth century, anchoresses were 'given the Carmelite habit' and enclosed in friaries of Carmelites—an Order which never had nunneries in England (Clay, *op. cit. s.v. Emma Stapilton*). In later publications (and *infra*) I shall return to the spiritual direction by English friars of contemplative women—which is something very

---

[26] Clay, *op. cit.*, pp. 77, 230–231.

[27] In the twelfth century, the Cistercians had sometimes been called "grey," as had the order of Savigny (*see* Dr. Coulton, in a review of my first article on the *Riwle*), *MLR*, xv (1920), p. 99. Later research by historians must clear up the references to the religious persons here called "*bis*."

[28] Clay, *op. cit.*, p. 140; Cf. Sir H. Maxwell, *The Chronicle of Lanercrost* (Glasgow, 1913), p. 151, translating and original *Sropesbiry* (J. Stevenson, *Bannatyne* Club, 1939, p. 151).

different from the direction of women of less advanced piety, with which friars are commonly associated. It is at least immediately clear that the case of Dame Emma illustrates a practical reason for some Franciscans to know the *Ancren Riwle*.

It was also about 1300 that the Corpus Christi Camb. MS 402, the unique copy of the full revision of the *Ancren Riwle* made *ca.*1225–1230 (and here called *Ancrene Wisse*) was procured for Wigmore Abbey almost certainly from Shropshire (*see* my letter to *LTLS*, February 8, 1936). In the material added in this version, reference is made to Shrewsbury and Chester, probably indicating that it was made for persons with connections on the Welsh border (Macaulay, *op. cit.*, p. 470).[29] It is noteworthy that it was a lady from this region, the most socially potent of medieval English anchoresses, Loretta, Countess of Leicester,[30] who gave enthusiastic patronage to the first Franciscans when they arrived at Canterbury in 1224; she lived in enclosure till at least 1266, in touch with court circles till the end. Her sister (Lady Mortimer, from Wigmore) also became enclosed. The new material added, *ca.*1225–1230, to the *Riwle* near the Shropshire district (as linguists seem to agree) makes clear that the twenty anchoresses addressed in *Ancrene Wisse* were in friendly contact—informally, not as spiritual daughters—with both Dominicans and Franciscans ('V̄re freres precheours & v̄re freres meonurs').[31] Hitherto no records of early recluses in Shropshire have been found. But Miss Ellis has lately brought to my attention an anchoress of the date, language-area, and historical associations reflected in *Ancrene Wisse*. The anchoresses Lady Leicester and Lady Mortimer (enclosed near Canterbury and Oxford, respectively) had one surviving sister in the world (their parents and brother having been destroyed through King John); she was the wife of the magnate Walter de Lacy. Miss Ellis points out to me the highly interesting fact that at Lacy's death in 1240 an anchoress was being supported

[29] On the dialect of *Ancrene Wisse, see* M. S. Serjeantson, *London Medieval Studies*, I (1938), pp. 225–248.

[30] *See* F. M. Powicke, in *Historical Essays in Honour of James Tait* (Manchester, 1933), pp. 247–272.

[31] *See* Macaulay, *op. cit.*, pp. 467, 471. It seems quite clear that the twenty anchoresses were not under the spiritual direction of friars.

at his castle of Ludlow (*Liberate Rolls*, II, p. 72). In another paper I shall discuss this fact, with other historical facts of some interest for our understanding of the background of *Ancrene Wisse*. It hardly seems likely that the Trinity compilation will show the influence of that text (the importance of which has been so graphically brought out by Professor Tolkien); reminiscences of the personal circumstances of the three anchoresses for whom the *Riwle* had been written remain in the *Uie* as a sign of affinity to the Titus-Nero MSS, rather than to the revision made for twenty recluses found in the *Wisse* (cf. Quot. F).

The fact that the Trinity compilation shows Franciscan influence, with the retention of the older type of text, is to my mind one of its most interesting features; thus seems to be demonstrated the widespread association of the early friars with anchoresses—which cannot be narrowed to one Order or locality. I shall later expound my belief that the extant group of early manuscripts of the *Riwle* (an older work) are in a sense a memorial of the religious revival brought about by the friars. They established no nunneries for many years. Miss Ellis first pointed out to me that their first feminine converts are likely often to have become enclosed. It seems to me on many grounds impossible that the *Riwle* could have been first written by a friar (a class of religious person not included in the categories there included); the recent textual studies cited in my note 34 confirm this opinion, by carrying back, at least a considerable distance behind the extant manuscripts, the associated 'Katherine Group.' Through three hundred years we see the *Riwle* used, in varying degrees, as a practical rule of life—being adapted in some way to suit special circumstances of a person or a group, by friars among others. It would be natural that revival of interest in so eloquent and congenial a work would follow in the wake of the great religious awakening which accompanied the early friars—without providing any convents in which their female devotees could be incorporated in their Orders. The 'expansion' of the *Riwle* which was the direct source of the Trinity 'compilation' (probably prepared by a Franciscan or some one closely associated with Franciscans), even though 'non-sectarian' in its appeal, must have been primarily addressed to persons of very advanced piety. Anchoresses and anchorites would use it, even though specially devout friars and even monks would do so likewise.

Associations of the early Franciscans with anchoresses might make it likely that a copy of the *Riwle* would be found at the Franciscan reclusory established at Norwich *ca.*1300. If more copies were extant, or if all the extant ones bore such evidence of linguistic and historical localization as *Ancrene Wisse*, it is likely that some would show Norwich provenance, perhaps from the reign of Henry III from which we have the magnificent group of five English copies. For, contemporary with the 'recluse countess' and with Bishop Grosseteste of Lincoln (d.1253, the special patron of the Franciscans) was Bishop Suffield of Norwich (1243–1257), historically famous for having directed the 'Norwich Taxation' of all ecclesiastical property for the pope. Miss D. M. B. Ellis points out to me that Suffield was a notable patron of recluses (as he was of friars); his own niece was enclosed in Norfolk.[32] Some early impetus to the recluse life in the county is likely to have come through Suffield. It will be a matter to me of great interest to see whether linguists will later find it possible that the language of the Titus MS may show some East Anglian influence. It stands apart from the better known group, MSS Corpus, Cleopatra, and Caius, according to Macaulay's summary (p. 148). Hall wrote (p. 373) of this copy that it stood 'nearest in dialect to the original' (which, in his opinion, arose in Lincolnshire). But it must never be forgotten how widely medieval persons of importance—ecclesiastical and secular—traveled, and manuscripts brought from far may have been used in Norwich reclusories—especially those written in Latin and French. Friars were of course regularly itinerant. So were the families of magnates.

I do not know of any evidence as to a personal interest in the anachoretical life on the part of Bishop Grosseteste. But his reforming zeal might incite those who had come under his influence to undertake such an instrument of conventual betterment as the Trinity compilation. I have in the past so often encountered Grosseteste's name attached to works of popular religious instruc-

[32] *See* Blomefield, *Norwich*, i (his *Norfolk*, iii), 486–491.

tion in Anglo-Norman, or even English, that many years ago I conjectured that the bishop may have taken active measures to stimulate vernacular writing as a means of raising the standard of contemporary piety;[33] hence, that the ascriptions to him of various vernacular works (usually verse) may represent a confused tradition, to some degree resting on facts. It is possible that new light may be thrown on a possible relation of episcopal action to the production of Anglo-Norman literature through the monumental labors, on all the manuscripts ascribed to Grosseteste, of Professor Harrison Thomson, and through the new edition of Wilkins's *Concilia*, under way by a group of eminent English historians. The *Manuel des Pechiez* was explicitly ascribed to Grosseteste fifty years after his death by Robert Mannyng, the canon of Bourne (co. Lincs.) who translated it into English. A sister of the bishop was a nun and in touch with the Oxford Franciscan Adam Marsh, who was himself in touch with Bishop Suffield of Norwich (*Rolls Ser.* 25 [1861], pp. 43 sq.; 4 [1858], index, *s.v. Juetta* [loosely called 'a recluse'], and p. 389). It should be noted that Grosseteste's diocese included Oxford, which was a center of reclusion in his time. But unexpected evidence has come to light proving a considerable circulation for the compilation—beyond that first traced for the section incorporating 'Grosseteste.' This fact introduces a new element of uncertainty into the problem of the localization.

The librarian of Trinity College referred to me in this connection Mr. C. J. Robson of Christ Church, Oxford, who generously wrote me as follows:

> I should like to call your attention to a second copy of this work which is in the Bodleian Library, MS. Bodley 90. Unfortunately it is incomplete, the scribe having abandoned his task on f. 77 in the middle of the seventeen points of true confession. About the first third of the work has been copied. As some of this corresponds to the *Ancren Riwle*, it may be of value for the establishment of the text. I hope it is not too late!
>
> There are also two Anglo-Norman opuscules which have some relation to this

[33] See *RR*, *loc. cit.*, pp. 444–449 (I should mention that I have since seen the manuscript described on p. 444, as has [independently] Mr. Charlton G. Laird, who, I hope, will describe it); also my article, *PMLA*, xxxii (1917), pp. 144–147, where I discuss systematic works of religious instruction in England in the vernacular.

work. One is the xvii points of confession in Camb. Univ. Lib. MS. Gg. 1. 1. The other is a summary of the seven sins and their various forms, the seven sacraments, the twelve articles of faith, and the ten commandments. The first part of this (and perhaps the last) is, like the xviii points, a *précis* from the work found in R. 14.7 and Bodley 90. It is found in about eight manuscripts, and seems to have been very popular [letter of 10. x. 38]. [Bodley 90 was the manuscript described, for its possible relations to the Parson's Tale, by Mark Liddell, in the *Academy*, xlix (1896), pp. 447–448, 509.]

I find it very gratifying that *Ancren Riwle* and Chaucer studies have now at last met—though only through Anglo-Norman analogues and derivatives. In work on the Parson's Tale, Professor Cline discovered a Paris MS of interest as an analogue. This was brought by Mrs. Dempster to the knowledge of Miss Dean, who recognized it as a copy of the Trinity compilation (a relation later confirmed through collation by Mrs. Dempster). Mrs. Dempster proved that its text was superior to that in the Paris MS (also of English origin). She is giving extracts from the Trinity MS in her chapter on the Parson's Tale in *Sources and Analogues of Chaucer's Canterbury Tales*. In recent correspondence which she has had with Mr. Robson, he describes his research on English penitentials in a way to make me hope that it will help to elucidate not only the background of the Parson's Tale but also that of the *Ancren Riwle*. Through my study of the Trinity compilation I have come to realize that the Angevin masterpiece of English mystical piety must have borne a part in the preparation for the confessional of the French-speaking upper classes of thirteenth-century England—in proportion to its spiritual and literary virtues, far beyond the limits of the contemplative life, for which it had been written. So many copies of the compilation have now come to light without special search having been made that it is likely that more are extant. Though this work was compiled for 'gent de religion' some copies will probably have been used for the same sort of devout lay person with whom we must associate Wynkyn de Worde's *Treatise of Love*.

The quotations which support my remarks on the Trinity compilation will follow. They have been kindly read with Mrs. Dempster's film (at her suggestion) by Professor W. H. Trethewey. He has generously consented to collaborate with me in the article in which I shall later present textual variants of the compilation, of interest for my studies of the *Riwle*, and will there expound his method used in transcribing from the work. I hope that he may decide to ask to edit this text. Through Mr. Adams, the librarian, permission was given by Trinity College in 1936 to the Early English Text Society to arrange the edition, and to me to print extracts.

Quot. A

A ses trechers freres et sueres en ih*es*u crist e a tuz iceus e celis ki lirru*n*t cest escrit v deuoteme*n*t e de bon quer de autre lire loru*n*t, saluz, e sancte de alme e de cors en lui k*e* est uerrai saueour de tuz (f. 1 c. 1—the opening of the tract on the Seven Deadly Sins);
A ses chers freres e soers en ih*es*u c*ri*st, serfs e anceles deu, e n*ost*re douce dame seinte marie, e a toz iceus e celes k*e* cest escr*i*t lirront ou p*ar* autre lire orrunt, saluz, e sante de alme e de cors en lui k*e* e*st* u*er*rai sauueour de toz iceus k*e* sauuez serront (f. 35 c. 2—the opening of the tract on Penance);
A ses chers freres e suers en deu, a tuz iceus e celes k*e* ceste co*m*pileson lirrunt ou de aut*re* lire le orrunt, saluz, e sancte de alme e de cors el duz ih*es*u c*ri*st k*e* est n*ost*re u*er*rai sauueour (f. 111ᵛc. 2—the opening of the ninth part of the tract on Penance, which is also found separately in Arundel MS 288, f. 84. An almost identical opening is given at the beginning of the tract on the Ten Commandments, f. 115ᵛc. 1; the slight variations elsewhere might give added evidence of individuality);

Isci com*en*ce li prologe de la uie de gent de religion, ke deiuent uiuere apres reule. Cest a dire k*e* il deiuu*n*t estre dedenz e dehors si reulez k*e* de p*ec*che boosce ne seit troue en eus. Si ad deus perografs. *Recti diligunt te.* A ses duz chers freres e suers en deu, hom*m*es e fem*m*es de religion, e a tuz icels e celes [ke] cest escrit lirront ou de autre lire le orrunt, saluz, e sancte de alme e de cors en duz ih*es*u crist k*e* est u*er*raie sauueour de trestuz ceus e celes k*e* leaument lui eiment. Duz chers freres e suers en deu, ieo v*us* ai cest escrit de la uie de gent de religion conpile de diuers lius de sei*n*te escripture al honur deu e sa douce mere e a sauuacion des almes (f. 124ᵛ c. 2—the 'consecutive' borrowing from the *Riwle*. The latter part of the rubric which here precedes *Recti* is restored by an insertion at the bottom of the page. In the Paris MS it is *in situ*.)

Quot. B

. . . especes k*e* de eus uienent e descende*n*t, ausint co*m* v*us* apertement trouez enz en la compeleison des set p*ec*chez morteus (*Uie*, f. 154 c. 2). [Cf. *A. R.*, p. 196: hore attri kundles, þet beoð her efter inemmed.]

Quot. C

. . . cest escrit auom n*us* p*ar* la grace n*ost*re duz seigniur ih*es*u crist co*m*pile, ceo est co*n*quilli ensemble, des set p*ec*chez morteus, e de lur esspeces, si come nus les auom t*ro*ue en seinte esc*ri*pture, p*ur* apre*n*dre les leaume*n*t e sanz feintise a tote genz, mes especiaume*n*t, e par deuant tuz autres, a hom*m*es e a fem*m*es de religioun, k*e* ceo escrit a salu de lur almes soue*n*t escuteront e uolu*n*ters e ente*n*-tifueme*n*t le lirront hu p*ar* autri buche lire le orrunt (f. 1 c. 2).

Quot. D

. . . si v*us* le lisez ou lire le facez deuant v*us* souent. Car autreme*n*t eusse ieo p*er*du mout de tens k*e* ieo ai mis [MS m-mis] entour ceo, a coiller le ensemble de plosours esc*riz*, al hon*ur*, etc., *ut supra* (f. 111ᵛ c. 1). [The compiler is here using only a part (ll. 11–14) of the conclusion to the *Riwle*, which he uses complete (p. 430, ll. 11–22) as the ending to this whole treatise (ff. 115–115ᵛ). But the lines just quoted do not constitute the ending to this section, which runs as follows (at the bottom of the same column), without mention of St. Francis, but with an echo of *A. R.* (p. 430, ll. 28–30)]:

Jeo v*us* en p*ri* par seinte charite k*e* ausi souent co*m* v*us* auez rien leu sur ceste liu*e*re, k*e* v*us* saluez n*os*tre duce dame seinte marie ou un salu, Ceo est, ou une Aue marie, p*ur* celui k*e* tant t*ra*uailla entour cest escrit, al hon*ur* deu e sa douce v*ir*ge mere, e de tuz seinz e seintes, e au saluacion de uos almes. Amen. [The piece immediately following (*Penance*, Pt. IX, translating a work ascribed to Grosseteste) continues (after the address already cited) in the plural ('N*us* en-tendoms p*ar* la grace n*os*tre duz seign*ur*.' . . .); *Penançe* began in the singular ('Isci v*us* mustrai . . . E ieo u*us* di p*ur* uoirs,' f. 35 c. 2); the *Ten Commandments* begins in the plural again ('Nus parlerom a v*us* par la grace deu en cest co*m*-pileison' . . . f. 115ᵛ c. 1). Later students may be able to trace these differences far enough to determine whether they have any significance. 'We' is of course common form in sermons, but I note that the first person is a characteristic of the four most distinctive of the *Lambeth Homilies*, in which I pointed out likenesses to the *Riwle* (cf. *PMLA*, xliv (1929), 671–678). The first person is so conspicu-ously used in the *Ancren Riwle* that it might temporarily divert from his own habitual usage a compiler borrowing extensively from that work].

Quot. E

E se u*us* moigne ou chanoine ou u*us* frere ki k*e* u*us* seez, ou blanc, ou bis, ou chaucez, ou nupiez, ou u*us* en sac, ou u*us* noir ou u*us* gris ou u*us* nonein blanche, ou bise, ou u*us* recluse noire, ou grise, ou v*us* autre aut*re* [marked for deletion], hom*me* ou fem*me* de religion ki k*e* v*us* estes, si v*us*, dedenz u*os*tre ordre ou dehhors, trauauz e meseises endurez e peines suffrez. . . . Mez donc uolu*n*tiers, v*us* hom*me* e v*us* fem*me* de religion, par le dur chemin e par le aspre e p*ar* le greuein, uers la tres g*ra*nt feste e la tres noble, du ciel, la ou nos freres e nos suers, nos chers amis en deu e nos chers amies, n*os*tre uenue attendunt (*Uie*, f. 152ᵛ c. 1). [Cf. *A. R.*, p. 188: Ȝif ȝe þolieð wo ȝe habbeð wurse of-earned; & al þet ȝe þolieð al is for ou suluen. Goð nu þeonne gledluker bi stronge wei & biswincfule, touward þe muchele feste of heouene, þer ase ower glede ureond ower cume ikepeð.]

Quot. F

Cotton Titus MS D. xviii (quoted by Macaulay, *op. cit.*, p. 159, n.): Mine leue childre þe nesche dale is to drede swiðe as is te harde of þeose fondinges þat arn uttre ihaten, As is plente of mete oðer of clað & of swiche þinges. Olhtninge oðer hereward mihte sone make sum of ow fulitohen ȝif ȝe neren þe hendere. Muche word þat is of ow; hu gentille ȝe beon, ȝunge of ȝeres ȝulden ow, & bicomen ancres, forsoken worldes blisses, Al þis, etc. [I have modernized the punctuation here and later].

Cotton Nero MS A xiv (edited by Morton, p. 192): [after unique personal details of the three anchoresses addressed] Ȝe muwen more dreden þe nesche dole þene þe herde of þeos fondunges þet is uttre ihoten. Vor uein wolde þe hexte cwemen ou, ȝif he muhte, mid oluhnunge, makien ou fulitowen, ȝif heo nere þe hendure. Muche word is of ou hu gentile wummen ȝe beoð, vor godleic & for ureoleic iȝerned of monie, & sustren of one ueder & of one moder, ine blostme of ower ȝuweðe, uorheten alle worldes blissen, & bicomen ancren. Al þis is strong temptaciun, & muhte sone binimen ou muchel of ower mede . . . þis is Godes word þuruh Isaie.

Trinity MS f. 153 c. 2: Queles temptacions font mouz a doter. Mes tres chers enfanz, douz freres e suers, la sueue mort e la mole, fet a doter ausi bien com la dure mort [a variant in my opinion superior, but, in view of its originality, likely to become corrupt, as through *deað* becoming *dole*]. Icestes te*m*ptacio*n*s k*e* sont apellez foreines, si co*m* e*st* ple*n*te [153ᵛ c. 1] de mang*er*, e de boiuere, sup*er*fluite de richesces, e de uesture, e de chaucheure, e habundance de te*m*pore*us* biens, e iteles choses, e ausint fauour de la gent, ou haute fame, e los, e g*ra*nt pris, u*us* porreient tost fere desafetez, e desafetees, se v*us* les plus sages e les plus queintes ne fusez. La g*ra*nt renomee k*e* est de u*os*tre genterise, e de u*os*tre fame, e u*os*tre bele iuuente, e k*e* v*us*, iofnes e de petit age en religio*n* v*us* rendistes; e k*e* v*us*, monie, ou chanoine, ou frere blanc ou bis ou noir, ou nonein, ou recluse, ou en autre man*ere* de religion, v*us* hom*me* ou v*us* fem*me* v*us* rendistis en la p*ri*son dampne deu, v*us* renduz, ou v*us* rendue deueinstes, e iceste cheitifue fause ioie seculere du tot deguerpist*es*, e longement en religion en seruice deu demorrez estes. Totes icestes deu*an*t dites choses sunt fortes temptacions, e v*us* porreient tost tolir mout de uostre louer ke v*us* deussez de dampne deu auoir. Car issint le dit nostre sire memes, par Ysaie . . .

Quot. G

Uie de gent de religion—table of contents [supplied by Professor Trethewey, who collated the text with the Paris MS.]

Trinity MS f. 124ᵛ c. 2 [directly following the opening address printed above, Quot. A]: Come*n*t v*us* poet tost t*r*ou*er* en esc*r*it ceo du*n*t v*us* au*er*et mest*er*, e k*e* v*us* puissez tost trou*er* en cest escrit ceo k*e* v*us* querrez, ieo v*us* ai mis a deua*n*t en le prologe les parties par ont v*us* poez tost t*r*ouer q*ua*nk*e* v*us* au*er*ez mester. La p*ri*mere partie parout de deus reules de deuinite, ceo est de seinte esc*ri*pture, des queles la une rectefie le quer dedenz, e lui autre rectefie le cors dehors: de la profession k*e* genz de religion deiuu*n*t fere, e equel est dreit ordre e uerraie religion. La secunde p*ar*tie v*us* aprent coment v*us* deuez par uos cinc sens garder uos quers, la ou ordre e religion e uie de alme est enz. La tierce p*ar*tie est de une manere de oiseus, ceo est a sauer, de le pellican, del egle, de la fresoie, del moisson, a quels en seint escripture sunt comparez genz de religion. E apres mustre ap*er*tement par essamples de la uelz loi e de la nouele, k*e* il est bon a hume de estre hors de la noise de ce perilus mond. E puis mustre par plusurs resons k*e* hom*m*e p*ar* droit deust fuir le mond e entrer en religion. La quarte partie parout de charnele temptacion e de espiritele am[b]edeus, e de conforz encontre cels, e de pureture del alme. La quinte p*ar*tie parout des set mortels p*ec*chez e des mals [f. 125 c. 1] ke de eus uienent, e de remediis encontre cels. E au derein dit les medecines gen*er*aument encountre totes te*m*ptacions. La sime p*ar*tie parout de penance. E ceo primes parout de penance generaument, e puis de contricion, de confession, de satisfaccion; k*e* checun hom*m*e deit fere penance, e uoluntiers; e de la seinte penance de gent de religion; e de net quer e de cler; par quei e come*n*t hom*m*e deit ih*es*u crist am*er*; e quei n*us* tout sa am*ur* e quele chose deueie li amer. La setime p*ar*tie parout des dis comandemenz deu, p*ar* quels hom*m*e doit deu [MS ben] am*er* sur totes choses e soen prome si co*m* sei meimes. La oitime p*ar*tie est de p*ur*gatorie e de ses peines, du iour de iuise e des peines de enfern, e des [set] glories des sauues e des confusions des dampnez. La nouime p*ar*tie est de la reule foreine p*ar* dehors, k*e* parout p*ri*mes de manger e de boiuere religiousement, e des autres choses k*e* cheent illoc entur. Apres ceo si parout des choses k*e* v*us* poet receiuere e queles choses v*us* poez garder ou auer; des uos uestures e de celes choses co*m* a ceo affierent; de uos eures, de la reule des serganz de genz de religion. Au derein u*us* aprent coment v*us* les deuez enseigner e ap*re*ndre, blamer, chastier e reprendre; com*en*t cest escrit deit estre liu. Ore v*us* p*ri* ieo ducement k*e* v*us* regardez cest escrit isci au comencement souent e atret le lisez ou deuant v*us* lire [le] facez. E metez i uostre quer e v*us* i poez ueer e oir uerraiment se v*us* uiuet religiousement e amez deu leaument si co*m* dit le auctorite au comencement. Ore do*n*c metez ci uostre quer e desk*e* a la fin ent[ent] iuement escutez e deuotement oez quels sunt k*e* u*er*eiement eimunt deu e leaument. Nus lisom en seinte escripture k*e* la seinte espuse deu, cest la seinte alme, dist a deu soen espus en cantikes: "Issi les dreiz, ces s*un*t les dreiturels k*e* uiuu*n*t apres reule, v*us* eimunt." *Recti, inquid, diligunt te: uerba ista in canticis dicit sponsa ad sponsum et fidelis anima ad christum.* V*us* deuez sauer k*e* plosours reules sunt troues si co*m*e reu[f. 125v c. 2]les de gramarie e reules de geomet*ri*e e reules de theologie, cest de seinte esc*ri*pt*ur*e. Sachez donc k*e* deus reules su*n*t de seinte esc*ri*pture des quels n*us* parlerom a v*us* en cest escrit e les autres lerrom. *Inuenitur enim rectum multiplex, est enim rectum gramaticum, rectum geometricum et rectum theologicum et sunt differencie totidem. De recto theologico, aliis omissis, est nobis sermo ad presens.* Deu par sa seinte grace me doint issi de cestes deus reules a v*us* parler k*e* il seit al honur de lui e a sauuacion des almes. AmeN.

III

I have left till this last section all comment on the most important characteristic of the Trinity compilation for my problem of tracing the source of the *Treatise of Love:* though the Trinity MS bore an unexpected relation to other extant volumes, from the text which it had been expected to resemble, it diverged surprisingly. As I noted in my letter, already quoted, this French derivative of the *Riwle* does not reproduce the French version in Cotton Vitellius MS F vii, which has been long known. That badly damaged relic of the Cotton fire was most expertly transcribed by Mr. J. A. Herbert through the aid of my grant from ACLS. He has been editing the transcript (with the help of the ultraviolet ray) for the edition of the Early English Text Society. When the Trinity MS was identified, the librarian at once consented to take it to London for collation by Mr. Herbert, with the Cotton French text then already at press. It proved to be of no more direct use for the diplomatic edition of the latter than the English manuscripts, but rotographs were taken of the 'borrowings' for general use by the various editors working (respectively) on the various manuscripts and versions of the *Riwle.*

I give at the end of my series of 'Quot. F' the most important of various passages which have brought me to the opinion that the 'Trinity version' should be printed also diplomatically—broken up, interpolated, and expanded though it is. Until it is studied in detail, perhaps no final judgment can be given on its relation to other manuscripts. But, as the case appears now, certainly the divergence from the Cotton version seems far too serious to be explained as the result of long circulation, as can the continual variations in the English copies. (Cf. n. 34 *infra.*)

Thus there appear to have been two independent versions of the *Riwle* in French, a fact which carries with it the strong presumption that the original was not French. I put this independence of the Trinity and Cotton texts with other historical considerations which seem to make almost certain an English original: I refer to the existence of five English copies from that francophile period, the reign of Henry III (an astonishing phenomenon, cogently discussed by Professor Chambers); I also refer[34] to the elevated social position of persons who owned this work in English in the thirteenth century;[35] also to the fact that it was the English version which was chosen as the basis for the Latin by a great churchman, *ca.*1300.[36] Against such historical considerations as these, any new textual considerations which will come to light during the preparation of the new edition can have very little weight. Special difficulties are raised for the scholar attempting to prove the original language of the *Riwle* on textual evidence, by the fact that the writer was in any case certainly bilingual, writing in a world using French at least as much as English. His literary use of either language would therefore naturally be somewhat affected by his familiar use of the other. It seems certain that he wrote for women reading English, hence almost certainly of English blood—in spite of their high level of culture.

But many new textual considerations are, in my opinion, likely to be brought forward, and to alter the textual study of the work so far made. Already, a note by Dr. Mack in 1936 (though she herself made no such assertion) seems to me to support one textual interpretation of Mr. Macaulay's against the belief of Miss Dymes. When 'the Trinity text' came to light in 1936—and the

---

[34] The writers on the problem of the original language of the *Riwle* used for my ensuing discussion are: Macaulay, *op. cit.*, pp. 64–70; Hall, *op. cit.*, ii, 377; D. M. E. Dymes, *Essays and Studies by Members of the English Association*, ix (1924), 31–50; R. W. Chambers, *RES*, I (1926), 6–14; F. M. Mack, *EETS*, O. S. 193 (1934), pp. 73–74; R. M. Wilson, *Early Middle English Literature*, Methuen's Old English Library (1939), pp. 135–136. The last named writer (in the excellent work which has just come from the press) does not use Dr. Mack's note.—I have also had recently the advantage of discussing various of the textual problems of the Cotton French text with Mr. Herbert, as his transcript and edition have proceeded.—To the works cited above should be added Miss d'Ardenne's *Seinte Iuliene*, Liége and Paris, 1936; she discusses (pp. xliv–v) the same repetition in *Seinte Marharete* of the much-discussed translation of a Latin distich (*A. R.* p. 240) as was discussed by Miss Mack independently. Miss d'Ardenne's comments on Professor Tolkien's study of *Ancrene Wisse* are of particular value since she worked with his encouragement. Her remarks on the tradition of her text should be taken in conjunction with Miss Everett's review of Miss Mack's *Seinte Marharete* (*R.E.S.* II (1935), pp. 337 sq.).

[35] *See* my letters to *LTLS* of March 22, 1934, February 8, 1936, and my note, *MLR.*, xxviii (1933), pp. 485–487.

[36] *See* Macaulay, *op. cit.*, pp. 70–78.

Treatise of Love now follows with evidence that another French compilation from the *Riwle* has once existed—if that text had reproduced the Cotton French version on which Macaulay founded his belief that the work was first written in French, a new check would also have been given to the effort to prove absolutely an English original. I repeat that I do not find that the textual studies so far made prove anything positively conclusive, for, after discussing them with other scholars and considering them myself over a period of many years, I have found that new explanations and cruces crop up, and that the arguments adduced tend to be taken by various scholars variously.

I should record here that many years ago Professor E. S. Sheldon was kind enough to investigate the literature of the controversy; he made the tentative suggestion (which he gave me permission to print) that the same author might have written a French version as well as one in English. This hypothesis would solve some of the difficulties. But the signal historical fact that it was the English text that seems to have been considered authoritative would remain to be accounted for. It seems to me possible that this interesting historical phenomenon might be due to the continued memory that the work had been written for women of English blood—probably of known family—a memory which would carry with it the presumption that only the English text was original with the author. I make these tentative remarks, in the hope that they will be kept under consideration by other scholars who may help to test their validity. But I wish to emphasize at the same time the positive fact that the *Riwle* had been written not as a literary treatise, primarily for impersonal general use, but (even though we can never recover their names) for three women who once lived; in its genesis it falls into the category of history rather than of literature, and that fact is occasionally very significant for the scholar—studying it for the literary and linguistic importance which were actually accidental.

Mr. Macaulay, as Professor Chambers has pointed out, made a serious historical error in speaking of 'the a priori probabilities' as being in favor of a French original: 'probabilities' in this case are certainly on the other side, as the fundamental historical considerations, which I have reviewed above, prove. And the contribution which the divergence of the Trinity from the Cotton text makes to the problem of the original language—as one more 'historical' consideration in favor of an English archetype—can be reinforced by an analogy: when two unrecorded Latin manuscripts came to light (my *op. cit.*, 1919 and 1922), they reproduced the two already known (it is a singular fact that, in the diplomatic edition of *EETS*, the Latin translation, which is being edited by Professor D'Evelyn, is the only one for which an edition with collations is planned). The translation made by Bishop Ghent for one of the most fashionable nunneries in England—which must have been roughly contemporaneous with the transcription of Dom Wroxham's copy of a French derivative of the *Riwle*—would seem to have been recognized as a standard.

The provenance of the Trinity and the Cotton French versions were such (respectively) as to raise the presumption that, where these volumes were written, an authoritative French text would have been known, had such existed. The Trinity compilation probably arose—as it certainly circulated—in the highest ecclesiastical circles; the other, in all likelihood, in the highest secular (as did, though the period is uncertain, the source of the *Treatise of Love*). The Cotton French text, in *ca.*1433–1441, was given to Eleanor Cobham, Duchess of Gloucester, almost certainly by the Countess of Kent—a descendant of the noble owner of the English Cleopatra MS *ca.*1280; see my letters in *LTLS*, March 22, 1934, February 8, 1936. The Anglo-Norman devotional tracts (which must be studied), with which the Cotton French text is found, show that the volume was originally written (slightly later than the Trinity MS) for pious and cultivated readers, who (if more learned) would probably have used the *Riwle* in Bishop Ghent's Latin. To the period *ca.*1300 we can now assign two extant copies of the *Riwle* in Latin (same text), and two in French (divergent). The fact that the newly discovered French derivative (widely circulated) embodies most of the text for conventual use proves a wide French currency of the work at that period, which aids the assumption that more Anglo-Norman derivatives may come to light. With each new 'borrowing' more become likely, since, with fashions, 'like begets like.' The *Ancren Riwle* must have been carried through the thirteenth century by a continuity not only of English prose but also of French—in which its rich imagery and persuasive eloquence were not lost. By further evidence of circulation in French, the historical probability that the original was English could not now, in my opinion, be impaired.

Thus, study of the two derivatives of the *Riwle* has shown a circulation for the work—through a conventual compilation and an early printed book—at once extensive in scope and influential in kind. The text of the 'borrowings' (and this is sure to apply to those earlier noted) would repay detailed study. It is significant that it is the Titus MS of the *Riwle*—a very interesting, but supposedly not influential text—which seems related to two derivatives of the *Riwle* so far found: the inference is that presumptions of relative importance founded on the relations of the extant copies are unsound. Even the far-descended *Treatise of Love* can be shown to offer some textual variants of historical interest. The alteration of *Giwerie* to *vsurye* has been noted. Again, I owe to the paraphrase, by which the *Treatise* (A[3]c.1) renders 'earthen castle,' the realization that the latter phrase in the original probably refers to the ancient Norman 'motte and bailey,' an 'earthwork,' of which the defensive force must have been still at least a vivid memory, at any date when the *Riwle* can have been written; though by 1493 the translator was so puzzled by a castle 'made of full feeble matter' that he did not even catch the *double entendre* (of the soul besieged in an 'earthy' body) probably intended by the author.'[37]

The single quotation of length which I have given from 'the Trinity version' serves the double purpose of illustrating the extraordinary range of religious persons toward whom 'the compiler' directs his discourse, as also the occasional extraordinary in-

[37] Cf. F. M. Stenton, *English Feudalism 1066–1166* (Oxford, 1932), p. 196: "The extent to which the Anglo-Norman aristocracy had given itself to the work of castle-building cannot be determined by written evidence alone. The remains of its castles still exist in every part of the country and in great number. For the past thirty years it has been generally recognised that the common type of earthwork . . . the motte and bailey of archaeological literature—represents a French castle of the eleventh or twelfth century." This work was brought to my attention by Miss Joan Wake.

terest of the textual variants of this much watered-down copy. It is of course obvious that for the long quotation F a manuscript of the *Riwle* has been used which contained the details of the personal circumstances of the three sisters for whom the work was first written, as given in the Titus MS (otherwise, only—in fuller form—in the Nero). Where the personal details of the source end and the compiler's generalizations begin is hard to say, but it at least seems very possible that he found in his source a reference to the 'sisters' having entered religion in 'petit âge' and remained there for a long time before the book was written. This text, which came to light in August 1936, gave curious provisional corroboration—so to speak—of my note of September 1935 (*PMLA*, L, 899–902).

Here I stated that, on the same sort of circumstantial evidence which made me first put forward the hypothesis of an origin of the work at Kilburn, I must now decide that the three Kilburn anchoresses were likely to have been 'the three daughters of Deorman'—an identification which allowed the retention of my theory that the *Riwle* was likely to have been written for this trio, only because I had found 'no address to the sisters in the *Riwle* that certainly implies their youth at the moment' (*ibid.*, p. 901, n. 10). I will mention here that I have later come upon a reference which would allow us to assign the 'three daughters of Deorman' to a period consistent with a composition for the work (if written for them) in the first decade after the coming of the Cistercians—as I had first postulated. *See* C. Horstmann, *Nova Legenda Anglie* (Oxford, 1901), II, 640, where a miracle is given, from the report of Osbert, prior of Westminster (a founder of the Kilburn cell), as to 'prediues vrbis Londonie mercator nomine Deormannus'; it is undated. If this very prominent Deorman of London was the father of the trio giving land in London to Westminster by permission of a brother '1107–c.1115,' his becoming a monk at Bury (here cited) must have preceded that date. The conspicuous Anglo-Saxon family of 'Deorman of London' of Domesday (who may have had a son of the same name) held an estate near Bury (through marriage with the great Norman family of Clare) by at least the last years of Henry I, or the first of Stephen. In the thirteenth century this family was linked to notable persons of church and state (in the court circle).

The implications of the quotation from the Trinity MS should not pass unnoted, yet the hope that we are on the eve of having available all the manuscripts of the *Riwle* makes me now more than ever desirous of holding loosely all theories in its connection —even the working hypothesis which I still find worth further investigation. If the present international disasters do not prevent, we shall in our time be able to give this exceptional monument of medieval English culture the thorough study which its literary, historical, and lingustic interest deserves.

SOME NOTES ON THE CIRCULATION OF LYRIC POEMS IN SIXTEENTH-CENTURY ITALY

WALTER Ll. BULLOCK

The University of Manchester

ONE of the most obvious and most frequently used types of evidence in the tracing of literary influences or the making of literary comparisons is based on a consideration of the dates of printing of the works involved. For the twentieth century, this method will in most cases conduce to tolerably accurate results; for the nineteenth century, too, it may generally be followed with success: in both these centuries a work (other than a learned study!) is likely under normal circumstances—unless its author be especially unlucky or inept—to be published very soon after it is actually completed. But for the first two centuries, at least, after the invention of the press, save in very exceptional cases, conclusions based on the date of a first printing are unsafe, above all where lyric poetry is concerned.

This has not always been realized. As an example of the kind of error into which scholars have sometimes fallen in the matter, one might cite, for the Italian lyric field, the discussions which arose some years ago over Sannazaro's sonnet *Simile a questi smisurati monti . . .* , translated, probably in the third or fourth decade of the sixteenth century, both into English (by Sir Thomas Wyatt) and into French. In trying to fix the date of Wyatt's translation, Professor E. W. Olmstead suggested that it could not have been written in the third decade 'if as Torraca affirms, the sonnet by Sannazaro was first published in 1533.'[1] As a matter of fact, the sonnet had been printed at least twice before that date by Zoppino, in editions of Sannazaro's *Rime* at Venice in 1531 and 1532; Miss A. K. Foxwell was nearer the mark bibliographically when she stated that 'The earliest date for Wyatt's translating the poem is during 1531,' because, of Sannazaro's poems, 'the first edition

[1] *The Sonnet in French Literature* (Ithaca, N. Y., 1897), p. 23.

appeared in 1531.'[2] But even had these scholars been perfectly accurate in their bibliographical data, their conclusions would have been unsound: there is no reason whatever why Wyatt should not have got hold of a manuscript copy of the sonnet, and indeed of all Sannazaro's *Rime*, when he was in Italy in 1527; or even, through some other traveller, at a much earlier date. One may well say that the attention of a sixteenth-century writer is likely to have been especially attracted in some definite year to a volume printed during that year; but it is quite unsafe to say, without further evidence, that he could not have known a lyric poem before the date of its first printing—even assuming that date to be beyond all question.[3]

Errors of this kind are less likely to be made today than earlier in our century; though an elaborate study by a far more recent writer than those cited above still assumed that a court preceptor and secretary of the early Cinquecento, Mario Equicola, having full access to the rich collections at Ferrara, Mantua, and elsewhere, 'must have used' this or that early printed edition of various works he had studied, ignoring the far greater probability that

[2] *The Poems of Sir Thomas Wiatt* (London, 1913), II, 46.—This statement also is not quite correct. It is true that the *Simile* . . . sonnet was apparently first printed in 1531, but the first edition of Sannazaro's *Rime*, which did not include that sonnet, was in 1530, if not earlier.

[3] Quite outside the lyric field we have several examples in sixteenth-century Italy of refutations—sometimes elaborate treatises—printed years before the works which they were written to answer; also criticisms of poems printed long before the poems themselves. The *Discorso* of the elusively pseudonymous 'Ridolfo Castravilla' against Dante, which gave rise to a long series of works for and against the *Commedia*, was composed and widely circulated about 1572; a number of the treatises deriving from it were printed in the last three decades of the century, but the *Discorso* itself was not in print until 1608. Again, Denores's attack on the *Pastor Fido* in his *Poetica* (Padova:Meietti, 1588), Guarini's defence of his "tragicommedia" in *Il Verrato* (Ferrara:Caraffa, 1588), and Denores's reply to that defence (*Apologia* . . . , Padova:Meietti, 1590) were all in print before the work which had called them forth was either printed or produced: it was known, of course, in manuscript. Other similar cases might be cited; it is also perhaps worth noting that although a few of the *menanti* (sixteenth-century propagators of "news-letters" of the type to which we have lately seen a curious reversion) began quite early in the century to have their wares printed, others continued to copy them out (or have them copied out) by hand at least well into the second half of the century. Various papal bulls aimed at the regulation of their activities make this abundantly clear.

he used a ducal manuscript.[4] But though few scholars now would fail to take due account of the likelihood of transmission by manuscript throughout the sixteenth century and later, no general discussion of the way in which newly composed works were passed about in the Cinquecento seems ever to have been attempted. It is the purpose of the present paper, joining in the general homage now being so happily offered to Carleton Brown (to whom the learned world is so deeply indebted for many scholarly contributions in his own chosen field, for all that he did to facilitate the publication of learned studies in every field of the modern literatures through the remarkable expansion of *PMLA* under his editorship, and for much else), to illustrate in some detail the extent to which lyric poems were circulated in manuscript form in Cinquecento Italy.

For sonnets, canzoni, and the like were constantly sent about, sometimes quite extensively, long before their earliest printing. Indeed, living poets whose lyrics saw the light of type in the early decades of the century were comparatively few, and these emphatically popular in tone (even if occasionally aristocratic in social position) rather than seriously literary: 'l'Altissimo,' del Carretto, Cei, Filosseno, Olimpo, Sasso, and such others. Only towards mid-century did printing come to be normal and expected. Benedetto Varchi's *Rime*, for example, existed in a quite copious manuscript collection at least as early as 1531/2: in that winter he sent almost all of them to Annibal Caro for the latter to copy for himself, Caro sending back the originals as fast as the copies were done.[5] But though so early collected and communicated, the first printed edition of them known to us is that of 1555, nearly a quarter-century later.—We may safely say that up to 1530 poets very rarely saw their lyrics printed. In that year there appeared in their first edition the poems of the master of the contemporary (erudite) lyric movement, Pietro Bembo, of whom it has been aptly said that at this time, lyrically speaking, 'there was no God but Petrarch, and Bembo was his prophet.'[6] During the next ten or

---

[4] Cf. *PMLA*, XLVI (1931), 443 n.

[5] Cf. Annibal Caro, *Delle lettere familiari* ... (Bassano, 1782), III, 16.

[6] Less concisely it has been said of Venice in the same period that "Venezia poteva allora

fifteen years publication through the press was no longer unfashionable, though it was still rare, especially for the more literary poets; but after 1545, when the spread of *Raccolte* began,[7] early printing became a commonplace, though not yet a matter of course. For occasionally, throughout the century, well-known collections of *Rime* by distinguished poets remained permanently unprinted: the much discussed lyrics of Giambattista Pigna are a case in point.

It should be borne in mind, of course, that in the earlier decades there was a strong tendency in many aristocratic circles (a tendency that did not entirely die out until much later) to regard a machine-made book much as one regards today, for example, machine-made lace or embroidery. When Margaret of Angoulême desired in 1540 to have a copy of Vittoria Colonna's verses, there was no thought of sending her a copy of any of the four or five editions which had already been printed: a beautiful manuscript was at once prepared.[8] After all, the handmade thing has almost always greater worth, except perhaps among savages.—For this reason too, then, many works of the first half century which might well have been printed remained in manuscript.

But while most of the multitudinous lyrics then being written stayed in manuscript, they often circulated widely and variously. A cursory examination of the letters written from beginning to end of the Cinquecento[9] will suffice to show how constantly verses

---

dirsi la reggia del Petrarca, adorato dai sudditi, produttori inesaurabili di rime e di canzoni; primo ministro Pietro Bembo." (P. Molmenti, in *Nuova Antologia* for January 16, 1927, p. 139.)

[7] The first important anthology (leaving out of account the early popular collections in which poems by half a dozen or so of the cruder poets might be brought together, as well as the famous *raccolta* of the early Italian poets printed by the Giunti at Florence in 1527 and reprinted by the brothers Da Sabbio in Venice, 1532) was issued by Giolito at Venice in 1545. Of fourteen of the more important anthologies published in 1545–1565, some account will be found in J. Vianey, *Le Pétrarquisme en France au XVIe siècle* (Montpellier, 1909), pp. 378–384. Numerous other anthologies of the century are listed *passim* in the extremely useful but by no means exhaustive bibliography of H. Vaganay: *Le sonnet en Italie et en France au XVIe siècle* (Lyon, 1903).

[8] Cf. D. Tordi, *Il codice delle rime di Vittoria Colonna . . . appartenuto a Margherita d'Angoulême* (Pistoia: G. Flori, 1900).

[9] The use of contemporary letters as evidence must, needless to say, always be made with caution. For sixteenth-century Italy such letters fall into two main categories: those

were being sent about by all sorts and conditions of men. For this activity was by no means confined to recognized poets and men of letters: youths, and sometimes those of riper years, would be suddenly seized with the notion that perhaps they too could write poems, so they would labor out a sonnet and send it off to the literary master whom they thought least unapproachable, asking for criticism and hoping for encouragement. Since such sonnets usually took the form of a fulsome complimentary address, the recipient was often put in an embarassing position; as a rule the simplest solution would be to temper encomium with an exhortation to slow and careful work, by way of discouraging the deluge. Bembo was particularly adroit at this sort of defensive appreciation; Aretino was rather easier. One who wrote to the latter after the clever manner of Cornelio Frangipane could be certain of a favour-

---

which were printed in their own century (a surprisingly large group); and those which remained in archives, sometimes to find publication centuries later, sometimes not. These latter may usually be assumed to represent not perhaps the actual facts, but either what the writer believed to be true or at least what he wished and expected his correspondent to believe. Letters, however, which were printed in the century itself were usually "edited" for the occasion, not only with stylistic corrections, but also with such additions, subtractions, and modifications as may have seemed desirable for reasons of politics, friendship, enmity, or religion. A few cases in which we have both the original letter and the sixteenth-century printing of it make this clear; as (e.g.) for some of the letters of Pietro Aretino. Occasionally what appears on the surface to be a genuine collected printing of a man's correspondence is a sheer fabrication or a hoax: the *Pistole vulgari* of Nicolò Franco (Venezia, Antonio Gardane, 1539, etc.), for example, were probably written purely for the printer, never sent as letters; while the *Lettere toscane* of Frosino Lapini (Bologna, Giaccarelli, 1556) are simply essays with a conventional superscription and signature added as a sort of afterthought. On the other hand, the *Lettere della molto illustre Sig. la Sra. Donna Lucretia Gonzaga . . . a gloria del sesso feminile nuovamente in luce posta* (Venezia: Gualtero Scotto, 1552), and the anthology of feminine correspondence *Lettere di molte valorose dame nelle quali chiaramente appare non esser ne di eloquentia ne di dottrina alli huomini inferiori* (Venezia: Giolito, 1549) were almost certainly not the work of their seeming authors, but composed out of whole cloth (or very nearly so); both volumes by the whimsical Ortensio Lando. And there were other cases of the kind.

But while it would be rash to trust the contemporary letter collections as proof, unless corroborated, of exact dates or precise details, they yet offer invaluable evidence of the general tendencies and manners of the time, social, literary, and political. For the purposes of the present paper, which aims at a general picture, it is fidelity of impression rather than exactness of detail which is paramount; possible inexactitudes or even deliberate misrepresentations by the authors of the letters here referred are thus comparatively unimportant.

able reply, especially if, like Frangipane (who had, it should be noted, already achieved some prominence in the world of affairs), he paved the way by a preliminary letter of unmixed adulation: 'I would like you,' he wrote, 'with the eye of your fine judgment to read over these two sonnets, and with your free spirit to judge if they merit death or are worthy of life, and I will act accordingly. And I beg of you send me your two written to the King and Queen of France.'[10] And one Guglielmo Boccarini, a youth of 23 from Arezzo, ventured to send Messer Pietro a sonnet for approval, with a marvellous letter of explanation, apology, and appeal whose structural intricacies might put even James Joyce to the blush.[11] Aretino's replies hardly ever offered any detailed critical comment; Bembo, on the other hand, frequently suggested minor emendations, though his criticisms were almost always considerate and tactful in the highest degree. A typical example of his delicacy in correction may be found in a letter which, among other things, discusses his correspondent's use in a sonnet of the word *celeste* as a noun, a use which Bembo did not like. 'I do not remember,' he wrote, 'having at any other time seen that word *celeste* used absolutely as you have used it in that line of yours *al bel del suo celeste*, but always as a word qualifying another. However, if you know of any other example, that is enough. If you do not, and wish to use it in this way on the authority of your own poetic feeling, why, I realise too that great men have always been allowed to innovate judiciously and in moderation.'[12] Annibal Caro, on the contrary, was often quite severe to the senders of unsolicited sonnets: to Captain Piero Bonaventura, for instance, whom he evidently thought more fitted for the soldier's than the poet's trade, he was decidedly outspoken. He corrected the poem, as desired, although (he adds) he did it against his will; he trusts his correspondent will pardon him if the corrector should appear to have made too much of a hash of his work; if the alterations seem excessive, let him learn not to apply for criticism to honest people or to true well-wishers.[13]—There was evidently a strong strain of the misanthrope

[10] *Lettere scritte a Pietro Aretino* (Bologna, 1875), II, ii, 116. Cf. *ibid.*, 114–115.

[11] *Ibid.*, pp. 320–322.

[12] To Girolamo Cittadino, May 1527. Bembo, *Opere* (Venezia, 1729), III, 234.

[13] *Op. cit.*, II, 133.

in Caro; we get it again, for example, in his letter to Tommaso Machiavelli: 'The sonnet that you have sent me has some good points, but I do not think it very remarkable, as the idea seems to me an ordinary one. . . . '[14] It must be observed, however, that this sort of severity appears chiefly in Caro's later life; the two letters quoted above were written after the middle of the century. Somewhat earlier, in 1543, he had written to one Lorenzo Foggini: 'There are some changes I would like made in your sonnets . . . , but distrusting my judgment I am not in the habit of ever touching anyone's work, and I do not dare to do so.'[15]

Far more frequently, however, it is writers of established reputation whom we find communicating their lyrics to each other for criticism and correction. Veronica Gambara, Lady and (after her husband's early death) castellan of Correggio, frequently sent sonnets to Bembo for revision, even a quarter of a century and more after her first diffident approach to him in verse had laid the foundations of their long literary friendship. Bembo's replies were at times rather noncommittal,[16] and it must be admitted that the vast bulk of the lady's verse is neither inspiring nor inspired; but on occasion he could wax almost ecstatic, answering one of her requests that he would courteously correct a sonnet for her: '. . . I have kissed it many times, in gratitude to the happy genius that composed it and the fair hand that writ. . . . As to correcting it, as you suggest I should, may Heaven forbid! . . . It is so charming and delightful that nothing could be added to it that would not spoil it, making it less lovely. . . . '[17]—Bernardo Tasso, Bernardo Cappello, and other well-known poets of the time also sent poems to Bembo asking for corrections, while Bembo himself was among the many who sought critical aid from Trifon Gabriele, an interesting *arbiter elegantiarum poeticarum* who wrote extremely little

[14] *Ibid.*, 157.

[15] *Op. cit.*, I, 112.

[16] As, for example, in his reply to her letter of October 29, 1540, which had enclosed a sonnet and begged him after looking it over to 'do with it what its plainness merited.' See *Rime e lettere di Veronica Gambara* (Brescia: Rizzardi, 1759), p. 127; Bembo, *op. cit.*, III, 325–326.

[17] Bembo, *op. cit.*, III, 324; cf. Veronica Gambara, *op. cit.*, p. 115.

but corrected and revised much for other poets. So Caro, again, sent sonnets to Guidiccione for counsel, and was answered with singular tact;[18] while a letter of his to that active polygraphic editor, Girolamo Ruscelli, thanking him for suggested alterations, makes it clear that some Cinquecento critics were less delicately considerate than others: '. . . If your worship should see anything else that does not satisfy you, I beg you to advise me of it; for I shall always consider it a favour to be corrected by a man of your stamp—and, in God's name, by anyone rather than by Castelvetro, who does it neither like a friend, a scholar, or a gentleman!'[19]

Occasionally poems would be submitted for correction as by an anonymous author. Della Casa, for instance, author of the famous Cinquecento 'Book of Good Manners,' *Il Galateo*, was once drawn into a rather harsh criticism of a sonnet, the author's name not having been mentioned. Later he evidently grew suspicious and tried to hedge, demanding also that the identity of the author be revealed. 'I thought,' he says, 'I had written to you that I considered the sonnet you sent me a good one; but it seems according to your letter that I did not do so. It is true, indeed, that I said it was stolen; but I did not mean by that to condemn it.—You have not yet told me the author's name.'[20] This was in 1525. Half a century later, Battista Guarini, while the printer was working on his *Pastor Fido*, found himself in a very similar predicament when asked by the *Cavaliere e Segretario* Vinta of Florence to give his opinion of some lyrics by an unnamed author. Guarini was careful not to say too much, though he seems to have been sure that at

[18] Caro, *op. cit.*, I, 42.

[19] *Op. cit.*, II, 111. By Caro's reference to Castelvetro there hangs, of course, a tale, and a very long one. But the story is well enough known: Castelvetro, it will be remembered, had rather severely criticized a canzone of Caro's, and had let his criticism get into wide (though of course manuscript) circulation; Caro was furious, and wrote a bitter anonymous volume refuting and counter-attacking. Friends joined in on both sides, and the dispute became violent and disastrous: Caro's last years were certainly saddened by it; and Castelvetro, accused of murder and heresy—largely because of the resentment he had roused in Caro's friends—was forced to flee to Switzerland and eventually to die in exile. For an elaborate account of the quarrel, *see* V. Vivaldi, *Una polemica nel Cinquecento . . .* (Napoli: A. Morano, 1891).

[20] Letter to Carlo Gualteruzzi of July 27, 1525. *Opere* (Venezia, 1752), II, 237.

least the poems were not the work of his correspondent.[21] Men were always chary of criticizing verses of unknown authorship; even praising them might sometimes lead one to regret. Daniello Barbaro (author, among other things, of an elaborate commentary on Vitruvius) once heard a sonnet recited by Gasparo Colonna and praised it highly, under the impression that it was by one of the Colonna family. It was afterwards revealed, however, as an effusion by Pietro Aretino, somewhat to Daniello's chagrin, for he appears to have been one of those who rather scorned the Aretine genius. Messer Pietro heard of the incident, and took occasion to write a philosophical letter on the subject to Barbaro, enclosing one of his avowed sonnets with the hope that it would please his correspondent no less than the one he had heard anonymously.[22] This reminds us of Messer Federico's story in the *Cortegiano:* 'Not long since, there being introduced here certain verses under the name of Sannazaro, they seemed very excellent to all, and were praised with wonder and admiration; then, it being known for certain that they were by another, they immediately lost their reputation, and seemed not even mediocre.'[23] Later in the century, Benvenuto Cellini in his sonnet *Ben molti si son messi a far sonetti* . . . declared that it made no difference how good a poem was: the one question men of letters asked was 'Who wrote it?' And their judgment of it would depend entirely on the answer. This was not the case, he observed with an artist's complacency, in the realms of painting and sculpture.[24]

Poems were also—indeed much more often—sent about in the mere way of friendship; so Aretino sent sonnets to numberless men; Molza to Veronica Gambara and various others; Bernardo Tasso to Speron Speroni, Antonio Gallo, and many more; Bembo to Lodovico Beccadello, Giovammatteo Bembo, Cola Bruno, Bernardo Cappello, Vittoria Colonna, Trifon Gabriele, Veronica

---

[21] *Lettere del Signor Cavaliere Battista Guarini* . . . (Venezia: Ciotti, 1615), p. 19. The letter is of March 20, 1590.

[22] *Lettere di M. Pietro Aretino* (Paris, 1609), IV, 121–122.

[23] *Il Cortegiano*, II, xxxv.

[24] *Le rime di Benvenuto Cellini* (Torino: Paravia, 1890), p. 222.—The extension of this critical criterion to the plastic arts must have come since Cellini's day.

Gambara, Cammilla Gonzaga, Girolamo Negro, Girolamo Quirino Francesco della Torre, and the rest. Lists could be drawn up like this for scores of poets throughout the century; besides Aretino, Bembo, and Bernardo Tasso, the letters of such men as Caro, Della Casa, Nicolò Martelli in the first half of the century, or G. C. Capaccio, Girolamo Catena, Giuliano Goselini, Angelo Grillo, G. B. Leoni, etc., in the second (to cite only some of those actually printed in the Cinquecento) show them all constantly sending, requesting, and receiving poems—usually sonnets—to be criticized, copied, or passed on. The whimsical Anton Francesco Doni touches fantastically on the matter in a quaint anecdote which he relates of Lodovico Domenichi. Some fellow from whom Domenichi had hoped to get certain savoury comestibles sent him a message regretting that they had unhappily spoiled on account of the meteorologic conditions; he was very sorry, and did not know what to do about it. Incidentally, he would be grateful if Domenichi would let him have some of the sonnets he had written the month before. Domenichi sent back word regretting that all the sonnets he had composed that month turned out to be rotten because they had been made up in the wane of the moon; he would try to be more careful in future. . . .[25]

Verses, however, were not only thus communicated from individual to individual; they were frequently meant to be passed on. Sometimes they were sent with the deliberate idea of broadcast distribution; and a general expansion of this kind, even when not specifically requested, was constantly expected. Veronica Gambara sent Bembo a sonnet through Girolamo Gambara to be given to the pope.[26] Caro informed Varchi that 'M. Matteo will let you have a sonnet of mine to Guidiccione.'[27] Aretino enclosed some verses in a letter to Claudio Tolomei, who did so much to establish standard spelling for Italian, asking him, if he thought them good, to pass them on to Rome;[28] at another time he wrote to the Abbate Vasallo: 'Here, father abbot, is the best sonnet my ability could

---

[25] A. F. Doni, *Canto: dialogo della musica* (Venezias:Scotto, 1544), f. 6.

[26] Bembo, *op. cit.*, IV, 325–326.

[27] Caro, *op. cit.*, III, 31.

[28] Aretino, *op. cit.*, V, 34.

achieve on the portrait of his most excellent and exalted Highness Marc'Antonio Trevisiano. Please communicate it to everyone who is fond of verse and respects princes, just as you did that other one. . . .'[29] And on yet another occasion he asked Giovan Tommaso Bruno to show a sonnet he had written 'to everyone that wishes the continued life and not the death of Charles V.'[30] We have also a curious letter from Aretino to one Antonio Anselmi requesting him to make copies of one of his sonnets, because such was the beauty of Messer Antonio's handwriting that copies so made would have a far greater value than the mere wit of Messer Pietro could confer upon the verse.[31]

But whatever part calligraphy may have played in the matter, there is no doubt that the circulation of poems in manuscript went very far. Men were frequently jealous of others who got hold before they did of sonnets written by their friends. Bembo, learning that his secretary had sent to others sooner than to his friend Bernardo Cappello copies of his latest poems, hastened to send Cappello another one brand new, that he is to be the first to see.[32] And Cammilla Gonzaga once asked Bembo specifically, as a special favor, to let her be the first to see whatever he might write.[33] Complex situations would sometimes arise in this way; in January 1533, for example, Caro wrote to Varchi: 'I have seen a fine sonnet of Bembo's to you, in the hands of Messer Carlo; but he did not want to give it [i.e., a copy of it] to me, because he says that Bembo has not yet sent it to you.'[34] Caro himself undertook obligations of the same kind: we find him apologizing at length to Monsig. Ardinghello in February 1538 for not having sent him a copy of a certain sonnet, although he had promised him copies of all he should write.[35] And some years later he wrote to Giuseppe Giova: 'I send you the two sonnets I happen to have written last; for, having been forced to let them get about, I should not like

[29] *Op. cit.*, VI, 204.

[30] *Ibid.*, p. 212.

[31] *Ibid.*, p. 165.

[32] Bembo, *op. cit.*, III, 128.

[33] *Ibid.*, p. 328.

[34] Caro, *op. cit.*, III, 44.

[35] *Ibid.*, I, 13.

them to come to your attention through anyone else. . . .'[36] In 1560 he had arranged to have all his sonnets sent to Varchi;[37] and that speedy circulation was the normal course of events is clearly implied in a further letter of his, in which he encloses two sonnets which, though not his last, 'have not,' he thinks, 'yet got into circulation.' A curious letter to Dionigi Atanagi to Giacomo Cenci —undated, but probably written about 1550–1560—again illustrates the lengths to which jealousy over the first view of a poem could ultimately extend. 'Messer Bernardo Cappello,' he writes, ' . . . has sent to ask me for a sonnet which he says he has understood you to have written for him. Although it seemed to me rather hard that you should, contrary to your custom, have shown it to others before I even knew it was written, yet in order to keep up the dignity which I seemed to acquire through his believing me to be your tiro and to be able to dispose of your works as I do of the gifts of Fortune, I answered that it was true that you had written it, but that it was not yet quite to your liking, and that for this reason you had not yet sent it to me. I hoped you would not be willing to do me the unkindness of letting him have it through other hands than mine.'[38]

From all this it is abundantly evident that, even if the poets of the time did not print their lyrics early, their friends and acquaintances (and often enough strangers or foreigners too) had ample opportunity to grow familiar with their work. For men passed about others' poems as freely as their own, sometimes for the benefit of persons quite unknown to them; so Claudio Tolomei to one Pierantonio Pecci on July 21, 1543: 'I send you ten sonnets to communicate to that friend of yours who is so interested; six are by Guidiccione and four by Caro.'[39]—Then copies would be made from copies, and these by the fourth or fifth generation would have multiplied as rabbits. A correspondent of Aretino once told him that above thirty copies had been made from one copy of a sonnet of his within two or three days; and the process was a common

[36] *Ibid.*, II, 195.

[37] *Ibid.*, 183.

[38] *Lettere volgari di diversi . . . , Libro Terzo* (Venezia: Aldus, 1564), f. 183.

[39] *Delle lettere di M. Claudio Tolomei* (Venezia: Giolito, 1553), f. 234 v.

one.—When such poems came to be printed, two marked characteristics of the Cinquecento lyric are to be directly traced to this ceaseless manuscript circulation: the numerous variant readings, and the constant misascriptions.

To give examples of the variant readings so incessantly encountered in the *raccolte* and *canzonieri* of the Cinquecento is hardly necessary. When one of the *raccolte* appeared (perhaps Giolito's *Libro Secondo*, printed in 1547), Claudio Tolomei wrote a long letter to Fabio Benvogliente, thanking him for a copy, but pointing out many errors—several pages indeed—in the readings of his own poems included in it.[40] And a comparison of the *raccolta* versions with the works of any poet as published in his own subsequent volume will invariably show numerous discrepancies. Sometimes the very opening words will be so metamorphosed as to make it impossible to locate a given poem from the table of first lines. A certain poem of Bembo's appears in one version (that followed, for instance, by the Milano *Classici* edition of 1809) as *Vago augelletto ch'al mio bel soggiorno* . . . ; in another (followed, e.g., by Serassi in 1745, and by the recent U.T.E.T. edition, s.a.) as *Picciol cantor ch'al mio verde soggiorno* . . . ; and one could multiply examples without difficulty. Differences of reading could readily enough arise in the course of endless transcriptions, and since, as often as not, the printer would use a manuscript which was not that of the original author, there was every room for confusion. A certain practice of the authors themselves made the existence of variants not only possible but unavoidable: this was the common habit of sending out poems hot from the pen, and then, after maturer consideration, sending on later a list of corrections or alterations to be made by the holders of the first copy. When, as was frequently the case, a number of copies of that first copy had already been made and scattered abroad, the chances of the corrections being made in every case were clearly very slight. Bernardo Tasso (in February, 1553) sent to the Bishop of Troyes a revised version of one of the lyrics he had written for Margaret of Valois;[41] Bembo enclosed in a letter to his nephew Giovammatteo a corrected form

---

[40] *Ibid.*, ff. 235 ff.

[41] *Delle lettere di M. Bernardo Tasso* (Venezia: Giolito, 1560), II, 67.

of one of his sonnets, saying: 'To content you, I let you have the sonnet for Messer Geronimo Quirino before I had revised it to suit me. Give him this other copy that I enclose, and see that he destroys the first.'[42] Aretino once wrote to Girolamo Molino: 'Most noble Signor Girolamo, Here is the sonnet (in due honour of Monsignor Della Casa) slightly revised and amended';[43] and Monsignor Della Casa himself was seriously upset when one of *his* sonnets got into circulation before he had given it its final polishing: he had only sent a copy of it to Carlo Gualteruzzi, and yet it had got about all over Rome. It was one of those on the portrait of Isabetta Quirini which had cost him such pains to produce; and there the first copy had got into circulation, though he had later changed it in a thousand places where it had not been right at first—and even now it was not perfect![44]

That the existence of more than one version in manuscript circulation should cause divergent readings between the different

---

[42] Bembo, *op. cit.*, III, 427.—This sonnet had a curious history. Quirino had asked Bembo through Giovammatteo to write a consolatory letter and a sonnet for him on the death of his father-in-law. Bembo refused the letter, on the ground that in the first place the decease was a stroke of luck, not a misfortune, for Quirino, and that in the second place it would create an awkward precedent, forcing him to write more than one such letter. Someday, perhaps, he would write him a sonnet. . . . Two weeks later he wrote to Giovammatteo again, badly wanting him to secure from one of the Diedi a carved stone tablet; if Giovammatteo did this, it would inspire his uncle to produce Quirino's sonnet instantly, otherwise he would never be able to write it. Apparently the tablet was duly forthcoming, as the sonnet was produced almost immediately—so hastily, in fact, that, as we see, it needed revision. Cf. the whole series of letters from Bembo to his nephew, *loc. cit.*

Bembo's revisions, it must be noted, were not always made on purely aesthetic or stylistic grounds; they were sometimes forced on him for other reasons. He was compelled to alter his phrasing of the sonnet he had written in lyric compliment to Elisabetta Quirini, *Se stata foste voi nel colle Ideo / Tra lor che nude Pari a mirar ebbe* . . . , on account of the lady's vigorous protest at his impertinence in imagining her—and communicating his thought to others—as a nudist, no matter how exalted the company might be in which he so placed her. His revised phrasing avoided all reference to the costume for the contest, but it runs far less smoothly: *Se stata foste voi nel colle Ideo / Tra le dive che Pari a mirar ebbe* . . . . *See* his letter to Antonio Anselmi of July 15, 1538: *op. cit.*, III, 296; and cf. II, iii, 32, 214.

[43] *Op. cit.*, VI, 62 (February, 1552).

[44] Della Casa, *Opere* (Venezia, 1752), II, 162. Cf. *ibid.*, 154 ff.—The lady of the portrait is the same that caused Bembo so much trouble over a sonnet; *see* note 42 above.

printed editions when these appeared was made more inevitable by the fact that a sixteenth-century author's poems were so frequently printed in Italy, when the time came, without his knowledge or consent;[45] though in many cases the statement to some such effect in a printer's or editor's dedication or preface is probably to be taken as a convenient fiction agreed upon between author and publisher to preserve for the former a certain semblance of conventional modesty, and to enable him to foil all hostile critics (should the occasion arise) by declaring that the printed version did not represent his final draft. But the fact remains that manuscript collections, partial or complete, of almost every poet's work, as well as of individual sonnets and other pieces, were so widespread that it was simple enough for a copy to find its unauthorized way to the printer.—So in August, 1536, Veronica Gambara expressed the fear that much against her will (though her unconventional correspondent Pietro Aretino urged her not to hesitate) she might have to send corrected copies of her poems to be printed,[46] apparently because versions of dubious accuracy were available to the printer and would almost certainly be used if she did not herself supply an authorized text. And a year or so after (as we learn from a letter of Annibal Caro dated January 10,

---

[45] The case of Tebaldeo's *Rime*, printed without his knowledge by his cousin Iacopo at the close of the fifteenth century, is the classic instance of this (see *Giornale Storico della Lett. Ital.*, XXXV, 204, etc.). A more curious example is provided by the *Canti carnascialeschi* of Giambattista dell'Ottonaio published by Lasca (Antonfrancesco Grazzini) in his elaborate anthology of such *canti* (Firenze: Torrentino, 1559). Messer Giambattista was no longer alive and could make no objection himself; nor (as far as we know) were his verses as Lasca printed them made the object of any hostile criticism. But a brother of his made so much ado over the matter, insisting that the printed versions were unauthorized and inaccurate, that he succeeded in getting the edition officially suppressed; or rather the hundred pages in it (298–398) devoted to Ottonaio were cut out of every copy, save for one or two (now *arcirarissimi*) which had already got into circulation. Next year the brother duly published his authorized version, which Lasca stigmatized as atrociously incorrect, from the same press.—*See* Lasca's amusing letter to Luca Martini on the subject, printed in the *Raccolta di prose fiorentine*, IV, i (Firenze, 1734), pp. 76–79.

[46] Cf. her letter to Aretino, *Rime e lettere . . .* (Brescia, 1759), p. 283, asking him to prevent the printing if he could, and if not to help her to revise the best of her lyrics for this publication. Presumably her efforts to prevent the printing in that case were successful; at least I know of no printing of her poems until seven or eight years later.

1538) that brilliant but tragically dissipated poet Francesco Maria Molza was unwilling to let any of his poems out of his own sight since his stanzas to Giulia had come out in unauthorized print.[47]

These are two out of many examples which present the author's side. More interesting in their varied ingenuity are those which give the editor's or publisher's point of view. Lodovico Domenichi, editor of many works for various printers (in connection with which he at one time fell foul of that whimsical Florentine eccentric, Anton Francesco Doni, who conferred on him a quantity of extravagant abuse), in 1547 saw through the press the poems of Remigio Nannini, usually—as in that volume—called simply 'Remigio Fiorentino.' In a curious dedicatory letter to Giovan Battista Besalu, Domenichi sets forth the circumstances: Nannini apparently had promised (indeed, had actually given, but then got back) a manuscript of his poems to Besalu. Domenichi subsequently borrowed it from Nannini, pretending that he merely wanted to read the poems, but intending from the first to hand the manuscript over to Besalu, whom he considered to have a valid claim to it. Having it in his hands, however, he proceeded instead to have the poems printed, though Nannini had more than once made clear his unwillingness not only that they should be printed, but that they should be even seen by any but his closest friends. To Besalu Domenichi sent one of the printed copies, adding that, since Nannini had in the first place broken his promise to Besalu about the manuscript, he was not in a position to show too much indignation over Domenichi's breach of confidence, different as it was, in having the poems published.[48] Ten years later, again,

---

47 Caro, *op. cit.*, III, 28–31.—Giulia is, of course, the famous Giulia Gonzaga, beloved of Cardinal Ippolito de' Medici of tragic story, and friend of the great English Cardinal Pole, of Juan Valdes, of Vittoria Colonna, and of many other reforming spirits, some of whom, like Bernardo Ochino for example, were subsequently pronounced heretical. Molza's annoyance may have been partly due to the fact that a number of stanzas by Gandolfo Porrino, Giulia's secretary and a very inferior poet, had been appended by the printer as a part of his work!

48 *Rime di M. Remigio Fiorentino* (Venezia: Bindoni e Pasini, 1547), f. 2. Remigio was a Dominican friar, author of numerous works (including a translation of Petrarch's *De remediis* . . . , and one of Ovid's *Heroides* which was frequently reprinted and even in the nineteenth century regarded as a classic), of which the *Rime* was the first to appear. His

the printer Torrentino of Florence was about to publish an edition of the poems of Pietro Massolo, an interesting Venetian gentleman who had shortly before murdered his wife and become a Benedictine monk, taking the cloister name of Lorenzo. This printing, too, was to be made without the author's knowledge; but Torrentino was reproved by friends for planning such an action. In consequence of this, he declares, he approached the author before beginning to print, and was fortunate enough to obtain not only the desired consent, but also an improved and corrected version of the poems for his press.[49]

A letter written in 1553 by Girolamo Ruscelli, like Domenichi an editor of countless works for sundry publishers in Venice, throws an interesting light on the methods sometimes used in compiling the lyric anthologies which in the second half century became so numerous. 'I happen to have seen through the press a few days since a number of admirable poems by various Brescia authors,[50] which I had been collecting, if not against their will, at least without their knowledge; and I had among them some seventy-five by Marco Mantova, which the gifted and charming Messer Giovan Antonio Sacchetto had shortly before, with great diligence, taken from him by stealth and sent to me. But he found out about it, and most urgently begged me in letters, and had me requested by various persons, on no account to wrong him by publishing them; because he had not yet corrected or revised them as

---

later works were mainly religious, and in 1569 he was (according to Poccianti, *Catalogus scriptorum florentinorum*, Florentiae, 1589, p. 159) appointed by Pius V to direct the revision and annotation of the works of Aquinas.

[49] *Sonetti morali di M. Pietro Massolo* . . . (Firenze: Torrentino, 1558), p. 3.—Torrentino had apparently planned a simple reprint of the Aldine edition of the year before (Bologna: Antonio Manuzio, 1557), which he abuses in his preface as unauthorized. All available evidence, however (including the dedication of the Aldine edition by Massolo himself, as well as sonnets addressed by him to Paolo Manuzio), seems to indicate that the earlier edition, in spite of Torrentino's statement, was by no means lacking in authority. Yet it must be noted that when a vastly expanded edition of Massolo's *Rime* appeared six years later, it was Torrentino who printed it.

On Massolo in general, *see* P. Molmenti, "Un poeta uxoricida del sec. XVI," *Nuova Antologia*, LXII (January 16, 1927), 129. His mother was Elisabetta Quirini: cf. above, n. 42.

[50] Doubtless the *Rime di diversi autori bresciani* . . . (Venezia: Pietrasanta, 1554).

he wished to do, and because, besides that, he had planned to publish them himself together with a number of other poems. . . .'[51] Ruscelli did not include Mantova's sonnets in his anthology, but, as their author died just as it was passing through the press, he published them in a slender volume of their own.

These are examples which could be multiplied at will.[52] The very emphasis sometimes laid upon such phrases in a title page as 'dal proprio originale dell'autore,' 'nuovamente rivedute dal proprio autore,' 'da lui medesimo reviste e corrette,' and the like, obviously imply that it was extremely common for second- or third-hand copies to be used, and for the author himself to take no part in the publication. And not only was printing, even when with the author's consent, frequently not from the author's manuscript, but an authorized publisher would sometimes include in the accepted edition pieces which the author had suppressed, but which had fallen into his hands from some outside source. A flagrant case in point was that of Marcolini, who, printing in 1536 the *Rime* of Antonio Mezzabarba, eliminated much of his Petrarchesque and Platonic work and gave full space, against the author's will, to the 'rime lascive ed oscene,' though admitting in his letter to the reader that Mezzabarba, a distinguished Venetian jurist, ever kept this part of his work, as far as he could, suppressed.[53]—This sort of thing anticipated in its way the sufferings of the twentieth-

---

[51] *Rime di M. Domenico Mantova* . . . (Venezia: Pietrasanta, 1554), pp. 5–6.

[52] In 1564, Stefano Blado tells us that although various works by Rinaldo Corso had been printed time and again in the past sixteen years, no printer had ever seen any manuscript of a single composition of his written in his own hand (R. Corso, *Fondamenti del parlar thoscano* [Roma: Blado, 1564], printer's dedication "agli amatori della thoscana favella."). Again, the editors of Vitale Pappazoni's *Rime* (Venezia: Domenico Nicolini, 1572), two of his friends, frankly admit in their dedication (f. a6) that they had not asked his permission for the publication, fearing that he might refuse it; they had decided to have the volume printed merely without his knowledge, rather than directly contrary to his probable command. The editor of Curzio Gonzaga's poems, on the other hand, frankly admitted that, having secured copies in a roundabout way from a lady who had them, he had asked the poet's permission to print and been refused it; nonetheless he proceeded with the publication. *See* Dedication of the *Rime dell'Illustriss. Sig. Curtio Gonzaga* (Venezia: Al Segno del Leone, 1591). And so for many more.

[53] Cf. A. Corbellini, *Di un rimatore pavese-veneziano del secolo XVI* (Pavia, 1913), p. 28.

century author from false emphasis, in a film version, on the more trivial episodes in his book.

Small wonder, then, that with the author so often left in the lurch, variants became innumerable. The task of any modern editor of a Cinquecento poet is under these circumstances far from easy; it is made even harder by the occasional obscurancy of some of the poets themselves. One of Bembo's letters to Vettor Soranzo reveals a quaint case of disingenuousness. The three new sonnets he is sending should not be shown to any one but Messer Carlo, he requests, and should be kept close. 'The reason for which I do not want you to let these sonnets out of your hands is not only because I have only just composed them and may make alterations in them, but also for this: that the subject matter is not appropriate to these years, specially in the two first, and I am thinking of including them one day among my Juvenilia.'[54] Another inconsiderate usage on the part of certain poets was the not infrequent revamping of an old sonnet to suit a new love or a different situation. Diomede Borghesi once did this; Luigi Alamanni did it several times;[55] and Tullia d'Aragona changed her sonnet for Ugolino Martelli (*Piú volte, Ugolin mio, mossi il pensiero . . .*) to fit Girolamo Muzio (*Ho piú volte, signor, fatto pensiero . . .*); etc. The most expert internal critic might thus be misled, unless the key information is in his hands, should he attempt to date the composition of a sonnet on the basis of internal evidence.

Another literary phenomenon of the Cinquecento directly traceable to unrestricted manuscript circulation is, as we have noted, the large number of misascriptions. Bernardo Tasso noted that a canzone and a sonnet of his (to Vittoria Colonna) were credited to Gandolfo Porrino in the *Rime di diversi eccellentissimi autori* of Venice, 1550.[56] Bembo was sent by Cola Bruno in 1525 various manuscripts of poems alleged by those who had copies of them to be by him, but found that only two were really his.[57] Four poems

---

[54] *Op. cit.*, III, 155; letter of July 19, 1530. Bembo was then sixty.

[55] Cf. H. Hauvette, *Luigi Alamanni . . .* (Paris, 1903), p. 162, n. 2.

[56] *Op. cit.*, II, 141.

[57] *Op. cit.*, III, 298.

ascribed to Vittoria Colonna by Dolce in a *raccolta* of 1556, and also by Ruscelli, following Dolce, in his later *Fiore delle rime* . . . , go everywhere else under the name of Veronica Gambara. To Molza was ascribed and printed with his collected poems a sonnet by Bembo (*Amor che vedi i piú chiusi pensieri* . . .), as well as one by Caro (*Vibra pur la tua sferza* . . .). The sonnet *Voi donna ed io per segni manifesti* . . . is generally ascribed to Cariteo, and is undoubtedly his, but in the *Secondo volume dlle* [sic] *rime scelte di diversi autori* (Venezia: Giolito, edit. of 1586, p. 560) it appears, with only the most trifling changes, under the name of Broccardo. Again, the well-known sonnet on jealousy, normally attributed to Tansillo, *O d'invidia e d'Amor figlia si ria* . . . is ascribed in the 1546 and 1549 editions of the Giolito *Rime diverse* . . . *Parte Prima* to Antonio Mezzabarba; and an unusual case of such error in the same anthology leads to the printing of one sonnet (*O stelle, o cielo, o fiero mio pianeta* . . .) twice, among the poems of two different authors: Giovan Andrea Gesualdo on p. 31, and Tommaso Castellani on p. 47. A final example of at least partial misascription, this time involving modern scholarship, is provided by two sonnets which Capasso found some twenty odd years ago in a manuscript of pasquinades: a *Libro delli Pasquilli* . . . now Cod. Ottobon. 2811 in the Vatican. One of these poems is on the conference between Pope, Emperor, and King of France at Nice in 1538, the other on the Turkish invasion of Hungary in 1543. They are clearly much finer than the vast majority of their fellows, and far more serious in tone; Capasso comments, with surprised admiration: 'Here is a living voice of the People raised to bear witness to the efforts of the Pope. . . .'[58] But was this in truth a voice of the people? Both these sonnets (though no one to this day seems to have noticed it, and Capasso published them as *inedite*) have from the middle of the sixteenth century always been printed with the poems of Molza. And Molza's they probably are, though they *may* have got his name attached to them in the first instance by sheer accident, and have retained it by inertia ever since. In any case, they are certainly the work of a man of letters; though

[58] C. Capasso, "Pasquinate contro i Farnesi nei Codd. Ottobon. 2811–2812," in *Studi dedicati a F. Torraca* (Napoli, 1912), p. 407.

this, it must be remembered, does not make it any less likely that they were actually posted up anonymously in Rome beside the torso of Messer Pasquino, and subsequently copied down thence with the rest.

This list of examples could be indefinitely drawn out; it was almost inevitable that such errors should constantly occur. When a short poem was hastily copied down, the name of the author—known perfectly well at the moment—would not always be written in: it was not needed *then*. But the sheet, taken to the copier's library, would be laid aside for a time, subsequently placed among many other copied poems, and finally its origin be lost to memory. In absence of other identification it would naturally be attributed by the owner to the author of the poem nearest to it; so the mis-ascription would begin, only to be continued and extended as copies were made from his collection. At other times—a case still more likely to lead to confusion—poems seem to have been actually stolen. Bernardo Tasso frequently complains of such losses, caused by the carelessness of a courier; Bembo cannot find some sonnets that had been sent to him by Vittor Soranzo, and fears Prioli [probably Luigi Prioli] may have made off with them;[59] and again, having been sent a sonnet by Benedetto Varchi, he regrets that he has not yet seen it, because it was stolen from Messer Lorenzo Lenzi, who was to bring it.[60] With poems thus often lost, stolen, or strayed, our chief surprise must be that the original authors managed to retain so many! And at times on this point too the poets themselves are to blame; they sometimes shut the door on an unwanted sonnet. We have a letter from Caro to Varchi written in 1562 about a particular poem of his which he had resolved to disown: 'As to the sonnet *Gaddo* . . . , it is true that I have it in a notebook of mine with the others, but I do not remember ever having told anyone that I planned to print it as my work. . . . And I do not want it ever again to be said to be mine: I wish I could get rid of all the others I have written likewise!'[61]

From beginning to end of the Cinquecento, then, lyric poems

---

[59] *Op. cit.*, III, 153.

[60] *Ibid.*, p. 282.

[61] Caro, *op. cit.*, II, 183.

were constantly communicated from one individual to another for comment and criticism, and were also sent about with the specific idea of their being shown to others. Not infrequently a poet undertook to send out a copy of every new poem which he might write, sometimes to a number of different friends or admirers; in every case further copies were normally made, and in brief process of time multiplied and widely circulated in manuscript form. Such manuscript circulation on a very wide scale is a familiar enough characteristic of the Middle Ages; but we sometimes forget that it continued to flourish, and actually increased (especially for lyric poetry), during far more than a century after the invention of printing might have been expected to put an end to it. And the fact that it wenton for so many generations side by side with multiplication through the press made the situation—until eventually printing achieved a practical monopoly—extremely complicated. This fact is largely responsible for the frequent variant readings and the numerous misascriptions which we find whenever the Cinquecento lyric appears in print. It also made it possible for writers and others, even abroad, to have knowledge of poems by men whom personally they may never have known long before the first printed edition of those poems had appeared.

MANUSCRIPTS OF THE 'ISLANDS VOYAGE' AND 'NOTES ON THE ROYAL NAVY'

(in relation to the printed versions in Purchas and in Ralegh's 'Judicious Essayes')

HELEN ESTABROOK SANDISON

Vassar College

FOR *A larger Relation of the . . . Iland Voyage*[1] [of 1597], Purchas used a manuscript, as is proved by blanks left where certain words were undecipherable. 'This booke,' Purchas asserts in his first sidenote, 'was written *A.* 1607. and dedicated to . . . Prince *Henry;* the Epistle to him and the Preface I haue omitted in regard of our long volume. . . . [The Author] added also Notes touching the Nauie Royall, which are . . . perhaps not to be permitted to euery vulgar and notelesse eye.'

The manuscript probably bore the date 1607, for the author, Sir Arthur Gorges, was in the habit of dating his manuscripts, and having scribal copies dated. The account may have been originally composed somewhat earlier, not long after the disgrace of Ralegh, to whom Gorges was a loyal kinsman and adherent—possibly about 1604.[2] The events of the voyage proper, as Corbett remarks in *The Successors of Drake*, are 'clearly taken from an accurately kept journal,' an assumption supported by the wording of Purchas's title: *A . . . Relation . . . written by Sir* ARTHVR GORGES *Knight, collected in the Queenes Ship, . . . wherein he was then Captaine.* The Relation includes certain added discourses, marine and martial, as Purchas's title puts it. The manuscript had as addendum the Notes on the Navy which Purchas omitted in discretion.

The papers that Purchas actually handled may have disappeared beyond recovery. But at least three copies of them, slightly revised, and written between 1612 and 1650, survive. They

[1] *Purchas His Pilgrimes*, 1625, Part II, Bk X, ch. xiv, 2, ed. Glasgow, 1905–1907, XX, 34. Quotations are from the 1625 edition.

[2] On Gorges, see *PMLA*, XLIII, 645–674.

preserve the title that Purchas altered, and sidenotes comparable to those that Purchas added (see below). They preserve also the Dedication and Preface, omitted by Purchas, though in the manuscripts these exist in a new and despondent form, substituted after the prince's death; in this Preface the author confirms the supposition that the basis of his narrative was a day-by-day journal: 'this[e] Seafaringe Collections and stormebeaten papers that I scribbled a shippboard.'

Moreover, a comparison of the manuscripts with the printed versions of the *Islands Voyage* in 1625 (Purchas) and of the *Notes on the Navy* in 1650 (in Ralegh's *Judicious and Select Essayes and Observations*) establishes the fact that the two items, Voyage and Notes, remained in conjunction as a manuscript unit from the time of their composition until as late as 1650. It proves that the 'Maritimall voyage' which Ralegh mentions in the 1650 edition of the Notes is not one of his lost works, as has been supposed (by Brushfield, for instance, in his Ralegh Bibliography, ed. 1908, item 254), but is his cousin's *Islands Voyage.*

These three manuscripts are all unprinted: SPDom. Jas. I, Add. 36, f. 225 (here called SP);[3] the manuscript in the Harmsworth collection at Bexhill, formerly Leconfield 83 (H); and Bodl. Ballard 52, f. 64 (B). All are post-1612; B is post-1634. H and B have both Voyage and Notes; SP, seriously mutilated, almost certainly had both, but now lacks the Notes as well as the latter part of the Voyage. All three have identical sidenotes, similar in arrangement and frequency to Purchas's, but different in substance and wording: a variation not easy to explain. Even more puzzling, SP and H (but not B) have marginal hands serving as N.B.'s to noteworthy passages; but though these passages sometimes coincide, at others they do not, with the 'Discourses' that Purchas signalized in his edition by italics (which for some reason are not reproduced in the excellent Glasgow edition of Purchas).

Each of the three bears some external suggestion of a careful presentation copy, prepared perhaps for influential officials. SP is among the Conway papers in the Record Office; it and H are so

[3] Corbett, *Successors of Drake*, 169, n, mentions this MS, and questions the date suggested in the Calendar: 1604.

nearly identical that they seem to be both copies of a single version which had been revised by Gorges himself (for a few characteristic spellings appear to betray his hand). And H is a de luxe gift copy; it is similar in binding, and identical in the ribbon used for ties, to Gorges's *Seafight*, inscribed 'Given by Sir Arthur Gorges'; the latter, like the *Islands Voyage*, was preserved until recently (MS. Leconfield 48) at Petworth House, and was a gift presumably either to Northumberland, or, perhaps more likely, to Lord Admiral Howard,[4] before 1619; in either case, preservation at Petworth would be natural (see *Hist. Mss. Com. Report VI*, 287). Even B, a dependable, utilitarian copy, lacking only the pointing hands, has been written seemingly by the same scribe as copied the *Seafight* in SPDom. Jas. I. XVII, 103; and B occurs in a volume devoted to naval treatises, one of which may be closely related to a Northumberland manuscript at Alnwick (see *Hist. Mss. Com. Report* III, 115, Sir W. Slyngisbye, 1596).

The history of the combined Voyage and Notes during Gorges's lifetime comes out fairly clearly: about 1607 or before, when Ralegh was in the Tower, and Gorges fallen from all favor, Gorges probably put together his account of the Azores voyage, drawing on his own memories, and on comments and 'discourses' taken from talk with Ralegh, or even from pages of Ralegh's writing, but drawing also on his own notes, scribbled on shipboard back in '97. To this narrative he appended at the same time the *Notes on the Royal Navy*, which Purchas was later cautiously to omit, and which from a complex of signs, external and internal, are assignable to Ralegh's authorship. (It is perhaps significant that Gorges claims them in versions H and B as only 'gathered and sett downe' by him.) Ralegh would readily enough countenance the addition of his Notes to the account of a voyage in which his fortunes were deeply involved, and which, as the Notes declare, 'did most of all others, discover unto us these experiences and tryalls in the Royall Navy' (1650 text).

A copy of this manuscript, dated 1607, came to Purchas, one

---

[4] Buckingham is ruled out as recipient of the Petworth *Seafight*, inasmuch as a copy exists in Stowe 426, extensively revised in Gorges's writing; it is freshly dated March 1619, and expressly directed to Buckingham, just made Lord Admiral.

would suppose among Hakluyt's papers, except that Purchas has assigned no 'H' to this article, as he was careful to do for Hakluyt's items.[5] Meantime, further copies were made of the Voyage and Notes, with some revisions designed for this eye or for that, as Ralegh and Gorges plied their suits, especially after 1612, for the restoration not only of their own fortunes, but also of English naval prestige.[6]

In 1625, the year of Gorges's death, the Voyage section first saw print. Purchas's prefatory sidenote remarks: 'I haue not added a word of mine, but the Title and Marginall Notes.' The title he is merely altering to suit the context. The marginal notes he probably composed, adding them in conformity to his practice throughout the *Pilgrimes*, a usage which he inherited from Hakluyt. Similar sidenotes occur in all three post-1612 versions, in opposition to Gorges's custom; none of his other writing employs them (nor was it apparently a habit of Ralegh's). Gorges may have got wind of the insertion of notes in the 1607 copy—may even have seen them—and may have taken up the idea, though preferring to compose his own notes. One can only guess.

Purchas continues: 'nor [haue I] defalked any [word] of the Authors (after my wont in others, not to make their writings mine, but thine, the tediousnesse in so often repetitions by often relators, and the superfluities being such as would deterre the Reader).' Why? Was it that Purchas recognized Ralegh's part—even sometimes his reflected wordings—in this narrative, and, sharing Hakluyt's admiration of that great man, kept all of the text as 'worthy the noting'? This seems likely, for he is at pains to explain further: 'The Discourses I haue vsually put in another letter [i.e., kept, and set in italics][7] to distinguish them from the History; the one the Eyes obseruations, the other the Minds,

---

[5] G. B. Parks, *Richard Hakluyt and the English Voyages* (1928), pp. 226–227.

[6] Reasons both political and personal presumably guided the changes: one interesting instance is Gorges's omission after 1612 of passages criticizing Grenville's rashness at Flores, and praising Lord Admiral Howard's discretion in 1588 (both printed by Purchas, ed. Glasgow, pp. 103, 106). Collation of the versions will be undertaken in my projected edition of Gorges's works.

[7] Hakluyt frequently has "Note" (or "Nota" for Latin texts) in his margins, though with no change of type in his black-letter text. With Purchas "Note" is frequent.

and both worthy both thine eyes and minds best obseruation.'

Marginal hands point to discourses, it will be recalled, in the post-1612 versions; possibly again Gorges adopted the Hakluyt-Purchas method, and some of his actual selections, though choosing to substitute some of his own.

At the end of his note Purchas explains that the Notes, though 'worthy the noting,' he has omitted, being 'loth' to 'reap the reward of a busiebody . . . [and] to buy repentance.'

These Notes, thus discreetly omitted from the print of 1625, were finally published, *in their 1607 form*, in 1650, as one of Ralegh's *Judicious and Select . . . Essayes*. There, significantly, the word 'Notes' lingers in the title, though in the post-1612 forms its place is taken by the more elaborate 'Observations and Overtures.' There—and there alone among these 1650 essays—appear the familiar sidenotes; examination shows them to be quite in the Purchas manner and tone, and once 'Nota,' reminiscent of Hakluyt and Purchas, appears. The genesis of the 1650 text is becoming clear.

But it is the opening sentence of the 1650 *Notes* that plays the final telltale: 'Having formerly (most excellent Prince) discoursed of a Maritimall voyage, and the passages and incidents therein, I thinke it not impertinent nor differing from my purpose, to second the same with some necessary relations concerning the Royall Navy.'[8] The 'former discoursing' is Gorges's *Islands Voyage*, in the 1607 form that Purchas used; it is not another 'lost work' of Ralegh.

This fact is reflected elsewhere in the 1650 *Notes:* in the reference under 'Ordnance' to 'this last journey to the Islands,' which immediately makes sense if taken to mean 'last-mentioned journey,' though as 'this latest journey' it conveyed nothing in a 1650 text; likewise in the 'passages and incidents therein' of sentence one, which may be seen as a flash back to the title, as it reads in the manuscripts, 'according to the accidents and occurrences

[8] This simple opening address contrasts sharply with the substitute in the post-1612 revising (H B), which attempts no connection with the Voyage, and seeks to justify the private subject who urges the reformation of naval affairs, an effort in which it is plainly ill at ease. The substitute introduction is printed below (from B, f. 125).

obserued . . . with . . . some pass[ag]es and Collateral discourses incident vnto the matter.'

Thus the 1607 Notes finally found their way into print in 1650. Their publisher, Humphrey Moseley, speaks of 'these . . . papers [that] came to my hand,' as 'legitimate issue' of Sir Walter, which he offers now to the son, Carew Ralegh, as fittest protector.[9]

The history of the *Islands Voyage* and the added *Notes on the Navy* has here been carried from the time of their composition, early in the reign of James, past various copyings that kept the two items always together, to their separate appearances in print, the one in 1625, the other in 1650. The original Dedication and Preface to the Voyage, written in the still hopeful days before 1612, may never be recovered; the original unpretentious address to the prince, which opened the Notes, we still have in the 1650 *Essayes*. For all three of these addresses, substitutes were offered in sober mood after Henry's death; these have survived in the group of manuscripts here considered, and are here given to print.[10]

f. 64] A true Relation of the Voyage

To the Iles of *Azores* by the Nauie and Forces of the late Queene Elizabeth of famous Memorie, vnder the Conduct of the Right Ho*noura*ble Robert Deuorux Earle of *Essex* and Ewe. M*aste*r of the horse and Ordinance, Lord High Marciall of England one of her Ma*iestie*s priuy Councell and Knight of the Order of the Garter, In the yeare of o*ur* Lord 1597 and about the 25th of Iune after the English accompt Collected and written according to the accidents and occurrences obserued from time to time in the Royall shipp called the Wastspight by S*ir* *Arthur Gorges* K^t. the Captaine of the same

With a briefe description of those Ilands and some pass[ag]es and Collaterall discourses incident vnto the matter as occasion is offered

---

9 This credible testimony as to Ralegh's authorship enforces other external evidence and that afforded by the substance of the Notes themselves.

10 From MS B (Ballard), a reliable copy, used here because SP is fragmentary. By the courtesy of Lord Leconfield, and subsequently of the late Sir Leicester Harmsworth, I have had opportunity to examine H, though not to make transcriptions of it.

Wherevnto are alsoe annexed certaine obseruations and ouertures concerninge the Royall Nauie and Seaseruice gathered and sett downe by the same Author:/

Fides fortibus fraus formidolosis.

The Epistle Dedicatorie of the Author.

f. 65] To the /: o Noble England:/ my deare and Natiue Countrey and to thy Hono*ur* doe I dedicate this labo*ur* of myne, beeing a Nauall discourse of the famous action attempted and performed by *Queene Elizabeth* thy late Souereigne M*istres*s of happy memory. For to whom can the glorie thereof and of many other Heroicall atchieuments more properly belong the[n] to thy bounteous self that didst both breed the men [ms. *man*] and gaue the meanes to effect those Noble enterprises in the Raigne of a mayden Queene, that w*i*th such Martiall renowne and glorie hath flowne throughout the world, whilst thou (the whilst) didst entertaine thy selfe w*i*th that Maiesticall calme and peace, w*hi*ch at home supported thy saftie, pleasure and plentie. Vouch[s]afe therefore to receaue from the hand of one of thy loyall and loueinge Children this offeringe of Zeale and deuotion proceedinge from the free and sincere disposition of that minde w*hi*ch neither expecteth nor desireth any other returne or gratuitie then that Seauen foote of earth, w*hi*ch thou at last bestowest on those whom thou hast brought into the worlds light, inclosinge them in thy fruitfull wombe, when all other friends and fortunes doe forsake them &c:/ .

[THE PREFACE]

f. 66.] The Voyage to the Iles of the *Azores*

The vnpartiall penns of those famous writters that haue reported truly of ages past, w*i*thout humoringe the present haue allwaies been to posteritie most profitable, and yet in experience wee finde that this sincere course is commonly rather praised then p*re*ferred and therefore the less in request. Notw*i*thstanding the generous spiritt that loues vertue for it selfe, likes better to be knowne for the vnfortunate follower of truth, then the graced seruer of time makeinge his contentment his comfort, and his comfort his Reward, w*i*th a mind soe p*re*pared doe I aduenture to expose to the Curtesie of publique Censure this Seafaringe Collections and stormebeaten papers that I scribbled a shippboard in the voyage sett out to the Iles of the *Azores* by o*ur* Late famous Soueraigne M*istress* Queene Elizabeth vnder the

Conduct of the Noble /: but vnfortunate:/ Earle of *Essex* wherein I haue vsed neither art nor eloquence beeing my self a meere stranger to those perfections and therefore haue shadowed the defects of an vnskillfull penn, vnder the shelter of a faithfull relation, w*hi*ch I hold to bee the chiefe ornament of an Historie, And in regard thereof I need not seeke to defend the creditt of this small pamphlett w*i*th anie superfluous apologie. For what is more pr*e*valent then truth ag*ains*t the w*hi*ch who soe spurneth receaueth a greater blowe then hee giueth, Neither doe I by the dedication thereof to any great personage seeke to insinuate myselfe into publique opinion or grace well knowinge the worke to bee of noe such meritt, and my frostbitten fortunes allreadie to much distasted[,] now to relish those Sunshininge

The Course of the author farr from flattery or p*ar*tiall respects

fancies[.] Only the p*r*eserued memorie of these fore passed actions, I leaue to the hono*u*r of my Countrie and the Glorie of an excellent Queene who now resting in the graue can neither returne for the same thanks nor reward, you therefore may free mee from all puta*ci*on of flatterie. But for that the successe of this Noble enterprise held not in all points Correspondent either w*i*th the expectacon or pr*e*paracou*n* if perhaps it bee therefore censured vnworthy of Record I doe thus answeare. That seeinge her late Ma*ies*tie and the State were not wantinge in anie thing on their parts that might giue authoritie life and meanes to the action, They should haue much wrong /: in my opinion:/ to be depriued of the honourable memorie due to soe Heroicall a resolu-

Strossy & the French w*i*th the Portingales beaten at the Iland. Good Counsells are not to be judged only by the successe.

*ci*on against so mightie an Ennemie, wherein the Combined forces of other Nations had been formerly repulsed and beaten) only because the winds and weaues (w*hi*ch noe mortall [power] can gouerne) were eminent letts to the compleat effecting thereof[,] besides to detract from the meritts of braue attempts, disgested and concluded by graue and deliberate Counsells because they are impugned and crossed by sinister successe and dismall encounters, wherevnto perimtorily to warrant a certaintie of future euents in humane actions, then the w*hi*ch nothinge is more absurd. To passe ouer therefore such prophane conceipts this wee are most sure of, that as all thinge vnder heauen are fraile, and vncertaine soe the euents and accidents of warr of

The Euents of warr most Casuall

all other most casuall, and especially those of Seaseruice, wherein two soe vnconstant Elements as the winds and weaues are so powerfull and violent Commanders, Let thee worst therefore that can bee objected against this journey stand for a blemish it will plainly appeare that notw*i*thstanding the impediments and discomforts that stumbled and wharted [corr. to *thwarted*,

SP] vs by long Contrary winds and tempestuous Seas wee performed the voyage to the places appointed, possessed most of the Ilands, greatly damnified the Ennemie both by Sea and Land, brought away spoiles and Artillerie taken from him burnt and sunck shipps laden w*i*th rich Marchandize and wealth more in value, then ten tymes the charges of the whole imployment, went out and returned home euen in the very face of the Spanish Coast vnmated or vnchect. Notw*i*thstandinge that the *Andalantado* was then pr*e*paringe their great Forces to encounter vs and to waft home the Indian treasure then dayly expected. Now admitt (as noe doubt there were) some Errors committed by vs in the pursuite of this affaires (*Errare enim humanum est*) is therefore the whole accon and enterprise w*i*th the circumstançe fitt to be [for]gotten and supprest? Noe sure, for hee that hath read and obserued the Ancient manner and method of the most famous and truthfull Histories of the most glorious Empire that euer was shall plainlie find and see that they did euer, as carefully and exactly sett downe in their stories their owne defaults their Cowardize, their disgraces and ouerthrowes, as their pollicies their valo*u*r their victories and triumphs whereof infinite store of examples doe rifely swarme and abound, as that it were but a worke of sup*er*[er]ogation, to cite anie more of a Million then the Streights of *Candium*, the Battells w*i*th *Pyrrhus* before Heraclea [ms. *Heractea*] *Terentius Varro* [ms. *Vano*] at Cannas field, *Aulus Posthumus* against *Iugarth*. M. *Crassus* against the *Parthians* and *Titurius Sabinus* in his winteringe Campe against the *Gaules*. All most excellently sett out by *Caesar Sallust*, *Liuie*, *Plutarch* and others. Those worthie witts in their deepe and considerate Iudgements wisely forsawe that the time present is duely admonished, when the age past is duely taxed for the same fault, And that there cannot be a more profitable meanes to reforme errors at home then by discoueringe the effects that they haue wrought abroad. For allthough experience be tearmed the instruction of fooles, yett is shee not to be esteemed a foolish instructo*u*r. But I presume not to make this slender [ms. and H *slendler*] taske of mine worthie anie other regard in obseruac*i*on, then by the bouldnes of myne aduenture, w*i*th soe weake forces to stirr vp men of greater faculties and skill beeing *Actors* themselues vppon the like occasions to affoord a little leasure and labo*u*r for the hono*u*r of the Age, wherein they liue, and allsoe for the benefitt of posteritie wherein they may be remembred when they are dead. For little hath industrie donne to make men excellent, if vertue

A breefe of the atchieuements of this voyage.

The faithfull manner of the Roman histories in their Relations.

The obserueinge of former Erro*u*rs profitable to after times

Experience a wise Schoole Mistris.

haue not as much power to giue it Co[u]ntenance, neither were it any glorie to doe worthilie if *ou*r Memories should end w*i*th our liues or *ou*r names (as often as enuy or malice endeauo*u*rs to obscure them) to be buried w*i*th *ou*r bodies And therefore to neglect in *ou*rselues, or to depraue in others an Office soe generally beneficiall, were rather an argument of rancker or sloth then an argument or euidence of Modestie or discretion, For as it is a great hono*u*r to performe an excellent worke soe is it a great honestie duely to praise that w*hi*ch is excellently performed. And allthough I knowe that manie of *ou*r notable and profitable actions and voyages haue beene of late yeares sett forth by men of vertue and learning (to their great paines) wherein they haue right well deserued reputac*i*on and reward yett beeing noe personall Actors themselues they could sett downe noe more then by hearesay and relac*i*on they had receaued and therein many times bee plunged w*i*th doubts and distracted w*i*th the difficulties of various and partiall reports, whereas if care and diligence had euer heretofore beene vsed by some of those that haue beene eyewittnesses of the many great expedicons, vndertaken and effected w*i*thin this Fortie and fower yeares of her late Ma*iestie*s Raigne, those presente obseruations and faithfull records should bee better able to testifie, that though wee had long breathed vnder the mild and happie gouernment of a gratious Ladie, yett wee were not lesse exercised in Militarie discipline abroad then in peaceable pleasure at home and that the politique Regiment, and Heroicall actions of a Mayden Queene, haue Rarely since the Conquest beene exceeded by anie of her most famous progenitors. For be it either in the wise reforminge, or wunderfull establishinge of Christian Religion, wherein shee shewed noe lesse stedfast constancy then true sinceritie or else in continuall confortinge and liberall assistinge her distressed Neigbo*u*res and allies (whereof shee euer had a Royall and charitable regard) or else in resolute repellinge, and fortunate inuadeinge her mightiest ennimies wherein shee was allwaies blest from aboue w*i*th happie and victorious successe) the w*hi*ch shee out of her owne only forces from time to time did enterprise and atchieue, was soe heroicall and glorious, as that in regard thereof her Councello*u*rs were reputed graue and prudent, her people loyall and valiant the Realme florishinge and powerfull and herself Magnanimious and renowned amongst the greatest Monarches of her tyme. But this Ocean of her great and farre spreadinge fame is to high growne for my weake witt to Nauigate and therefore I will her[e] take about and w*i*th a

Worthie actions deserue memorie.

The vncertaintie of relations in great attempt[s] where y[e] reporter was noe eye wittnes

Many braue actions & great imployments in the Raigne of Queene Elizabeth

The praise of Queene Elizabeth.

lowe sale apply to lay the land for w*hi*ch I am now bound. And because that this followinge discourse hath relation chiefely to those Iles of the *Azores* I will briefly touch them soe farr forth as moderne writters and experience doth warrant, for I doe not find that Antiquitie hath made anie mention or description of them w*hi*ch were to be presumed they would haue done if they had beene but as well knowne vnto them as theis Iles, w*hi*ch they named the Fortunate Ilands, *Hesperides*, *Orchades*, *Hebrides*, *Thule* and diuers others.

The Iles of *Azores* not knowne to antiquitie

f. 125]

Obseruations and Ventures [for *Ouertures*] concerning the Royall Nauye and Seaseruice.

To writt of matters concerninge o*u*r shipping & other Marine affayres I confesse is a taske the more difficult for that the alterations defect*es* and abuses of the same by practise and dayly experience of late yeares haue beene found to bee great and diuers (as it falls out many times in the Circumstance and accidents of land Armies, and that kind of seruice by the change of armes diuersities of fortificacon and alteration of discipline. Soe as for the reformacon of o*u*r Nauall affaires many things are necessary and particularly to bee spoken of and considered in their order in regard whereof I will first beginne w*i*th the Officers, and therein craue pardon if in speaking playnly and truely in a matter of soe great importance, I doe sett aside all priuate respect*es* and partiallitie, For in that w*hi*ch concernes the seruice and benefitt of my Prince and Country I will say w*i*th *Cicero* Nil mihi *charius*, And therefore not justly to be taxed w*i*th anie pr*e*sumption for medlinge w*i*th matters wherein I haue noe dealings nor charge for that in such affaires as concerne the strenght and defence of the kingdome euery good Subject is deeply interessed and bound both in Conscience and duty both to saye and doe his best, And as for such as can or will doe better in this kinde neither doe I nor this myne opinions hinder them but wish all good successe to their worthy indeauo*u*r that shall putt their hands to the ploweinge of these furrowes and that the fruits thereof may happely prosper./.

SHAKESPEARE REMEMBERS HIS YOUTH IN STRATFORD

C. F. TUCKER BROOKE

Yale University

THE Elizabethans, and Shakespeare among them, habitually saw Italy as a land of high social civilization, where the wealthy classes—however their morals might fester—could at least be sure of suavely perfect service in their homes. The antithesis of all this which one observes in the household of the Capulets at Verona is striking enough to suggest several questions about the play of *Romeo and Juliet.*

We are first struck by the deplorable domestic situation at the Capulets' when (in the second scene) we observe the master of the house entrusting a list of invitations to Sunday supper to a servant so ignorant that he can't read the addresses and so green that he doesn't know how to excuse himself—so naïve also that he doesn't hesitate to add a couple of guests on his own authority. In the next scenc the approach of supper brings the whole staff, and indeed the family also, to the verge of hysteria. Says the butler to Lady Capulet:

'Madam, the guests are come, supper served up, you called, my young lady asked for, the nurse cursed in the pantry, and everything in extremity. I must hence to wait; I beseech you, follow straight!
Lady Cap. We follow thee! Juliet, the county stays!' (Exit running.)

A glimpse into the butler's pantry in scene five shows the servants facing the tasks of removing joint stools, shifting trenchers, and looking to the silver in an agony of noisy desperation. One of the footman's guests, Romeo, inquires Juliet's name of a servant who seems to be so fresh from the employment agency that he hasn't yet identified the family he is working for. On the Tuesday following, the master of the household, planning a modest wedding breakfast for his daughter, despatches one messenger with invitations, and another to the 'Help for Hire' office: 'Sirrah go hire me twenty cunning cooks.' A moment later it develops that there are no servants left in the Capulet mansion, and the master has to carry his own message to the County Paris. At three o'clock the next morning Capulet is frightfully busy in the pantry, bidding Angelica 'look to the baked meats' and 'spare not for cost,' exchanging badinage with the log carrier and resisting the Nurse's efforts to send him to bed.

Now it is evident that no consideration of tragic art is served by misrepresenting the Capulet family as a group of amiable bounders; and I can think of no honest reply that Shakespeare could have made, if Lord Southampton had asked him why in the world he thought the Capulets lived thus, except 'Ignorance, my Lord, pure ignorance.'

Steevens suggested something like this long ago in one of his notes, and you will find in the Furness *Variorum* a long record of the snubbing Steevens received—invariably, so far as I have observed:

> Steevens turns up his nose aristocratically at Shakespeare for imputing 'to an Italian nobleman and his lady all the petty solicitudes of a private house concerning a provincial entertainment'; and he adds very grandly: 'To such a bustle our author might have been witness at home; but the like anxieties could not well have occurred in the family of Capulet.' Steevens had not well read the history of society (Verplanck, etc.)

It is seldom safe to snub Steevens so lightheartedly; and, at the risk of being snubbed myself, I venture to suggest that the only visible reason for the picture of frontier manners which the domestic scenes of *Romeo and Juliet* portray is that when Shakespeare sketched the background of the tragedy he was by no means so familiar with urbane social life as he was when in 1594 he wrote his friendly dedication of *Lucrece* to Southampton—or even as he was when in 1593 he offered his first timid addresses to that nobleman; in fact, when Shakespeare conceived the play, his most vivid idea of large hospitality *was* what Steevens called 'a provincial entertainment'; that is, doubtless, a high bailiff's feast at Stratford.

It is natural to ask how far Capulet, who vitalizes and unifies these scenes of rustic merriment, may be John Shakespeare himself. I do not know, but Capulet emerges as a very living and likable person, rather surprisingly like the John Shakespeare that we come to know in Mr. Fripp's *Minutes and Accounts of the Corporation of Stratford:* incorrigibly obstinate, and on matters of principle or prejudice impolitic, but generous, solidly beloved by his neighbors, and, for all the risks he took, not unprosperous. At least, he is much closer to this than to the old picture of John, phrased by Sir Walter Raleigh: 'an energetic, pragmatic, sanguine, frothy man, who was always restlessly scheming and could not make good his gains.'

The pseudo-aristocratic background of *Romeo and Juliet* is chiefly supplied by the picture of the Capulet household which I have discussed and by the figure of Mercutio. This last is, of course, one of Shakespeare's great successes, but certain interesting things appear when one examines the materials he has drawn together to create the impression of a gallant and witty nobleman. Mercutio speaks a little over two hundred and fifty lines of assorted prose and verse. With one remarkable exception his speeches are short, averaging less than four lines each; and with the same exception they handle only two themes: smut and fencing. So much has not often been made of smut and fencing; but these are rather trite materials out of which to construct the full character of a Renaissance princeling, and one may wonder whether Shakespeare would not have given Mercutio some other interests if he had been more at home with persons of his type. I think that the suspicion is strengthened when we look at Mercutio's one highly exceptional speech—the forty-one-line declamation that he so surprisingly devotes to Warwickshire folklore. As Pope might have said:

> The things, we know, are *amply* rich *and* rare,
> But wonder how the devil they got there.

The tone of this description of Mab, her equipage, and her pranks is beautifully Mercutian, but the theme is not a little strange, and seems forcibly lugged in by Romeo's sudden remark: 'I dream'd a dream to-night.'

I will not take your time with arguments over the possibility that Mercutio's words about Mab *might* be later than *A Midsummer Night's Dream:* that they *might* show Shakespeare utilizing a residue of native folklore left on his hands after Mab was displaced by Titania and the Stratford fairies went classic. Shakespeare sometimes worked in this way; but it is much easier to believe that Mercutio's description—adhering so precisely to English village atmosphere, and showing so much closer relationship to Drayton's *Nymphidia*—preceded *A Midsummer Night's Dream* and contains the germ of that play. It is unnecessary to labor this point, for surely a Shakespeare who knew his noblemen as Shakespeare shows that he knew Theseus in *A Midsummer Night's Dream* would not have needed to leave the social environment of his Capulet and Mercutio so incorrect and patchy.

We come finally to the Nurse's famous line, ''Tis since the earthquake now eleven years,' repeated a little later: 'And since that time it is eleven years.' Do we have to remember (as some commentators have urged us to do) that there was an earthquake in Ferrara in 1570? Or should we suppose (as others would have us) that the Nurse—always so proudly meticulous and so correct about statistics, from teeth to birthdays—was grossly misreckoning on this occasion?

There was only one earthquake that the English public of the 1590's would remember, and few would not remember the date of that: 1580. 'The 6th of April,' says Stowe, 'being Wednesday in Easter week, about six of the clock towards evening, a sudden earthquake happening in London and almost generally throughout England, caused such amazedness of the people as was wonderful for that time, and caused them to make their earnest prayers unto Almighty God.'

> Shake, quoth the dove-house. 'Twas no need, I trow,
> To bid me trudge:
> And since that time it is eleven years.

To me this sounds like an authentic experience. I rather fancy there was a real dove-house to shake, and a sixteen-year-old boy to observe and trudge, and later to incorporate his remembrance of the incident in a passage that gave a sense of lively contemporaneity to his play. If this is so, and Shakespeare was writing *Romeo and Juliet* in 1591, it is not surprising to find the tragedy still marked by evidences of social inexperience that would be hard to account for after 1594.

COMEDY VERSUS OPERA IN FRANCE 1673–1700

H. CARRINGTON LANCASTER

The Johns Hopkins University

A TENDENCY to introduce music into plays is obvious in Molière's lifetime, finding expression in such comedies as *le Bourgeois Gentilhomme* and *le Malade imaginaire* as well as in more spectacular productions of the period. This tendency was hampered after his death by the fact that Louis XIV gave to Lully the monopoly of opera, which was interpreted as forbidding actors to employ outside singers. The edict, first promulgated on April 30, 1673, little more than two months after *le Malade imaginaire* was first produced, was renewed on March 21, 1675, shortly after Thomas Corneille's spectacular *Circè* was first shown to the public, and again on July 30, 1682, when the actors were reviving Pierre Corneille's *Andromède* to compete with an opera that Lully had brought out on the same subject. The significance of the dates is obvious. Actors' protests availed little. On December 1, 1676, the registers of the Guénégaud note the payment of 61 francs, 10 sous, to defray the expenses of a trip to Compiègne, undertaken in order to get the king's permission for two singers in a play that was being given at that theater.[1] At the end of a court entertainment five years later La Grange, speaking for his comrades, declared that nothing pleased spectators so much as a play that made use of music.[2] But Louis XIV did not take the hint. If actors broke the rule, they ran the risk of serious consequences.[3] Baron expressed their irritation by introducing into the prologue of his first play the remark, 'il y a long-tems que

[1] Cf. also La Grange, *Registre*, p. 182.

[2] Frères Parfaict, *Histoire du théâtre françois*, XII, 273.

[3] Dancourt's *Trois Cousines*, first played on October 18, 1700, has a prologue in which a musician sings and which was suppressed when the comedy was given on January 15, 1701. The protests of the parterre were answered by an official with the explanation that his action was taken "par rapport au privilège del l'Opéra." Nevertheless, the troupe had occasionally employed professional singers.

l'on sait qu'il nous est défendu de savoir ni chanter ni danser.'[4] There was, however, a means of revenge, one by which they could make of opera material for comedy. They could laugh at it.

If Molière had been alive, he might have taken action more promptly, for he had shown his ability to make the most of an obstacle by holding up to ridicule the young gentlemen who crowded his stage. Even as it was, the movement began in a play devoted to his memory. Brécourt's *Ombre de Molière*, first produced in 1674, introduces not only many of Molière's victims, but Quinault, who had begun to write operas. He is described as lamenting that he is among the shades, probably because he was still alive at the time, as recalling the fact that he had always been considered 'la douceur mesme,' as repeating a phrase from his *Alceste*, 'Hélas, Caron, hélas!' and as being accused of making very pretty boys out of Greek heroes. The criticism is not severe and is directed at Quinault rather than Lully. Still less objectionable to the Italian composer was Hauteroche's *Crispin musicien*, a comedy played in the summer of 1674 and subsequently called *l'Opéra de l'Hôtel de Bourgogne*, for its representation of persons who are deeply interested in music or would like to be thought so is not an attack upon opera, but an advertisement of its popularity. *Les Opéra*, written in England by Saint-Evremond, would be important in this connection if there were any evidence that it was known in France during the seventeenth century, but, though composed in 1676, it was not published until 1705 and was not referred to by authors who wrote for Parisian troupes. He had already expressed the idea that opera is a strange combination of poetry and music in which the poet and the musician, equally impeded each by the other, labor mightily to produce an inferior composition.[5] In his play he showed lovers crazy over the opera, to such an extent that the girl has substituted song for speech, and persons who discuss the work of Cambert and Lully and protest against the structure of operas and the use of music throughout them.

---

[4] *Le Rendez-vous des Thuilleries*, acted in 1685. Baron exaggerated, for members of the troupe danced and even sang.

[5] Cf. his letter to Hévart, published in *RHL*, XXIX (1922), 406–407, and his treatise "sur les Opéra."

It is after the union of the two French troupes in 1680 that the attacks become numerous and frequently severe. At the end of that year there is merely the fact that the hero of Poisson's *Foux divertissans* enters an insane asylum by pretending to have lost his mind over opera, but in 1685 Dancourt turned to parody of opera, already employed to a limited degree by actors of the Théâtre Italien,[6] and composed his *Angélique et Médor*, in which the *Roland* of Quinault and Lully is the subject of comic imitation and there are various uncomplimentary remarks about opera. According to this play, the streets are full of opera singers, but good ones are hard to find; dancers are an essential element of opera; musicians and poets work together with difficulty; casts are absurdly large; operatic knights wear tin armor. A professional singer is introduced in order that he may display his insolent manners. A girl of fifteen, who knows no music but is very pretty, is encouraged to offer her services, for 'on feroit un fort joli opera avec une demi-douzaine de filles comme cela.' There is comment on the violence of opera when one of the characters pretends to have played the dying Hercules and to have dashed out a man's brains against a wall: 'Tout le monde étoit charmé de cela.' The climax is reached when the wealthy bourgeois who has proposed to give an opera in order to please the girl he hopes to marry discovers that she has eloped while pretending to rehearse *Roland*. Unconsciously he imitates the deceived hero of the opera by casting off his hat and wig and unbuttoning his doublet, just as Roland had thrown off his arms and put himself 'dans un grand desordre,' while the servants who have deceived him sing the words of the opera, 'Il s'agite.—Il menace.—Il pâlit.—Il soupire,'[7] and an onlooker exclaims, 'Morbleu cet Opera me fait crever de rire.'

The next year Dancourt renewed his attack with *Renaud et Armide*, in which he has two characters that are devotees of the

---

[6] In *Arlequin Mercure galant* (1681) four lines are sung to an air of the illustrious "M. de Lully." Allusions to Quinault's *Cadmus* and *Phaéton* are found in *Arlequin Prothée* (1683). A *chaconne* from his *Amadis* is parodied in *Arlequin Jason* (1684). The dates are those of first performance. It is possible that the references to the opera were not in them at the time, for the earliest texts of these plays that we have are those published in 1694.

[7] Cf. *Roland*, IV, 7, and *Angélique et Médor*, sc. 20.

opera and parodies Quinault's *Armide*, the merits of which are summed up by the maid as follows: 'Le Prologue m'ennuit, le premier Acte m'assoupit, cet endroit du Sommeil m'endort, et je ne me réveille qu' à ce grand tintamare de la fin.'[8] He continued to disparage the opera in subsequent productions and a number of authors, writing for the Comédie Française or the Théâtre Italien, followed his example. One of the most amusing was Palaprat, who, in his *Ballet extravagant*, described a projected opera on Roman history (sc. 16):

> Toute l'histoire Romaine est le sujet de l'Opera dont le Balet que vous allez voir, fait un divertissement. . . . Il me tarde que vous entendiez le chœur des Oyes qui sauvérent le Capitole. . . . L'histoire d'Enée en fera le Prologue; d'abord le théatre représentera la ville de Troye en flâmes, Enée paroîtra portant son pere sur ses épaules, tenant son fils Ascagne par la main, et perdant dans la confusion sa femme. . . . Ensuite il s'embarquera, il y aura une tempête; mais une tempête à faire dresser les cheveux. Les vents, les éclairs, une nuit, un tonnerre, bouroulouIou, bouroulou: la tempête finira par une entrée d'Alcions; c'est de quoi on n'a pas encore oüi parler sur le Théâtre, et où, sans vanité, je me suis surpassé. Point de Tritons, point de Sirennes, cela est trivial: mais des monstres les plus singuliers, parmi lesquels je ne laisserai pas de mêler une danse galante de petits poissons, jusques aux maquereaux et aux solles. . . . Je ne vous parle point de la chasse des cerfs, des harpies, de sa descente aux Enfers; car un Opera sans lutins, sans ombres, sans furies et sans enfers, ne vaut pas le diable. Mais sautons le reste du Prologue. Premier Acte, la fondation de Rome. Romulus la fait bâtir. Troupes de Maçons et de Charpentiers. Il établit le Sénat. On verra paroître avec de longues barbes, et de larges robes fourrées, cent hommes vénérables, à qui je fais danser des rigaudons. Ce sera une danse grave et majestueuse celle-là: mais la plus variée à mon gré, et que j'ai choisie sur toutes pour vous faire voir aujourd'hui, c'est celle qui représente l'enlevement des Sabines.

The increasing interest in contemporary manners, so noticeable in the last two decades of the century, supported this effort to derive from the opera comic material. The following operas are mentioned in comedies of the period: Quinault's *Fêtes de l'Amour et de Bacchus*, *Cadmus*, *Alceste*, *Thésée*, *Atys*, *Isis*, *Proserpine*, *Persée*, *Phaéton*, *Amadis*, *Roland*, and *Armide;* Thomas Corneille's *Bellérophon*, Campistron's *Acis et Galathée*,[9] Fontenelle's

---

[8] Sc. 15; cf. *Armide*, II, 3, "Renaud s'endort sur un gazon," and V, 5, "les Démons détruisent le Palais enchanté, et Armide part sur un char volant."

[9] The music of these fourteen operas, produced in 1672–1687, was by Lully.

Thétis et Pélée, La Fontaine's *Astrée*, Mme de Sainctonge's *Didon*, La Motte's *Europe galante*.[10] Parody, concerned with a number of these operas, was extended to two of the singers, Du Mesnil and la Rochois, who were mimicked by actors of the Théâtre Italien in *l'Opéra de campagne*. Imaginary operas, besides the one devoted to Roman history, were described. There was to be one derived from *Clélie* in which a ballet was to be danced by the various localities indicated on the map of Tendre.[11] There was to be another in which the dying Cato was to hum melodiously a treatise on the immortality of the soul.[12] A third, which would have pleased Stravinsky, was to be an opera of the Pont-Neuf, the music of which was to fit the characters: pickpockets, charlatans, and a trio of men who had been hanged.[13]

Another device for rendering opera absurd was to have ridiculous characters infatuated with the institution or taking part in preparations for a production. In the *Ballet extravagant* the mother wishes to form an operatic troupe and tour the provinces. Dancourt described a peasant operatic troupe in his *Opéra de village*. In Dufresny's *Opéra de campagne* we see such a troupe enter a village in a wagon piled high with costumes, boxes, decorations, weights, cords, etc., and followed by a humpback who carries a musical score on his hump. The author adds that

> tous ces gens-là sont habillés avec des habits d'opera les plus plaisans qu'on ait pu imaginer; et lorsque le chartier veut aller à droite, à gauche, avancer, ou reculer ses chevaux, il s'exprime toujours en chantant et sur divers tons, suivant les divers mouvemens qu'il demande de ses chevaux, et tous les instrumens l'accompagnent; si bien que tous les termes des chartiers, comme *à dia*, *hureau ori*, et les autres, sont toujours prononcés par le charetier en musique, et le chœur ensuite les reprend.

Parisian mockery spread to Lyons, where, too, an operatic troupe had been competing with actors. When the former company failed, Marc-Antoine Legrand composed a comedy called the *Chute de Phaéton* in which the fall of the opera was compared

---

[10] The music of *Thétis* (1689) and of *Europe galante* (1697) was by Campra; that of *Astrée* (1691) by Colasse; that of *Didon* (1693) by Desmarest.

[11] *Ballet extravagant*.

[12] *La Fontaine de sapience*, attributed to Louis Biancolelli.

[13] Regnard's *Divorce*.

with that of Phaeton. But the allusions to opera at Paris and Lyons are not all unfriendly. Opera may be attacked by one character and defended by another. Bordelon[14] makes Molière point out the absurdity of having persons sing while they are deeply moved, but Quinault reply that this is no more absurd than to have them, under similar circumstances, speak in verse. In Legrand's *Comédiens de campagne* the complaint is made that operas are noisy, that the singing interferes with the declamation and the action, and that it is against nature to 'faire chanter les passions.' But another character argues that expression of emotion has always been the aim of music, that he approves of 'ce merveilleux dans les sons qui charme l'esprit' and 'ce passionné qui saisit le cœur, et le tourne du côté de la passion qui est traitée par le musicien.' If the opera fails, it is not the fault of music, but of the musician, always excepting the incomparable Lully, who fits his music so cleverly to songs that most of these would lose their force without him. Usually, however, when opera is attacked, there is no one to defend it.

Reference has been made to criticism of the structural looseness and lack of verisimilitude that characterize the *genre*. Operas are also said to bay the moon,[15] to have no new airs, and to employ monkeys instead of poets and musicians.[16] Mechanical devices for aerial flights at the opera are considered dangerous.[17] Their operation, it is implied, is greeted by whistling from the audience, or, since whistles, though satisfactory for disturbing plays, are not loud enough for opera, bells have been substituted.[18] The building is a good place for flirtation.[19] *Chanteuses* have dubious reputations.[20] The fate of a singer when he loses his looks and is in danger of losing his wife is pitiful.[21] The institution is demoralizing. Indeed, Penelope's lovers, after trying many snares for her virtue,

---

[14] *Molière aux Champs Elisées.*

[15] *La Thèse des dames*, attributed to Louis Biancolelli.

[16] Mongin, *les Promenades de Paris.*

[17] Delosme de Monchesnay, *les Souhaits.*

[18] Regnard, *le Divorce.*

[19] Baron, *l'Homme à bonne fortune.*

[20] Dancourt, *Moulin de Javelle* and *Vendanges de Suresnes.*

[21] Palaprat, *Arlequin Phaéton.*

employed as the most promising device the opera.[22] Since Vergil made Dido 'peu cruelle,' she can now be the heroine of an opera.[23] The opera is a hermaphrodite, half sense and half nonsense.[24] Its chief value is found in the dancing, or in the costumes, or in the love-making.[25] A character in Regnard's *Divorce* asserts that he is never bored at the opera, 'les habits sont si beaux.' Only in three comedies are kind words said for the music![26]

How much exaggeration there was in all this satire it is hard to say. The opinions expressed by the dramatists certainly contrast sharply with most of those collected from other sources by M. Mélèse.[27] But, whether justified or not, the criticism had little effect upon the future of French opera. The extensive use of parody by its enemies is, indeed, evidence of its popularity. On the other hand, opera helped Parisian actors, both French and Italian, by giving them a new object of ridicule, one that had for an excellent reason escaped the satirical thrusts of Molière.

---

[22] Delosme de Monchesnay, *le Phénix*.

[23] Delosme de Monchesnay, *les Souhaits*.

[24] L. A. D. S. M., *Ulysse et Circé*.

[25] Dufresny, *Opéra de campagne*.

[26] *Les Opéra, Molière aux Champs Elisées, les Comédiens de campagne*. I would add J.-B. Rousseau's *Caffé* except that the character who in that comedy praises opera for the variety of emotions it excites seems chiefly interested in the danseuses.

[27] Cf. his *Répertoire* (Paris: Droz, 1934). The remarks that he reproduced are highly favorable to most of the operas, less so to *Atys*, *Isis*, *Phaéton*, and *Didon*, unfavorable to *Astrée*.

THE 'MEMORIAS' OF FELIPE FERNÁNDEZ VALLEJO AND THE HISTORY OF THE EARLY SPANISH DRAMA

JOSEPH E. GILLET

Bryn Mawr College

MANUEL CAÑETE, the distinguished yet sadly unfulfilled historian of the early Spanish drama, was apparently the first, in 1862, to draw attention to a manuscript entitled: *Memorias i disertaciones que podrán servir al que escriba la historia de la iglesia de Toledo desde el año MLXXXV en que conquistó dicha ciudad el rei don Alonso VI. de Castilla*, written about the year 1785 by Felipe Fernández Vallejo, Canon of the Cathedral of Toledo and for two years, until his death in 1800, Archbishop of Santiago.[1] The content of the manuscript, of great importance, Cañete implied, was to be divulged at a later time. In 1867, in his edition of Lucas Fernández,[2] the dramatic critic even more tantalizingly reverted to the subject with a mention of *la escena ú Oficio de Pastores y la Sybila de la noche de Navidad, traducida de versos latinos en castellanos á fines del siglo XIII*, adding that *De ambas escenas litúrgicas da circunstanciada razon, reproduciéndolas íntegras en latin y en romance.*

These highly interesting documents, together with the sixteenth-century plays, also unknown to all others, of which he revealed only the titles and the beginning lines,[3] were to be ornaments of the history of the early Spanish drama which was con-

[1] Cf. Cañete, *Discurso acerca del drama religioso antes y después de Lope de Vega* (September 28, 1862), pp. 10 f. Reprinted in *Memorias de la Real Academia española*, I (1870), 368–412.

[2] Madrid, p. lxxvii, n. 1.

[3] Lucas Fernández, *Farsas y églogas*, pp. lix ff. We now realize that Cañete knew no more about most of those plays than was revealed by the notes which Gallardo had taken from the catalogues of Ferdinand Columbus in the *Biblioteca Colombina;* in the introduction to Carvajal's *Tragedia Josefina*, p. xlvi, however, the illusion was heightened by twenty-five lines from an unknown play by Alonso de Salaya (cf. *PMLA*, LII, 1937, 16–67) of which a copy had actually been discovered in the library of the Marqués de San Román.

fidently expected of him (an expectation, incidentally, which blighted all other research in the field) but of which not even an outline has come to light.

When Cañete first saw the manuscript of Vallejo it belonged to the library of the notable bibliophile Gallardo. Eventually Gallardo's nephew and heir, Juan Antonio Gallardo, seems to have granted a glimpse of it to a few favored scholars (*muy pocos eruditos*!). One of these was Amador de los Ríos,[4] who probably had little opportunity of studying it, if one may judge from his meager report. Later the manuscript appeared in the library of the Marqués de San Román (owner of the unknown play by Salaya), and there it was consulted by the onetime Spanish Ambassador in Washington, D. Juan F. Riaño, who described it in an appendix to his critical and bibliographical *Notes on Early Spanish Music*,[5] singling out for notice 'an interesting poem translated from the Latin in Spanish verse of the end of the XIIIth century on the Sybil and Shepherds on Christmas eve, with its music,' and adding that 'examples are also given of the music which served in the dramatic representations, which were given in olden times in the Cathedral of Toledo.' Thereafter, more references appeared: an allusion in the Madrid daily, *El Universo*, on December 24, 1905, set Juan Moraleda[6] wondering in 1911 whether the *obra inédita* mentioned there might not contain information on the costume of the religious dancers known in Toledo and Seville as the *Seises*. Again, in 1920, Ricardo del Arco mentioned the *Memorias*[7] without being able to quote from them, and a year later González and Palencia[8] raised utterly false hopes by declaring that the manuscript was in the *Biblioteca Nacional*. Simultaneously, the late Professor G. G. King, in a study on

[4] *Historia crítica de la literatura española* (Madrid, 1861 . . .), III, 17, n. 2.

[5] London, 1887, p. 135. In 1893, R. Beer, in his *Handschriftenschätze Spaniens* (*Sitzungsberichte d. K. K. AK.*, Wien, Phil.-Hist. Kl., vol. 129, p. 27 f.), reported the manuscript in the same library.

[6] *Los Seises de la Catedral de Toledo, Antigüedad, Vestidos, Música y Danza* (Toledo, 1911), p. 34, n. 2.

[7] "Misterios, autos sacramentales y otras fiestas en la Catedral de Huesca," *RBAM*, XLI (1920), 265 n.

[8] *Historia de la literatura española* (Madrid, 1921), p. 125.

Gil Vicente's *Sibyl Cassandra*,[9] expressed a desire to see Vallejo's manuscript in print *if it can be found by searching the archives*. Finally in 1926, Mr. J. B. Trend[10] in the most casual manner indicated the presence of the elusive manuscript, which he did not further discuss, in the library of the *Academia de la Historia*, in the center of Madrid.

Indeed, there it was, and presumably still is: a folio manuscript numbered up to 707 pages, with the signature 2-7-4 Ms. 75; very legibly written and showing all the earmarks of being ready for the printer. In a letter dated June 28, 1785, and bound in with it, Canon Vallejo was complimented on his achievement by Pedro Manuel Hernández, *bibliotecario de la Arzobispal*. There are a number of drawings in ink, or pencil and ink, sometimes with touches of ink-wash, some signed *Palomares del* ᵗ or *Palomares junior*, dated 1783 or 1786 (this was evidently the artist who designed the framework of the title page, in pencil, ink, and water color); some signed *Morales* or *Pedro Morales*, one of the latter being dated 1784.[11]

Vallejo's manuscript has never been properly studied or made readily accessible to students. In spite of its comparatively recent date it contains materials of unquestionable authenticity so far utilized only by a few scholars, mostly *aficionados*, and practically unknown to systematic research. The records of the medieval drama in the Peninsula, with the exception of a few tropes, begin in the middle of the twelfth century with the startling *Auto de los Reyes Magos*, entirely in the vernacular and so far advanced in characterization and metrical skill as to imply a considerable previous development. A rich dramatic life is reflected by the warnings of King Alfonso el Sabio in the *Siete Partidas* (13 c.), yet the history of the Spanish drama is practically a blank until the first dramatic attempts of Iñigo de Mendoza at the end of the fifteenth century. There the scholar is confronted with the puzzle of a fully elaborated stage dialect for the rustics. It is clear that

---

[9] *The play of the Sibyl Cassandra* (Bryn Mawr, 1921), p. 17.

[10] *The Music of Spanish History to 1600* (New York), p. 183.

[11] The drawing, signed Pedro Morales, reproduced with this article, opposite p. 272, and measuring 15.9×10.7 cm., was to be inserted in the manuscript after fol. 584.

anything which may help to fill in such amazing historical gaps may be considered as more than intrinsically important.

The part of Vallejo's manuscript which is of major interest to literary historians is the section entitled *Disertacion VI. sobre las Representaciones Poeticas en el Templo, y Sybila de la noche de Navidad.* It extends from f. 587 to f. 643 and falls into three parts which we shall severally discuss, while singling out in a running commentary such personal remarks or quotations by Vallejo as still appear to have value for the historian. From the preceding chapter, *Disertacion V. sobre la Musica* (ff. 477 *ff.*), we shall, moreover, take the description and text of a medieval Christmas performance in the Cathedral of Toledo.

I. *The 'Auto de los Reyes Magos'*: A certain antiquarian interest attaches to the earliest and far from perfect copy (ff. 591–599) made from the original manuscript of the *Auto de los Reyes Magos*, then marked *Cax. 6, 8* in the *Biblioteca del Cabildo*, Toledo, now, and since 1868, marked *Hh-115* in the *Biblioteca Nacional*, Madrid. Vallejo misread a number of words and frankly desisted in a number of difficult places, but he made an attempt to reproduce some of the curious markings of the original, which have not yet been satisfactorily explained, and guessed that these *puntos, señales, circulos, semicirculos y Cruces* were indications not only of *la diversidad de interlocutores* and *la diversidad de scenas* but were also *advertencias de inflexiones de voz, y actitudes de cuerpo* (f. 599). He tried to visualize its performance: *me represento los tres Personages con Cetros, y Coronas, saliendo cada uno de lugar diferente de la Iglesia, seguidos de criados que llevan los dones: hablando con Herodes, y á este de resulta del Coloquio, airado, consultando á sus sabios, en una palabra, me parece veo el tropel de gente, que con motivo de este spectaculo devoto está lleno de admiracion* (ff. 599 f.).[12] Here, as in other parts of the manuscript, there are occasional dis-

[12] Before Cañete, who had not yet seen the original manuscript of the *Auto*, could have published Vallejo's copy, Amador de los Ríos, guided probably by the catalogue of the Toledo Chapter-Library prepared by the Augustinian monk Frías ("*Al fin hay un romance a los reyes magos escrito a renglón seguido, como si fuere prosa*") had made a somewhat better transcript from the original in 1849, which he published in 1863 among the *Ilustraciones* of vol. III of his *Historia crítica*. A much better copy was prepared soon afterwards by

creet notes by Vallejo, based on such authorities as Blas Nasarre's prologue to the *Comedias* of Cervantes (1749), Riccoboni's *Réflexions historiques et critiques sur les différens théâtres de l'Europe* (1738), and mingled with references to the seventeenth-century *Rhytmica* of Caramuel de Lobkowitz[13] and the original texts of Timoneda and Gil Vicente. Of greater interest are his quotations from the collections of Synod- and Council-decrees, from the Toledo *Actas Capitulares* and from rare local *relaciones* of early festivities. Canon Vallejo did not look with a jaundiced eye on all dramatic festivals; indeed, he imagined an age in which church performances could be so supervised as not to allow *el menor gesto, la mas minima descompostura, ó accion que desdigese ál Santuario* (f. 601); but, living in an atmosphere of neoclassicism, he was keenly conscious of the abuses which had been gradually undermining the popular religious drama. Without forgetting *los vicios de los Juglares y Farsantes Publicos* (f. 600), he emphasized a point generally overlooked; namely, the effect of the inadequate cultural resources of small places: *Los vicios, é impropiedades de estas Representaciones nacieron en los Pueblos cortos. Emulos de las grandes Poblaciones querian solemnizar como ellas sus funciones Eclesiasticas, no tenian proporcion de Actores, ni vestidos y empeñandose en la execucion, insensiblemente declinaron los Dramas devotos en Actos bufonescos. Los Representantes eran hombres á quienes por sus actitudes era mas facil hacer reir, que llorar: eran ignorantes, á quienes costaba menos discurrir patochadas que decorar el papel, y eran Aldeanos pobres, que suplian la propiedad del Trage con disfraces ridiculos* (f. 602). Referring to a sixteenth-century *relación*[14] he pictures a village-Malchus slashing Peter, the Angels in shirts, the executioners (*sayones*) half-naked, the three Maries loaded with coral beads, the Apostles in borrowed dalmatics (f. 603). On

---

Escudero de la Peña, which Lidforss used in 1871 and Hartmann in 1879. Baist printed a diplomatic text in 1887 and finally Menéndez Pidal's edition of 1900 gave the little masterpiece the setting it deserves.

[13] Cf. Gillet, "Caramuel de Lobkowitz and his commentary (1668) on Lope's 'Arte Nuevo de hacer comedias,'" *PQ*, VII (1926), 122 ff.

[14] *Relacion verdadera de lo que aconteció en la Villa que se llama Tordehumos en Castilla el dia del Sanctissimo Sacramento en este presente año de 1572.* Unknown to Alenda or Palau.

the other hand, Vallejo charitably adds, the authors were betrayed by their concern for verisimilitude: *Pensando guardar los caracteres de las Personas en la fiesta del Nacimiento, entre los Pastores ponian un Bato, que hacia de gracioso, en la del Prendimiento un Judas vomitando blasfemias, y en la de la Resurreccion unos Soldados, ó guardas del Sepulcro echando brabatas* (f. 605). In order to delight and terrify, the stage managers elaborated decorations, machinery and figuration of heaven and hell, and statues of saints came to be rigged like marionettes, so that: *para conmover á las gentes sencillas en los actos mas serios de Religion moviesen las imagenes ojos, manos, ó cabeza por cuerdas y resortes* (f. 606).

The great period for religious performances in the Cathedral of Toledo, Vallejo continues, was the sixteenth century. It seems worth while, pending an eventual survey of such *Actas Capitulares* as may still be consulted, to reproduce Vallejo's extract on the exact location of the performances in and outside the Cathedral, as provided by the Chapter-decree of November 17, 1511: *Entre los dos Choros: entre la Capilla de S. Eugenio y D. Luis Daza: Otra en saliendo de la puerta de la Iglesia, que se vea desde las Casas del Arcediano de Toledo: otra en la Capilla Muzarabe, y la Casa del Dean: a la puerta del Perdon, y a la lonja de la esquina de la Claustra: otra en los Cambios, Lazareto, Zapateria, Zocodover* (f. 607).[15]

Quoting from the *Descriptio Templi Toletani* (1544) of Blas Ortiz who mentioned the storeroom in the *Claustro baxo* (*officina ubi multa intrumenta servitio Ecclesiae, et representationibus Actuum qui Festis solemnioribus fiunt, reponuntur*), he enlarges on the elaborate organization provided for the yearly festivals: *A este fin Diputaban dos Canonigos que nombraban Comisarios, ó Mayordomos de la Fiesta del Corpus, y del cuidado de estos era escribiesen los Poetas mas celebres las Piezas que se habian de Representar: Que los Actores las ensayasen entre las dos Pasquas: Que acudiesen los Musicos y*

---

[15] Apparently to be added to this quotation as a note are the following lines, written on a piece of paper pasted to the bottom of the page: *Estas Representaciones serían mui breves, y acaso serian lo que en algunas partes llaman* Dichos, *que se reducen á ciertas coplillas que dizen los que van vestidos de farsa: De otro modo no es posible que en una misma mañana, y durante la Procesion se representasen diez.*

Cantores á los ensayos: Que multasen al que faltase, ó despidiesen al que reusase asistir: Que hiziesen preparar el Teatro entre los dos Coros, y los tablados para el Cavildo y Ciudad. . . (f. 608).

In the course of time, also, greater demands were made on the writers. The *Actas Capitulares* registered contracts for *autos sacramentales* with P. Remón,[16] with Valdivieso (*sic*) on June 26, 1608,[17] and with unspecified *Autores de las Compañias comicas* on May 30, 1609 (actors from Valladolid), and on June 8, 1613. Under June 4, 1592, the *Actas* reveal that it had been uncertain *si el Autor mas famoso deveria venir á Toledo, ó ir al Escurial*, and under May 30, 1609, they record that a *Carta de súplica* had actually been sent to Madrid in order to obtain the freedom of an imprisoned actor.

II. *Cardinal Juan Martínez Siliceo:* Such concern with plays and players meets with severe censure on Vallejo's part; but worse yet, and inexcusable in his opinion, are church performances devoid of religious significance: *por la Coronacion de un Rey, por la entrada primera de un Prelado, ó por un ascenso de este.* As an example of the latter type he quotes (ff. 611–621) from the manuscript of Baltasar Porreño's *Historia de los arzobispos de Toledo* the description of the dramatic festival held in the Cathedral on May 31, 1557, to celebrate the elevation to the Cardinalate of D. Juan Martínez Siliceo.[18] This has already been reprinted elsewhere.[19] It is difficult to understand Vallejo's indignation at this

[16] That is, Fr. Alonso Remón (cf. La Barrera, *Catálogo*, pp. 315 ff.); the space for the date was not filled in.

[17] Maestro José de Valdivielso; cf. La Barrera, *loc. cit.*, pp. 412 ff., and Milego, *El teatro en Toledo* (Valencia, 1909), pp. 128 ff.

[18] Porreño, T. II, f. 232 (Cap. 21, num. 10, 11).

[19] The Conde de Cedillo (D. Jerónimo López de Ayala y Alvarez de Toledo) in his *Discurso* before the *Academia de la Historia* in 1901 entitled *Toledo en el siglo XVI después del vencimiento de las comunidades*, pp. 169–175, has reprinted Porreño's original text. The text of the *entremés* was reprinted by Barrantes in his *Aparato crítico para la historia de Extremadura* (Madrid, 1875–1877), I, 146–149, and there is a brief description of it in Lucas Fernández, *Farsas y églogas*, ed. Cañete, pp. lxxxiii and C, in Picatoste's *Los Españoles en Italia* (Madrid, 1887), I, 51, and in Creizenach's *Geschichte des neueren Dramas*, ed. Hämel, III (1923), p. 64. The same festival was described by Sebastián de Horozco, whose account has been reprinted by the Conde de Cedillo in *Algunas relaciones y noticias toledanas que en el siglo XVI escribió el Licenciado Sebastián de Horozco*, first published in

description of what must have been an impressive ceremony (*de las mas solemnes que se han visto en esta Iglesia*, said Porreño) and a charming *entremés*, in which the actor impersonating the aged Archbishop reviewed a devoted career in smoothly flowing lines reminiscent of the best dramatic eclogues:

O! que hato y que rebaño,
que arboleda, y que olivas,
O! que prado tan extraño,
nunca vi prado tamaño,
plantado de piedras vivas.[20]

Vallejo was irked by the boy, dressed in blue, who played the part of *Zelo de la Fee*, and of the *bobo* who said nothing but *Padre, Papa, Papa, Padre*, 'quando venia bien.' He was not impressed by the homage to the Archbishop by the *Siete Artes Liberales*, nor by the *Danza de Salvajes* and the more solemn dance of the *Seises* capped with their *morriones*.

With excellent common sense Vallejo asked: *Que importa que los Poetas escribiesen Piezas alegoricas, devotas y edificantes, si los Executores las adulteraban con sus gestos y pantominas!* And as to the emotionally starved audience: *El mas bien educado disputaba el puesto: el mas taciturno hablaba: el mas serio reia; y el mas devoto volvia la espalda al Altar.* The Canon therefore recounts with satisfaction the struggle which in Toledo put an end to the *autos sacramentales* as early as 1614 (f. 626), long before their suppression throughout the nation by the Royal decree of 1778.[21] The first to voice a serious protest in Toledo, as recorded by *Actas Capitulares* under May 23, 1572, was apparently the Canon D. Pedro González de Mendoza, and his action seems to have closed the Cathedral for a time to all performances: *pues pasado algun tiempo resolvieron se hiziesen en la Calle los Autos* (f. 622). But under pressure from the Corregidor, it would seem, the ancient custom was reëstablished in 1581, *acordando. . . . Que no se hiziesse*

Boletín de la Sociedad española de Excursiones, XIII (1905), 182 f., and separately (Madrid, 1906), p. 27.

[20] The last line, of course, alludes to the prelate's name, Martínez *Guijarro*, latinized into *Siliceo*.

[21] The details supplied by Vallejo may be added to the scanty information supplied by J. Milego, *El teatro en Toledo*, pp. 82 ff.

innovacion de las Representaciones del dia del Corpus, que queria el Corregidor que no se hiziessen fuera de la Iglesia. This secular resistance was countered in the following year by the Provincial Council of Toledo, in Decreto 38, concerning tragedies and comedies *etiam de argumentis sacris;* yet because the Cathedral-chapter was not in agreement with certain other decrees of the Council and made these the subject of an appeal to the King, the whole matter was left in suspense: *se halló medio para no observar por entonces lo decretado* (f. 623). There was, moreover, the argument, used by certain *Metafisicos* after a decree of the Provincial Council in 1566, that the objection applied only to performances which interrupted the Divine Office, as had notably been the case with the performance in honor of Archbishop Siliceo. And secular forces continued to uphold the ancient custom: indeed, at Corpus in 1596, before the heir presumptive, Prince Philip, *concluida Prima se representaron dos Autos, y por la tarde despues de Visperas entraron en el Coro ocho quadrillas de Danzantes.* Later: *En el dia de la Octava del mismo año representaron otros dos Autos. En el año de 1603. mandaron representar quatro, dos por la mañana, y dos por la tarde, y asi subcesivamente* (f. 624). But victory over *toda Farsa Sagrada en Iglesia, Calles y Teatros Publicos* was finally achieved in 1614, and so decisively that, as Vallejo reports from personal knowledge: *á ciertos Comediantes que se atrevieron á hacer una Representacion en la Iglesia del Convento de Monjas de Santa Isabel la Real de esta Ciudad á 3. de Diciembre del año 1653. los castigó el Consejo de la Governacion, y . . . aprobó su providencia la Real Chancilleria de Valladolid* (f. 624).

III. *The Sibyl of Christmas Eve:* It would be a mistake, as we said, to assume that the learned historian was opposed to all sacred festivals, but his situation was evidently a difficult one when he came to discuss the age-old performance of the *Sibila de la Noche de Navidad,* one of the glories of the Cathedral. Then he had to decide, in sober conscience, whether this performance, with its *Musica, Tablado, Poesia en lengua vulgar, y disfraces,* was not also *uno de aquellos juguetes pueriles* (f. 631), . . . *un Acto de los que se acostumbraban á hacer en los Siglos poco ilustrados,* or, on the contrary, *una ceremoni[a] antiquissima, y venerable, que en*

THE SIBYL OF CHRISTMAS EVE IN THE CATHEDRAL OF TOLEDO

lo substancial no ha padecido alteracion; y que debemos conservar interin no se vicie, ó introduzca en ella alguna novedad reprehensible (ff. 627 f.). He himself had inclined to the former view *antes de reflexionar mucho*, but later he came to think of it more favorably, and his conscientious description of the ceremony, which he knew so well, and the arguments which he presented for its preservation are worth reprinting with diplomatic fidelity.[22]

[f. 628] *En nuestra Santa Iglesia la noche de la Natividad de nuestro Señor Jesuchristo, concluido el himno Te Deum laudamus,*[23] *sale de la Sacristia un Seise vestido á la Oriental representando á la Sybila Herophila, ó de Eritrea. Acompañanle quatro Colegiales Infantes :dos que con albas, Estolones, guirnaldas en la cabeza, y espadas desnudas en la mano dicen hacer papeles de Angeles, y otros dos con las ropas comunes de Coro, y con el fin de que por las hachas encendidas* [f. 629] *que llevan sean mas visibles los tres Personajes. Suben todos cinco á un Tablado que esta prevenido al lado del Pulpito del Evangelio, y colocados como representa la lamina que he puesto por Cabeza de la disertacion,*[24] *esperan se concluyan los Maytines, y principia la Sybila á cantar las siguientes coplas:*

Sybila— Quantos aqui sois juntados
ruegoos por Dios verdadero
que oigais del dia postrimero
quando seremos juzgados.
Del Cielo de las Alturas
un Rey vendra perdurable
con poder muy espantable
á juzgar las Criaturas.

Haora los Angeles que han tenido las Espadas levantadas, las esgrimen, y la Musica canta en el Coro:

Juicio fuerte
sera dado

[22] There is a paraphrase of the description, with none of the text, in Felipe Pedrell's *Cancionero musical español* (Valls-Cataluña [1914]), as part of a musical study on *El canto de la Sibila*, pp. 91–99. In reprinting this part of Vallejo's text we shall include his notes, marking them with (V.)

[23] Quando se seguia el el (*sic*) Breviario antiguo Toledano se hazia esta Ceremonia despues de la 6ª. Leccion de Maitines. (V.)

[24] Reproduced in this article opposite p. 272; for a description of the original, cf. *supra*, p. 266. The appearance of the Sibyl, in a dress more reminiscent of late sixteenth-century fashions than anything oriental, will have to be discussed more fully when the iconography of this figure, together with her literary history, shall have been reliably established. The Sibyl's traditional garland of laurel seems to have been transferred to the sword-bearing acolytes, but she is still adorned with the heavy necklace and earrings which she wears on some ancient bronzes.

[f. 630] *cruel y de muerte.*

Sybila— *Trompetas, y sones tristes*
diran de lo alto del Cielo
levantaos muertos del suelo
recivireis segun hizistis.
descubrirse han los pecados
sin que ninguno los hable
á la pena perdurable
do iran los tristes culpados.
Musica—Juicio fuerte
sera dado
cruel y de muerte.
Sybila— *A la Virgen supliquemos*
que antes de aqueste litijo
interceda con su hijo
porque todos nos salvemos.
Musica—Juicio fuerte
sera dado
cruel, y de muerte.

[f. 631] *Concluido todo esto bajan todos del Tablado y dando un*[*a*] *buelta por dentro del Coro se van.*

The ceremony here described Vallejo would like to preserve because of the *conducto puro por donde llegó á nosotros* (f. 632), that is, because of its transmission, as he believed, through the Church Fathers, the *Monges de Oriente* (*pues tambien la observaban varias Iglesias de Africa*) and so through the French Benedictines of the eleventh century into Spanish tradition; also because he considered it a wholesome warning *para que ninguno alegue ignorancia, ni excusa quando se le tome residencia de sus obras* (f. 633); and even because he had been emotionally affected by it: *que es preciso mueva el animo de los oientes una voz delgada, y lamentable, que con pausa, y gravedad predice el dia tremendo del Juicio* (f. 633).

He admits, however, that there may have been in the course of time some modification in the original performance, and indeed that the vestigial remains of the Latin lines: *Judicii signum* . . . , which the Sibyl wears on a placard from the left shoulder, may represent the original text:

[f. 634] . . . *bien creo que al principio se haria en nuestra Iglesia como en la de Roam, Paris ó Narbona, y que se cantarian en latin los versos Sybilinos, bien fuese segun la version que pone S. Agustin en la Ciudad de Dios, bien segun lo que pone Eusebio Cesariense en la Oracion de Constantino, ó bien segun la que ponen otros muchos, pues todos convienen en la substancia. La prueba de esta conjetura es que nuestra Sybila los lleva como por adorno escritos en una tarjeta, que se le prehende en el hombro izquierdo, y son como se sigue:*

Judicii in signum tellus
sudore madescet;
[f. 636] *Et Rex Eternus summo*
descendet Olympo:
Scilicet ut carnem, mundum
ut Judicet omnem
Vnde Deum fidi, diffidem-
tesque videbunt
Summum cum sanctis in
Secli fine sedentem.[25]

Pero como el fin de esta Ceremonia era instruir ál Pueblo, y cantando los versos en latin, y en el Coro por algun Psalmista las gentes rusticas no entendian la fuerza de ella quisieron sensibilizarla mas vistiendo un Niño á la Oriental, y poniendo en la boca de este unos versos Castellanos, que en el concepto dixesen lo mismo que los otros. Favorecia á los que pensaron asi el uso de nuestra Iglesia, que desde el siglo XIII. cantaba los milagros de nuestra Señora varios dias, y estos estaban arreglados á Musica, idioma y Poesia de aquel tiem- [f. 636] *po como se conoce del Libro Cantigas del Rey D. Alfonso que se guarda en nuestra Biblioteca, y tambien les favorecia para tratar en romance los asuntos mas Sagrados, la version de la Biblia, que el mismo Rey Sabio mandó hacer, y las Representaciones de los Misterios de nuestra Religion, que ya eran comunes en los Templos. Como á los fines del Siglo XIII. ó principios del XIV. infiero es la traducion del sentido de esta Profecia Latina ál idioma vulgar, pues aunque hoy parece su estilo, y locucion mas moderna, se dexa percebir la hán ido acomodando ál Siglo presente, y suavizando las voces juntados por* aiuntados, *hijo por* fijo, *litijio por* litijo, *y hablar por* fablar. *No obstante acomodaron el genero de rima quanto pudieron á la similitud de los otros. . . .*

Emphatically this is no idle, gradually corrupted *juguete* to flatter the senses. The music, for one thing, is unearthly: *tan patetica, y poco grata á los oientes, que no hay uno que no desée se concluia quanto antes* (f. 637); and here the historian intended to reproduce it, but it was never written into the blank bars provided for it in the manuscript.[26]

[25] For the best known version of the famous acrostic cf. Augustinus, *De Civitate Dei*, I, XVIII, c. 23. For Eusebius of Caesarea's version cf. his *Werke*, ed. Heikel (Leipzig, 1902), I, 179 f. The implications of the Toledo version (*Olympo!*) will be examined in a study on the Sibyl in Spain.

[26] Barbieri, *Cancionero musical de los siglos XV y XVI* (Madrid), no. 243 reproduced what he calls "la música original de Toledo"; this may be the music which Vallejo intended to write in, and which Mr. J. B. Trend (cf. *The Music of Spanish History*, n. 67) found in the "Libros de Polifonia, No. 21, Obras extravagantes, f. 30" of the Chapter Library in Toledo.

Vallejo insists on the *musica inocente, sin bajo, sin acompañamiento de instrumento* (f. 639), on the simplicity of the text, the necessity of the escorting angels, their harmless use of borrowed vestments.[27] And the reader may try to realize the eerie effect on the shadowy crowd of worshipers, at dawn, when the stark childish voice rose through the gloom of that enormous nave, while torches glinted from the naked swords and the choir somberly answered:

Juicio fuerte
sera dado
cruel y de muerte.

IV. *The Christmas Play:* Hardly less interesting for the historian of the Spanish drama, although principally written for the musicologist, is the *Disertacion V. sobre la Musica* (ff. 477 *ff.*), for it contains the description and text of a primitive traditional performance on Christmas Eve at Toledo, which has so far remained almost unnoticed.[28]

[f. 495] . . . *Desde el principio de la Misa salen del Sagrario los Clerizones vestidos de Pastores, y van ál Altar mayor por el Postigo, y estan arriba en lo plano mientra se dice esta Misa danzando, y bailando: y acabada la Misa toman Capas los dichos dos Socapiscoles Racioneros para hacer el Oficio de las Laudes, que se empiezan luego en el Coro, á las que habrá tañido el Campanero, segun es costumbre, por la señal que le hizieron, quando se dixere el Hymno* Te Deum laudamus, *con la cuerda del Coro: y dicho por el Preste:* Deus in adjutorium, *desde su silla, se empieza primero la primera antiphona, que es:* Quem vidistis Pastores? *y la dicen toda, y luego los Clerizones hechos Pastores ministrandolos su Maestro* [f. 493] *Claustrero dicen en el Choro mayor debajo de la Lampara de plata á Canto-llano el verso* Infantem vidimus Pannis involutum, et Choros Angelorum laudantes salvatorem, *y tornan en el Choro á decir toda la antiphona:* Quem vidistis? *y los Pastores responden entre los dos Choros debajo de la Lampara de enmedio el verso* Infantem vidimus, ut supra, *y despues dicen en el Choro tercera vez toda la antiphona* Quem vidistis? *y responden los Pastores desde la Puerta del Coro del Arzobispo el verso* Infantem, *y luego salen los Socapiscoles con las Capas de brocado, y Cetros, y llegan á los lados del Aguila del Choro del Arzobispo, y alli los Cantores á Canto-llano les hacen las preguntas siguientes, y los Capiscoles asen de las manos á*

---

[27] By quoting from Martene the answer of the monks of Cluny: *Habemus alvas non sacratas.*

[28] It was reprinted by the Benedictine P. Luciano Serrano in an article entitled "Historia de la Música en Toledo," *RBAM*, X (Tercera época) 1907, pp. 219–243, also issued as a pamphlet the same year in Madrid. Father Serrano modernized spelling and punctuation and omitted several sentences. For the lines reproduced by Moraleda cf. *infra*, n. 36.

dos de aquellos Pastorcicos, y les preguntan juntamente con los Cantores lo siguiente:

Canto-llanistas. *Bien vengades Pastores,*
[f. 494] *que bien vengades.*
Pastores do anduvistes?
decidnos lo que vistes?
Cantores. *Que bien vengades.*
Canto-llanistas *Pastores del ganado*
decidnos buen mandado.
Cantores. *Que bien vengades.*
Melodicos.[29] *Vimos que en Bethlen Señores*
nasció la flor de las flores.
Cantores. *Que bien vengades.*
Melodicos. *Esta flor que hoy ha nascido*
nos dará fruto de vida.
Cantores. *Que bien vengades.*
Melodicos. *Es un Niño, y Rey del Cielo*
que hoy ha nascido en el suelo.
Cantores. *Que bien vengades.*
Melodicos. *Está entre dos animales*
embuelto en pobres pañales.
Cantores. *Que bien vengades.*
Melodicos. *Virgen ,y limpia quedó*
la madre que le parió
Cantores. *Que bien vengades.*
Melodicos. *Al hijo, y Madre roguemos*
les plega que nos salvemos.
Todos. *Que bien vengades.*

En la substancia se hace hoy esta Ceremonia como la refiere el Racionero Arcayos. La Danza en el plano del Altar mayor se habra omitido por evitar excesos, por considerarla abuso, y porque siempre procura el Dean ó Presidente se execute con la mayor seriedad.

Vallejo then disclaims the intention of commenting for the nonce on this text, adding that the original *Oficio de Pastores* came to Spain *de los Monasterios Benedictinos*. Unfortunately he continued:

Ni tampoco quiero detenerme á probar que las coplas castellanas que se la añadieron en el siglo XIII. y acaso por D. Lope de Loaysa[30] *son una parafrasis de la Profecia*

[29] For the distinction between the *canto melódico*, or *melodía*, also called *Eugeniano*, and the *canto llano* and, incidentally, an adverse opinion on Vallejo's authority as a musicologist, cf. Rojo and Prado, *El Canto Mozárabe*, Barcelona, 1929, p. 148 ff.

[30] Serrano printed *Jofré* de Loaysa, and his silent correction may be right. Jofre Gaufredo de Loaisa, archdeacon of Toledo in the thirteenth century, is known to have also been a historian. Cf. Amador de los Ríos, *Historia crítica*, IV, 66 ff.

de la Sybila Eritrea que llamó á Christo flor *conviniendo con Isaias, y de la antiphona* Quem vidistis *que usa la Iglesia en el oficio de aquella noche. Todo esto pide mas tiempo, y tratarse mas de proposito.*

If Vallejo could have disposed of the collection of liturgical texts which has been gathered since his time, even though mostly outside of the Peninsula, he might have tentatively placed this combination of a Latin trope with a somewhat fuller paraphrase in the vernacular approximately in the eleventh century as to its first part, and in the thirteenth, perhaps, as to the second.[31] On the other hand, the polymetric verse is of the greatest interest: outside of the recurrent choral refrain they show a series of rhymed couplets, first two heptasyllabic ones, followed by six octosyllabic ones. The refrain has two lines, of respectively seven and five syllables—all in all an arrangement not so varied as the twelfth-century *Auto de los Reyes Magos,* yet possibly based on the same tradition. At any rate Vallejo's actual guess, assigning the Castilian part to the thirteenth century, may not be much amiss.[32]

In his account of the *Sybila* of Christmas Eve, Vallejo evidently mingled what he knew at first hand and what he had learned from manuscripts and printed documents, and from such historians as were accessible to him; but his description of the *Pastores,* a performance still practised in his time, he copied from the manuscript of one of his predecessors, Juan Chaves de Arcayos, of whom Vallejo himself gave the following account:

---

[31] The latin antiphon is close to the earliest forms of the *Quem vidistis* type, cf. Young, *Officium Pastorum,* Wisconsin Academy, XVII (1914), 344; Böhme, *Das lateinische Weihnachtsspiel* (Leipzig, 1917), pp. 30 ff.; and even the phrase *et Choros Angelorum laudantes salvatorem,* which distinguishes the Toledo text from these forms, was used in the eleventh century (cf. Young, *loc. cit.,* 351). In Spain the later *Quem queritis* type (Young, *loc. cit.,* 300 n.) appears somewhat later: in Huesca (XI–XII c.), Plasencia (XII c.), or Vich (XII–XIII c.). The vernacular part is evidently based on the interrogation *Pastores, dicite, quidnam vidistis?,* also used in the Cathedral of Valencia (cf. Sanchis Sivera, *La Catedral de Valencia,* Valencia, 1909, p. 466), finishes with a lyric in praise of the Virgin, and may well be compared with a *berrichon* trope of the thirteenth century (cf. Young, *loc. cit.,* 350 f.) still entirely in Latin. Definite conclusions, of course, will not be possible until more Spanish evidence has become accessible.

[32] For linguistic evidence we shall have to await the possible publication of a less evidently modernized text. It may be noted, however, that the rhyme in line 12 calls for *ha*

Juan Chaves de Arcayos, que fué Capellan de Coro, y despues Racionero y Repartidor, hombre sumamente laborioso, pasó su vida trasladando noticias, ya de las que hallaba en memoriales antiguos, y ya de las que sucedian en su tiempo. Como vivió mucho, y casi sesenta años en nuestra Iglesia, pues murio el de 1643, y havia entrado en ella á ser Capellan de Coro el de 1589. resultaron entre otros muchos quadernos, que se conservan, fruto de un trabajo material, dos volumenes folio, que al primero llamó él: Casos sucedidos en diversos tiempos en la Santa Iglesia de Toledo, desde el año de 1433. sacados de los libros Capitulares, *y al segundo:* Sucesion de Prevendados. *Estos dos volumenes que en su original*[33] *estan de mala letra en la Libreria, mandó el Cavildo en 13. de Setiembre de 1765. se trasladasen y la Copia que comprehende quatro volumenes folio es la que sirve. Arcayos fué fiel en lo que trasladó, pero si son suyas algunas especies, se advierte corta instruccion, y genio nimiamente credulo* (ff. 27 f.).

The original manuscript of Arcayos was still available in Vallejo's time, and the four-volume transcript of 1765 was still in the Chapter Library in 1911.[34]

Arcayos himself, however, compiling his materials between 1589 and 1643,[35] used older documents which he designated as *antigua costumbre*. These are among the sources which we hope may yet come to light when bonafide students, properly vouched for, may find the huge portals of the Chapter Library no longer irreducibly closed. The documents may have perished, of course, but there are recent records of two manuscripts, quite probably still extant, which have been in the hands of a local historian, neither of them, so far as we know, utilized by Arcayos or Vallejo, and which might represent, directly or indirectly, the *antigua costumbre* or parts of it.[36] It is impossible to guess how far back into time either of these manuscripts, or others that may have been used by

---

nascida, or rather *es nascida*, since agreement of an intransitive construed with *haber* is probably out of the question.

33 Cax. 67. num. (V.). The number was not given.

34 Moraleda, *Los Seises*, p. 19; possibly also the original two volumes: the reference in Moraleda (*estos libros*) is not quite clear.

35 According to Moraleda "1568 and 1643," but the first date is probably a misreading.

36 The first is the *Musica y letra de la Sibila . . . , cuaderno . . . en 4º apaisado con 10 hojas y 8 en blanco, mide 15 centímetros y medio de alto por 22 de ancho* (Moraleda, *loc. cit.*, p. 40). To this description was added a small photographic reproduction of one page of the manuscript, 12.2×9.5 cm., in which the text can barely be deciphered. The second is the manuscript of the *Cancion de Pastores* which occupies the last two pages of a *libro de pergamino pintado en colores—siglo XVI—en 4º con 28 hojas*, with the title: *Psalmi qui in*

Arcayos, would carry the latter's authority and, through him, that of Vallejo.

We shall have to trust in the favor of time and peace, which may yet establish good will and throw open to students all the treasures of the peninsular archives and eventually make possible for medieval Spain a record of drama and stage comparable to that of other European nations.

---

al / ma Eclesia Toletana consuescunt dici, in / Vesperis et com / pletorio ad organ / num; canticum Veate / Marie Virginis / Luce primo Cap. Moraleda has taken from this six bars of music together with some lines of the *Pastores* in an arrangement differing from that of Arcayos.

THOMAS CARLYLE AND CHARLES BUTLER OF WALL STREET

LeROY ELWOOD KIMBALL

New York University

IT would appear that the biographers and editors of the letters of Thomas Carlyle have not mentioned the name of Charles Butler of Wall Street, New York, who for fifteen years rendered a gratuitous service as investor of the author's savings in this country. However, the friendship is recorded by two writers[1] outside of the Carlyle biographies and collections of letters, and recently more details of this friendship were found in a benefactor's papers in a university's archives.

When Charles Butler died in 1897 at the age of 95 years, the newspapers of New York justly praised his memory. *The New York Daily Tribune* for Tuesday, December 14, 1897, contains a column and a half obituary with a portrait, and a half-column editorial which begins as follows:

> Charles Butler is dead. He had lived nearly a hundred years. He had attained distinction in a great profession. He had amassed an ample fortune. He had assisted conspicuously and efficiently in founding several institutions of National beneficence, and for more than three score years had devoted time, labor, knowledge and money without stint to the strengthening of their foundations and the extension of their good works.

He had been for sixty-one years a member of the Council, or Trustees, of New York University. Elected in 1836, four years after its founding, he served until the day of his death. During the last eleven years of his life he was president of that body.

Charles Butler's middle years came at a time when land was the medium for speculation, new States talked of repudiating their bond issues, and railroad and canal owners and operators were in constant litigation. He was an able lawyer, whose brother,

---

[1] George Lewis Prentiss, *The Union Theological Seminary in the City of New York; Its Design and Another Decade of Its History. With a Sketch of the Life and Public Services of Charles Butler* (Asbury Park, New Jersey, 1899).

Francis Hovey Stoddard, *The Life and Letters of Charles Butler* (New York, 1903).

Benjamin Franklin Butler, seven years his elder, was the founder of the New York University School of Law and Attorney General of the United States under Presidents Jackson and Van Buren. But Charles Butler's flare was not for public office; it was for the practice of law with all of the financial responsibilities, and opportunities, which went with it in those expanding years. He did act as confidential adviser to several federal administrations, but his only public activity came early in life, at the age of twenty-four years, when he took the place of his law partner, District Attorney Bowen Whiting, as public prosecutor in the famous William Morgan case, and secured the indictment of the four alleged kidnappers, when Whiting could not act because he was a Mason.

Butler bought land in Chicago in 1833 on almost the very day the citizens voted twenty-seven for, and one against, becoming a town, and he wrote home: 'If I were a young man [he was then thirty-one] I would settle in Chicago.' He did the next best thing; he had his brother-in-law, William B. Ogden, settle there in charge of the Butler land interests and saw him elected first mayor of Chicago at its incorporation as a city in 1837.

When Mr. and Mrs. Butler first went to England for the latter's health in 1838, they did not meet Thomas Carlyle. It was in the summer of 1853 that Butler was introduced to Carlyle through Miss Delia S. Bacon of Ohio, the recipient of his philanthropy, who had been sent to Carlyle by Ralph Waldo Emerson in the matter of the treatise she was writing to prove Shakespeare never existed. Carlyle was 68 years old and had begun work on *Frederick* in his reconstructed attic at No. 5 Cheyne Row; Butler, who had passed his fifty-first birthday, wrote home: 'I ought to have mentioned that I spent last evening with Miss Lynch at Carlyle's by special invitation through Miss Delia Bacon. We found Mr. and Mrs. Carlyle very interesting and pleasant. I was very much delighted with both of them.'

At the time Butler and Carlyle met in the summer of 1853, it is apparent the latter spoke to the financier concerning a one thousand dollar State of Illinois bond which he had purchased years before and with which he was having difficulty. Mr. Butler offered to be of assistance as he was then representing the foreign and domestic holders of bonds of the State of Indiana, and had previously acted in the same capacity with the bonds of the State of Michigan. Then, too, the railroad, in which he had a personal interest, the Terre Haute, Alton & St. Louis, had rights of way in Illinois and he was negotiating with Russell Sage for the sale of two locomotives from Mr. Sage's Minnesota Central Railroad.

Mr. Carlyle wrote to Mr. Butler from 5 Cheyne Row, Chelsea, London, under the date of January 17, 1854:

Your very obliging letter came in due course of post, but except a silent record of thanks for your goodness, I was not at that time able to do anything with it. I had been called into Scotland; my dear and excellent old mother was passing away from me by the road we have all to go:—that unforgetable event took place on Christmas day; and ever since, there as here, I have been occupied as you may fancy. It was not till yesterday that I could get a proper copy of the Illinois bond; and to-day I hasten to send you the original, that you may dispose of it for me, according to your kind purposes, in the way you judge most advantageous.

The copy, so far as I can examine, is exact to the original now sent: Bond for $1,000. State of Illinois, No. 324 with thirty-warrants of interest of $30 each, attached to it, the first dated July, 1843, the last, July, 1860, by means of which, I suppose, the original could be replaced, should any accident happen to it.

As to management of the affair, I have only to say that the money is not at all wanted here at present; and that I will leave the matter wholly to your *skill* and friendliness, well aware that there can be no course nearly so good for me and it. Had I once got notice from you that the bond has arrived safe, I shall dismiss it from the list of my anxieties, and wait with very great composure indeed for what issue you will educe from it. So enough on that subject.

Miss B has gone away from us—soon after you went—to St. Albans, the great Chancellor Bacon's place: there we suppose her to be elaborating the Shakspeare discovery! but have heard almost nothing since, and have seen absolutely nothing. The painter whom my wife spoke of has at length, I believe, actually got to sea, and will probably be in New York the week before this arrives: he has a note to Miss Lynch and you from my wife; and as he is both a really superior artist, and a very honest, modest, kindly and interesting man, we doubt not you will be good to him as opportunity offers. A lively remembrance of that pleasant evening survives here, too; it is not always that one falls in with human figures of that kind either from our side of the water or from yours! I beg many kind and respectful regards to Miss Lynch, whom I shall long remember.

And so adieu for this time,

Yours sincerely,

T. Carlyle.[2]

[2] Prentiss, *op. cit.*, p. 515.

The painter mentioned in the letter is Samuel Laurence, who was a house guest of the Butlers during his entire stay in New York, and made several sketches and paintings of Mr. Butler and members of his family. On the 3d of March Mr. Carlyle wrote at some length from Chelsea, London:

My Dear Sir:

A week ago I received your kind and pleasant letter, intimating to me, among other welcome things, that you had received the Illinois Bond safe, and would, as your beneficent purpose had been, take charge of it in due business form, which is all right and a real favor done me; which in fact, as it were, absolves my lazy mind from any farther thought or trouble about that matter; there being evidently nothing half so good I could have done with it, and therefore in the meanwhile, nothing further whatever that I have to do with it. With many sincere thanks, let it so stand therefore! I have only to add that the 3 coupons you inquire about are quite gone beyond my reach or inquiry. I suppose them to have been given off for 3 installments of interest, which were, (as I can remember) paid to me in regular succession, long years ago, when a worthy friend, a merchant in the city, now deceased, had charge of the Bond for me; if that was not their fate, I cannot form a guess about it; but in any case, they are to be held, these 3 coupons, as extinct for us, and finally gone. And this is now all I have to say upon the Illinois Bond. Requesting you only not to bother yourself with it, beyond what comes quite in your way in the current of far wider operations, I will leave that rather memorable Document now at length well lodged in your repositories, and dismiss it again quite into the background of my own remembrances.

We are struck with a glad surprise to hear you have been so supremely hospitable to our voyaging painter. To snatch him, the thin-skinned, sea-worn man, from the horrors of a stranger hotel or boarding-house, and bid him come and rest in safety, under soft covers and protection, in the house of a human friend; this is indeed a high and fine procedure; but it is far beyond what is demanded or expected in these later unheroic ages! I can only say we find a beautiful 'politeness of the old school' in all this, and in the way all this spoken of and done; and do very much thank Miss Lynch and yourself for all your kindnesses; and shall (if we be wise) silently regard the existence of such a temper of mind, thousands of miles away from us, as a real possession in this world.

Miss B. sends no sign whatever from St. Albans; we suppose her to be, day and night, strenuously wrestling down in her own peculiar way, that monstrous problem she has got; poor lady, I really wish I heard of her safe home again, and well out of it, on any terms. Your Minister here has done a notable thing the other day: entertained, or rather been partner while the Consul entertained, the 6 or 5 select pearls of European Revolutionism, Kossuth, Ledru-Rollin, Mazzini, Garibaldi, etc., I do believe the most condensed Elixir of modern Anarchy that could have well been got together round any earthly dinner table, which has caused a perceptible degree of laughter, commentary and censure in certain circles; now pretty much fallen silent again. Undoubtedly a diplomatic mistake (in a small way) on the part of Mr. B.; which, however, it is expected he will amply redeem by and by.

Adieu my dear sir; with many kind regards, from both of us, to both of you, I remain,

Yours always truly,

T. Carlyle.[3]

Not quite three months after he wrote his March letter, Mr. Carlyle acknowledged with appreciation the financial solution which Mr. Butler had worked out for the much discussed bond when he wrote on May 28 from his usual address in Chelsea:

My Dear Sir:

It must be at once admitted, and ought to be always gratefully remembered, you have stood a real father to that poor down-broken bond; and have set it up triumphantly, with victorious kindness, on such a footing as it never had before! I think (so far as vague recollection serves), it bears now almost the value, and yields about twice the interest that was originally attached to it, which is a result valuable to me, in more ways than one. The money is worth something in this ever-hungry world; and as to the transaction which the money now comes from, that is one with a value in it higher, probably, than any money. I may long recollect that pleasant brief evening, and the chivalrous procedure that has arisen out of it.

By all means, leave the document where it is, if you will still be so kind as to trouble yourself with the keeping of it. If you continue to think the investment safe, I may send you some more in the course of years; the interest, in August or any time, will find uses for itself here. And so, with many thanks, let the matter lie arranged.

We are in our usual state here, little different from what you saw, except that I am dreadfully overwhelmed this long while with an ill-fated Prussian enterprise in the Book way, the ugliest I ever undertook, and the thankless and hopeless, in which, except the unwillingness to be flatly beaten in one's old days, there is no adequate motive to persevere. This is really a sore job, and I have often fallen nearly desperate upon it. One needs 'The obstinacy of ten mules,' as I sometimes say, 'in this world.' However, I now do begin, in cheerful moments, to see promises of daylight here and there through the abominable black dust-whirlwind where my dwelling has so long been; and expect to get out of it alive after all, doing a bad Book, the best I can, since a good one is not possible in the case.

Of Miss B., I am sorry to report that I know absolutely nothing for many

---

[3] *Ibid.*, p. 516.

months past, perhaps above a year, when she made her last visit here, and promised to come back soon, but never came. She lives about four miles from us (in a street leading off Hyde Park Gardens, towards the Paddington region, at least there she did live, when I called long since and found her gone out). I am so held to the grinding-stone, I never, by any chance, get away to such distances, and indeed, hardly make visits at all, this long while. I have often asked myself, and ask all American friends, what poor Miss B. is about? but nobody knew her, nobody can tell. Her very address I have now lost; could find the place, I think, from the physiognomy of the street, were I there in person, and from some recollections of 'twelve' as being the number of the house. Poor lady! I fear she is in a very abstruse condition; engaged in an enterprise which is totally without rational basis, and getting more and more exasperated that she does not (as she cannot by possibility) succeed in it.[4]

Laurence need not write to me 'till his demon fairly bids him;' I am satisfied to hear of his prospering so among you; for which, I doubt not, the good, meritorious man is thankful. Such 'hospitality'—I have often thought of it with loyal wonder; it is like the hospitality of the heroic ages, and rebukes common mankind of our day!

My wife joins with me in kind regards to Miss Lynch (among others of the Chelsea party of that evening) whom I very well remember, and still like. My notion is the Sardinian professor may have done an extremely wise thing, in staying where he was on those terms. Easily go farther and fare worse.

What a narrow providential miss of the uttermost calamity was that of you and yours.

We do well to recognise such things as mercies of a Special Power that has pity on us. Great pity withal is shown us in this universe, where so much rage and cruelty also are—the soil of it only getting arable by little and little. Accept our united regards. I remain always,

Yours sincerely,

T. Carlyle.[5]

The 'narrow providential miss' refers to the fact that the Butler party had taken passage to America on the ill-fated *Arctic* and, at the last moment, were led by an unexpected incident to give up their staterooms and await the next steamer.

Upon receipt of the news from Mr. Butler of the death on June 6, 1856, of his only son, A. Ogden Butler, who had graduated with honors from New York University in the Class of 1853, Mr. Carlyle wrote his New York friend:

Alas, I can too well understand what a blank of utter sorrow and desolation

---

[4] L. E. Kimball, "Miss Bacon Advances Learning," *The Colophon*, II, no. 3, 338–354.

[5] Prentiss, *op. cit.*, p. 518.

that sad loss must have left in your household, and in the heart of everybody there. Your one son, and such a son, cut off in the flower of his days; so many high hopes for himself and others, suddenly abolished forever! It is hard for flesh and blood—and yet is must be borne; there is no relief from this; and all wisdom of all ages bids us say, 'good is the will of the Lord,' though that is hard to do.

You do well not to slacken in your labors: to keep doing so long as the day is, the duty of the day. I know no other remedy so sure of ultimately helping in all sorrow whatsoever. Let us work while it is called to-day. In a very little while we too shall follow into the silent kingdom the loved ones that have already gone; and one divine eternity will hold us all again, as God may have appointed for them and for us. I will say no more on this sad subject; upon which you feel at present all speech to be mostly only idle.[6]

The copies of the letters from Mr. Butler show the great care which he gave to the increasing amounts which Carlyle sent him for investment. Mr. Butler wrote from his office at No. 12 Wall Street under the date of 3d of May, 1859:

My Dear Sir:

Your letters of the 8th & 13th of April have been received. The letter enclosing Certificate of Deposit for one thousand pounds sterling of your money to me for investment and management of your account and for your benefit. This remittance is all safely administered as after results may testify to you. The sober second and proper business thought of your letter of the 13th quite relieved me as I am sure you would have found the machinery proposed in your letter of 8th cumbrous & possibly expensive. The methods of remittance between the two countries are now so simple and the facilities of intercourse so constant and rapid that you may consider New York but at the other end of a steam ferry and this thought will help you to feel that you have not transferred your treasure beyond speedy reaching if occasion need. I shall before long advise you of the investment that I shall make of your money and attend to the payment & regular remittance of the dividends to you. I have also to acknowledge with many thanks to you the receipt since I last wrote to you of the copy of your life of Frederick the Great in two volumes, with your own autograph sign manual on the fly leaf which book I am now reading to my daughters with interest & gratification. I trust that you will be able to accomplish the residue of this task to your own great relief and satisfaction: as my work lies in a different direction having to do more with the material things such as railways & canals than is convenient at times. I can yet sympathize fully with one whose work lies in fields of literature and history where I doubt not they find many hard places & trying experiences to work through & out of—and yet it is doubtless true of us all that in these our working cares rightly considered & improved we find our chief blessing to spring. As the

---

[6] *Ibid.*, p. 506.

mail closing is at hand I send you this to relieve your anxiety as speedily as possible in respect to the safe arrival of your remittance.

With kindest regards to Mrs. Carlisle, I am, dear Sir,

Truly yours,

Charles Butler.[7]

Another letter dated the 17th of August, 1859, is strictly business, and gives an interesting account of an American railway security eighty years ago:

Thomas Carlyle, Esq.
Chelsea, London
My dear Sir:

Enclosed I hand you draft on Union Bank for 14£ or $70 dividends due on your bonds on 1 August which would have been sent forward a few days earlier but for absence from the city in these dog days.

Your remittance of one thousand pounds sterling I cashed at Duncan Sherman & Co. on the 3 May and received the avails in our currency at par viz $4,883.83 four thousand eight hundred and eighty three dollars and eighty three cents—the interest on this sum computed up to 1 August inst. was $84.30 making $4,968.13 which I have invested in $5,000 of the First Mortgage Sinking Fund Bonds of the Chicago and North Western Railway Company bearing 7 per cent interest payable semi-annually on the 1 August and 1 February in each year in this city. These bonds are secure beyond a reasonable doubt being at the rate only of eleven hundred pounds sterling per mile upon the road which is the great north western road out of Chicago & on the first day of October will be about two hundred miles in length and the cost of which exceeds eight thousand pounds sterling per mile. Hereafter your interest will accrue on 1 Feby & 1 Augt 7% on $7,000 at 7% or $490 per annum and $245 each semi annual remittance.

The bonds which I hold for you I deem it proper to have registered on the books of the company in my name as trustee for T. Carlyle which will provide for the contingencies of fire, or death, and transmit to you the proper certificate of the company to this effect which will be a voucher in your hands. I am just on the point of leaving the city again for a few days on a visit to the sea shore & confine this letter strictly to the business transaction.

With my best regards to Mrs. Carlyle, I am, dear Sir,

Truly yours,

Charles Butler.

Memo. for Mr. Carlyle

3 May 1859 Rec[d] proceeds of draft on
Duncan Sherman & Co
for 1000 Sterling par $4883.83

[7] New York University Archives.

1 Aug^t. / 59 add int from 3 May to it—7%	84.30
	$4968.13
1 Aug. / 59 To invested 5000$ in purchase of 5 Sinking Fund 1 Mortgage Bonds of Chicago & North Western Railway Company	5000.00
Balance due C. B.	$31.87

This balance will be deducted from the dividend 1 Feb 1860—

C. Butler[8]

Mr. Butler remits an interest payment and reports that his family circle has read the presentation volumes of Carlyle's *Frederick:*

New York, 10 Feby 1860
12 Wall St.

My dear Sir:

I have collected for you two hundred & forty five Dollars interest ($245.) due on the first day of this month of February on 7000$ of securities—From this I have deducted a small balance of thirty one dollars & eighty seven cents due to me in August last as per my letter to you in that month leaving $213.13 your due which amount I now send you in a sight bill on London for £42.12.6 and which I hope will find its owner safely. I also enclose certificate of Secretary of Chicago & North Western Rail Way Company that these bonds are registered in my name in trust for you which document should be in your possession as showing the fact in the event of anything happening to me—there are two classes of securities enumerated in this certificate—those denominate the sinking Fund being the superior or higher, the other 2 being inferior in point of security but both good and a reference to my letter of August last will give you the particulars in respect the first class herein mentioned.

Since writing you last the two volumes of Frederick have been read in my family circle with absorbing interest and gratification and we shall look for the forthcoming third volume with quickened desire. I trust that the summer and autumn & these first winter months have found you able to continue your labors and that you have not found them too wearisome. I also hope that Mrs. Carlyle has regained her health and that I shall hear good accounts of you both.

We are looking from this side of the water with gratified interest to the progress of events on the Continent in France and Italy and it seems to me as if the Emperor had really entered into the spirit of the thing and would give freedom to Italy and at the same time a mighty impulse to commercial and industrial

---

[8] *Ibid.*

activities throughout Europe—that his programme of reform, in abolishing or modifying the restrictive & prohibitory system which has so fettered France—and establishing such free interchange with England will earn for him greater fame than all his great battles.

With kind regards to Mrs. Carlyle

I am dear Sir

Truly yours

Charles Butler[9]

Carlyle's Scotch bankers are asked for a promised remittance:

Robert Adamson, Esq.
Dumfries, Scotland
Dear Sir:

My friend T. Carlyle of London in a letter written in November last requested me to remit to you the semi annual interest on certain securities which I hold in trust for him to be placed by you to his credit in your Bank. I have the pleasure to hand you enclosed first sight bill of Exchange for 49£ Stg (the proceeds of 245$ interest coupons accrued on the first instant) to your order on Union Bank of London which please place to the credit of Mr. Carlyle. In same letter Mr. Carlyle advises that he had requested you to make a further remittance to me of 1000£ Stg for his benefit. I allude to it to say that I have not received any such remittance and if any has been made it has not reached me but has miscarried. I should have written sooner but absence from this city for some time in the west has delayed it. You can not fail to look at events transpiring in this country with profound interest. We yet hope for a solution of this slavery question short of dissolution and in any event without civil war. The great industrial interests of the northern states will not be seriously damaged. Public sentiment is sound and there is no trouble any where save in the unhappy south where they have a festering sore for which it is indeed difficult to find a remedy—Property & securities in the northern states must be strengthened and established while those of the south must in the nature of things be weakened. The present appearances are favorable to an adjustment which will save the border slave states at least from the impending ruin.

Very respectfully

Your obt servt

Charles Butler[10]

Memo.

Bill Duncan Sherman & Co. on Union Bank of London for £49 Stg to order of Robert Adamson Dumfries. Dated Feby 5th 1861—sight exchange—enclosed—for T. Carlyle.[10]

---

[9] *Ibid.*

[10] *Ibid.*

Further instructions concerning the thousand pounds sterling:

New York 15 Feby 1861
12 Wall St.

Robert Adamson, Esq.
Dumfries, Scotland
Dear Sir:

Enclosed I hand you *second* bill of exchange Messrs. Duncan Sherman & Co on Union bank of London for £49 Stg 245$ interest coupons on account of & for Thomas Carlyle of Chelsea London.

On the 5th inst I had the pleasure to enclose to you the first of this exchange on same account. Since then I have received a letter from Mr. Carlyle under date of 21st Jany in which he says that the 1000£ Stg awaits in your hands my order. You will remit it by exchange in usual form to credit of Duncan Sherman & Co for my use. They keep account with the Union Bank London & a deposit of the amount in *that* Bank to *their* credit for my use is a simple mode of remittance.

Our political affairs look better and all that is required is time for the working out of the difficulties which I confidently anticipate will be without serious conflict, tho not without shock to industrial interests in the southern states particularly.

In haste very respectfully
Your obt servt
Charles Butler[11]

The money is received and the beginning of the Civil War is reported:

New York, May 1861
12 Wall Street

Samuel Adamson, Esq.
Dumfries, Scotland
Dear Sir:

I have received through Messrs. Duncan Sherman & Co. one thousand pounds sterling deposited by you in the Union Bank of London to credit of above house for my use on account of Thomas Carlyle and the proceeds ($4,822.22) are in my hands to credit of & to be invested for Mr. Carlyle.

Since I had the pleasure of writing to you in February events of the most thrilling character have taken place in this country as you see by the public papers involving us in civil strife. But I think you cannot fail to be impressed with the position of our government and the extraordinary unanimity which prevails in all of the free states in favor of maintaining the integrity of the Government, and the union at any and every cost. The intensity of this union feeling with the people is wonderful, & any amount of men & money will be furnished by the free

[11] *Ibid.*

states to sustain the government. So far all movements on the part of the Government have been judiciously taken, and tho we have reason to deplore this state of things & the spectacle exhibited to the civilized world, still we have hope that the issue of it will be to strengthen & establish the credit & character of our Government & to settle a question that has been festering in our Southern states for more than a quarter of a century & which has now come to a head in this insurrection to overthrow our government. Our railways in the northwestern states are doing a good business and the prospect of another good crop is at this time promising.

Very respectfully,
Your obt servant,
Charles Butler[12]

Two letters forwarding semi-annual interest and the views of a Northerner:

New York, 13th August, 1861
12 Wall Street

Sam'l Adamson, Esq.
Dumfries, Scotland
Dear Sir:

Enclosed I hand you draft on the Union Bank London. for 49£ (245$) for account of Thomas Carlyle of London being semi-annual interest.

A further remittance to his credit will be made about first of November next. I wish it were in my power to say that the political troubles of our country were approaching a satisfactory solution. At present we cannot predict when we shall have peace but there is a universal conviction at the North that we shall effectually put down the rebellion and maintain the union and Government intact: indeed no one in the north entertains any thought of a different result. With great respect, Dear Sir, Yours truly,

Charles Butler

New York, 28 Feby. 1862
12 Wall Street

Samuel Adamson, Esq.
Dumfries, Scotland
Dear Sir:

Enclosed I hand you sight exchange on London for 80£ Stg for Thomas Carlyle.

I have delayed this remittance for quite 28 days (it should have been on 1 Feby) on account of the state of exchanges. The rate being very high at present (15% for sight exchange) but I dared not delay longer.

I have no doubt that exchange will fall here shortly below present rates. Please place the enclosed to credit of Mr. Carlyle to whom I shall shortly write.

[12] *Ibid.*

I am happy to assure you that the terrible conflict that has been preceding in this country between the Government and the slave holders of the south is rapidly drawing to a close. The rebellion will be effectually crushed and the government and union will be maintained and preserved intact. No intelligent man who understands the real state of the case can for a moment doubt the result.

With great respect
Dear Sir:
Truly yours,
Charles Butler[13]

During these years, when Mr. Carlyle's health had faltered in his effort to finish his *History of Frederick II of Prussia*, Mr. Butler wrote several times to Carlyle's brother, Dr. John A. Carlyle, who was living intermittently with the author and caring for his affairs. Mr. Butler wrote him on August 17, 1865:

My Dear Sir:

Inclosed I hand you statement brought up to the 1st August, 1865, showing the state of your brother's affairs in my hands at that date. Since the previous statement the exchange has declined very much, and I think we may count on its continuing to do so.

I concluded to invest the balance in hand by the purchase of two bonds of $1,000 each at 8% which I regard as very favorable. The interest of these two will be now added to the account. Their purchase required a small advance over the amount standing to the credit of the account, which will be reimbursed to me out of the accruing interest in Feby next. I shall write your brother shortly not only on the termination of the war here in this country, whereby commercial relations are left to return to their usual & natural condition, but also on the termination of his great work, the History of Frederick, whereby his peace of mind must be restored & himself freed from a great burden,

I am,
Dear Sir,
Truly yours,
Charles Butler[14]

On April 14, 1868, after fifteen years of gratuitous financial assistance, Mr. Butler, following a decision not disclosed in the correspondence, dispatched all of Mr. Carlyle's securities to Dr. J. A. Carlyle, who acknowledged them on May 6 as follows:

My Dear Sir:

Last week before leaving Dumfries I wrote to you, acknowledging receipt of

---

[13] *Ibid.*

[14] *Ibid.*

your letter of the fourteenth of April, with notarial packages of eighteen bonds, for one thousand dollars each which up to that date you had purchased for Thomas Carlyle, my brother. These bonds are now lodged in his name at Dumfries in the British Linen Company's Bank. And since my arrival here I have got your second letter of April twenty-first, with notarial certificate (copy) of statement of account up to that time, and bill for £34.8s.6p. which balances it finally and which I have had paid to my brother's London banker. The statement is quite clear to me and corresponds with all earlier ones. I enclose that of August, 1865, (4), signed by you and declaring what bonds you had in trust at that time; and if there by any later declaration of the sort at Dumfries, I will have it cancelled at once.

I need hardly say that my brother feels extremely obliged for all your kindness and work on his behalf through so long a series of years. I find him looking at least as well as last year, and he is occupied at present in preparing for a new library edition of all his works. It will be a useful and not too severe occupation for him in the coming month. He may, perhaps, add a post-script to this, though to-day he is entangled with preliminaries for settling with printers as to the forms of that edition.

I remain,
Most sincerely yours,
J. A. Carlyle[15]

The author brother did not write a postscript, and instead wrote this letter, under the same date, May 6, 1868:

Dear Sir:

I cannot let my brother despatch this final document, and altogether satisfactory closure of the affairs, there have been between us, without testifying in my own words what a pleasant and grateful feeling I have now, and all along have had, for the whole of your conduct, from first to last, in regard to all that. I was a stranger, and I felt that you took me up as a friend; and, sure enough, you have throughout acted conspicuously in that character; caring for my interest with a constant loyalty, sagacity and punctuality, as if they had been your own; manifesting at all times the qualities of a perfect man of business, and of an altogether singularly generous, faithful and courteous benefactor:—in short, making good nobly, in all points, the reading we took of you here, that evening, long years ago, when, alas, it was still 'we,' not as now only one, who could recognize men and love them!

Words of thanks are of little use, but it is certain I shall all my days remember you with gratitude, with honest satisfaction, and even a kind of pride, which will or may, whether talked of or not, be a real possession to us both. I do not yet renounce the hope of seeing you again this side the sea. Meanwhile, I enclose (by same mail) a little bundle of new photographs, which may gain a few glances

---

[15] Prentiss, *op. cit.*, p. 521.

from your ladykind on an evening, and occasionally bring me to mind. May all good be with you and yours, dear sir. I remain yours with lasting esteem and good will,

T. Carlyle.[16]

In the Gould Library at New York University, among the volumes containing presentation inscriptions by Thomas Carlyle to Charles Butler, there is a message of three years later, inscribed at the top of the title page of the 1869 edition of *Sartor Resartus:* 'To Charles Butler Esq., Wall Street, N. York: with many good wishes & grateful regards, T. Carlyle (Chelsea, 27 June, 1871).'

E. Lyulph Stanley, who with Matthew Arnold, Charles Kingsley, James Anthony Froude, and Goldwin Smith formed but a small part of those from the other side of the Atlantic who accepted the hospitality of Charles Butler at his New York home, wrote to Mr. Butler's daughter at the time of her father's death: 'Among the many more worthy tributes to his memory which you will receive I can only add what Mr. Carlyle said in giving me the letter of introduction to Mr. Butler: "The truest gentlemen I ever knew."'

[16] *Ibid.*, pp. 522–523 (letter in facsimile).

THE MEDIAEVALISM OF HENRY ADAMS*

OSCAR CARGILL

New York University

THE Archangel loved heights.' Behind this audacious opening sentence of *Mont-Saint-Michel and Chartres* lurks the apologetic figure of Henry Adams in the guise of a charitable and much traveled 'uncle' volunteering his services as guide to a kodak-snapping 'niece' for a summer sojourn in France. Much significance may be harvested from this seriocomic contrast of the soaring angel on his lofty pedestal and the mouselike little man, pendant but dignified, accompanying some adopted Daisy Miller down the gangplank of an exhausted Cunarder at Cherbourg or Havre. Yet this significance must be gathered quickly, for a scudding cloud may obscure the Archangel and the seemingly substantial girl may melt into thin air, leaving us only the lonely globe-trotter and connoisseur of cathedrals—as enigmatical as ever.

Of the symbols—man and maid, and austere angel poised on the summit of the tower that crowns his church—the stone image is most easily guessed at. Indeed, Adams himself obligingly furnishes us an interpretation from the eleventh century:

> . . . The Archangel stands for Church and State, and both militant. He is the conqueror of Satan, the mightiest of all created spirits, the nearest to God. His place was where the danger was greatest; therefore you find him here. For the same reason he was, while the pagan danger lasted, the patron saint of France. So the Normans, when they were converted to Christianity, put themselves under his protection. . . . So soldiers, nobles, and monarchs went on pilgrimage to his shrine; so the common people followed, and still follow, like ourselves.[1]

* Quotation is made from material in copyright by the kind permission of the publishers: from *The Education of Henry Adams*, from *Mont-Saint-Michel and Chartres*, from *Letters of Henry Adams* and *A Cycle of Adams Letters* (both edited by Worthington Chauncey Ford), from *Charles Francis Adams: An Autobiography*, and from *Letters to a Niece and Prayer to the Virgin of Chartres* by the Houghton Mifflin Company; from *The Letters of Mrs. Henry Adams* (edited by Ward Thoron) by Little, Brown and Company.

[1] (Boston, 1913), p. 1.

Yet what interest has the artless girl in this ancient protector of the Normans? Has she not Adams? And why the humility of her guide who could not, in all seriousness, have thought of himself as one of 'the common people' and possibly would not have respected her as such? The thought is almost obscene that he should bring her to Mont-Saint-Michel merely to pamper her passing passion for photography. Besides, the winged image of Saint Michael is beyond the reach of the sharpest Graflex lens, even in the possession of the most athletic American miss. Perhaps he has chosen the Archangel merely as a text for a vainglorious display of his learning—surely a temptation to a former Harvard University professor and president of the American Historical Association? Yet Adams is not exactly in his dotage and is still possessed of wit enough to be amused by our suggestion that both image and niece will vanish precipitately with his first rolling period.

No, we must fetch our imaginations up to the style of our author if we are to perceive the necessary connection of things. In a word, we must start several hundred feet off the ground and clear of all of the encumbrance of sober facts to get anywhere at all with the symbolism. It is breath-taking, but we are good for it, since reason tells us that the empyrean should furnish the better view. Very well then—the Archangel is not Saint Michael but Yggdrasil, Niece Daisy is not herself but the Little Lamb, and Adams is plainly Ishmael. Further, these images have a tendency to interfuse and mix.

I

When Henry Adams returned in 1868 from London with his papa, who had been an extraordinarily useful servant of the Republic at the Court of St. James during our Civil War, he was a brilliant but spoiled boy. To be sure, one does not gain this impression if one confines his study of Adams to *The Education*, even though one of the two chapters covering the interlude between the close of the War and the home-coming of Ambassador Charles Francis Adams is entitled 'Dilettantism' and even though the author admits that he had 'reached his twenty-seventh birthday without having advanced a step, that he could see, beyond his twenty-first.'[2] One comes away from *The Education* so infected with the author's pessimism that a conception of him as a light and purposeless fellow approaching thirty with no fixed career is all but impossible, despite the careless admissions of the author himself.[3] That his chief anxiety in going to Washington was that the city 'stood outside the social pale'[4] is a sufficient indication that our knowledge of the elder Adams has engulfed our perception of the boy. We do better to thrust *The Education* into some dusty corner and forget it while we form our knowledge of Henry Adams on the *Letters* which Mr. Worthington Chauncey Ford has edited with discrete omissions.[5] Instead of the acute analysis of British politics during the time when intervention in our War seemed imminent—an analysis which makes several chapters in *The Education* the liveliest sort of reading—*The Letters* show Henry merely to reflect his father's emotions and anxieties without any very sharp perception of what was going on.[6] 'I don't know what we are ever going to do with this damned old country,' he wrote his brother Charles who was enduring a 'long siege in mud and rain' in Virginia in 1863; 'some day it will wake up and find itself at war with us, and then what a squealing there'll be. . . . '[7] The same letter boasts that he has been 'put up for a Club in St. James's Street, by Mr. Milnes'—a boast more revealing of his preoccupations than his prior outburst of emotion against England. 'The *Trent* affair . . . destroyed all our country

---

[2] *The Education of Henry Adams*, Riverside Library (Boston, 1930), p. 208.

[3] "[Immediately after his return] he went to Newport and tried to be fashionable. . . . Newport was charming . . . and one enjoyed it amazingly. . . . " *Ibid.*, pp. 243 f.

[4] *Ibid.*, p. 243.

[5] *Letters of Henry Adams: 1858–1891; 1891–1918*, 2 vols. (Boston, 1930, 1938).

[6] During the Mason and Slidell affair, Henry wrote Charles: "This nation (England) means to make war. Do not doubt it. . . . *Our good father is cool but evidently of the same mind as I am.*" *A Cycle of Adams Letters*, ed. Worthington Chauncey Ford, 2 vols. (Boston, 1920), I, 76. Henry's letters in *A Cycle* must strike the reader as less thoughtful and considered than those of his brother and father, whose correspondence makes up the bulk of the volume—an indication that Mr. Ford reached this conclusion, too.

[7] *Letters*, I, 96. "What a bloody set of fools they are," he writes in regard to the English in *A Cycle*, I, 83.

visits,' he had earlier complained to his soldier-brother.[8] Subsequent letters from London, in the year of Fredericksburg, Chancellorsville, Gettysburg, Vicksburg, and Chickamauga, show Henry Adams to be having 'a very tolerable time' in the British capital though he feels 'the want of that happy absurdity' he has enjoyed in American society.[9] 'We are dragging our weary carcasses to balls and entertainments of every description,' he sighs in a letter to Charles on June 25, 1863, and two weeks later, while 'the rush and fuss of society is still going on,' he gives his brother a more detailed account of his fearful regimen:

> One rides in the Park two hours in the morning, dines out in the evening, and goes to a ball; rises to a breakfast the next day; goes to a dance in the afternoon, and has a large dinner at home, from which he goes to another ball at half after eleven.[10]

Despite the generous excisions of Mr. Ford, we may gather from the *Letters* that Henry Adams was not unsusceptible to feminine influence. On a sojourn in Italy in the April of Lincoln's assassination he was commissioned by Lady Frances Gordon to purchase for her 'some stones of turquoise-blue.'[11] One letter to Charles Milnes Gaskell mentions Adams's discomfiture at Mrs. Story's, where he had attempted to introduce himself to 'a pretty blonde in blue' only to find her a 'monosyllabic Hebe' and closes with a request to Gaskell to tell a Miss Montgomery that 'she looks like the Venus of Medici.'[12] Another missive to the same correspondent, after Adams's return to Portland Place, reveals that the author is regarded by his friend as shrewd enough to evaluate an object of the other sex: 'By the way I did the Argyll girl, and rather liked her. She has a pretty complexion; and is very fresh and unaffected; at least, so I thought after ninety seconds conversation.'[13] Though 'regularly done by those brutes of tailors,' Adams is worried that too great attentiveness to a matron will make the young ladies think him a bore. At Baden-Baden, he finds the females 'enough to make one's hair stand out in all di-

---

[8] *A Cycle*, I, 104. [9] *Letters*, I, 99.

[10] *Ibid.* [11] *Letters*, I, 119.

[12] *Letters*, I, 117–119. [13] *Letters*, I, 130.

rections.' Cora Pearl, the notorious vampire,[14] is there, and Adams readily adjusts his morals to the atmosphere of the resort, chiding Gaskell because the latter cannot 'distinguish between *l'infidélité du corps et l'infidélité du cœur*.'[15] Back in London, Adams has the pleasure of taking a 'lovely one,' whom Gaskell had evidently marked as his own, to dinner, and he teases his friend by telling him 'we were . . . somewhat gay. You can measure it by the fact that we became sentimental and poetical before we rose from table. I gave a short discursive sketch in about fifteen minutes, of the nature and objects of love. She blushed and listened. Of course I spoke only as your representative.'[16] Another dinner, out in Bayswater, at the home of an American girl who had married an Englishman, furnishes Adams with a happy release:

> . . . I admired her as a girl; she was fast but handsome and lively. I had a dinner there last night which carried me off my legs. I talked all the time, ate all the time, drank all the time. In short I was *en train*. I drank a great deal too much and fell desperately in love with my hostess and told her so. There are oases in the desert of life. Such a one was Inverness Terrace last night. . . . [17]

Here, surely, was a lighter Adams than the whole chronicles of that illustrious family had hitherto provided. And here perhaps was an Adams who might have some difficulty in adjusting to the rougher exigencies of American life.

In the *Letters* there is no evidence to show that Henry Adams thought even once of a career for himself during all the while that he was assistant secretary to his father in London. He had apparently pinned his hopes on the expectation that in his father's political future—Charles Francis Adams was as likely a presidential possibility in 1868 as any one—lay ample provision for himself. Landing in July, Henry Adams spent a few weeks in Quincy and Boston,[18] and then sought the solace of America's most fashionable resort:

> So far, life has been really pleasant. After finishing my article on Lyell which occupied me to the end of August, I went down to Newport which is a very gay sort of Torquay, and there I performed the butterfly with great applause, for a week. Everyone was cordial and the young women mostly smiled on me more

[14] *See* Ernest Boyd's introduction to *Nana*, Modern Library (1928), p. vi.

[15] *Letters*, I, 134.

[16] *Letters*, I, 137.

[17] *Letters*, I, 138.

[18] Not three or four months as in *The Education*, p. 241.

beamingly than I had been accustomed to, during my residence among the frigid damsels of London.[19]

In *The Education* Adams reports a bitter sense of being on the auction block with no bidders in sight,[20] but the correspondence hardly shows him seriously troubled about his future. Again, looking backward to 1868, Adams remembered that he and his brother Charles had struck a bargain in Quincy for one to pursue the railroads and the other the press, in the hope that they would play into each other's hands; and that he had gone to Washington as affording the shortest path to New York journalism.[21] The *Letters* do not reveal any such working harmony in the Adams family.[22] In response evidently to an urgent letter from Charles to hurry up a political article, Henry asserts that he 'may be a year or two in working it up,'[23] and, in point of fact, he never completed it. Four or five months later when Charles has charged him again with dilatoriness, Henry takes a high tone in his reply:

> . . . your ideas and mine don't agree, but they never have agreed. You like the strife of the world. I detest and despise it. You work for power. I work for my own satisfaction. You like roughness and strength; I like taste and dexterity. For God's sake, let us go our ways and not try to be like each other.[24]

Most biographical sketches of Henry Adams imply that he acquitted himself well while in Washington from the middle of October 1868[25] till the beginning of October 1870.[26] In those two years, however, his total output as a 'journalist' was not over half a dozen articles,[27] any one of which could have been put together

---

[19] *Letters*, I, 145. Contrast *The Education*, pp. 241–242: " . . . he failed as fashion."

[20] "He was for sale, in the open market. So were many of his friends. All the world knew it, and knew too that they were cheap; to be bought at the price of a mechanic. There was no concealment, no delicacy, and no illusion about it." *Op. cit.*, 240.

[21] *Ibid.*, pp. 242–243.

[22] "I have not thought it worth while to answer your remarks about my judgment in the Governor's case, because you and I are wider apart than the poles." H. A. to C. F. A., Jr., January 8, 1869. *Letters* I, 149. "I can't get you an office. . . . " *Idem*, I, 157.

[23] *Letters*, I, 150.

[24] *Letters*, I, 160.

[25] *Letters*, I, 147.

[26] *Letters*, I, 194, 195.

[27] Possibly an unsigned paper "A Look Before and After," in the *North American Review*, for January 1869, was by Adams; "The Session," *N. Am. Rev.* (April 1869); an article on "American Finance," *Edinburgh Review* (April 1869); and "Civil Service Reform"

in a week at the outside. 'I dawdle here,' Henry wrote in March 1869. 'The life is pleasant, rather than otherwise, and I am more contented here than I could be elsewhere.'[28] The truth seems to be that the way of Henry in Washington is still the way of the dilettante. 'Society accepts all sorts of impertinences from me, without showing its teeth,' he could boast, like the Beau of Bath.[29] His first 'Session' paper in the *North American Review* provoked a response which must have hit pretty near home, judging from his past. This is his own account in an epistle to his English confidante, Gaskell:

> . . . I enclose to you a long slip from a Massachusetts paper, probably the most widely circulated of all these Massachusetts papers, in which I am treated in a way that will, I think, delight you. Of course it is all nonsense. I am neither a journalist nor one of the three best dancers in Washington, nor have I a profound knowledge of the cotillon, though I confess to having danced it pretty actively. But you see I am posted as a sort of American Pelham or Vivian Gray. This amused me, but the part of the joke which pleased me less, was to come.
>
> This leader was condensed into half a dozen lines by a western paper, and copied among the items of the column 'personal' all over the country. In this form it came back to New York. Hitherto my skill as a dancer was kept a mere artistic touch to heighten the effect of my 'brilliant' essay. Now however the paragraph is compressed to two lines. 'H. B. A. is the author of article, etc., etc., etc. He is one of the three best dancers in W.' The next step will be to drop the literary half, and preserve the last line, and I am in an agony of terror for fear of seeing myself posted bluntly: 'H. B. A. is the best dancer in W.' This would be fame with a vengeance.[30]

The Pelham-Vivian Gray character is enlarged by other 'confessions.' In January 1870, Adams was supposed to be attentive to

---

N. Am. Rev. (October 1869). "The Session," *N. Am. Rev.* (April 1870); and "The New York Gold Conspiracy," *Westminster Rev.* (July 1870). See *Letters*, I, 149, 153, 157, 169. Also *DAB*. The best article, "Chapter on Erie," *N. Am. Rev.* (April 1870), is signed "Charles Francis Adams, Jr." Adams writes Gaskell, "I have brought all the respectable old fools of the country down on me by a mighty impudent article published in the April *North American* under my name though I was only half author." *Letters*, I, 186. This estimate is of solid articles requiring work. It does not include whatever is covered by Adams's apparently exaggerated statement: "At the same time I write about two articles a month in the *Nation*, and if I want to be very vituperative, I have a New York daily paper to trust." *Letters*, I, 181.

[28] *Letters*, I, 153.

[29] *Letters*, I, 177.

[30] *Letters*, I, 159.

a young woman bringing a dowry of £200,000. In his eyes 'her only attraction is that I can flirt with the poor girl in safety, as I firmly believe she is in a deep consumption and will die of it. I like peculiar amusements of all sorts, and there is certainly a delicious thrill, much in the manner of Alfred de Musset, in thus pushing one's amusements into the future world. . . . Is not this delightfully morbid?'[31] With the coming of spring in 1870 he grew fatuous: 'The young maidens no doubt adore me, but I am obdurate. . . . Have some one nice to flirt with me at Wenlock.'[32] Dining with 'Jephtha's daughter'[33] and muckraking Congress brought, however, their inevitable reward, and Henry Adams was properly scored on in a reply to his second 'Session' article by a western senator in a phrase which he remembered for many a long day:

> His article on the Session in the July *North American* had made a success. . . . It had been reprinted by the Democratic National Committee and circulated as a campaign document by the hundred thousand copies. . . . His only reward or return for this partisan service consisted in being formally answered by Senator Timothy Howe, of Wisconsin, in a Republican campaign document, presumably to be also freely circulated, in which the Senator, besides refuting his opinions, did him the honor—most unusual and picturesque in a Senator's rhetoric—of likening him to a begonia.
>
> The begonia is, or then was, a plant of such senatorial qualities as to make the simile, in intention, most flattering. Far from charming in its refinement, the begonia is remarkable for curious and showy foliage; it was conspicuous; it seemed to have no useful purpose; and it insisted in standing always in the most prominent positions. Adams would have greatly liked to be a begonia in Washington, for this was rather his ideal of the successful statesman. . . . [34]

In *The Education* the villain of Henry Adams's Washington career is President Grant. When Grant announced the make-up of his Cabinet in 1869, Adams knew that he himself had made 'another inconceivable false start. . . . Grant had cut short the life which Adams had laid out for himself in the future. After such a miscarriage, no thought of effectual reform could revive for at least one generation, and he had no fancy for ineffectual politics.'[35] The General is roundly abused: Grant 'had no right to exist. He

---

[31] *Letters*, I, 178. [32] *Letters*, I, 185.

[33] *Letters*, I, 183. [34] *The Education*, pp. 291 f. *See* also *Letters*, I, 200.

[35] *The Education*, pp. 262, 263.

should have been extinct for ages. . . . The progress of evolution from President Washington to President Grant, was alone evidence enough to upset Darwin.'[36] yet the blunt-fingered General, conqueror of Lee, can hardly be said, even metaphorically, to have crushed the wings of this lovely butterfly. There is every indication that Adams's family came to the conclusion that his stay in Washington was utterly purposeless and made provision for him to leave. Indeed, in his disarming and invalidating fashion, Adams freely admits as much. While he was visiting at Wenlock Abbey in the summer of 1870, President Eliot had written offering an assistant professorship in history at Harvard College—an offer Adams at once declined.[37] But the 'begonia' attack apparently spurred on the family, which chose to think the 'Session' article provoking it hardly an important contribution to American politics:

> . . . No sooner had Adams made at Washington what he modestly hoped was a sufficient success, than his whole family set upon him to drag him away. For the first time since 1861 his father interposed; his mother entreated; and his brother Charles argued and urged that he should come to Harvard College.[38]

Adams capitulated, and, with rancor in his heart and with surely no especial inclination toward his subject, began to teach medieval history at Harvard.

II

No act of Charles W. Eliot in 'reforming' Harvard College is superficially in greater need of justification than the appointment of Henry Adams to teach medieval history. Adams had never written a word upon it nor upon an allied subject. He had shown no aptitude as a scholar, standing well down in his Harvard class and abandoning the study of law in Germany because he could not learn the language. His few articles were on scattered subjects —not to one of them could the epithet 'learned' be applied. And at thirty-two he had twice been nationally advertised as frivolous

[36] *Ibid.*, p. 266. [37] *Ibid.*, p. 291.

[38] *Ibid.*, pp. 292–293. The contradiction between Adams's disappointment at leaving Washington and his earlier resignation after the announcement of the Grant Cabinet should be duly noted. The Adams "Session" articles appear to this writer to be fashioned on the summaries of Parliament in the *Edinburgh Review*.

and a lightweight. Why, then, did Dr. Eliot, an astute and far-seeing administrator, appoint him?

Not over eager for the appointment, Adams himself challenged the President of Harvard on his selection. 'But, Mr. President,' urged Adams, 'I know nothing about Mediæval History.' With the courteous manner and bland smile so familiar to the next generation of Americans, Mr. Eliot mildly but firmly replied, 'If you will point out to me any one who knows more, Mr. Adams, I will appoint him.'[39] The exact measure of Henry Adams's knowledge of his subject is indicated by the fact that he could think of no American to fill the place which he himself did not want.

The bland smile of Doctor Eliot concealed, of course, an administrative economy and strategy. Ephraim Whitney Gurney, his overworked professor of ancient history and the university's first dean, was making, in the fall of 1870, what might be called a successful marriage, to wealthy Ellen Hooper of Boston, and felt no longer any necessity to conduct the *North American Review* for the stipend it brought.[40] Furthermore, he and Professor Torrey could no longer compass unassisted the range of history demanded by the influx of students and the new styles in curricula.[41] Eliot saw an opportunity to 'sandwich-in' a tyro between the energetic Gurney (who was one of the leading reformers at Harvard) and the capable Torrey; and he also saw a chance to make the *North American Review* carry a part of the financial burden of the experiment.[42] Whoever was chosen must be selected with both the review and the college in mind; that person, furthermore, must be acceptable to Gurney. That Dr. Eliot was ruled by the latter is an obvious inference.[43] Justification of the appointment, then, de-

---

[39] *The Education*, pp. 293–294.

[40] Ward Thoron, ed., *The Letters of Mrs. Henry Adams* (Boston, 1937), Preface, p. xiv.

[41] *The Education*, p. 300.

[42] "Now, I am, I believe, assistant professor of history at Harvard College with a salary of £400 a year. . . . I am fitting up rooms regardless of expense. For I should add that what with one thing and another my income is about doubled, and I have about £1200 a year. With the professorship I take the *North American Review* and become its avowed editor." *Letters*, p. 194. This would indicate that the review paid about £200, or a third of Adams's total salary.

[43] "It was Gurney who had established the new professorship." *The Education*, p. 293.

pends upon an analysis of Gurney's motives. How far was he influenced by a desire to strengthen his department at Harvard and improve the review, and how far was he persuaded by gentle pressure from the Adams family?

Debatable as are some of the issues raised by Henry Adams's appointment, the notion that he was established as editor of the *North American Review* for the improvement of that journal is utter nonsense. He had no editorial experience, and Gurney must have foreseen that either he or Lowell (a former editor) would have to overlook Adams's work as an editor. As a matter of fact, the *North American Review* was changed in no important particular while Henry Adams had nominal control of it. Vital changes were made in it as soon as he resigned.[44] The only factor influencing Henry Adams's selection as editor of the review was that he would not be likely to interrupt the important contributions on the railroads begun by his brother in 1867.[45] So far as the *North American Review* was concerned, then, the promotion of the ambitions of Charles Francis Adams, Jr.,[46] is the clearest assignable cause for the installation of Henry Adams.

Did Ephraim Gurney consider Henry Adams to be potentially a first-rate medieval historian? One ought not to shout at the idea, for such skepticism makes of the president of Harvard either an idiot or a hypocrite. Where could Eliot have got his opinion that Adams knew as much about the subject of medieval history as any one, except from Gurney? And was Gurney completely deceived? Adams has a revelatory statement in regard to himself in *The Education* that seems to need enlargement: 'He knew no

---

[44] Frank Luther Mott, *A History of American Magazines*, 3 vols. + (New York and Boston, 1931—) III, 31; "it took the editorial boldness of Allen Thorndike Rice to lift the review out of its rut in 1878. . . . " *Ibid.*, III, 23. In 1875 Adams expressed the fear that it would die on his hands or "go to some Jew," *Letters*, I, 267.

[45] *See* H. C. Lodge "Memorial Address" pp. xxxiii–xxxvi in *Charles Francis Adams: An Autobiography* (Boston, 1916); *The Education*, p. 307: "For seven years he wrote nothing; the *Review* lived on his brother Charles's railway articles."

[46] We must remember that both Charles and Henry had before them the inescapable fact that their father had made his first political capital out of journalism—with the publication of *An Appeal from the New to the Old Whigs* in 1835. *See* "Adams, Charles Francis," *Enc. Brit.*

history; *he knew only a few historians. . . .*'[47] Henry Adams could claim acquaintance with Stopford Brooke, chaplain-in-ordinary to Queen Victoria and later author of *English Literature from the Beginnings to the Norman Conquest* (1898), and intimacy with 'Frank' Palgrave, the eldest son of Sir Francis Palgrave, deputy-keeper of the public records and author of the *History of England: Anglo Saxon Period* (1831) and the *History of Normandy and England*, 4 vols. (1851–1864).[48] 'Frank'—Francis Turner Palgrave—was married to the sister of Adams's friend, Charles Milnes Gaskell, and Adams was sufficiently intimate with the Palgrave-Gaskell circle, probably, to talk glibly about the concerns of English medieval historians, in particular about the controversy between the supporters of Sir Francis and those of Edward A. Freeman over the effect of the Norman Conquest on English institutions. We must allow for the possibility that his chatter impressed the less fortunate Ephraim Gurney and that this was the basis of his recommendation to Dr. Eliot. Despite the presence of Norton and Lowell, Harvard College was pleasantly rustic and provincial in 1870.

On the other hand, it will not do to ignore the powerful influence of the Adams family on both Eliot and Gurney. Charles Francis Adams was the most distinguished son of Harvard College in politics in 1870,[49] and Henry's older brother was to become one of the overseers of the institution at the end of the decade. 'There is a tradition in the (Hooper) family,' writes Ward Thoron, who married into it, 'that Gurney, after successfully tutoring Brooks Adams, Henry's younger brother, was recommended by Minister Adams to Dr. Hooper as an excellent person to teach his eldest daughter, who wished to study Greek.'[50] If there is any truth in this story of how Gurney met Ellen Hooper (to the improvement of his fortunes), then his gratitude to the father of Henry Adams must be counted a factor in the appointment.

---

[47] *Op. cit.*, p. 293. [48] *DNB.*

[49] Possible exception might be noted in Charles Sumner, close friend of Charles Francis Adams. Was the elder Adams president of the board when Henry was appointed to teach at Harvard? S. E. Morison, *Three Centuries of Harvard* (Cambridge, 1936) p. 340, seems to indicate as much. [50] Thoron, p. xiv.

If there was no 'influence' exerted in Henry's behalf, we have to grant that he displayed a capacity for 'politics' on assuming his post that there is no warrant for in his previous career. At the close of his first academic year he wrote Gaskell, 'As I have managed to get into the "inside ring," as Americans say, the small set of men who control the University, I have things my own way.'[51] This was 'progress' with a vengeance. Is it not easier to assume that Adams was favored from the start because of his 'connections'?

Though the author of *The Education* points out that 'it could not much affect the sum of solar energies whether one went on dancing with girls in Washington, or began talking to boys at Cambridge,'[52] the *Letters* indicate that Adams felt definitely that his sun was obscured by the clouds in the college town. To Gaskell, he immediately confessed, 'I lose by the change. The winter climate is damnable. The country is to my mind hideous. And the society is three miles away in Boston. . . . '[53] He had definitely been 'rusticated.' Significantly, he celebrated his first holiday—the Christmas recess—by rushing off to Washington.[54] Yet for want of social exercise he went to work. His epistles groan with his labors as he sought to keep ahead of his students in his courses.[55] 'My reputation for deep historical research is awful,' he whimsically remarked, and we should understand the whimsey of it. He needs must be superficial, but his protection was that his students did not detect how superficial he was:

> . . . As yet I have seen no society. I am too busy and have to read every evening as my young men are disgustingly clever at upsetting me with questions. Luckily I have a little general knowledge which comes in. I gave them the other day a poetical account of Wenlock in relation to Gregory VII and Cluny. You see how everything can be made to answer a purpose.[56]

Wenlock, it must be explained, was a Shropshire abbey converted into a residence (where Adams had frequently stayed) by the

---

[51] *Letters*, I, 212. *See* also I, 194: "I am brought in to strengthen the reforming party in the University, so that I am sure of strong backing from above."

[52] *The Education*, p. 293. [53] *Letters*, I, 195.

[54] *Letters*, I, 201. [55] *Letters*, I, 195, 198, 199, 202, 210.

[56] *Letters*, I, 199.

Gaskells. The young instructor had knocked about enough to know how to extemporize successfully when necessary. Furthermore, he possessed a ready wit which proved a cheval-de-frise in an emergency. 'How were the Popes elected in the eleventh century?' asked Ephraim Emerton in Professor Adams's course. 'Pretty much as it pleased God!' was the reply in the instructor's 'characteristic and somewhat nasal drawl.'[57] The best thing that can be said for Henry Adams is that he did not deceive himself as to his limitations:

> . . . You can imagine me giving lectures on mediæval architecture, cribbed bodily out of Ferguson and Viollet le Duc. Precious lucky it is that Palgrave isn't here to snub me for my intolerable impudence. If he could hear me massacre the principles of historical art, he would . . . brain me where I sit.[58]

So passed the first year of his 'professing.' He began the second 'feeling much more at home in my Mediæval chair than I did a year ago.'[59] He still complained of work, but he felt freer to have his fling in society. He found it a 'trifle monotonous . . . one is too well known in such a place as this. I am sure every idiocy I ever committed as a boy, is better remembered here than I remember it myself.'[60] Adams tried to improve the society of Cambridge himself by innovating new fashions:

> . . . Only last Saturday I made a sensation by giving a luncheon in my rooms here, at which I had the principal beauty of the season and three other buds, with my sister to preside; a party of eleven, and awfully fashinable and larky. They came out in the middle of a fearful snowstorm, and I administered a mellifluous mixture known as champagne cocktails to the young women before sitting down to lunch. . . . They made an uproarious noise and have destroyed forever my character for dignity in the College.[61]

Continuing, Adams intimated to Gaskell that American society could never have the dash of European:

> . . . In this Arcadian society sexual passions seem to be abolished. Whether it is so or not, I can't say, but I suspect both men and women are cold, and love only with great refinement. How they ever reconcile themselves to the brutalities of marriage, I don't know.[62]

---

57 Emerton "History," *The Development of Harvard University*, ed. S. E. Morison (Cambridge, 1930), p. 154, note 2.

58 *Letters*, I, 204.

59 *Letters*, I, 215.

60 *Letters*, I, 221.

61 *Letters*, I, 222.

62 *Letters*, I, 222.

Adams's next letter to Gaskell, on March 26, 1872, told of his engagement to Marian Hooper, sister to Ephraim Gurney's wife and her father's favorite daughter.[63]

In the same year Henry Adams ran his first tilt against a full-fledged medieval historian. 'Glance at my notice of Freeman's *Historical Essays* in my next number, if you see it,' he begged Gaskell. 'I think I have caught him out very cleverly, but I would like to know what you say.'[64] Edward Augustus Freeman's *Historical Essays* (1871) is a very important book if one has the object of revealing the whole political background of the scholarly crusade which sought to show the determining influence of German institutions upon the Anglo-Saxon. Incorporating articles written during the Franco-Prussian War, the *Historical Essays* openly takes the side of Germany and castigates Napoleon III for his imperialistic designs. We at once perceive that more than mere scholarship separates the classical school of English historians—Lingard, Hallam, Macaulay, Palgrave, *et al.*—and the Germanist school of Kemble, Freeman, Stubbs, and Green.[65] On one side are arrayed the lovers of ancient and medieval Rome, whose influence they believe spread over Europe and reached England through the invasion of affected races: the particular thesis of Palgrave (the historian most vital to us) being that even the Britons were Continental migrants infected with the ideas of Roman imperialism rather than innocent Celts.[66] Instinctively this school is allied to France, and some of its members to the Roman Church. On the other side, the contention is that all of the free institutions of England are prefigured in German tribal customs, that the Norman Conquest had no effect upon these institutions, and that the normal allegiance of England should be with Germany.[67] Freeman's *Historical Essays* is primarily an anti-French, pro-German tract, with historical studies in Anglo-Germanic history and contemporary political essays significantly intermixed. It is a hand with all the pips exposed.

Adams should have treated the book lightly, perhaps using it

---

[63] *Letters*, I, 223. [64] *Letters*, I, 220.

[65] *C. H. E. L.*, XIV, Pt. 3, pp. 56 ff. [66] *Ibid.*, p. 75.

[67] I am well aware that this is stated overboldly.

to discredit in America the Germanists as a school. Instead he belabored it like Orlando Ponderoso. His partisanship, we feel, is determined wholly by his friendship with the Palgraves and Gaskells.[68] After a conventional and meaningless compliment to Freeman, Adams remarks that the contents of his book 'are rather necessary to an elementary education than to the attainment of any very advanced knowledge.'[69] 'More than half the volume concerns points of continental history,' the reviewer continues, 'and Mr. Freeman's special grievance . . . is that French ideas of continental history are utterly distorted, and that Englishmen, and we may add Americans, are profoundly ignorant of anything except French ideas. This is not a very lofty aim for an historian of Mr. Freeman's rank. . . . '[70] Adams complains that Freeman assaults the French Empire 'with a very vicious temper.' He calls Freeman's assertion that Louis Napoleon had used the verbs *révendiquer* and *réunir* in claiming territory which he wished to add to his empire a 'wilful, malicious, and unjustifiable calumny of Louis Napoleon Buonaparte, a calumny which must add a considerable sting to the sufferings of that unfortunate man.'[71] The critical notice closes with a blast against the competence of Freeman as an historian, a thing hardly warranted by the book under review:

> Barring Mr. Freeman's most inveterate prejudices, he is, when there is neither a French Emperor to abuse nor an Anglo-Saxon king or earl to worship, a hard student and an honest workman. That he is or ever can be a great historian, in any high sense of the word, is difficult to believe. He has read the great German historians, and he probably admires them, but he has certainly failed to understand either their method or their aims. He shows only a limited capacity for critical combinations, and he has a true English contempt for novel theories. In spite of his labors, the history of the Norman Conquest and an accurate statement of Anglo-Saxon institutions still remain as far from realization as ever. . . . [72]

---

[68] "Although I have seen so little of Palgrave these last twenty years, I never forgot how much I owed to him at the beginning of life, and how strongly he affected my tastes and pursuits. Thirty-five years have passed since you first made me acquainted with him, but in all that time I have never found myself obliged to change any of the opinions he taught me to hold, or to correct any of the rules I got from him." *Letters*, II, 134 (October 25, 1897).

[69] *N. Am. Rev.*, CXIV (January 1872), 193. [70] *Ibid.*, 193.

[71] *Ibid.*, 195. [72] *Ibid.*, 195.

Could it be allowed that Adams is right in some particulars, his review nevertheless is insulting and scurrilous. Perhaps his friends made him feel it was at least undignified. At any rate, the publication of a revised American edition of Freeman's *The History of the Norman Conquest* in 1873 gave him an opportunity to appear better mannered and more erudite. He was well enough pleased with the critical notice which he produced to initial it 'H. A.' contrary to the practice of his journal.[73] 'I have been writing for the next number another little notice of Freeman, calculated to improve his temper as I guess . . . ,' he confided to Gaskell.[74] It was a poor guess, if not meant ironically. How did he suppose Freeman would take a review which began with the observation that his major work was 'far from attaining its aim so completely' as his *Early English History for Children?*[75]

With raised eyebrows Adams claims 'the right to confess a slight feeling of amused disappointment on examining this new and revised edition. The amusement is due to the fact that Mr. Freeman should have discovered in his revision so little to revise; the disappointment to the fact that he should have found nothing to improve.'[76] Adams objects to Freeman's overenthusiastic statement that 'Aelfred . . . is the most perfect character in history' and to Freeman's attempt to exonerate Earl Godwine from responsibility in the death of another Aelfred, son of Aethelred II. He contends that both the Anglo-Saxon Chronicle and Florence of Worcester establish Godwine's guilt, and that Godwine's 'compurgation' later was not equivalent to 'acquittal' in any modern sense.[77] The critical notice closes with another prophecy, very similar to that of the first review, dismissing Freeman as an historian:

> . . . If Mr. Freeman proposes to go through all mediæval history in this genial manner, acquitting every man from offence who has ever availed himself of the privilege of compurgation, he will end by offering to the public one of the most

---

[73] *N. Am. Rev.*, CXVIII (January 1874), 176–181.

[74] *Letters*, I, 257. [75] *N. Am. Rev.*, CXVIII, 176.

[76] *Ibid.*, 176–177. Adams must have known that the "revision" was a mere "reprint," yet to acknowledge this would have deprived him of the privilege of "reviewing" the book. This practice was general until the twenties in America.

[77] *Ibid.*, 177–181.

considerable lists of hardly treated ruffians and perjurers that has been seen even in this generation, to which the sight of rehabilitated criminals is so common. But the public patience will hardly last to the end of the list. Its judgment will be that the historian who resorts to such arguments has by the very act abdicated his high office and is no longer entitled to the name. He has become an advocate, and not a very strong one.[78]

Adams has, of course, taken a relatively small incident in *The History of the Norman Conquest* and given it major significance. No one today would presume to say whether Godwine knew that Harold, to whom he surrendered Aelfred, intended to kill the prince, so terse and contradictory are the records. Yet one thing is clear, Freeman had searched the probabilities more thoroughly than had Henry Adams. In the Preface to the third English edition of his work, after an extended rejoinder to Mr. Pearson, Freeman briefly notices his American assailant:

If I were to examine any anonymous criticism, it would be an article signed 'H. A.' in the *North American Review*, in which I am blamed for maintaining the innocence of Godwine, though his guilt is asserted in 'the Saxon chronicle.' It would almost seem as if 'H. A.' had written this without either looking at the Chronicles themselves or at the examination of their witness in my appendix. Indeed it would seem that, even in such respectable quarters as the *North American Review*, the idea still lingers that there is a single book called 'The Saxon chronicle.' I need hardly say that strange havoc would be made of history, as strange havoc often has been made, by any one who did not stop to compare the wide difference in statement and feeling between Abingdon and Peterborough.[79]

That Henry Adams was innocent of the fact that there was more than one version of the Anglo-Saxon Chronicle is not the improbability which it seems. In January 1873, he wrote to Henry Cabot Lodge, from Cairo, whither he had gone on his wedding journey, 'I have got to learn to read Anglo-Saxon, but that is too much to expect from you or anyone not obliged to do it.'[80] Six months later he had just begun the study of the language, which he found 'quite amusing.' In the same letter, however, he expressed the hope that Lodge would have 'more facility' with

---

[78] *Ibid.*, 181.

[79] *The History of the Norman Conquest*, 3d. ed., 6 vols. (Oxford, 1877), I, ix. The title of Florence of Worcester's *Chronicon ex Chronicis* explains adequately why Freeman did not bother to touch the "evidence" which Adams cited from it.

[80] *Letters*, I, 237.

'Latin and Saxon' than he had—though he saw no necessity for 'working very laboriously even at this.'[81] Making due allowance for the fact that he was bent on seducing a younger man to pursue a given course of study, one cannot believe that Adams was armed against the egregious blunder he triumphantly produced at the end of the year—for how else may his review be styled?

A three-year interval separated Adams's critical notice and Freeman's Preface, during which time the editor of the *North American Review* and his assistant, Henry Cabot Lodge, scolded the Germanists without effect (as they supposed) in their journal. 'I have myself devoted ten pages in my July number to a notice of Prof. Stubbs's unconscionably dull *Constitutional History*,' Adams wrote Gaskell in 1874. 'And I have ventured to assert some opinions there which I fear that dignified Professor will frown upon. Luckily for me, a good, heavy-bottomed English University Don rarely condescends to notice criticism, and never American criticism. Even Mr. Freeman now ignores my poor comments.'[82] There is an unattributable notice of Sir Henry Sumner Maine's *Lectures on the Early History of Institutions* in the *Review* for April 1875, and 'H. C. L.'—obviously Lodge (who had sole charge of that issue)—has a notice of Kenelm Edward Digby's *An Introduction to the History of Real Property* in the October 1875 number.

These reviews are important as they contain ideas later developed in full in *Essays in Anglo-Saxon Law*, the last carronade that Adams or his students were to discharge at the Freemanites. 'The great German historian, Sohm, has described more clearly than Professor Stubbs has done the peculiarities of the Anglo-Saxon political system,' declares Adams in his notice of *The Constitutional History of England*.[83] This is a matter of opinion, but it may be significant that no later student has sided with Henry Adams. 'So far as private law is concerned,' Adams remarks with a glance ahead, 'the early history of this great system is almost a blank. Neither Mr. Stubbs nor any other writer has seriously attempted it, and it is destined to remain untouched until Germany

---

[81] *Ibid.*, I, 253–254. [82] *Letters*, I, 260–261.

[83] *N. Am. Rev.*, CXIX (July 1874), 237.

has forced England into scholarship.'[84] Adams takes the ground that manorial jurisdiction in England was always a mere continuation of hundred jurisdiction. He denies by implication that the English constitution is descended from German tribal law—the Normans surely destroyed the Witan:

Neither Mr. Stubbs nor even Mr. Freeman would probably maintain that there is any evidence whatever to establish the existence of a legislative assembly under Rufus, Henry I, Stephen, Henry II, Richard, or John. The utmost that can be demonstrated is the occasional indication of a consultive body, which, to say the least, has no stronger affiliations with the Witan than it has with the Curia Regis or the Norman Court of Barons. Two whole centuries elapse between the last meeting of the Witan and the first meeting of Parliament.[85]

The review of Sir Henry Maine's *Lectures*[86] is marked by the reviewer's insistence that primogeniture was a part of the feudal, as distinct from the Germanic, heritage. He poses this query:

... Can Sir Henry demonstrate that at any period whatever the Teutons of the village communities were not absolute owners of the houses in which they lived and the close about those houses? And if English ownership is descended from the ownership of the tribal chief, why were the grants of land in such absolute ownership always acts of the political government, of the king and the people in a legislative capacity?[87]

Lodge, in examining Kenelm Digby's *An Introduction to the History of Real Property*,[88] remarks that 'Folcland, the usual stumbling block, has proved one to Mr. Digby'[89] who adopted the view of Kemble and Stubbs that such land was the common property of the nation out of which the king could carve dependent tenures.[90] Lodge holds that, as regards the law, 'William the Conqueror superimposed a fully developed system on a half-developed one of the same stock'[91]—the Palgravian thesis.

In these three reviews, whatever their merits and defects, there is the stirring of a small breeze that might have grown to a wind to dissipate the 'delusion' which Charles A. Beard has called 'one of the weirdest ... that has ever afflicted American intellectual

---

[84] *Ibid.*, 235. [85] *Ibid.*, 238.

[86] *N. Am. Rev.*, CXXI (April 1875), 435–437. [87] *Ibid.*, 436.

[88] *N. Am. Rev.*, CXX (October 1875), 430–433. [89] *Ibid.*, 431.

[90] This view was upset by Sir Paul Vinogradoff in 1893. *See* "Folkland," *Enc. Brit.*, 14th ed. [91] *Op. cit.*, p. 430.

life, namely, the Teutonic theory of history—the theory that the Teutonic race has been the prime source of political liberty and popular government and that the roots of Anglo-Saxon democracy are to be traced back to tun-moots of barbarians in the forest of northern Germany.'[92] Why did not Henry Adams develop his objections to the Freemanites into a general assault upon their master conception? Why was he content to lop off a few of the lower limbs when he might have destroyed it root and branch?

Adams has been extravagantly praised as an historian. 'He gave the first historical seminary in this country,' asserts Professor Morison. 'He was the greatest teacher that I ever encountered,' wrote Edward Channing—epitaph enough for any man.[93] The roll of his distinguished students adds lustre to his name—Lodge, Ernest Young, J. Laurence Laughlin, S. M. Macvane, Freeman Snow, Lindsay Swift, Henry Osborn Taylor, Ephraim Emerton, Edward Channing, and Albert Bushnell Hart.[94] Yet Adams undoubtedly missed his greatest opportunity as an historian and teacher. He had neither the strength nor the vision to oppose the Germanists fundamentally.

The contentions of Adams and Lodge in their handling of Freeman, Stubbs, Maine, and Digby in the *North American Review* were in a sense bold guesses. They needed to be substantiated by hard work. 'I took the ground in my notice of Stubbs that manorial jurisdiction was *always* a mere continuation of hundred jurisdiction,' Adams wrote Lodge in September 1874:

> In France the *haute justice* embraced felonies and the *inquisitio.* The constitutional character of English and French feudalism is nicely expressed in this contrast. So we must collect *all* evidence, especially in the reign of Henry II, who as succeeding the lawless reign of Stephen must have found manorial power stronger than ever it was again unless under Henry III. I think I see the way to a good monograph by you on this point.[95]

This letter, beyond illustrating the element of conjecture in the critical notices, indicates the beginning of doctoral studies in his-

---

[92] "Turner's *The Frontier in American History*" *Books That Changed Our Minds,* ed. M. Cowley and B. Smith (New York, 1939) p. 62.

[93] Both quotations from Morison, *Three Centuries*, p. 349.

[94] Emerton, *op. cit.*, p. 156.

[95] *Letters*, I, 264. Emphasis added.

tory at Harvard. Adams's next missive reports, 'Laughlin of '73 proposes to join our Ph.D. class.'[96] It was the principal work of this class to substantiate the reviews. Adams told Lodge to indicate to the university authorities that the course was a 'special study on the early English law as exhibited in Anglo-Saxon and Norman sources, with a view to ascertaining and fixing the share that Germanic law had in forming the Common Law.'[97] This description might imply a broader purpose than was ever realized by Adams and his students.

Employing German methodology,[98] they produced in the next two years four studies in Anglo-Saxon law, three of which were offered as doctoral dissertations. Their teacher, who bore the expense of publication,[99] supplied an initial study, and in 1876 the lot was printed under the title *Essays in Anglo-Saxon Law.*[100] 'This has been a really satisfactory piece of work,' Adams wrote Gaskell. 'I shall be curious to learn whether your universities think they can do better.'[101] Certainly there was nothing to compare with the book as a graduate study either in England or America at the time. As a permanent contribution to the history of English law, the book is called valuable by Winfield.[102] Though there are *lacunae* in the authors' knowledge,[103] there is no reason to dissent from this estimate. Our concern is that the book has

---

[96] *Ibid.*, I, 265. [97] *Ibid.*, I, 265.

[98] "He imposed Germany on his scholars with a heavy hand," *The Education*, p. 304. *See* also *Letters*, I, 235–237, 254, 287. [99] *Letters*, I, 286, 288.

[100] Boston, 1876. Four essays: Henry Adams, "Anglo-Saxon Courts of Law"; H. Cabot Lodge, "Land Law"; Ernest Young, "Family Law"; J. Laurence Laughlin, "Legal Procedure." [101] *Letters*, I, 300.

[102] Percy H. Winfield, *The Chief Sources of English Legal History* (Cambridge, 1925), p. 53.

[103] For example, Benjamin Thorpe's *Diplomatarium Anglicum Aevi Saxonici* (London, 1865) was apparently unknown to Adams. It is not in his bibliography nor was it drawn upon for his appendix of thirty-five legal cases, though it has some twenty cases not in J. M. Kemble's *Codex Diplomaticus Aevi Saxonici* (London, 6 vols., 1839–1848) on which Adams chiefly relied. It should be pointed out, too, that Adams made no effort to check MS readings. Professors F. A. Marsh of Lafayette College and F. J. Child of Harvard were called upon to assist in the translation of the charters, with which the authors had difficulty. *See* "Three Letters from Henry Adams to Albert Stanburrough Cook," *Pacific Review*, II (September 1921), 272–275.

no broad purpose. It is not the cornerstone of a structure to be erected athwart the path of the Germanists. Indeed, Adams can write, 'There is no higher authority on the subject of Anglo-Saxon law than Dr. Reinhold Schmid. . . . '[104] The book is instead a specific attack upon the Freemanites as an historical sect, without any reference to the larger issue, as citation from Adams's conclusion makes evident (he has just shown that the Norman-trained Edward the Confessor distributed powers, especially to the Church, *by writ*, with no reference to the Witan):

> With the hopeless confusion of jurisdictions which followed the collapse caused by the Confessor in the Anglo-Saxon system, this is not the place to deal. From the moment that the private courts of law become a recognized part of the English judicature, the Anglo-Saxon constitution falls to pieces, and feudalism takes its place. Yet whatever historical interest the manorial system possesses, as part of the English judicial constitution, is due to the fact that its origin was not feudal, but Anglo-Saxon. The manor was a private hundred so far as its judicial powers were concerned. The law administered in the manorial courts was hundred law; the procedure was hundred procedure; the jurisdiction, like that of the hundred, was controlled by the shire. The manor was but a proprietory hundred, and, as such has served for many centuries to perpetuate the memory of the most archaic and least fertile elements of both the Saxon and the feudal systems.[105]

That is, the effort of Adams and his students is an effort so to individualize and particularize Anglo-Saxon institutions by insisting on their archaic inflexibility that all liberal elements must be recognized as post-Norman. This could have been made momentous with no more than a turn of phrase, but that phrase was never written or uttered.

Adams, therefore, emerges from his Harvard studies as a mere controversialist. Yet this was precisely how he entered upon them—a partisan of the Palgraves. His quarrel with Freeman began because the publication of the latter's study of the Norman Conquest knocked Palgrave's earlier book off the stocks. Its superior merits Adams never admitted. Later, when the Freemans visited this country and the Adamses met them unexpectedly at the Bancrofts, the Americans appeared to have vied with the guests in being offensive, even in Mrs. Adams's jaundiced account:

[104] *Op. cit.*, 12. [105] *Ibid.*, 50.

At dinner, the great historian of the Norman Conquest was on my right; Henry, *one* removed from my left. Ye Gods, what a feast it was! No stylographic could relate it. Let us draw a veil over nine-tenths of it. When Freeman informed us that the Falls of Slap-Dash—or some such name—were better worth our seeing than Niagara 'for the reason that many streams like your States end in one great *fall*,' we let the vile insinuation pass, and Edmunds, with his best senatorial courtesy, said very gently and with no passion in his tones, 'Where is this fall, Mrs. Freeman?' 'On the *H*adriatic,' she said, as most Englishwomen would. There was a deathly stillness, unbroken save for the winter rain beating drearily against the window-panes. On we went. The canvasbacks entered. *Three* of them—fresh and fair, done to a turn; and weltering in their gore. Says Mrs. Bancroft, with a growing hauteur of manner as of a turning worm, 'Do you appreciate our canvasbacks, Mr. Freeman?' 'I cannot eat raw meat,' he said angrily, while a convulsive shudder shook his frame. Then the *picador*, which is latent in me when nature is outraged, rose in me, and I said to him, all unconscious of his theories and the scheme of his writing, 'I wonder that you do not like rare meat. Your *ancestors*, the Picts and Scots, ate their meat raw and tore it with their fingers.' At which he roared out, 'O-o-o-o! *Whur* did yer git that?' Unheeding, careless of consequences, I said, 'Well, your Anglo-Saxon ancestors if you prefer.' He thereupon pawed the air and frothed at the mouth.

The funniest remains to be told, but it must be done viva-voce. It was a dialogue between him and George Bancroft, when the latter was tired and sleepy and at the end of his forces, as the Gauls say. Never having read one line of Freeman, I did not know until the next day the exquisite point of my historical allusions. As I casually repeated them Henry became purple in the face and rolled off his chair, and he, the husband of my bosom, who is wont to yawn affectionately at my yarns, he at intervals of two hours says, 'Tell me again what you said to Freeman about the Picts and Scots and Anglo-Saxons.' I send this to you for Whitman; to me and to you it is probably without point or flavour. As *we* rose up to go Mrs. Freeman came up to me very kindly and said, 'We mean to go *back* to Cambridge before we sail for home to see our friends once more.' I smiled like one in a trance and said, 'I'm sure they'll be much flattered.' That's all; they are at the Arlington, next door, as it were, have been ten days or more, leave tomorrow, and we have neither of us called.[106]

III

Two quite different explanations are given in *The Education* why Henry Adams resigned his professorship and quit Cambridge for Washington: first, 'he regarded himself as a failure,' and, secondly, society in the college town was deadly—'a faculty meet-

[106] Thoron, pp. 331–332. Contrast the reception given the Adamses by Sir Henry Maine (Thoron, p. 132).

ing without business.'[107] Other motives are assignable from a study of his career: during his last two years at Harvard he had been permitted to offer a course in American history[108]—a course which heightened his already acute sense of the accomplishment of the Adamses. He may have conceived at this time his purpose of writing an historical work which should display the doughty John Quincy Adams as consistently virtuous, even in his 'desertion' of the Federalist Party. For this task and for the study of Gallatin upon which he was engaged,[109] the Washington archives were more rewarding than the libraries of Cambridge and Boston. It is likely, too, that if a realization of his limitations as a medieval historian never came to him, some real knowledge of the arduousness of the labors in that field had been borne in upon him.[110] Yet the motive with which he wanted most to impress Gaskell was that of founding a salon in Washington, as Rogers and Milnes had done in the London of an earlier time, and thus 'tone-up' society as they had done:

> ... The fact is I gravitate to a capital by a primary law of nature. This is the only place in America where society amuses me, or where life offers variety. Here, too, I fancy that we are of use in the world, for we distinctly occupy niches which ought to be filled. . . . One of these days this will be a very great city if nothing happens to it. . . . It will be saying in its turn the last word of civilisation. I enjoy the expectation of the coming day, and try to imagine that I am myself, with my fellow *gelehrte* here, the first faint rays of that great light which is to dazzle and set the world on fire hereafter.[111]

Henry Adams's vision of a Washington salon threw a burden upon his wife which life in Cambridge had not imposed. For the first time she assumes an eminence in the narrative not warranted before. Marian Hooper Adams, whom Adams had married in June 1872, was the daughter of the well-to-do Doctor William

---

[107] *Op. cit.*, pp. 304, 307. [108] *Letters*, I, 260.

[109] *Letters*, I, 300, 301, 303 *seq.*

[110] *Letters*, I, 265, 268, 271, 290. One suspects an awakened political ambition, too, despite Adams's denial: "The future is very vague to me. My political friends or one wing of them, have come into power, but under circumstances which prevent me from giving them more than a silent and temporary sympathy. Meanwhile I hob-nob with the leaders of both parties, and am very contented under my cloak of historian. I am satisfied that literature offers higher prizes than politics. . . . "

[111] *Letters*, I, 302. Slightly emended for brevity's sake.

Hooper and Ellen Sturgis Hooper, an heir to the Sturgis shipping fortune. Katherine Simonds, who in her article, 'The Tragedy of Mrs. Henry Adams,'[112] has done more towards illuminating our subject than any other critic, makes it clear that this vivacious young woman was a person of great charm and exceptional taste. Her elder sister was described by Henry James as the 'exquisite Mrs. Gurney of the infallible taste, the beautiful hands, and the tragic fate'; her brother, Edward William Hooper, treasurer of Harvard College for twenty-two years, was, like Henry Adams, a collector of Chinese paintings. Henry, it seemed, could hardly have done better for a wife; indeed, an acquaintance described theirs as 'a marriage of similarities.' Nor could so exacting a person as he have had a more satisfactory mistress for his salon.

'Mrs. Adams was an admirable ally to him in making their house a unique place in Washington,' writes the celebrated biographer of John Hay. 'Sooner or later, everybody who possessed real quality crossed the threshold of 1607 H. Street.'[113] Among the élite thus distinguished was an inner circle of friends still more exalted—a clique which included John Hay, William Evarts, and Clarence King.[114] This group became the critics of the Gilded Age, Adams contributing anonymously the novel, *Democracy*, in 1880,[115] and Hay, *The Breadwinners*, in 1883. Adams's novel, whatever its political consequence (and on that he seemed chiefly intent), has little merit as literature, and another novel, called *Esther*, published under the pseudonym 'Frances Snow Compton' in 1884, consoles the reader to the fact Adams wrote no more fiction.

Yet this novel *Esther*, if we follow Miss Simonds, determined

---

[112] *New England Quarterly* (December 1936), pp. 564–582. Except where noted, I am dependent in the next five paragraphs for my material to Miss Simonds. Professor Schlesinger, I believe, verified the fact of Mrs. Adams's suicide.

[113] William Roscoe Thayer, *The Life and Letters of John Hay*, 2 vols. (Boston, 1915), II, 55.

[114] "The Adamses, the Hays, and Clarence King formed an inner circle, which somebody named 'The Five of Hearts'!" *Ibid.*, II, 58. Another list of intimates is suggested in Thoron, p. 247.

[115] Note that a Miss Emily Beale thought herself satirized in *Democracy* (Thoron, pp. 284, 339). Adams, we shall see below, did not spare women, as women, in his fiction.

Adams's future, for Esther is a portrait of his wife. The novel itself is dull and trivial—the story of a woman who loves a popular minister, but, being a skeptic, cannot marry his church or submit to his faith. It is the severity of the portrait that stuns. Esther, or Marian Adams, is revealed as a creature of a 'gaiety almost too light,' a person who, according to Adams, 'picks up all she knows without effort, and knows nothing well, yet she seems to understand whatever is said.' Though she has 'a style of her own,' the author can never make up his mind whether he likes it or not. She appears to him to have too little conviction about anything to survive the ordinary tests the spirit is put to:

> . . . I want to know what she can make of life. She gives one the idea of a lightly sparred yacht in mid-ocean unexpected; you ask yourself what the devil she is doing there. She sails gaily along though there is no land in sight and plenty of rough weather coming.

One cannot say, however, that the portrait has no loving touches; on the contrary, Esther appears the product of an exacting love, the love that demands perfection in the object adored. Yet, if the person so portrayed did not comprehend the complex nature of the animus, *Esther* must have fallen as a heavy blow, and there is reason for supposing that Mrs. Adams was in a peculiar psychological condition at the time the book appeared. The devotion of the Adamses to each other is beyond all challenge,[116] yet they were not happy. They had been married twelve years and were still childless. A woman acquaintance says, 'Not having any was a greater grief to Mr. Adams than to her,'[117] yet this is not certain, for a great change had come to Marian Adams. As a young girl, we are told that, 'she did many kind and generous actions,' yet later, 'she had a reputation for saying bitter things and of unsparingly using her powers of sarcasm whenever an opportunity presented. She was feared rather than loved.'[118] Furthermore, Mrs.

---

[116] Note his little kindnesses, as recorded in her letters (Thoron, pp. 178, 282, etc.). Note that Henry objected to a short separation after they had been married eleven years. Thoron, pp. 272, 437, 441.

[117] *See* Adams's expression of fear (*Letters*, I, 166) that if he married without love he would be childless.

[118] Much of her character is revealed in "I prefer to receive no foreigners unless presented by their own ministers." Thoron, p. 345. *See* also p. 363.

Adams within a few months after the publication of the book was to lose her father, to whom she was greatly devoted.[119] In Adams's novel Esther likewise loses her parent, a man who, after his retirement, 'amused the rest of his life by spoiling this girl.' Esther's father, dying, tries in vain to bolster his daughter's courage and strengthen her faith:

> 'It is not so bad, Esther, when you come to it.' But now that she had come to it, it was very bad; worse than anything she had ever imagined; she wanted to escape, to run away, to get out of life itself rather than suffer such pain, such terror, such misery of helplessness.

Who can doubt that here was the suggestion for suicide, and that Mrs. Adams's death on December 6, 1885, from self-administered cyanide must have appeared to the author of the book as the one inevitable result of the portrait? Yet she took her life at a time which she ordinarily gave to writing letters to her father, and it was of him that she was probably thinking rather than of her husband, the author of *Esther*. Adams had no assurance of this, however, nor could he be certain that his disappointment in regard to children was not a factor in his wife's rash act.[120] Perhaps, too, the recollection of his persistent banter on the subject of sexual freedom,[121] with its unmeant implication of lack of satisfaction in his wife, may have oppressed Adams as a factor in her death:

> Such a quaint little society, you never saw or imagined. We do not even talk scandal. There is no scandal to talk about. . . . We are all of the Darby and Joan type, and attached to our wives. It is the fashion. . . . [122]

---

[119] The frequency of her letters to him establishes this beyond cavil. "My angel Pa," Thoron, p. 353.

[120] Mrs. Whiteside, close enough to Marian Adams to refer to her by her nickname "Clover," evidently thought that the suicide was partly chargeable to the Adamses' yearning for children, for she wrote, "How after we have spoken of Clover as having all she wanted, all this world could give, except perhaps children. And now at forty years old comes down a black curtain and all is over. . . . "

[121] How this may have affected Mrs. Adams can only be guessed at from such things in her letters as her refusal to meet Oscar Wilde (before any charges had been made against his morals), Thoron, p. 328.

[122] *Letters*, I, 309. Note Adams's admiration for King because of the latter's knowledge of women, particularly "robust" women. *The Education*, pp. 271, 272.

Yet if he ever chid himself for frivolity in talk on this subject, his intimates had no knowledge of it. When, in time, he was to reëstablish himself as a gracious host in Washington, John Hay could chaff him, without any idea of offense, on the score of his success with the ladies. '*Ces dames* are desolate without you.'[123] It is only when we see beneath the polished surface of *Mont-Saint-Michel and Chartres*, privately printed in 1904, and after wide circulation and discussion given to the general public in 1913, that we understand how hard Adams was hit.

To appreciate fully Adams's second excursion into medievalism we must pick up and follow a very faint trail. It begins in Paris in January 1891, when we find Adams trying to absorb the French Naturalists. 'Imagine my state of happiness,' he writes to Elizabeth Cameron, 'surrounded by a pile of yellow literature, skimming a volume of Goncourt, swallowing a volume of Maupassant with my roast, and wondering that I feel unwell afterwards.'[124] By his process of reading at least a volume a day, Adams came to Joris-Karl Huysmans, an author who may have repelled him, but in whom he maintained an interest for twenty years.[125]

Huysmans's career was to have certain parallels with Adams's own, parallels he could appreciate better than any one else, and Huysmans had treated, and was to treat, certain subjects of especial interest to Adams. Huysmans began his career as a Naturalist, a believer in Positivism, and a follower of Goncourt and Zola.[126] He had, at the outset, as firm a conviction in the value of science as Adams.[127] Then came the sophisticated and audacious satire of the Decadents in *À Rebours*, a volume which plausibly may have appealed to Adams because of its cynical tone and its profession of admiration for what was decadent.

At the time when Adams was reading yellow-backed novels in

---

[123] Thayer, II, 84. [124] *Letters*, I, 534.

[125] *See* citations in *Mont-Saint-Michel and Chartres* below; also *Letters*, II, 115.

[126] For Huysmans, *see* Arthur Symons, *Studies in Two Literatures* (London, 1897), *The Symbolist Movement in Literature* (New York, 1919), and Havelock Ellis, *The New Spirit*, 4th ed. (London, 1926).

[127] *See* Adams's demand for a "science of history" in a letter of December 12, 1894, to the American Historical Association, in *The Degradation of Democratic Dogma* (New York, 1919).

Paris, however, the Huysmans book which was most likely to fall into his hands was *La Bas*, over which Paris was still agitated,[128] though the volume had appeared the year before *Esther* was published. *La Bas*[129] is a disgusting book, an effort to pile refuse on the High Altar, and, while its skepticism may have appealed to Adams's mood, it could not have been this which permanently attracted Adams to the book. There is, first of all, in *La Bas* a hatred of the nineteenth century; even occultism, Huysmans insists, has degenerated since the Middle Ages. 'The people,' one character says, 'grow from century to century more avaricious, abject, and stupid.'[130] And again, 'Society has done nothing but deteriorate in the four centuries separating us from the Middle Ages.' *La Bas* denounces the 'Americanisms'[131] that Henry Adams detested in the America of Grant's administration. The Catholic general, Boulanger, so much like Grant, is denounced for 'American' methods of self-advertisement;[132] Huysmans even insists that Gilles de Rais's death at the stake is to be preferred to an 'American lynch-law' death.[133]

Very important in the book is Huysmans's attack upon Joan of Arc. If Joan had only stayed with her mother, France would not have become a heterogeneous nation; the Charles she saved was the leader of Mediterranean cutthroats, not Frenchmen at all, but Latins—Spaniards and Italians. Without Joan, Northern France and England would have remained united, a homogeneous nation of Normans.[134] Now this is a most important passage for the development of Henry Adams's thinking. When we are invited to visit Mont-Saint-Michel by the author, it is on the score that, if we have any English blood at all, we are also Norman, with an hypothetical ancestry of two hundred and fifty million in the eleventh century, ploughing the fields of Normandy, rendering military service to the temporal and spiritual lords of the region, and helping to build the Abbey Church. Adams was inordinately

[128] *Figaro* (July 30, 1892) reports conversion of Huysmans. Léon Deffoux, *J.-K. Huysmans sous aspects divers* (Paris, 1927), p. 42. Bibliographie, pp. 97–111.

[129] J.-K. Huysmans, *Oeuvres Complètes*, 18 vols. (Paris, 1928–1930), XII, Pts. 1 and 2.

[130] XII, Pt. 2, 231.

[131] XII, Pt. 2, 6–7.

[132] XII, Pt. 2, 58.

[133] XII, Pt. 2, 232.

[134] XII, Pt. 1, 73–75.

proud of his Norman ancestry,[135] and in that highly personal poem, *Prayer to the Virgin of Chartres*, which was found among his papers after his death, he even fancies himself 'an English scholar with a Norman name' returning to France in the thirteenth century to study in the schools and worship at the shrine of the Virgin.

Finally, Adams found in *La Bas*—though he may not have been immediately attentive to it—a skepticism in regard to science[136] more deeply felt than Huysmans's hostility toward the Church. In the nineteenth century, says Huysmans, speaking through the character Gevingey, 'People believe nothing, yet gobble everything.'[137] Positivism, the first love of Huysmans, is roundly denounced. Barbey d'Aurevilly had prophesied after reading *À Rebours* that Huysmans would choose either 'the muzzle of a pistol or the foot of the cross,' and to the discerning this choice was possibly even more apparent in *La Bas*. To Henry Adams, however, it must have come as something of a surprise to find that the irreverent writer who had fascinated him in *La Bas* had set off in 1892 to be converted at a Trappist monastery. He read the story in Huysmans's novel *En Route* (1895); and followed it through the highly symbolical novel, *La Cathedral* (1898), from which he several times quotes in *Mont-Saint-Michel and Chartres*;[138] reaching finally *L'Oblat* in 1903. *Les Foules de Lourdes* (1906), with its discussion of the many shrines erected in southern France to the Virgin, which to the casual reader seems most like Adams, came out too late to have exerted any influence upon him. If Adams interpreted the writing of *La Bas* as an act which drove Huysmans back to Catholicism in contrition, he could not but realize another parallel between himself and the Frenchman—both had written a novel of which they deeply repented.

Yet Adams could not readily produce a series of Catholic novels, as Huysmans had done, by way of atonement. His sin was in his eyes, perhaps, not specifically against the Church, but

---

[135] "I am sure that in the eleventh century the majority of me was Norman . . . " *Letters*, II, 79. [136] XII, Pt. 1, 158–159.

[137] XII, Pt. 2, 229. [138] *Op. cit.*, pp. 76, 83–84.

against Woman. Hence, *Mont-Saint-Michel and Chartres* is one of the most eloquent tributes to the power of Woman ever penned by man. For whatever she may have meant to the thirteenth century, and whatever she continues to mean to the devout, the Virgin symbolized for Adams Woman Enthroned.[139] He writes with scarcely less eloquence when he treats of the three great queens of France, Eleanor of Guienne, Mary of Champagne, and Blanche of Castile, at whose courts poetry and courtesy were born.[140] They brought to the political and social world the order and unity Adams so much admired. Whether he writes of the legendary windows[141] or of Nicolette and Marion,[142] it is the feminine influence on glass and 'chante-fable' that interests him. In the world that he reveals Woman is everywhere triumphant and supreme. The book, *Mont-Saint-Michel and Chartres*, should not be looked upon, possibly, as a study in medieval history, but rather as a cathedral of words—various, complex, and beautiful, yet designed to give a single impression—a cathedral erected by Henry Adams to the glory of Womankind.

Absurdly futile, then, the scholar's effort to show that Adams used in the main secondary sources for his book.[143] Equally futile also to suggest that Adams discovered a unity and order in France in the era of cathedral building which may not have been so apparent to contemporaries. And even a little ridiculous to charge Adams, as a modern historian, with neglect of economics in his study.[144] The reference ought not to be from *Mont-Saint-Michel*

---

[139] *Op. cit.*, pp. 89 ff.; pp. 179 ff.; pp. 251 ff. [140] *Ibid.*, pp. 198 ff.

[141] *Ibid.*, pp. 149 ff. [142] *Ibid.*, pp. 230 ff.

[143] Michelet, Hauréau, Viollet-le-Duc, Westlake, Molinier, Regnon, Rohault de Fleury, Rousselot, Ottin, Male, Lasteyrie, Lacroix, Labarte, Enlarte, Garreau, Corroyer, Bulteau, and Caumont. *See* Index, *Mont-Saint-Michel and Chartres* (Boston, 1913), for authorities cited and list of works. The list must be supplemented, of course. In his index, for example, Adams cites only Jean-Barthelemy Hauréau's *Histoire de la philosophie scolastique* yet he used also Hauréau's *Mémoire sur quelques chanceliers de l'Eglise de Chartres*, *Histoire littéraire du Maine*, and *Histoire littéraire du France*, etc.

[144] It is worth pointing out, however, that, though the tone of *Mont-Saint-Michel and Chartres* is sometimes like that of Palgraves's *The History of Normandy and England*, 4 vols. (1864)—note especially the beginning of Palgrave IV, viii, 385—Adams is not the moral bigot that Palgrave is. I have not space here to study the relationship of Henry

and Chartres to thirteenth-century France, to test Adams's accuracy, but to contemporaneous works of literature, to fix the place and meaning of the book, for Adams's creation is a prose poem rather than anything else. Yet the first and most obvious reference—to James Russell Lowell's *The Cathedral*[145]—is not very rewarding. Here Adams may have found approval for his love of Gothic Chartres,[146] the coupling of philosophy with aesthetic meditation, yet withal a stout protestantism which may have helped him to resist neo-Thomism.[147] There is just a chance, moreover, that he may have transmuted Lowell's 'genius,' whom the poet represents as feminine, into the ubiquitous American 'niece' whose presence is so very incongruous in *Mont-Saint-Michel and Chartres:*

> But she, my Princess, who will some day deign
> My garret to illumine till the walls . . .
> Dilate. . . .
> One feast for her I secretly designed
> In that Old World so strangely beautiful
> To us the disinherited of eld,—
> A day at Chartres, with no soul beside
> To roil with pedant prate my joy serene
> And make the minster shy of confidence.[148]

An utterly absurd idea—yet no more absurd than the presence of the niece herself, hence worth retaining.

The more we reflect upon it, the more it seems imperative to explain Henry Adams's choice of a companion for his last medieval excursion. An American niece! To be sure, Adams had nieces,[149] but one would not thoughtlessly take one's *own* niece into the

---

Adams's writings to those of Brooks Adams, but Henry seems to have been the guide. See *Letters*, II, 70, 163. [145] Boston, 1870.

[146] From pedantries past, present, and to come,
I looked, and owned myself a happy Goth.
Your blood is mine, ye architects of dream. . . .

[147] *See* Ch. XVI, "Saint Thomas Aquinas," *Mont-Saint-Michel and Chartres*, p. 363. Adams's poem, *Prayer to the Virgin of Chartres,* shows him abandoning science altogether for mysticism. [148] *The Cathedral,* ll. 150–151, 154, 176–180.

[149] *Letters*, II, 482 (Paris, 1907): "Just now I am victim of nieces. They swarm like honey-bees. . . . Three other nieces have budded into flower and fruit since I came away, and two more are notified as coming due." *See* also, of course, *Letters to a Niece . . . With a Niece's Memories* (Boston, 1920).

thirteenth century. She must have been, in Adams's imagination, some unattached Daisy Miller[150]—such as his friend Henry James invented and piloted with eleemosynary regard through Europe. Yet she must have potentialities which the novelist had not observed. Adams could not read James's novels.[151] 'James knows almost nothing of women but the mere outside; he never had a wife.'[152] James's heroines were crushed or absorbed by their European experiences; Adams wanted a young woman who could survive the text he chose for the day. He had much to accomplish still, and the years had taught him that, though he had the strength of the Archangel, he could accomplish nothing without her. A melancholy letter to Henry James, on November 18, 1903, elicited by the novelist's study of a '*type bourgeois-bostonien*,'[153] tells of Adams's discovery 'at least thirty years ago'—the time of the Washington salon—that they were but 'improvised Europeans.'[154] An American society could not be created by male shams. If his *ingenue*, however, were capable of learning enough from the women of the thirteenth century to go back to her own country to create a society which she through her sex should dominate, then Adams's life would not be as fruitless as it seemed. A sex-conscious Daisy might conquer the earth, and to awaken her it was worth while to parade the pertinent lore of a forgotten century. Was ever medievalism put to so exalted a purpose?

---

[150] "I am uncle to all the girls in the Atlantic Coast States." *Letters*, II, 205.

[151] *Letters*, I, 323, 333. [152] *Ibid.*, I, 354.

[153] *William Wetmore Story and his Friends* (Boston, 1903).

[154] *Letters*, II, 414.

A BIBLIOGRAPHY OF CARLETON BROWN'S WRITINGS

Books

1910 *A Study of the Miracle of Our Lady told by Chaucer's Prioress.* Chaucer Society Publications, 2d Series, 45. Pp. x+141. London.

1913 *Venus and Adonis. The Rape of Lucrece, and other Poems.* The Tudor Shakespeare. Pp. xxvi+200. New York: Macmillan. Poems by Sir John Salusbury and Robert Chester. Bryn Mawr College Monographs, XIV. Pp. lxxiv+86. Bryn Mawr, Pa.—1914 *Idem.* Early English Text Society, Extra Series, No. cxiii. Pp. lxxiv+86. London.

1916 *A Register of Middle English Religious and Didactic Verse,* vol. I. The Bibliographical Society. Pp. xv+528. Oxford.—1920 *Idem,* vol. II. Pp. xx+458. Oxford.

1919 *Selections from Old and Middle English.* Pp. 18. New York: The Century Company.

1920 *The Stonyhurst Pageants* (edition). Hesperia, Ergänzungsreihe vii. Pp. xxx+302. Baltimore and Göttingen.

1924 *Religious Lyrics of the XIVth Century.* Pp. xxiv+358. Oxford.

1932 *English Lyrics of the XIIIth Century.* Pp. xlii+312. Oxford. Foreword to *Three Chaucer Studies* by R. Krauss, H. Braddy, and C. R. Kase. Pp. vii+182, 101, 89. New York: Oxford University Press.

1935 Chaucer: *The Pardoner's Tale.* Pp. xl+63. Oxford.

1939 *Religious Lyrics of the XVth Century.* Pp. xxxii+394. Oxford.

1940 *A Manuscript Index of Middle English Verse.* [Completed.]

Editor

1920–1932 *PMLA,* Volumes xxxv–xlvii.
(The Secretary's Reports, 1920–1934, are listed in the Index, 1936.)

Articles and Reviews

1903 Cynewulf and Alcuin. *PMLA,* xviii, 308–334.

1904 The Author of the *Pearl,* Considered in the Light of his Theological Opinions. *PMLA,* xix, 115–153, 215.
Notes and Introduction to "The Long-Hidden Friend." *JAFL,* xvii, 89–100, 144–152.
(review) C. Abbetmeyer's *Old English Poetical Motives derived from the doctrine of sin. MLN,* xix, 221–231.

1906 Chaucer's *Prioresses Tale* and its Analogues. *PMLA,* xxi, 486–518.
Chaucer's *litel clergeon. MP,* iii, 467–491.

1907 The Autobiographical Element in the Cynewulfian Rune Passages. *ESt,* xxxviii, 196–233.

1908 The Etymology of *bicched bones. MLN,* xxiii, 126.
Additional Note on *bicched bones. MLN,* xxiii, 159–160.

1909 Irish-Latin Influence in Cynewulfian Texts. *ESt*, xl, 1–29. The "Lost Leaf" of Piers the Plowman. *The* (*N. Y.*) *Nation*, xciv, 298–299.

1910 The Vernon *Disputisoun bytwene a cristenemon and a jew*. *MLN*, xxv, 141–144.

1911 *Shul* and *Shal* in the Chaucer Manuscripts. *PMLA*, xxvi, 6–30.
The Prologue of Chaucer's *Lyf of Seint Cecile*. *MP*, ix, 1–16.
The *Cursor Mundi* and the "Southern Passion." *MLN*, xxvi, 15–18.
Another Contemporary Allusion in Chaucer's *Troilus*. *MLN*, xxvi, 208–211.

1912 (reviews) A. J. Barnouw's *Schriftuurlijke poëzie der Angelsaksen;* G. Binz's *Untersuchungen zum altenglischen sogenannten Crist;* K. Jansen's *Die Cynewulfforschung von ihren Anfängen bis zur Gegenwart*. *ESt*, xlv, 90–101.
The "Pride of Life" and the "Twelve Abuses." *Archiv* (Herrig's), cxxviii, 72–78.
Lydgate's Verses on Queen Margaret's Entry into London. *MLR*, vii, 225–234.
The Fifteen Conditions of a Good Horse. *MLN*, xxvii, 125.
Shakespeare and the Horse. *The Library*, iii (3d series), 152–180.

1913 Caiphas as a Palm-Sunday Prophet. *Anniversary Papers by Colleagues and Pupils of George Lyman Kittredge*. Pp. 105–117. Boston and London: Ginn and Company.
Lydgate and the *Legend of Good Women*. *ESt*, xlvii, 59–62.
(review) F. A. Patterson's *The Middle English Penitential Lyric*. *MLR*, viii, 215–218.
Manuscripts of William Lichfield's *Complaint of God*. *ESt*, xlvii, 317.

1914 A Textual Correction. *MLN*, xxix, 60–61.
(review) J. M. Booker's *Middle English Bibliography*. *MLN*, xxix, 153–156.
Chaucer's Serpent-Pit. *MLN*, xxix, 198–199.

1915 A Passage from *Sir Isumbras*. *ESt*, xlviii, 329.
(review) Blanche C. Williams' "Gnomic Poetry in Anglo-Saxon." *The* (*N. Y.*) *Nation*, c (June 24), 716–717.
A Homiletic Debate between Heart and Eye. *MLN*, xxx, 197–198.
Chaucer and the Hours of the Blessed Virgin. *MLN*, xxx, 231–232.

1916 The Towneley *Play of the Doctors* and the *Speculum Christiani*. *MLN*, xxxi, 223–226.

1917 (review) J. E. Wells, *A Manual of the Writings in Middle English, 1050–1400*, *MLN*, xxxii, 162–166.
(review) C. H. Turner, Early Worcester MSS., fragments of four books and a charter of the eighth century, belonging to Worcester Cathedral. *The* (*N. Y.*) *Nation*, cv, 263–264.

1918 Dialogue between a Clerk and a Husbandman. *MLN*, xxxiii, 415–417.

1919 (review) R. M. Garrett, *The Pearl:* an Interpretation. *MLN*, xxxiv, 42–45.
(review) *Death and Liffe*, an Alliterative Poem, ed. by J. H. Hanford and J. M. Steadman. *MLN*, xxxiv, 63–64.
Beowulf, vv. 1080–1106. *MLN*, xxxiv, 181–183.

1920 Mulier est hominis confusio. *MLN*, xxxv, 479–482.

1921 The Stonyhurst Pageants. *MLR*, xvi, 167–169.

1923 William Herebert and Chaucer's *Prioresses Tale. MLN*, xxxviii, 92–94.
(review) H. G. Leach's *Angevin Britain and Scandinavia. The Literary Review*, iv, b.

1925 An Holy Medytacion—by Lydgate? *MLN*, xl, 282–285.
Studies in the First Folio. *Christian Science Monitor* (June 20), p. 3.

1926 A Thirteenth Century MS. at Maidstone. *MLR*, xxi, 1–12.
The Maidstone Text of the *Proverbs of Alfred. MLR*, xxi, 249–260.

1928 Texts and the Man. *MHRA Bulletin*, ii, 97–111.
A Thirteenth-Century Manuscript from Llanthony Priory. *Speculum*, iii, 587–595.

1929 Somer Soneday. *Studies in English Philology in Honor of Frederick Klaeber.* Pp. 362–374.

1931 An Early Mention of a St. Nicholas Play in England. *SP*, xxviii, 594–601.

1933 A Survey of the First Half-Century of the MLA. *PMLA*, xlviii, 1409–22.
The Evolution of the Canterbury "Marriage Group." *PMLA*, xlviii, 1041–59.

1934 The Squire and the Number of the Canterbury Pilgrims. *MLN*, xlix, 216–222.
Sermons and Miracle Plays. *MLN*, xlix, 394–396.

1935 Chaucer's "Wreched Engendring," *PMLA*, L, 997–1011.

1936 [Has Chaucer's "Wretched Engendering" been found?] An affirmative reply. *MLN*, li, 296–300.
Presidential Address: The Attack on the Castle. *PMLA*, li Supplement, 1294–1306.

1937 The Man of Law's Head-Link and the Prologue of the *Canterbury Tales. SP*, xxxiv, 8–35.

1938 Beowulf and the Blickling Homilies and Some Textual Notes. *PMLA*, liii, 905–916.

1939 See Myche, Say Lytell, and Lerne to Saffer in Tyme. *MLN*, liv, 131–133.

1940 *Poculum Mortis* in Old English, *Speculum*. [Forthcoming.]
The Prioress's Tale, in *Sources and Analogues of Chaucer's Canterbury Tales*. Chicago: University of Chicago Press. [In proof.]

P.W.L.

LIST OF SUBSCRIBERS

LIST OF SUBSCRIBERS

(Carleton Brown once intrigued a class by announcing that since a midyear examination was required, but its nature not specified, he would conduct his by requiring the students to question him. This precedent for semantic gymnastics warrants, what a host of letters confirm, that *subscribers* here should be understood in a special sense. The list is a Tabula Gratulatoria of friends who join with New York University and the Modern Language Association in expressing their appreciation of Carleton Brown as a scholar and a man.—*P.W.L.*)

Nelson F. Adkins
Hope Emily Allen
Tempe E. Allison
Dorothy C. Alyea
Albert C. Baugh
Nita Scudder Baugh
Paull F. Baum
Joseph W. Beach
Allen R. Benham
Albert S. Borgman
Archibald A. Bouton
Haldeen Braddy
Lyman R. Bradley
William T. Brewster
William Dinsmore Briggs
C. F. Tucker Brooke
Leslie Nathan Broughton
William Frank Bryan
Milton A. Buchanan
Walter Ll. Bullock
Stephen H. Bush
T. Moody Campbell
Oscar Cargill
Mary Ellen Chase
Stanley P. Chase
Samuel C. Chew
George R. Coffman
Klara H. Collitz
Georgianna Conrow
Roberta D. Cornelius
F. A. G. Cowper
Hardin Craig
DeWitt C. Croissant
Genevieve Crotty
Henry C. Davis
L. V. Dedeck-Hery
Germaine Dempster
Charlotte D'Evelyn
Louise Dudley
Erika von Erhardt-Siebold
Hollon A. Farr
Dana H. Ferrin
J. D. Fitz-Gerald, II
Norman Foerster
Robert S. Forsythe
Frances Foster
Grace Frank
J. Milton French
James Geddes, Jr.
Joseph E. Gillet
Joseph S. Graydon
R. H. Griffith
Miles L. Hanley
Frederick Hard
Eleanor K. Heningham
J. A. Herbert
Urban T. Holmes, Jr.
Karl J. Holzknecht
Cecilia A. Hotchner
Richard F. Jones
Robert Porter Keep
May L. Keller
Robert J. Kellogg
LeRoy Elwood Kimball
Rudolf Kirk
George L. Kittredge
Edgar C. Knowlton
Hans Kurath
H. Carrington Lancaster
Ida Langdon

W. W. Lawrence
Irving Linn
Mary McDonald Long
Percy W. Long
Laura Hibbard Loomis
Roger S. Loomis
Marian L. S. Lossing
Claude M. Lotspeich
William F. Luebke
Thomas Ollive Mabbott
Kemp Malone
Mildred E. Marcett
Edward L. McAdam, Jr.
Bruce McCullough
Sanford B. Meech
Robert J. Menner
C. Bowie Millican
Arthur H. Nason
George H. Nettleton
George T. Niedert
William A. Nitze
Henry W. Nordmeyer
Walter Oliver
Mary I. O'Sullivan
Roscoe E. Parker
C. E. Parmenter
Cyril A. Peerenboom
Homer G. Pfander
Louise Pound
Robert Armstrong Pratt
George F. Reynolds
Fred N. Robinson
Robert K. Root
Helen E. Sandison
Margaret Schlauch
Colbert Searles
Percy Simpson
Alice D. Snyder
Edward D. Snyder
Helen P. South
David H. Stevens
J. S. P. Tatlock
Alwin Thaler
Oliver Towles
Frederick Tupper
Rosemond Tuve
W. Morley Tweedie
Herbert H. Vaughan
Willis Wager
Homer A. Watt
William W. Watt
Kenneth G. T. Webster
Minnie E. Wells
Florence Donnell White
Rudolph Willard
Karl Young